For the children who didn't quite make
it to the wicket

THE
BOUNDARY
BOOK

SECOND INNINGS

CONTRIBUTORS

EDMUND BLUNDEN · *HAROLD PINTER* · IAN WOOLDRIDGE
JOHN ARLOTT · CHRISTOPHER MARTIN-JENKINS · *A. A. MILNE*
MICHAEL AND NORMA PEARCE · *NORMAN HARRIS* · G. K. CHESTERTON
SIMON BARNES · PETER WEST · *DICK BRITTENDEN*
MICHAEL MELFORD · *SIR ARTHUR CONAN DOYLE* · BARRY TOOK
E. W. SWANTON · JOHN SNOW · *JOHN EBDON*
SIR LEONARD HUTTON · *COLIN ATKINSON* · LESLIE THOMAS
TIM RICE · SIR JOHN BETJEMAN · *CHRISTOPHER BOOKER*
IAN HISLOP · *MICHAEL PARKINSON*
ALAN ROSS · RICHIE BENAUD · *ANTHONY COUCH*
LESLIE FREWIN · *HARRY EAST* · JOSEPH S. F. MURDOCH
RICHARD KERSHAW · HUGH DE SELINCOURT · *J. B. BOOTH*
RALPH WOTHERSPOON · *E. B. OSBORN* · VERNON SCANNELL
RACHAEL HEYHOE FLINT · MOLLY SHIMEILD · *RITA MARSHALL*
A. A. THOMSON · *BILL FRINDALL* · MICHAEL COWARD
ALAN KNOTT · SIR JOHN MILLS · *W. J. FORD*
COLIN COWDREY · *SIMON RAVEN* · FRED TRUEMAN
FRANCIS THOMPSON · BASIL BOOTHROYD · *SCYLD BERRY*
RICHARD FORD · *GERALD BRODRIBB* · P. G. WODEHOUSE
RAYMOND ROBERTSON-GLASGOW · JACK POLLARD · *DAVID FRITH*
WILLIAM GOLDWIN · *C. L. R. JAMES* · LORD OLIVIER
ARTHUR MARSHALL · JOHN WOODCOCK · *DONALD TRELFORD*
LESLIE AMES · *RAMAN SUBBA ROW* · HAROLD ('DICKIE') BIRD
MILES KINGTON · CARDEW ROBINSON · *SIR NEVILLE CARDUS*
GEOFFREY WATKINS · *RAY ROBINSON*
BRIAN JOHNSTON · J. A. R. SWAINSON · *NORMAN GALE*
REG VARNEY · *BILL TIDY* · DAVID LANGDON
REG SMYTHE · JACKIE BROOME · *PETER USTINOV*
TOM NEWTON · *JACK WOOD*

A Lord's Taverners' Miscellany of Cricket

THE
BOUNDARY
BOOK

SECOND INNINGS

COMPILED AND EDITED BY
LESLIE FREWIN

With a Preface by
HRH The Prince Philip,
Duke of Edinburgh, KG, KT

PELHAM BOOKS
LONDON

All Editor's and Contributors' fees and royalties
from the sale of this book have been donated to
The Lord's Taverners' Charities to aid Disabled
Children and Youth Cricket

First published in Great Britain by
Pelham Books Ltd
27 Wrights Lane, Kensington, London W8
1986

British Library Cataloguing in Publication Data

The Boundary book: second innings.
1. Cricket
I. Frewin, Leslie
796.35′8′0922   GV919

ISBN 0 7207 1697 7

Printed and bound in Great Britain by
Butler & Tanner Ltd, Frome and London

CONTENTS

CARTOONS

His Royal Twelfthmanship

PREFACE

HRH The Prince Philip,
Duke of Edinburgh, KG, KT

The first Boundary Book appeared in 1962 and I understand it was a huge success both in Britain and in cricketing countries around the world. Thanks to this success it raised a large amount of money for the charitable activities of the Lord's Taverners.

Those readers who are unfamiliar with the Lord's Taverners should know that it is a heterogeneous collection of cricket enthusiasts who prefer to watch their favourite game from a public house with a view of Lord's cricket ground rather than from a seat in the stands. As might be expected, the members of the Lord's Taverners are, to put it mildly, different. For some hitherto unexplained reason, it seems that the members of those professions engaged in entertaining the public appear to require the comfort of a full tankard in order to enjoy a game of cricket. Whether this indulgence causes a prick of conscience, or for some other reason, Lord's Taverners have committed themselves to raise money to help young people to learn the game and to give handicapped children the chance to explore the world outside their

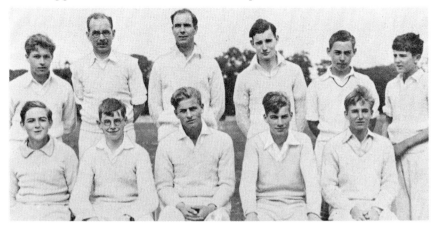

Cricket Eleven, Gordonstoun School, Summer 1938.
Captain: Prince Philip (centre front row).

homes. Needless to say, their methods of extracting money from the unsuspecting public are just about as original as the members themselves.

As I have said, the first Boundary Book was an outstanding success and bearing in mind the fact that the Lord's Taverners are largely drawn from the entertainment world, you will understand the reason for producing this 'Son of Boundary Book' but which has been graced with the more original title of 'The Boundary Book: Second Innings'.

I hope it has at least the same success as its predecessor and that it will encourage all who read it to give their support to this admittedly eccentric but very well meaning group of enthusiasts for a game that is almost as eccentric as its supporters.

BUCKINGHAM PALACE

LESLIE FREWIN

... The Taverners are remarkably adept in setting up what can best be described as usurious ploys ...

A LOOK BACK IN LANGUOR

Nearly a quarter of a century has passed since buoyant, if slightly barnacled, I landed myself with the task of creating the original *The Boundary Book* for the Lord's Taverners' charities. Here I am now, in 1986, 'at it again', having in turn been gently bludgeoned, pushed, nudged and persuaded to bring out this Mark II version.

If you hadn't already noticed, the Taverners are remarkably adept in setting up what can best be described as usurious ploys. These ploys take the form of insidiously infiltrating the defences of the fellow who, in reply to cunning invitations to apply himself again to a battle area like this book, roundly and decisively declares to all such entreaties, 'Sorry, old lads, it's not on. Haven't the time. Try so and so.' Such protestations are usually met with wistful whimpers and dull stares. As early I learnt, the Taverners, like the girl in *Chaimrent*, seldom take 'no' for an answer. They have a well-tried technique. They selectively fire an opening salvo; the noise reverberates and seemingly dies away. Then months, sometimes – as in the case of this book – years later, somebody from headquarters, or deputed from headquarters – the president, chairman, director or some odd bod from the Council – will casually loom up with the throwaway line, 'I thought we might think again on that idea we thought of some time ago'. '*We* thought of' inferring that you were part and parcel of the original thought!

As Peter Dobereiner said in his piece in the *Observer* on the Lord's Taverners' *Fifty Greatest Golfers*: 'They thought I might lend them a hand (or words to this effect) and suddenly I was landed with the whole blooming enterprise!' But, of course, the progenitors know full well that this is the point when they are closing the net. Further protests, 'Sorry, I'm travelling a lot. Time's the problem – I'm up to my neck', are totally ignored. Excuses go for naught. They simply wait and pounce again at the right moment. Which is precisely how, in 1986, I found myself in the middle again, snookered, landed like a helpless, floundering fish, totally unable to get away. Up there in the Chester Street warren they are at this point rubbing their hands gleefully, while you, poor wretch, rudely discover that you have committed yourself to a mountain of work, endless files of correspondence, a never-ending welter of telephone calls, innumerable meetings, undigested meals, untold miles of travel, lengthy research and an endless succession of Mogadon-popping nights. As the Twelfth Man wrote when he heard of this new book, 'It's going to be a lot of work'. But it's the ploy, d'you see? And if you don't see, take my word for it that it is pure, unadulterated Gamesmanship of the kind invented by my old friend Stephen Potter whom, aeons ago, along with John Snagge, I put up for membership of the Taverners. In short, they move you slowly – but oh, so slowly – to the edge and then with a gentle heave shove you in at the deep end. Then they look the other way while you scream, 'Save me!'

They did it before in the early sixties and I should by now have recognised the signs. This time, they blamed it on Dick Douglas-Boyd, the most pleasant of publishers, who allegedly said to them (and this was quickly passed on to me), 'Our sales people keep asking for another *Boundary Book*. Any hope?' Any hope, indeed!

Now, I am one of those types who refuse to live in the past. I'm usually too busy coping with the present. Having been lumbered, I sat down and asked myself: how does one follow the remarkable success – a success due *solely* to my distinguished contributors – of the original effort? Let's see, then. Let's go back to the original *Boundary Book*.

Who did that piece for me on *547 Useless Facts About Cricket?* Of course, it was Pip Youngman-Carter, Lord's Taverner Number 138, who also did that charmingly barmy essay *The Lord's Taverners in Literature*, and the nonsense about *The First Taverner*, as well as the frontispiece drawing of the Twelfth Man. In his home at Tolleshunt d'Arcy in full view of his talented wife Marjery Allingham, whose charm belied her amazing capacity to cook up a succession of best-sellers full of fiendish murder and mayhem, Pip got to work. And what about all those rude Lord's Taverners drawings like the one of the maiden aunt twisting the private parts of a nude Lord's Taverner, using the vital area as the tap of a tea urn? I remember calling Jackie Broome. 'Jackie', I think I said, 'I want you to do some drawings for *The Boundary Book*.' 'Meet you tomorrow at the Garrick at one,' came the reply. (He meant the Club, not the pub.) 'Let's talk about it.'

Beneath a menacing oil painting of Sir Henry Irving and other thespian knights, we duly talked about it. Jackie subsequently turned in a file of hilarious drawings. I had to drop the 'samovar' one. After all, ladies play cricket and ladies read cricket books and I hope I was fairly well brought up. But dear Jackie has gone to the outfield and times have changed. Thus, the 'samovar' drawing is herein included.

It's still very funny if you like your humour emanating from genitalised tea-urn taps...

How did the original book take shape? Let's, I thought, have a piece on Music and Cricket – after all, our Founder was originally an opera singer. This bright idea landed me up in a dressing-room in the Kingsway Hall, London. That's a lie. It was a room in a corridor where the caretaker made revolting cups of tea. John Barbirolli, a dear and valued friend, slumped near-exhausted in a chair after rehearsing his beloved Hallé Orchestra for a recording, pulled out a whisky flask from his hip pocket, gave me a swig, listened and said, 'I'll see what I can do.' Two months later, having winged its way across half the world, a mail packet thudded on my desk. It contained John's delightful piece on *Music and Cricket* – cricket as played by him and the Hallé team. 'It was necessary to add one or two new rules to the Hallé cricket team's operations,' he wrote. 'No Hallé batsman could ever be given out l.b.w. and should he be bowled out, I was under instruction to shout, somewhat belatedly, "No ball!"' Impeccable behaviour on the part of Lord's Taverner Number 7.

This missive was followed next day by a memorable evening of wine and chatter with Peter Sellers, nervous, twitchy as ever. It was an evening which started in his security-swamped eyrie above Clarges Street, Mayfair, and ended with a delicious dinner at Le Gavroche, both of which, I hope and believe, nudged him into producing the inimitable, staccato essay *Village Cricket* with Peter Munro-Smith.

You'll understand that to make the new *Boundary Book*, one inevitably had to go back in time. There were – on that first foray – more dinners, lunches, weekends in the country, letters – a prodigious amount of letters – telephone calls galore and endless meetings. Drinks with Sir Alan Herbert in his enchanting above-Hammersmith Thames-side abode; a memorable dinner party with John Marshall, he of Slindon Village where, he suggested, cricket began. The dinner party lasted until three in the morning at the old Criterion Restaurant in Piccadilly Circus. It was a party which prized out of John his superb *Big Cricket's Little Cradle* – Slindon, of course, – on the very day he took over from Reginald Willis as editor of London's *Evening News*.

And what about the peerless cricket writer and raconteur, John Arlott? Was it at that luncheon party I gave in a box at Lord's in the high summer of '62 that I persuaded John to pen his *The Man Who Never Encouraged Bowlers* for the original *Boundary Book*? I can't remember exactly; memory plays tricks. But it certainly was John who, with John Bridges and Alf Gover, provided the thrill of a lifetime – luncheon with the peerless and self-effacing Sir John Berry Hobbs at the Master's Luncheon Club above Henri's in Maiden Lane, Covent Garden, a luncheon that became a fine, photographic feature in *The Boundary*

Book. And the wonderful party at Lord's during the England–Pakistan Tests of 1962, when my box was graced all day by the formidable presence of that fine statesman and cricket lover, Sir Robert Menzies – which, in its turn produced his enchanting *The Gentle Art of Looking On*.

The original *Boundary Book* evokes, for all its intense work, many wonderful memories for me; talks with the gifted poet and don, Edmund Blunden; diverting telephone conversations with 'Plum' Warner, waning in body but quick-witted of mind; delightful letters from the talented Dennis Silk, then, as now, Warden of that fine public school, Radley; singular correspondence, too, with Samuel Beckett, no less, going to and from his secret lair in Paris; a long week-end at Esher with my old friend R. C. 'Bob' Sherriff – he of *Journey's End* fame – which got me *Badger's Green* for *The Boundary Book*.

And can one forget the series of delightful pub lunches with R. C. Robertson-Glasgow, the lovable 'Crusoe', a man of infinite wisdom and humour who shortly afterwards died much, much too soon in tragic circumstances. And those lunches, too, at the mausoleum-like Liberal Club in Northumberland Avenue with Neville Cardus, that master – past-master – of cricket prose who wrote of cricket with the same felicity as he wrote of music and life. Winsome, gentle in humour, graphic in prose, Neville gave me several things to print as I knew he would. Perhaps here I ought quickly to forget an excursion to the Emerald Isle, to Dublin, in the company of Art Buchwald, one of America's most accomplished humorous commentators on the human scene, which provided me with the right to publish *Are You Sure It's Cricket?* under his name. Perhaps the less said about that trip (as guests of film director John Huston), the better. Memory at times grows somewhat faint, doesn't it? Just as well!

Is it really nigh on a quarter of a century since Robin Marlar bounded up the stairs of my Mayfair house, two at a time (like my doctor, always ignoring the lift), to hand me his fine piece on *Lord's – The Game and It's Headquarters?* Yes, it *is* close on twenty-five years ago. And is it not a continuing delight that Robin is still writing his urbane cricket reports and articles for the London *Sunday Times* while at the same time directing his highly-successful business with offices in eight countries?

There were, too, many others who helped, who responded to my entreaties to contribute to the original *Boundary Book*. The peerless cricket dignitary and historian Harry S. Altham; the beloved Ray Robinson in far-off Australia; the always effervescent Alf Gover – 'Mr Cricket' – whom I had watched in action at the Oval as a boy, mesmerised by the sight of his run-up, with Andy Sandham crouched behind the wicket like a waiting eagle, hungry for its prey; the same bowler and man who years later was to teach my son and now my grandson how to hold a bat and thrash a ball. All these fine experts said 'Yes, of course' to my invitation to contribute, as did the scholarly Alan Ross; the gay, ever-smiling, incomparable stumper Godfrey Evans; the always impeccably-dressed, carnation button-holed Gordon Ross; the gentle, highly-knowledgeable novelist friend of long-standing, Ernest Raymond; the down-to-earth Frank Lee; the enthusiastic Raman Subba Row; the tall, imposing Stuart Surridge (*O, my Surrey, long ago!*). There were many others, too: Len Hutton, rightly sitting astride his bright and shining knighthood; the erudite Spike Hughes (whose evocative words taught me so many, many ploys of cricket!); Doug Insole, later to become an England Selector; Peter May, ditto; the rolling figure of John Snagge whom I lured away from the Thames to write for me; the irrepressible story-teller Brian 'Johnners' Johnston; John Clarke of the *Standard*; Bernard Hollowood, a fine cricketer, then head boy of *Punch*; the urbane Crawford White of the *Daily Express* and the civilised Michael Melford of the *Daily Telegraph*. These, and many more, like the quiet, pensive Thomas Moult, a diffident cricket poet of great talent, who gave me tea and penned a poem for me in his Essex cottage. How grateful one was, and still is, to them all. And to the fine cartoonists, too – Artie, Brockbank, Emmwood, Carl Giles, Jensen, David Langton, Millington, Doug Smith, Smythe, Ullyett and Reg Varney.

It is good that Prince Philip is as direct, pertinent and amusingly wry as ever in his observations in this book. When invited to write the Preface to the original volume, he responded with a delicious opening-over on both the Taverners and the old Tavern. Hear him again:

'Quite what it is which makes the Lord's Tavern such a very special place, I don't know. But there is something about this celebrated hostelry that can persuade an eminent Scottish playwright to stand and watch cricket in the company of perfectly strange Englishmen. What is it that causes staid theatrical producers to finish rehearsals early on some trivial excuse, only to find themselves, ten minutes later, rubbing shoulders with their own actors who should be studying their lines? And what prompts a renowned conductor to lay down his baton on a Saturday afternoon and look for a cab to St. John's Wood? Just cricket? Scientists may one day discover what controls the homing instinct of fish and birds but I hope they never try to analyse the urge of the Taverner to return to Lord's.'

Just so.

But what *has* all this nostalgia bit, this look back in languor, to do with the totally new *The Boundary Book: Second Innings*? Little, except that if you were to change many of the names included here, it could truthfully be said that it has been a similar tale creating and producing this Mark II version. It goes without saying that had it not been for the kindness, consideration and goodwill of the contributors (listed at the front of this book), I would not have been able to bowl even a first over, leave alone stay the course of the game. As the Twelfth Man said when he overheard me demurring from tackling the original book, 'It doesn't just happen. You've got to make it happen.' He'd got it right again.

I hope that *The Boundary Book: Second Innings* will follow the success pattern of its predecessor in cricketing countries throughout the world. If it does, lots of young people, many disabled and underprivileged, will be able to share a great deal of happiness as a result of the money this new book will raise; even before publication it has already pulled in a substantial sum, mainly through the generosity of Pelham Books.

Sometimes it is worth looking back if retrospect helps others to look forward. That, of course, is what Taverners' ploys are all about.

THE SEASON OPENS

A Tower we must have, and a clock in the tower,
Looking over the tombs, the tithebarn, the bower;
The inn and the mill, the forge and the hall,
And that loamy sweet level that loves bat and ball.

So a gray tower we have, and the centuried trees
Have arisen to share what its belfry-light sees,
The apple-plats richest in spring-song of all,
Kitchen-gardens and the field where they take bat and ball.

The stream with its moments of dance in the sun
Where the willows allow, runs and ever will run
At the cleft of the orchard, along the soft fall
Of the pasture where tourneys became bat and ball.

And now where the confident cuckoo takes flight
Over buttercups kindled in millions last night,
A labourer leans on the stackyard's low wall
With the hens bothering round him, and dreams bat and ball;

Till the meadow is quick with the masters who were,
And he hears his own shouts when he first trotted there;
Long ago; all gone home now; but here they come all!
Surely these are the same, who now bring bat and ball?

EDMUND BLUNDEN

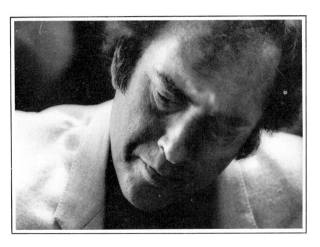

HAROLD PINTER

*The accomplished playwright sent this,
autographed, to the editor as recompense for
taking over his secretary in 1962 . . .*

HUTTON AND THE PAST

Hardstaff and Simpson at Lord's. Notts versus Middlesex. 1946 or 1947. After lunch, Keeton and Harris had opened for Notts. Keeton swift, exact, interested, Harris Harris. Harris stonewalled five balls in the over for no particular reason and hit the sixth for six, for no particular reason. Keeton and Harris gave Notts a fair start. Stott, at number three, smacked the ball hard, was out in the early afternoon. Simpson joined Hardstaff. Both very upright in their stance. They surveyed the field, surveyed themselves, began to bat. The sun was strong, but calm. They settled into the afternoon, no hurry, all in order. Hardstaff clipped to midwicket. They crossed. Simpson guided the ball between midoff and the bowler. They crossed. Their cross was a trot, sometimes a walk, they didn't need to run. They placed their shots with precision, they knew where they were going. Bareheaded. Hardstaff golden. Simpson dark. Hardstaff offdrove, silently, Simpson to deep square leg. Simpson cut. Hardstaff cut, finer. Simpson, finer. The slips, Robertson, Bennett, attentive. Hardstaff hooked, immaculate, no sound. They crossed, and back. Deep square leg in the heat after it.

Jim Sims on at the pavilion end with leg breaks. Hardstaff wristed him into the covers. Simpson to fine leg. Two. Sims twisting. Hardstaff wristed him into the covers, through the covers, fielder wheeling, for four. Quite unhurried. Seventy in ninety minutes. No explosions. Batsmanship. Hardstaff caught at slip, off Sims.

Worrell and Weekes at Kingston on Thames. 1950. The Festival. Headley had flicked, showed what had been and what remained of himself, from the thirties. Worrell joined Weekes with an hour to play. Gladwin and Jackson bowling. Very tight, very crisp, just short of a length, jolting, difficult. Worrell and Weekes scored ninety before close of play. No sixes, nothing off the ground. Weekes smashed, red eyed, past cover, smashed to long leg, at war, met Gladwin head on, split midwicket in two, steel. Worrell wanted to straight drive to reach his fifty. Four men at the sight screen to stop him. He straight drove, pierced them, reached his fifty. Gladwin bowled a stinging ball, only just short, on middle and leg. Only sensible course was to stop it. Worrell jumped up, both feet off, slashed it from his stomach, square cut for four, boundary first bounce.

MCC versus Australians. Lords 1948. Monday. On the Saturday the Australians had plastered the MCC bowling, Barnes one hundred, Bradman just short. On Monday morning Miller hit Laker for five sixes into the tavern. The Australians passed 500 and declared. The weather darkened. MCC thirty minutes batting before lunch. The Australians came into the field chucking the ball hard at each other, broad, tall, sure. Hutton and Robertson took guard against Lindwall and Miller. Robertson caught Tallon off Miller. Lindwall and Miller very fast. The sky black. Edrich caught Tallon off Miller. Last ball before lunch MCC 20 for 2. After lunch the Australians, arrogant, jocular, muscular, larking down the pavilion steps. They waited, hurling the ball about, eight feet tall. Two shapes behind the pavilion glass. Frozen before emerging a split second. Hutton and Compton. We knew them to be the two greatest English batsmen. Down the steps together, out to the middle. They played. The Australians quieter, wary, tight. Bradman studied them. They stayed together for an hour and then Compton was out, and M. P. Donnelly, and Hutton, and the Australians walked home.

First Test at Trent Bridge. The first seven in the English batting order: Hutton, Washbrook, Edrich, Compton, Hardstaff, Barnett, Yardley. They'll never get them out, I said. At lunch on the first day, England 78 for 8.

Hutton.

England versus New Zealand 1949. Hutton opened quietly, within himself, setting his day in order. At the first hour England 40 for none, Hutton looking set for a score. Burtt, slow left hand, took the ball at the Nursery End, tossed it up. To his first ball Hutton played a superb square drive to Wallace at deep point. Wallace stopped it. The crowd leaned in. Burtt again, Hutton flowed into another superb square drive to Wallace's right hand. Wallace stopped it. Back to the bowler. Burtt again, up. Hutton, very hard, a most brilliant square drive to Wallace's left hand. Wallace stopped it. Back to the bowler. The crowd. Burtt in, bowled. Hutton halfway up the pitch immediately, driving straight. Missed it. Clean bowled. On his heel back to the pavilion.

Hutton was never dull. His bat was part of his nervous system. His play was sculptured. His forward defensive stroke was a complete statement. The handle of his bat seemed electric. Always, for me, a sense of his vulnerability, of a very uncommon sensibility. He never just went through the motions, nothing was glibly arrived at. He was never, for me, as some have defined him, simply a 'master technician'. He attended to the particular but rarely lost sight of the context in which it took place. But one day in Sydney he hit 37 in 24 minutes and was out last ball before lunch when his bat slipped in hitting a further four, when England had nothing to play for but a hopeless draw, and he's never explained why he did *that*. I wasn't there to see it and probably regret that as much as anything. But I wasn't surprised to hear about it, because every stroke he made surprised me. I heard about Hutton's 37 on the radio. 7 a.m. Listened to every morning of the 46/7 series. Alan McGilvray talking. Always England six wickets down and Yardley 35 not out. But it was in an Irish kitchen in County Galway that, alone, I heard Edrich and Compton in 1953 clinch the Ashes for England.

Those were the days of Bedser and Wright, Evans, Washbrook and Gimblett, M. P. Donnelly, Smailes and Bowes, A. B. Sellars, Voce and Charley Barnett, S. M. Brown and Jim Sims, Mankad, Mustaq Ali, Athol Rowan, even H. T. Bartlett, Hammond and certainly Bradman.

One morning at drama school I pretended illness and pale and shaky walked into Gower Street. Once round the corner I jumped on a bus and ran into Lord's at the Nursery End to see through the terraces Washbrook late cutting for four, the ball skidding towards me. That beautiful evening Compton made seventy.

But it was 1950 when G. H. G. Doggart missed Walcott at slip off Edrich and Walcott went on to score 165, Gomez with him. Christiani was a very good fielder. Ramadhin and Valentine had a good season. Hutton scored 202 not out against them and against Goddard bowling breakbacks on a bad wicket at the Oval.

It was 1949 when Bailey caught Wallace blindingly at silly mid on. And when was it I watched Donnelly score 180 for the Gents versus Players? He went down the afternoon with his lightning pulls.

Constantine hitting a six over fine leg into the pavilion. Talk of a schoolboy called May.

A BOWLER'S BOWLER. Australian Raymond Russell Lindwall, MBE, played in 61 Test Matches, took 228 wickets for 23.05 each and scored two Test centuries. He boasted an incredibly smooth run-up followed by a beautiful arm action. Here he is practising in the nets at the Oval in September 1983 with the Old England Eleven v Old World Eleven. In the background is Sir Garfield Sobers.

IAN WOOLDRIDGE

*'I shall go for long walks and grow vines and
stop drinking at lunchtimes . . .'*

THE DAY CRICKET
STOOD STILL

For a man whose glorious imagery enthralled three decades of cricket listeners, John Arlott's valedictory sentence on Test match cricket was prosaic to the point of historic understatement.

There were no goodbyes, and no emotion tinged the deep rural voice that epitomised not only his game, but the very English way of life. All he said was: 'And now, after comment by Trevor Bailey, it will be Christopher Martin-Jenkins.' To the last the poet in him was ruled by sheer professionalism.

It was, of course, a desperately emotional moment, for Arlott has described every Test match played in England since the war not to mention plenty overseas, to audiences who regarded him not only as a sports commentator but as a national institution.

In the next few minutes he was to understand, at last, the esteem in which he has for so long been held. Behind him, in the tiny sound-proof box high in the Lord's Pavilion, his fellow commentators broke into spontaneous applause.

At the end of the over, Test cricket itself stood motionless in tribute. A loudspeaker announcement informed the crowd and cast of the Centenary Test that the great man had just uttered his last broadcast word on the international game. The Australians were in the field. They turned to the Pavilion and applauded. So did Geoffrey Boycott, an English batsman usually dedicated to turning a cold back on all distraction.

And so did the crowd, for down the years, in sitting rooms and motorcars and in dressing gowns on cold mornings, while listening to his voice home in from Sydney or Melbourne they have hung on to his syllables, marvelling at the similes and metaphors, the humour and the humanity that he could manifest over a simple ball game.

As if to honour him, even the cruel summer relented on his final day. Lord's, the greatest ground of all, was bathed in sunshine as he came

HIGH ABOVE THEM ALL. *The indomitable John Arlott in the commentary box at Lord's on 2 September 1980, the day of his retirement from broadcasting. His career in front of the microphones started in 1946 and continued without pause for thirty-four years.*

down the dark stairs from the Pavilion and walked up six more flights of stairs to the press box bar.

'A glass of Beaujolais, I think,' he said and grinned. Mr Arlott, purely in his other professional capacity as wine correspondent of the *Guardian*, of course, has never been averse to a drink.

My fondest memory of his whole career, in fact, was of a single sentence he spoke in a hotel lounge in Cambridge in circumstances far removed from covering cricket matches for unseen audiences. It was at the height of the huge controversy concerning whether or not England's cricketers were morally justified in touring South Africa and Arlott, a firm but restrained spokesman for those who stood against apartheid, had been asked to oppose some heated politicians in a debate at the Cambridge Union.

'They tell me,' said Arlott very quietly, 'that I only have to keep sober to win this one.'

The politicians waved fists clutching sheaves of notes. In due course Arlott rose to speak. He was wearing what appeared to be a sports jacket that had seen its best days on the grouse moors, and into its left pocket he plunged a fist, leaving his right hand to gesticulate occasionally.

He won the day not only with sane persuasion, but a faultless flow of English so beautiful in its construction that you could almost hear the commas and semi-colons fall into place. He sat down to a standing ovation.

Arlott's genius over more than three decades has been based on that mastery of the English language, allied to a wit epitomised by a pun he produced in his apprentice days at the microphone in 1947.

At Lord's, a crafty South African googly bowler named Tufty Mann was tying a Middlesex tail-end batsman named George Mann into such knots that the crowd was reduced to laughter.

When it occurred for the fourth time in a single over, John Arlott, apparently without a moment's thought, reported: 'So what we are watching here is a clear case of Mann's inhumanity to Mann.'

Not far from his seventies, he says with a modesty that has never left him, the puns and epigrams are becoming harder in the invention.

The output, both spoken and written, has been prolific, the life harrowed by the two deep personal tragedies of the early death of a wife and a son killed in a road crash. But, though still full of words and wisdom, his decision to retire reflects his respect for his profession.

'I wanted retirement to be my choice,' he said, 'not someone else's. Anyway, I've reached the point where I simply don't enjoy talking all day on the radio, writing my piece for the *Guardian*, driving 240 miles home and then getting up next morning to do it all over again.'

At the end of this month he will move from his rambling home in Alresford, Hampshire, with its 10,000 books and autographed first editions of Thomas Hardy, and the personally inscribed early works of his close friend Dylan Thomas, and its impressively stocked wine cellar, to the island of Alderney.

'I shall go for long walks and grow vines and stop drinking at lunchtime,' he forecast, without total conviction. 'Mind you, what I'm really up to is trying to extend this marvellous life by another 20 years.'

He will not, of course, stop talking. John Arlott only stops talking when he is writing, and the talk, if you had been privileged to be present at one of his 8 p.m. to 3 a.m. *soirées* round the bottle-laden refectory table at his home, is, surprisingly, only occasionally about cricket or John Arlott.

It is of Gladstone and bull-fighting, and the adored mother who encouraged him to the local library, and the social development of the English working class, and politics and topography and the thousands of books which have been the constant friends of his life.

'Cricket,' he says, 'has only been part of my life. It has never been an obsession.'

That, over the thirty-five years since his transfer from the BBC's Poetry Department for a trial in the commentary box, has been his ultimate strength.

The man who won a million friends for cricket always realised that war and poverty were reality and cricket, in the end, was only a glorious game.

JOHN ARLOTT

*'Do cricketers ever realise, I wonder – to how
many millions of people they will never know –
they are breakfast-table heroes?'*

CRICKET FOR BREAKFAST

Cricket is pre-eminently the breakfast-time sport, recognised and enjoyed all over the world, though nowhere quite so deeply nor so frequently as in England. In the life of the English county cricketer, breakfast is in many ways the symbol of his achievement. While other men are choking down a cup of tea and dashing out to be at work at eight or nine o'clock, the county cricketer is at his leisure. At away matches he strolls downstairs in the hotel without hurry – though not always with the entire approval of the dining-room staff – with the ease of a man who does not have to start work until half-past eleven. True, some captains call for a half-past ten report on the ground, but even that leaves time for relaxation, a three-course meal, an extra cup of coffee at the end; and above all, the paper.

You may always identify a county cricket team at breakfast in an English hotel because they are all reading the morning newspapers; not simply one apiece but passing them round so that they all see them all. They are, of course, reading the cricket scores and reports so that, by the end of the meal, most of them know – without consciously committing it to memory but from sheer interest – just what every team and individual did in the previous day's play. Being a county cricketer is not simply playing for a county; it is following all the other counties. These are the ultimate 'shop' men.

The conversation stirred by this morning study has an established and traditional form. 'I see' – comment on anything read in the paper always begins with 'I see' – 'I see old Fred got a hundred runs against Derbyshire: must have been a beautiful track for him to get runs against Alan Ward.' 'But perhaps Alan wasn't really fit – ?' 'Must have been, they gave him eighteen overs.' Every game is weighed up. They have not missed a trick. 'I see old Eddie got another star (a not out) against Sussex; bet that made Snowball mad.'

They know who is fit, who is playing well; they notice tactical details a hundred miles away: 'Why did Brian only bowl a dozen overs yesterday if it's a turner at Weston, then?' 'Why did he keep Skinny on for forty overs when he only took one?'

The difference between the first-class cricketers and their followers is that the players have longer to go about this delightful morning pursuit. Other games, such as football, produce morning reading only once or twice a week – and anyway it is not quite the same on Sundays. England is the best breakfast-cricket country because every day in the season there is a match to be reported somewhere. Since my childhood the special flavour of summer has always been the cricket scores in the morning. There was one brief period when, living in North Hampshire where the local club is called Basingstoke and North Hants, I thought we had two county teams – Hampshire and Northants – and was only relieved of the anguish of not knowing which to support in a match between the two by my father's explanation.

Like millions of other small boys, I knew all the county cricketers from the morning papers before I ever saw any of them play. There was no television then; cricketers were to be seen only in the papers – photographs, and Tom Webster, then in the heyday of his economic, laughing line – on cigarette cards, or in the mind. There were not even any evening scores on the wireless so that the rumour someone had heard from a man who saw it in the Stop Press of an evening paper, that Mead had been 77 not out in the afternoon, left us in a state of agonised suspense until next morning's news confirmed that he had scored his century (he usually did, though several of us were rendered uneasy for years after he got out in the nineties twice during the same fortnight).

Test Matches in Australia were tantalising; in the years before the relayed commentaries there was a terrible wait for the morning editions of the evening papers; they did not arrive until we had gone to school, there was no chance of a glimpse of one in the mid-morning break and it was horrid not to know even the worst until lunchtime.

It is never quite the same after one has grown up. Of course many breakfast-table cricketers follow their native counties faithfully all the summer through the morning reports. For them, though, the players themselves are not distant and unattainable: they simply do not bother to go to the matches when they might. For us, as boys, remote from the county grounds, the morning paper was the only link with those splendid creatures. The heavy tread of Armstrong's Australians echoed through England in that blazing summer and, all at once, though their game was not even a distant relation of our rough-ground skirmishes, they spellbound me. So each breakfast-time, when my father had gone out to work, leaving the paper for me, there was regular news of the

27

great: Jack Hobbs – until he fell ill, Hendren, Hearne, Russell, Woolley, Sandham, Tyldesley, E. Freeman, White, Macaulay, Rhodes, Parker, the destroying Australian fast bowlers, Gregory and McDonald, the splendid Macartney – and, of course, *all* the Hampshire players, but especially Tennyson, Mead and Brown, who almost alone defied the Australians. All of these I was to see and many of them I later came to know personally.

Many others, though, remain fresh in my mind, cricketers I followed through those distant summers, men I never set eyes upon, but whom I still remember (initials as well, if pressed) in the pictures my mind made of them all those years ago: Wells, Murdin and Buswell; Curgenven, Cadman and Bestwick; Coventry, Preece and Tarbox; Mounteney, Coe and Benskin; Gillingham, Perrin and Farnfield; and, from the 'new' county, Whittington, Hacker, Creber, O'Bree and Pinch. Do cricketers ever realise, I wonder – to how many millions of people they will never know – they are breakfast-table heroes?

HENDREN REACHES THE HEIGHTS!
Middlesex cricketer E. 'Patsy' Hendren batting in his heyday.

CHRISTOPHER MARTIN-JENKINS

*The BBC's Cricket Correspondent remembers his
schooldays – and a book . . .*

FROM THE (NEAR) NURSERY END

The Boundary Book was one of the first two cricket books I ever actually bought with my own money. The other was the 1963 *Wisden Almanack* and I bought them in the same bookshop in Marlborough High Street on the same day with money I had been awarded as winner of the School's Public Speaking prize. If I remember correctly, the speech was an imaginary one welcoming a party of students from the USA on their arrival in the UK. Thank goodness the script does not survive!

Once I had got over the excitement and vanity of seeing my own name in print in the Centenary Edition of Wisden, it took me time to appreciate the real treasures it contained. But *The Boundary Book* was at once a hallowed possession, that attractive green cover beckoning constantly like a pitch on a sunny day in May with the wickets set, the first ball of the match unbowled and hope springing, as ever, eternal in the breast of every player.

I had not then heard of the Lord's Taverners, but the book conveyed quite remarkably the sense of fun and deep devotion to cricket which the pioneers of our now rather more business-like organisation must have had. The sole recipient then, I see from the Duke of Edinburgh's characteristically thoughtful introduction, was the National Playing Fields Association. I sometimes wonder whether the present Lord's Taverners have lost sight of the original aim to stimulate *cricket* for the young and deprived. No cricket anthology up to that time can have had so wide and varied and distinguished a list of contributors. There was a happy mingling of serious and light-hearted pieces, not to mention informative ones. The use of verse, sketches and photographs was imaginative and entertaining. As an 18-year-old I was already so besotted with the game that it had not even occurred to me to spend my tensely-earned prize on something more academic which might have impressed the Schoolmasters as being more appropriate a donation for the highly intelligent and learned Master, J. C. Dancy, to present on Prize-Day. I lapped up every page of *The Boundary Book*, from the first article by Sir Robert Menzies, through the contributions of Arlott, Bradman and Cardus to the last piece of all, a prediction of what cricket would be like in 1984, by Raman Subba Row, the recently elected chairman of the TCCB.

Raman got some things right. He foresaw the (then imminent) ending of amateur status and professional cricket on Sunday. But promotion and relegation in the Championship has not come nor has his wish that professional cricketers should become part-timers, carrying on a 'normal' profession the rest of the time. Tours have not shortened as he thought they would and instead international cricket has grown too fast. Nor is there yet a fully residential hotel in the grounds of Lord's. There isn't even one at The Oval. But keep working on it, Raman!

Above all the first *Boundary Book* conveyed, as the game always should, a real sense of fun. Cricket has become too commercial and too political in the twenty-four years elapsing since the original *Boundary Book*, but no doubt this present volume will help to restore the balance.

STUMPS DRAWN!

He played cricket on the heath,
The pitch was full of bumps:
A fast ball hit him in the teeth,
The dentist drew the stumps.

ANON

THE FIRST GAME

There comes a Day (I can hear it coming),
   One of those glorious deep blue days,
When larks are singing and bees are humming,
   And Earth gives voice in a thousand ways –
     Then I, my friends, I too shall sing,
     And hum a foolish little thing,
And whistle like (but not too like) a blackbird in the Spring.

There looms a Day (I can feel it looming;
   Yes, it will be in a month or less),
When all the flowers in the world are blooming,
   And Nature flutters her fairest dress –
     Then I, my friends, I too shall wear
     A blazer that will make them stare,
And brush – this is official; I shall also brush my hair.

It is the day that I watch for yearly,
   Never before has it come so late;
But now I've only a month – no, merely
   A couple of fortnights left to wait;
     And then (to make the matter plain)
     I hold – at last! – a bat again;
Dear Hobbs! the weeks this summer – think! the *weeks* I've
lived in vain!

I see already the first ball twisting
   Over the green as I take my stand,
I hear already long-on insisting
   It wasn't a chance that came to hand –
     Or no; I see it miss the bat
     And strike me on the knee, whereat
Some fool, some silly fool at point, says blandly, 'How was that?'

A. A. MILNE

MICHAEL AND NORMA PEARCE

*– for over twenty-five years 'official' umpire and scorer
respectively for the Lord's Taverners.*

*'Wasn't it at Cranwell that Harry Secombe's
trousers split as he bent to field the ball?'*

THE OLDEST DOUBLE-ACT IN THE BUSINESS

NORMA: It's been fun, hasn't it?

MICHAEL: What has?

NORMA: Being associated with the Taverners all these years.

MICHAEL: Oh yes, a lot of fun.

NORMA: Did you know they want us to write about it?

MICHAEL: Write about what?

NORMA: Our memories of the games, the places we've been, the people we've met – you know – and some of the funny bits.

MICHAEL: Funny bits?

NORMA: Mmm – like Jack Rayfield's box slipping down his leg at Wisborough Green.

MICHAEL: Oh, that sort of funny bit.

NORMA: It's been a long time, hasn't it, since it all began?

MICHAEL: Certainly has – you started in the Fifties when people like Denis Castle, Tony Britton, McDonald Hobley, Jack Martin, Ben Barnett, Leo Bennett and Monty Garland

	Wells played regularly, as did Bill Edrich, Len Phillips, Alf Gover and Stuart Surridge.
NORMA:	And you umpired *your* first game on the Taverners' first trip to Scotland in 1964 at the Hamilton Crescent ground in Glasgow.
MICHAEL:	Let's have a look at the old scorebooks and programmes – they'll bring back memories.
NORMA:	Here – remember this game? – Ingham in 1964 against the Edrich Family – what a day! – 823 runs scored in four hours ten minutes in front of 8000 people, packed in solid.
MICHAEL:	Yes – and the ground could only hold 4000 at a pinch! I think Ingham's probably my favourite ground of all the ones to which we've been.
NORMA:	What – better than Poloc in Glasgow? Where they let us take our caravan for the weekend in 1969?
MICHAEL:	Ah yes, well, it *is* a bit difficult to decide, isn't it?
NORMA:	We surely have been to some lovely grounds – Broadhalfpenny Down, Meudon, Arundel, Shanklin, Exning, to name but a few – and the stately homes, Blenheim, Castle Ashby, Hatfield House, Longleat, Althorp, Badminton, Burghley, not to mention Lord's, The Oval and the other Test Match grounds.
MICHAEL:	What about Great Wichingham?
NORMA:	You're favouring Norfolk again, aren't you?
MICHAEL:	Well, I always did like the Broads.
NORMA:	We're not getting far with the funny bits, you know.
MICHAEL:	You mentioned Shanklin – what about the journey back on the ferry when Gertie Martin swapped fish and chips with Valerie Pitts for a bit of her Kitkat and Marjorie Gover and Betty Surridge had a holdall full of drink for the train journey only to find they hadn't a bottle opener!
NORMA:	I'll always remember RAF Cranwell when Prince Charles came out to bat on a polo pony.
MICHAEL:	Then he dropped a catch, Johnny Blythe called him 'Butterfingers' and he replied – 'To the Tower!'
NORMA:	It was marvellous of Martin Boddey to introduce us to Prince Charles afterwards, a very proud moment – the only trouble was I couldn't remember his bowling analysis when he asked me!
MICHAEL:	Wasn't it at Cranwell that Harry Secombe's trousers split as he bent to field the ball?
NORMA:	Yes – and a little WAAF lass had to make running repairs – literally!

MICHAEL: There was trouble with trousers this year, too, with both Fred Rumsey and John Price having to borrow a pair from Ollie Milburn and I don't think the fit did much for their image!

NORMA: We had a streaker once, didn't we?

MICHAEL: That was at GEC Coventry, but his performance fell rather flat, as I remember he was told to get off the field in no uncertain terms, only to find his clothes had disappeared, leaving his assets decidedly frozen!

NORMA: You know, if we listed all the people we have met, it would be a cross between *Wisden's* and *Who's Who in the Theatre*, with a bit of Debrett thrown in, but it's surprising, when we look back, just how long some of the Taverners have been around. Look at this – Jeremy Kemp was at Ingham in 1964, he's still going strong; and what about this one – Derek Ufton played against us at the Mote in 1961. Crumbs! Mr Pastry – Richard Hearne – was in that match – he was lethal with his cricket bat-throwing act. Hey, here's another programme dated 1958 and Uffers was in L.E.G. Ames' XI against us on that occasion, too!

MICHAEL: Let's see, ah, D. Ufton, stumped John Slater, bowled Vic Lewis 34.

NORMA: You've fiddled a few games in your time, haven't you, with judicious 'no balls' – I recall dear old Jack Robertson at Milton Keynes being caught quite brilliantly in the slips first ball and you called the bowler for throwing from square leg – he wasn't best pleased, was he?

MICHAEL: Not really, but the crowd were: Jack went on to give them an exhibition of elegant batting. John Conteh at Northwood was another example, when he was 'out' off the first two balls he received, but lived to fight on and I've lost count of the times when *I've* 'lost count' and given an extra ball or two in the final over just to make an exciting finish.

NORMA: Scoring positions have had their moments too, you know. I've perched on scaffolding at Ingham with Alan Curtis, climbed up a ladder at Poloc which was too short to reach the platform (coming down was fun), been on the flat roof of a half-demolished pavilion with 'Danger' signs all around, and at Broadhalfpenny Down once Harry Secombe kept telling limericks behind Alan and me, making our job nigh on impossible! Johnny Dennis had a similar problem at Skew Bridge a couple of years ago when the commentary/scoring spot was in the dressing room – Johnny's ON/OFF switch was put to good use that day! John McKelvie, Jack Rayfield and Johnny Blythe were regular commentators; now Henry Kelly, Tony Fairbairn and Bill Frindall all take their turn.

MICHAEL: Bill Frindall had trouble with the mike at Stratford that year, didn't he, when he thought it had gone up the creek?

NORMA: Yes, but Butch White and Fred Rumsey were fiddling the controls in the dressing room.

MICHAEL: Did he find out?

NORMA: Don't know, but if he didn't then, he knows now!

MICHAEL: Wasn't Bill's day, actually, was it, with Farokh Engineer hitting a six through his windscreen, to the amusement of all?

NORMA: Farokh certainly hits the ball hard. He's made quick runs for us many a time, though, mind you, we've seen some speedy batting like Fred Rumsey's 50 in twelve minutes at Cranwell, Ben Barnett's 100 in thirty-two minutes at Ingham, Butch White's 50 in 22 balls at Radbrooke Hall and many more too numerous to record.

MICHAEL: It's funny, though, with all the cricketers who've played, one of the best, in fact, I think *the* best bowling analysis, was by an actor – one Ian Carmichael, who took 5 for 27 at Egham!

NORMA: If performances are to be mentioned, what about Eric Morecambe? He was the 'superman' in the autograph and Polaroid enclosure. How he sat in there the hours he did, game after game, and still came up smiling, I'll never know; he was a lovely man.

MICHAEL: Of course, our current President David Frost first turned out in the Sixties, and over the last ten years or so personalities such as Bill Tidy, Ted Moult, Henry Kelly, Steve Davis, Leslie Thomas, Richard Kershaw turn out whenever they can and blend in with the cricketing fraternity very well.

NORMA: Very true – you know, we have been very lucky to have met so many lovely people and been to so many places, haven't we?

MICHAEL: We have indeed. And we have so many memories, we could talk about them forever. But which game of them all really sticks in your mind?

NORMA: Well, it's got to be the first Old England game at Lord's in 1962, where I was allowed into the Pavilion to have

	lunch with the players and Bill Edrich said that he might have known I'd be the first woman to break the rule!
MICHAEL:	It must have been a great thrill – as for me when I umpired at Lord's for the first time; there really is nothing quite like the feeling you get when you walk on to that 'hallowed turf'.
NORMA:	You realise we've come back in our thoughts to where the Taverners began all those years ago?
MICHAEL:	So we have – but what better way to finish. Certainly I can't think of one, can you?
NORMA:	Not really – I'll go and make the tea.

The cartoon below, drawn by Reg Varney for the original Boundary Book, *is reprinted with no apologies.*

NORMAN HARRIS

*A great cricket paradox is investigated by a
leading* Sunday Times *sportswriter.*

DAVID GOWER: RIGHT-HANDED!

David Gower is right-handed. He proves it by using his right hand to write a letter, hammer a nail and wield a tennis racket. Only in his left-handed dealing of cards does he show a glimpse of left-handedness. But it is only a glimpse. To all intents and purposes he is a right-handed person.

Tim Robinson is left-handed. He uses his left hand to write, to hammer and to play tennis. When he uses a broom or shovel, it's his left hand that is at the top of the handle, doing all the shoving. He's a left-hander at almost everything except cricket.

Since it's Gower who is the left-handed batsman, and Robinson the right-hander, the game of cricket is obviously not what it seems to be. Only when they bowl do most players reveal their true hand. It's when they bat that they deceive us most. Almost all those batsmen we call left-handers, and regard as unusually talented, are right-handed people – most of them, including the great West Indian left-handers, even more right-handed than Gower.

Clive Lloyd and Alvin Kallicharran are right-handed not only when they write, hammer a nail and swing a racket, but even when they

37

brush their teeth and unscrew a jar lid. And if it's true that most of these batsmen do also bowl with their right hand, even *they* were most surprised when they were told that they were all right-handed at almost everything.

More surprising still, our questioning of some 100 first-class cricketers revealed that it's the players who do everything on the field – batting, bowling and throwing – right-handed who show most experience of left-handedness.

Among these 'orthodox' right-handers there is Martyn Moxon who, like Tim Robinson, is left-handed at almost everything except cricket. So is Glamorgan's John Hopkins. Then there's Mark Nicholas who, though mainly right-handed, uses his left hand to write and also, if need be, to thread a needle. Jim Love and Neil Taylor are two who play snooker left-handed. Imran Khan is a left-sided rifleman and archer. And Ken McEwan can even bowl and throw left-handed.

Indeed, some of these players might easily have been left-handed cricketers. Robinson batted left-handed for a time when he was a small boy, and Derek Randall also says he 'could have played either way'.

So why didn't they become left-hand batsmen? Why, indeed, don't more right-handed people do what Gower, Kallicharran and company have done, and bat as cricketing left-handers – with their best hand at the top of the handle?

To get to the bottom of this puzzle, let's start with the observation of an American professor who knows a great deal about left-handedness, but knew little about cricket – until he studied photographs in a coaching manual.

'I'm not surprised to learn that some batsmen are very mixed-handed,' said the professor. 'Batting in cricket appears to require a bi-manual symmetry, the two hands working much more in unison than they do in baseball batting. To bat well in cricket, it must be an advantage to be somewhat ambidextrous.'

This might seem obvious, but many batsmen and coaches these days tend to think of the two hands almost as antagonistic: the strong, bad bottom hand working against the good, weak top hand. They want to restrict the influence of the bottom hand, which they fear will pull the bat away from the line on which the top hand wants to lead it. They want to strengthen the left hand to give it more influence at the top of the handle in shaping a pure cricket stroke.

But even if the right-hander does possess what he thinks is a strong bottom hand, the two hands may be in better balance then he realises, with the left hand being used at the top of the handle because, in a sense, it's *good enough* to be there.

The reverse of this coin is that those who are very right-handed have apparently been compelled to use that hand as the important one at the top of the handle. They've 'turned around' to make this happen, and become cricketing left-handers. In the same way, most players who bowl left-arm – and this group seems to be strongly left-handed – have also switched around to bat with their dominant hand uppermost, as cricketing right-handers.

As for those 'classic' left-hand batsmen, then, what are we now to make of their free stroke-play – those flashing cover-drives and wristy sweeps away to leg? We now see these not as the result of unusual talent, or flamboyant character, but simply of the better hand being used to 'lead' the stroke and the poorer hand to control it. The left-hand batsman can hardly play any other way than with a flourish.

Derek Randall says it all when describing how, as a boy, he could bat either way around: 'I was more fluent left-handed, but had more control right-handed.'

Perhaps we can find further evidence in the batting of Allan Border, for the Australian captain is one of a rare breed (the greatest of whom

David Gower watches the ball fly past Australian wicket-keeper R. W. Marsh at the Lord's Test, England v Australia, on 7 July 1981. Gower went on to score 89 before he was caught behind wicket.

was Garfield Sobers) who bat left *and* bowl left: mirror images, perhaps, of right-handers.

Border also plays racket games left-handed, but uses his right hand to write a letter and hammer a nail. With such considerable mixed-handedness, one would expect him to be a fine batsman but less free, more controlled, than other left-handed batsmen. Many would say that he is.

Player	CRICKET		PRIMARY INDICATORS					SECONDARY INDICATORS			
	Batting	Bowling	Write letter	Hammer nail	Tennis/ Squash	Strike match	Brush teeth	Use scissors	Deal cards	Thread needle	Unscrew lid
Clive Rice	Right	Right	R	R	R	R	R	R	R	R	R
David Gower	Left	Right	R	R	R	R	Either	R	L	R	L
Tim Robinson	Right	Right	L	L	L	L	L	L	R	L	R
David Thomas	Left	Left	R	L	L	Either	Either	R	L	R	R
Phil Edmonds	Right	Left	L	L	L	L	L	L	L	L	L
Norman Gifford	Left	Left	L	L	L	L	L	L	L	L	L

● *These six cricketers represent the span of left- and right-handedness in cricket; and the questions they all answered were based on a hand preference test made available by a leading authority on the subject, Dr Marian Annett of Coventry. Of the nine particular hand sections identified, five are regarded by Dr Annett as primary indicators, and four as secondary indicators.*

The awarding of points of both primary and secondary actions, together with other significant indications of left-handedness, suggested that right-hand batsmen, as a group, were two to three times more 'mixed-handed' than any other group.

FULL MARX . . .

14 August 1844. Baron Alderson, a few days since, addressed the following remarks to the grand jury of the county of Suffolk: 'In a neighbouring county which I passed through on the circuit this time, I had what I am afraid I shall not have here – a day of rest; and I went out into the country, and had the pleasure of seeing a match of cricket, in which a noble earl, the Lord-Lieutenant of his county, was playing with the tradesmen, the labourers, and all around him, and I believe he lost no respect from that course – they loved him better, but they did not respect him less. I believe that if they themselves associated more with the lower classes of society, the kingdom of England would be in a far safer, and society in a far sounder condition. I wish I could put it to the minds of all to think so, because I think it is true.'

Original Report

'LLOYD OF THE WEST INDIES' on his way to a magnificent century in the Prudential Cup Final, West Indies *v* Australia, at Lord's on 21 June 1975.

LINES ON A CRICKET MATCH

How was my spirit torn in twain
When on the field arrayed
My neighbours with my comrades strove –
My town against my trade

And are the penmen players all?
Did Shakespeare shine at cricket?
And in what hour did Bunyan wait
Like Christian at the wicket?

When did domestic Dickens stand
A fireside willow wielding?
And playing cricket – on the hearth,
And where was Henry Fielding?

Is Kipling, as a flannelled fool,
Or Belloc, bowling guns,
The name that he who runs may read
By reading of his runs?

Come all; our land hath laurels too,
While round our beech-tree grows
The shamrock of the exiled Burke
Or Waller's lovely rose.

Who ever win or lose, our flags
Of fun and honour furled,
The glory of the game shall stand
Stonewalling all the world,

While those historic types survive
For England to admire,
Twin pillars of the storied past,
The Burgess and the Squire.

G. K. CHESTERTON

SIMON BARNES

'There's even a mysterious reference to the sacred symbol of Anglo-Australian conflict...'

CRICKET
FROM BIBLE TO BUNYAN

Shakespeare was by far the finest cricket writer of them all. When I solicited hidden references to cricket in the literature of the ages, the response was startling. So many great writers have touched on cricket – even the Bible is filled with allusions, right from the moment when the Great Umpire started play and 'saw light, that it was good.' But Shakespeare is tops.

Many readers offered me that reference to the days when close catchers were slimmer than Botham and Gatting: 'I see you stand like greyhounds in the slips' (*Henry V*, III i). Even more offered me a biblical example of poor spelling: 'And Peter went out with the eleven, and was bold,' which they all claimed was *Acts* 2:14. It isn't, in fact, in the Authorised or the Revised Standard, but has achieved extraordinarily wide currency.

There is, however, a genuine Shakespearean precedent for Peter May's speaking out against the reverse sweep: 'This is the bloodiest shame, the wildest savagery, the vilest stroke' (*King John*, IV iii). And the bouncer is obviously no modern thing, but was in use centuries ago: 'You have broken his pate with your bowl' (*Cymbeline*, I iv).

Nor is the turmoil that affects one of the northern counties a thing of recent years only: 'Alas, poor York, I should lament thy miserable state' (*Henry VI part 3*, I iv). However, southern traditions of gentility have long given rise to hostility from outsiders – hence the reference to 'the filth and scum of Kent' (*Henry VI part 2*, IV ii).

A Midsummer Night's Dream contains a clear reference to the last Ashes series, a remark doubtless uttered by an Australian perplexed with the wiles of Edmonds and Emburey: 'Hence, ye long-legged spinners, hence.' Interesting too, to note that the googly was known in Roman times: 'He put it by with the back of his hand, thus' (*Julius Caesar*, I ii).

Antony and Cleopatra contains a nicely written – almost worthy of

Cardus – description of Lillee appealing for leg before: 'His legs bestride the ocean, his rear'd arm crested the world, his voice was propertied as all the tuned spheres, and that to friends; but when he meant to quail and shake the orb, he was rattling thunder.'

It is hardly surprising to find the rumoured excesses of the England team in the dressing room in New Zealand echoed in the Old Testament: 'Ben-hadad was drinking himself drunk in the pavilion' (I *Samuel* 2:9). Evidence, too, that all cricket is morally reprehensible: 'He that touches the pitch shall be defiled by it' (*Ecclesiasticus* 13:1).

Weather played as big a part in cricket matches in biblical times as it does now: there is a reference in the *Psalms* to a couple of boundary fielders exhorting each other to get back to the pavilion: 'Deep called to deep at the noise of the water spouts' (69:15). Yet as every cricketer knows, rain can be – a godsend: 'Thou, O God, sentest a gracious rain' (*Psalms* 68:1).

Then there is a mysterious reference to the sacred symbol of Anglo-Australian conflict: 'The priest shall put on his linen garment ... and take up the ashes ... and he shall put them beside the altar. And he shall put off his garments, and put on other garments, and carry forth the ashes without the camp unto a clean place' (*Leviticus* 6:10–11). The clean place referred to is the Lord's pavilion.

Dr Johnson was clearly a cricketer in Bothamesque mould: 'I never think I have hit it hard, unless it rebounds.' Elizabeth Barrett Browning, surprisingly, had a penchant for treating her copies of *Wisden* in a rather playful spirit: 'Do you see this square old yellow book? I toss i' the air and catch again.'

Bunyan knew a thing or two about cricket, and writes allegorically about the game: 'Then said Evangelist, pointing with his finger over a very wide field, Do you see yonder wicket? ... So I saw in my dream that the man began to run.'

A number of writers show an uncanny knack of predicting recent events. Shakespeare has it in *Pericles* that 'from ashes ancient Gower is come'; perhaps the man is older than he looks. In *Henry V* we have the undeniable, though unspectacularly expressed notion that 'Gower is a good captain, and in good knowledge', while Chaucer, writes: 'O moral Gower! This book I direct at thee.'

The moral problems of the game have fascinated writers for several millennia. Omar Khayyam, in *The Rubaiyat*, tells us:

> The ball no question makes of ayes or noes,
> But right or left as strikes, the player goes;
> And he that toss'd thee down into the field,
> He knows about it all – he knows, he knows!

PETER WEST

Denis Compton – the dashing cavalier of cricket

ON 'COMPO'

If I were asked to nominate the half-dozen or so players who have given me most pleasure in my cricketing life I would without hesitation put Denis Compton, Keith Miller, Gary Sobers and Ian Botham at the top of my list and then have the very dickens of a job to decide about the others. I wrote a piece about Denis Compton in the *Daily Telegraph* in celebration of his sixty-sixth birthday in 1984 and it may bear repetition here as a salute to the genius of a cricketer the like of whom this and future generations will be very fortunate to see.

My mind goes back to the golden summer of 1947 when the names of an illustrious Middlesex duo, Compton and Edrich, seemed for ever linked in the headlines. Between them, in all matches against the touring South Africans, they plundered more than 2,000 runs. With 18 hundreds and a season's aggregate of 3,816 Compton set seasonal records that will never be surpassed so long as cricket's present first-class structure remains.

The records, stunning though they were, and the bare statistics meant very little to an ever modest, dashing cavalier who tailored every innings to his side's needs and never played a selfish one. There was an eternal freshness, a gaiety, a sense of fun, enjoyment and challenge about his batting that provided his box office appeal and made him a folk hero of his time. An entertainer supreme, and always an impeccable sportsman. To his marvellous eye (the priceless gift of 'seeing the ball early') were added instinctive timing, balance, flexible wrists, nimble

'Compo' in action during the Middlesex v Leicester match at Lord's on 24 June 1954. After he had scored 33, V. G. Jackson was responsible for his dismissal.

footwork, a complete armoury of strokes and a rare capacity for audacious improvisation. If he had 'specialities', these were the sweep which got him out sometimes when the bounce was uneven but brought him countless runs (no one has played this shot more effectively), the cover drive and a delectable late cut. There have been more powerful and elegant cover drivers – the names of Walter Hammond and Everton Weekes spring to mind, to name but two – but no one reduced cover points to such distraction as he opened or closed the blade to frustrate their latest move.

In other respects Denis Charles Scott Compton, CBE, was less well organised. In spite of his stout assertion, with glint in eye, that he seldom ran anyone out, it has to be said that he was not the greatest judge of a run, and he cannot deny that he achieved the rare distinction of running out his brother in Leslie Compton's benefit match! John Warr (Cambridge University, Middlesex and England) has always maintained that Denis is the only player to call his partner for a single and wish him luck at the same time. The erstwhile county captain also holds that conversational par for the course would go as follows: 'Yes . . . no . . . wait . . . sorry . . . oh my gawd!'

If Denis arrived on time for a day's cricket – something that could never be taken for granted – it was always possible that he turned up without some vital piece of clothing or impedimenta. How many of his hundreds, I wonder, were made with borrowed bats? I am told that he made one of them against India without his socks on.

He suffered lapses of concentration in the field where in his athletic prime he was an outstanding all-round performer. It was always said that he could catch anything, provided he happened to be looking. Another endearing weakness was his inability to say 'No' to any worthwhile request. Having invited him one summer to play for my MCC side againt my old school, I was somewhat put out to discover in due course that he had accepted two other invitations for a game on the same day. I had to adopt the sternest line with the great man, and it stands greatly to his credit that he drove himself through London to reach Cranbrook a mere five minutes late. He subsequently enriched the scene with a 70 made in the most Stygian gloom forlorn.

How many first-class runs, how many hundreds (in addition to the 123 he finished with) would he have made but for years lost to the war and a creaking knee – legacy of an old football injury in Arsenal's colours – that frustrated mobility in the later years of his career and finally impelled his premature retirement? That injury played no part in his slightly ungainly, rolling gait. E. W. Swanton has shrewdly observed that it was as though, when the construction of this creditable machine was completed, no one thought to go round and give the nuts and bolts a final turn.

DICK BRITTENDEN

doyen of New Zealand cricket writers.

*'... It was 82 for 6 when Sutcliffe, swathed in
bandages, absolutely ashen, returned ...'*

BERT SUTCLIFFE – THIRD BALL UNLUCKY

To some in the northern hemisphere, New Zealand could well be a South Pacific atoll, with fish and coconuts as the principal source of sustenance. But if it is a small and distant country, its people do not spend their days sitting in the sunshine. They share all the problems and pleasures of the old and new world, political and social. New Zealand also has in common with its ancient antecedents an adulation of its sports heroes.

There are large, craggy and meaningful All Blacks, each and every one a household name. Peter Snell and John Walker brought particular distinction on the track; Susan Devoy has won obeisance from the nation by taking the British and world squash titles. It is a long list, for a people of little more than 3,000,000, and there are cricketers among them.

The feats of Richard Hadlee have had elderly ladies dancing about their television lounges; the same sort of emotional outbursts had them throwing their shoes at their screens when Trevor Chappell bowled his underarm. Yet the cricketer who is most admired and respected is a man who played his last first-class game twenty years ago. Bert Sutcliffe has survived all the challenges thrown up by the salesmanship and razzmatazz which goes with modern cricket. He remains a perfect example of what a sportsman was expected to be. A cultured, charming, charismatic batsman, he never by word or deed hinted that he was aware of his stature, or of the adulation in which he is held. New Zealand cricket has made a considerable advance in the last few years, but Sutcliffe's mana is undiminished – this although he never played in a Test-winning New Zealand team.

As a youngster he showed much promise, but the cricket world was not really aware of him until he made a century in each innings of an Otago–MCC match in 1947, showing memorable displays of high art. In England in the golden summer of 1949, he had scored only 331 runs in 14 innings before the first Test, but finished the tour with 2,627 which, if memory serves, left him second only to Bradman in tour aggregates.

At home in 1949–50, he scored 355 for Auckland against Otago, and three years later a world record for a left-hander, 385 for Otago against Canterbury. Sutcliffe ended his career with 44 centuries, the most by a New Zealander except for Glenn Turner, who had the advantage of a long and successful career for Worcestershire.

For all his success, the innings by which Sutcliffe is best remembered is one of 80 not out at Johannesburg in 1953. This was New Zealand's first tour of South Africa; Johannesburg was the venue for the second Test.

On the first day, South Africa scored 259 for eight. On the second, before play had begun, word was received of a dreadful rail disaster in New Zealand; among the dozens who died was the fiancée of Bob Blair, the New Zealand fast bowler. Blair stayed behind in the team hotel when his comrades went to the ground. The South African innings was wrapped up quickly – a clearing of the stage before the playing of the most dramatic act in New Zealand, perhaps in all Test history.

It was a spiteful pitch, from which the big, strong, twenty-year-old Neil Adcock could get savage lift from a length. Murray Chapple was bowled off his gloves and chest. Sutcliffe played two balls and was then felled by one which flew at him. He was hit on the left ear, and the ambulance men ran out. He was able to get to his feet and staggered from the field with a blood-stained glove to his head. He went to hospital and collapsed twice during treatment. There was an announcement that he would be unable to bat again.

At Ellis Park, the carnage continued. Lawrie Miller was also hit and left the field, coughing blood. He was not expected to bat again. Matt Poore was hit, and bowled. John Reid, in an innings of 25 minutes, was struck five sickening blows. At lunch New Zealand had reached 41 for four, with two batsmen out of action.

Miller won the hearts of everyone by batting again, but it was 82 for six when Sutcliffe, swathed in bandages, absolutely ashen, returned, to a tremendous reception. The South African players applauded him, every one of them.

The third ball Sutcliffe faced was from a talented swing bowler, Dave Ironside. Sutcliffe struck it for six. All audacity, he then put Hugh Tayfield over the fence and repeated the treatment two balls later. With a resolute Frank Mooney as his partner, 50 were added in a half-hour of graceful violence. With eight down, and Guy Overton as his companion, Sutcliffe hit his fourth six, again off Tayfield, but when the score was 154 Overton was out and the players moved towards their dressing rooms.

Then there was a sudden, almost chilling silence, as Blair came out to bat, giving a dramatic day its most poignant moment. He had heard at his hotel that his team was in trouble, and somehow summoned the courage to come to the ground. It was distressing to see how much trouble he had trying to get his gloves on, how he had to brush them over his eyes as Sutcliffe came to meet him in the sunshine, and to put an arm about him.

Then it was all action. With the sweetest of timing, the most deft of footwork, Sutcliffe hit three more sixes in an over from Tayfield, then took a single from the seventh ball. Blair clearly did not feel in need of such protection. He hit the last ball far into a half-demented crowd.

They were together only 10 minutes but added 33 before Blair was stumped. So they went off together, arms about each other's shoulders, into the tunnel and history: Sutcliffe 80 in 90 minutes, with seven sixes.

Little wonder that New Zealand's junior manhood then wanted to bat left-handed, that he became a national hero. What would he have done today, when a top New Zealand player can make a very good living playing, writing and appearing in television advertisements, and is as

Bert Sutcliffe ... 'unable to bat again'.

50

familiar on the small screen as any prime minister?

Sutcliffe would have been the same relaxed, modest, cheerful and charming performer. That view was certainly held by members of the Auckland Cricket Society, when Sutcliffe was a guest at the 1985 annual dinner.

Quite unknown to Sutcliffe, a 'This Is Your Life' function had been arranged. The society always has a guest of honour at this gathering; Sutcliffe thought it was just another familiar occasion.

He sat at a table on a brightly-lit stage. The guests in a remarkable parade came in, at intervals, from an ante-room through a darkened part of the hall. First there was his 84-year-old mother, then a succession of men who had shared his triumphs, and had come to pay tribute to him – his school first eleven captain, his first Auckland captain; other New Zealand skippers, including Mervyn Wallace and Geoff Rabone; New Zealand players such as John Hayes and Eric Petrie. From Australia came Alan Davidson and New Zealand's other great left-hander, Martin Donnelly; finally, a telegram from his best-known companion-at-arms, John Reid, now living in Johannesburg.

It was brought in by a fearsome-looking gorilla, led on a chain, and that requires some explanation. On the boat going to South Africa, Reid and Sutcliffe had won a prize at the fancy dress ball, as a gorilla and his keeper. Reid had long had a strong addiction to the works of Edgar Rice Burroughs and, indeed, had 'M'Bogo' for a nickname, derived partly from his taste in literature and partly from his primitive if good-natured ways of handling those he alleged had offended him.

So there was a telegram, for which Sutcliffe was obviously grateful. But when this cavorting creature removed its head-piece, there was Reid himself, to give the evening a memorable moment.

That these men had come from overseas to share in the tribute to Sutcliffe speaks eloquently of the esteem in which he is held. It was, someone said, an evening knee-deep in nostalgia; there were hundreds there, with one mission in mind – to let Sutcliffe know how they felt about him. In an age of sport marred so often by outbursts of acrimony, was there not some point in paying homage to one who had set the very highest standards and examples?

MICHAEL MELFORD

'What I do remember is the bellow with which Johnston triumphantly swept off the bails. It is said to have frightened the cows three villages away ...'

'JOHNNERS' AT THE HELM!

Those who played under the captaincy of Brian Johnston at Widford in Hertfordshire in the 1950s and 60s ran the gamut of cricketing experiences.

We were the guests of John Pawle, on whose family ground the village club played, and he was wont to invite Johnston to bring an assorted bunch of players to take on the village. There must have been a tradition of eccentricity on this lovely ground, for there is a famous story about John's fierce but absent-minded father captaining a side here. He kept a fast bowler on for so long that, as the poor chap became hotter and hotter and slower and slower, another player, plucking up courage, said to the captain: 'Don't you think he's tiring, Major?'

'Yes, I agree,' replied Major Pawle. 'I can't think why they don't take him off.'

Johnston's visits were usually on the Sunday of the Lord's Test and, when possible, representatives of that season's touring side and their Press party were included.

There were one or two unwritten courtesies to be observed. The first was inspired by an incident when square leg was knocked over while waiting under a catch to which the wicket-keeper, Johnston himself, aspired. Thereafter it was the rule, before attempting to catch a skier almost anywhere on the field, to ascertain whether the shouting emanating from Johnston was merely wishing the catcher good luck or was an indication that he himself was on his way to take the catch.

The other courtesy was to make way for others if you reached 50. There was one occasion when Johnston sent in Gerry Gomez, no less, with instructions to run out a distinguished cricket writer who was considered to have batted too long. Alas, Gomez, calling dutifully for an impossible run, was sent back by an unmoving partner and he it was who perished.

To avoid such mishaps, the custom of considering 50 enough was explained to newcomers, but one year, through an oversight, was not communicated to a guest artist who went on ominously towards 100. Eventually our captain could stand it no longer and instructed us to break into loud applause when the batsman scored his next run. This outburst of appreciation was taken up by attendant wives and children and the batsman, having momentarily looked puzzled, doffed his cap in acknowledgment of this generous acclaim of his 100. He had, in fact, just scored his 93rd run. Just to make absolutely sure, he hit the next ball for six and then got out. The outraged expression on his face as the figure 99 went up on the scoreboard was immensely satisfying to those waiting to bat. It was, of course, the work of a moment for the captain to find subsequently that a run had incorrectly been recorded as a leg-bye and to reestablish goodwill all round.

I recall two Pakistanis who, some years apart, were bemused by the idiosyncrasies of village cricket under Johnston. One was M.E.Z. Ghazali, a member of the 1954 side, who was relishing the opportunity of making runs in a wet summer when he was adjudged lbw to a ball a foot outside the leg-stump. His surprise grew when in the next over his successor nicked the ball hard to the wicket-keeper, turned and walked off, only to be told as he passed square leg that he had been given not out. He returned in embarrassment and, attempting to do the decent thing and rectify the matter by giving his wicket away, played one of his finest innings.

The other Pakistani, still more mystified, was Major Rahman, assistant-manager of the 1963 side. Whereas in other years the village team were far too good for us, on this occasion they were below strength and were clearly not going to come near our total. When they had lost four wickets to different bowlers, nothing would satisfy Johnston but to see that all 11 – we were playing 12 aside – fell to different bowlers.

Somehow the plan was not fully explained to Major Rahman and his amazement at being taken off as soon as he had taken a wicket in his second over only diminished as subsequent bowlers met a similar fate. Those who took a wicket early in an over ran the risk of severe censure from the captain behind the stumps if they threatened to take another.

I note from the scorecard which we were all sent that Robin Marlar had to bowl a second over before he took a wicket whereas Trevor Howard needed only one over and conceded only one run. Russell Endean also needed only one over but conceded six runs. I see that I bowled the only maiden but I suspect that after I had removed one batsman, the next received nothing within reach.

The climax came when John Woodcock, the eleventh bowler (or ninth change), began his fateful over. It had not been allowed to escape anyone that the one name missing from the scorecard so far was that of Johnston.

I do not remember by what guile Woodcock lured his man down the pitch. It would be churlish to give credence to the theory that the batsman was pushed from behind, especially as the scorecard mentions a brilliant legside stumping.

What I do remember is the bellow with which Johnston triumphantly swept off the bails. It is said to have frightened the cows three villages away.

STEADY, M'LORD ...

30 1840. A match of cricket was played at Ballinasloe on Wednesday, between the Teetotallers and the Whiskey Drinkers, which caused considerable amusement. The Temperance men mustered strong, and were backed by Lord Clancarthy and Admiral Trench. After a well contested game, the patrons of the mountain dew won the match by 35, and celebrated their victory in the evening by illuminating their houses, bonfires, &c., much to the discomfiture of the Mathewites, who fought a hard battle.

The Times

THE TERRIBLE TWINS!

Dennis Keith Lillee was born in 1949. A magnificent right-arm fast bowler, he has taken more wickets than any bowler in the history of Test cricket. Adept at mixing leg-cutters with out-swingers, Lillee is regarded in Australia as a matinee idol. At times a controversial and provocative player, his fearsome pace is legendary: he is indisputably among the greats of cricket history.

INSET: Jeffrey Robert Thomson, or 'Tommo', is a shock bowler of sling-shot. Born at Greenacre, Sydney, in 1950, he is the son of a Newtown cricketer, one of five boys whose aggressive action is renowned. Facing 'Tommo' on a fast wicket can be a daunting experience for the most accomplished batsman. He seldom swings the ball, and his incredible pace and delivery may have something to do with the fact that he trained to throw javelins in his early youth!

SIR ARTHUR CONAN DOYLE

*'Droppers, I call them – Spedegue's droppers –
that's the name they may have some day ...'*

SPEDEGUE'S DROPPER

The name of Walter Scougall needs no introduction to the cricketing public. In the nineties he played for his University. Early in the century he began that long career in the county team which carried him up to the War. That great tragedy broke his heart for games, but he still served on his county Club Committee and was reckoned one of the best judges of the game in the United Kingdom.

Scougall, after his abandonment of active sport, was wont to take his exercise by long walks through the New Forest, upon the borders of which he was living. Like all wise men, he walked very silently through that wonderful waste, and in that way he was often privileged to see sights which are lost to the average heavy-stepping wayfarer. Once, late in the evening, it was a badger blundering towards its hole under a hollow bank. Often a little group of deer would be glimpsed in the open rides. Occasionally a fox would steal across the path and then dart off at the sight of the noiseless wayfarer. Then one day he saw a human sight which was more strange than any in the animal world.

In a narrow glade there stood two great oaks. They were thirty or forty feet apart, and the glade was spanned by a cord which connected them up. This cord was at least fifty feet above the ground, and it must have entailed no small effort to get it there. At each side of the cord a cricket stump had been placed at the usual distance from each other. A tall, thin young man in spectacles was lobbing balls, of which he seemed to have a good supply, from one end, while at the other end a lad of sixteen, wearing wicket-keeper's gloves, was catching those which missed the wicket. 'Catching' is the right word, for no ball struck the ground. Each was projected high up into the air and passed over the cord, descending at a very sharp angle on to the stumps.

Scougall stood for some minutes behind a holly bush watching this curious performance. At first it seemed pure lunacy, and then gradually he began to perceive a method in it. It was no easy matter to hurl a ball up over that cord and bring it down near the wicket. It needed a very correct trajectory. And yet this singular young man, using what the observer's practised eye recognised as a leg-break action which would entail a swerve in the air, lobbed up ball after ball either right on to the bails or into the wicket-keeper's hands just beyond them. Great practice was surely needed before he had attained such a degree of accuracy as this.

Finally his curiosity became so great that Scougall moved out into the glade, to the obvious surprise and embarrassment of the two performers. Had they been caught in some guilty action they could not have looked more unhappy. However, Scougall was a man of the world with a pleasant manner, and he soon put them at their ease.

'Excuse my butting in,' said he. 'I happened to be passing and I could not help being interested. I am an old cricketer, you see, and it appealed to me. Might I ask what you were trying to do?'

'Oh, I am just tossing up a few balls,' said the elder, modestly. 'You see, there is no decent ground about here, so my brother and I come out into the Forest.'

'Are you a bowler, then?'

'Well, of sorts.'

'What club do you play for?'

'It is only Wednesday and Saturday cricket. Bishops Bramley is our village.'

'But do you always bowl like that?'

'Oh, no. This is a new idea that I have been trying out.'

'Well, you seem to get it pretty accurately.'

'I am improving. I was all over the place at first. I didn't know what parish they would drop in. But now they are usually there or about it.'

'So I observe.'

'You said you were an old cricketer. May I ask your name?'

'Walter Scougall.'

The young man looked at him as a young pupil looks at the world-famous master.

'You remember the name, I see.'

'Walter Scougall. Oxford and Hampshire. Last played in 1913. Batting average for that season, twenty-seven point five. Bowling average, sixteen for seventy-two wickets.'

'Good Lord!'

The younger man, who had come across, burst out laughing.

'Tom is like that,' said he. 'He is Wisden and Lillywhite rolled into one. He could tell you anyone's record, and every county's record for this century.'

'Well, well! What a memory you must have!'

'Well, my heart is in the game,' said the young man, becoming amazingly confidential, as shy men will when they find a really sympathetic listener. 'But it's my heart that won't let me play it as I should wish to do. You see, I get asthma if I do too much – and palpitations. But they play me at Bishops Bramley for my slow bowling, and so long as I field slip I don't have too much running to do.'

'You say you have not tried these lobs, or whatever you may call them, in a match?'

'No, not yet. I want to get them perfect first. You see, it was my ambition to invent an entirely new ball. I am sure it can be done. Look at Bosanquet and the googlie. Just by using his brain he thought of and worked out the idea of concealed screw on the ball. I said to myself that Nature had handicapped me with a weak heart, but not with a weak brain, and that I might think out some new thing which was within the compass of my strength. Droppers, I call them. Spedegue's droppers – that's the name they may have some day.'

Scougall laughed. 'I don't want to discourage you, but I wouldn't bank on it too much,' said he. 'A quick-eyed batsman would simply treat them as he would any other full toss and every ball would be a boundary.'

Spedegue's face fell. The words of Scougall were to him as the verdict of the High Court judge. Never had he spoken before with a first-class cricketer, and he had hardly the nerve to defend his own theory. It was the younger one who spoke.

'Perhaps, Mr Scougall, you have hardly thought it all out yet,' said he. 'Tom has given it a lot of consideration. You see, if the ball is tossed high enough it has a great pace as it falls. It's really like having a fast bowler from above. That's his idea. Then, of course, there's the field.'

'Ah, how would you place your field?'

'All on the on side bar one or two at the most,' cried Tom Spedegue, taking up the argument. 'I've nine to dispose of. I should have mid-off well up. That's all. Then I should have eight men to leg, three on the boundary, one mid-on, two square, one fine, and one a rover, so that the batsman would never quite know where he was. That's the idea.'

Scougall began to be serious. It was clear that this young fellow really had plotted the thing out. He walked across to the wicket.

'Chuck up one or two,' said he. 'Let me see how they look.' He brandished his walking-stick and waited expectant. The ball soared in the air and came down with unexpected speed just over the stump. Scougall looked more serious still. He had seen many cricket balls, but never quite from that angle, and it gave him food for thought.

'Have you ever tried it in public?'

'Never.'

'Don't you think it is about time?'

'Yes, I think I might.'

'When?'

'Well, I'm not generally on as a first bowler, I am second change as a rule. But if the skipper will let me have a go—'

'I'll see to that,' said Scougall. 'Do you play at Bishops Bramley?'

'Yes; it is our match of the year – against Mudford, you know.'

'Well, I think on Saturday I'd like to be there and see how it works.'

Sure enough Scougall turned up at the village match, to the great excitement of the two rural teams. He had a serious talk with the home captain, with the result that for the first time in his life Tom Spedegue was first bowler for his native village. What the other village thought of his remarkable droppers need not influence us much, since they would probably have been got out pretty cheaply by any sort of bowling. None the less, Scougall watched the procession to and from the cowshed which served as a pavilion with an appreciative eye, and his views as to the possibilities lying in the dropper became clearer than before. At the end of the innings he touched the bowler upon the shoulder.

'That seems all right,' he said.

'No, I couldn't quite get the length – and, of course, they did drop catches.'

'Yes, I agree that you could do better. Now look here! you are second master at a school, are you not?'

'That is right.'

'You could get a day's leave if I wangled with the chief?'

'It might be done.'

'Well, I want you next Tuesday. Sir George Sanderson's house-party team is playing the Free Foresters at Ringwood. You must bowl for Sir George.'

Tom Spedegue flushed with pleasure.

'Oh, I say!' was all he could stammer out.

'I'll work it somehow or other. I suppose you don't bat?'

'Average nine,' said Spedegue, proudly.

Scougall laughed. 'Well, I noticed that you were not a bad fielder near the wicket.'

'I usually hold them.'

'Well, I'll see your boss, and you will hear from me again.'

Scougall was really taking a great deal of trouble in this small affair, for he went down to Totton and saw the rather grim head-master. It chanced, however, that the old man had been a bit of a sport in his day, and he relaxed when Scougall explained the inner meaning of it all. He laughed incredulously, however, and shook his head when Scougall whispered some aspiration.

'Nonsense!' was his comment.

'Well, there is a chance.'

England *v* Australia Past Players at a special match at the Oval, 27 August 1980.
(L to R) BACK ROW: Fred Trueman, Jim Parks, Godfrey Evans, Colin Cowdrey, Ken Barrington, Tony Lock and Frank Tyson. FRONT ROW: Basil d'Oliviera, Peter Richardson, John Edrich, Mike Smith, Fred Titmus (the England Past Players team).

England *v* New Zealand at Lord's, Second Test, 21 June 1958.
The England team after their Second Test win. (L to R) BACK ROW: P. E. Richardson (Worcs.), F. S. Trueman (Yorks.), M. J. K. Smith (Warwicks.), M. C. Cowdrey (Kent), P. J. Loader (Surrey), G. A. R. Lock (Surrey).

THE BIRDIE!

The celebrated Gentlemen's Team of 1962.
(L to R) BACK ROW: R. M. Prideaux, D. B. Pithy, O. S. Wheatley, A. R. Lewis, A. C. Smith, E. J. Craig. FRONT ROW: R. W. Barber, T. E. Bailey, E. R. Dexter, Revd D. S. Shepherd, M. J. K. Smith.

The Old Firm.
Australian Test cricketers Macartney, Carter and Taylor, 13 April 1926.

'Nonsense!' said the old man once again.

'It would be the making of your school.'

'It certainly would,' the head-master replied. 'But it is nonsense all the same.'

Scougall saw the head-master again on the morning after the Free Foresters match.

'You see, it works all right,' he said.

'Yes, against third-class men.'

'Oh, I don't know. Donaldson was playing, and Murphy. They were not so bad. I tell you they are the most amazed set of men in Hampshire. I have bound them all over to silence.'

'Why?'

'Surprise is the essence of the matter. Now I'll take it a stage farther. By Jove, what a joke it would be!' The old cricketer and the sporting schoolmaster roared with laughter as they thought of the chances of the future.

All England was absorbed in one question at that moment. Politics, business, even taxation had passed from people's minds. The one engrossing subject was the fifth Test Match. Twice England had won by a narrow margin, and twice Australia had barely struggled to victory. Now in a week Lord's was to be the scene of the final and crucial battle of giants. What were the chances, and how was the English team to be made up?

It was an anxious time for the Selection Committee, and three more harassed men than Sir James Gilpin, Mr Tarding and Dr Sloper were not to be found in London. They sat now in the committee-room of the great pavilion, and they moodily scanned the long list of possibles which lay before them, weighing the claims of this man or that, closely inspecting the latest returns from the county matches, and arguing how far a good all-rounder was a better bargain than a man who was supremely good in one department but weak in another – such men, for example, as Worsley of Lancashire, whose average was seventy-one, but who was a sluggard in the field, or Scott of Leicestershire, who was near the top of the bowling and quite at the foot of the batting averages. A week of such work had turned the committee into three jaded old men.

'There is the question of endurance,' said Sir James, the man of many years and much experience. 'A three days' match is bad enough, but this is to be played out and may last a week. Some of these top average men are getting on in years.'

'Exactly,' said Tarding, who had himself captained England again and again. 'I am all for young blood and new methods. The trouble is that we know their bowling pretty well, and as for them on a marled wicket they can play ours with their eyes shut. Each side is likely to make five hundred per innings, and a very little will make the difference between us and them.'

'It's just that very little that we have got to find,' said solemn old Dr Sloper, who had the reputation of being the greatest living authority upon the game. 'If we could give them something new! But, of course, they have played every county and sampled everything we have got.'

'What can we ever have that is new?' cried Tarding. 'It is all played out.'

'Well, I don't know,' said Sir James. 'Both the swerve and the googlie have come along in our time. But Bosanquets don't appear every day. We want brain as well as muscle behind the ball.'

'Funny we should talk like this,' said Dr Sloper, taking a letter from his pocket. 'This is from old Scougall, down in Hampshire. He says he is at the end of a wire and is ready to come up if we want him. His whole argument is on the very lines we have been discussing. New blood, and a complete surprise – that is his slogan.'

'Does he suggest where we are to find it?'

'Well, as a matter of fact he does. He has dug up some unknown fellow from the back of beyond who plays for the second eleven of the Mudtown Blackbeetles or the Hinton Chawbacons or some such team, and he wants to put him straight in to play for England. Poor old Scougie has been out in the sun.'

'At the same time there is no better captain than Scougall used to be. I don't think we should put his opinion aside too easily. What does he say?'

'Well, he is simply red-hot about it. "A revelation to me." That is one phrase. "Could not have believed it if I had not seen it." "May find it out afterwards, but it is bound to upset them the first time." That is his view.'

'And where is the wonder man?'

'He has sent him up so that we can see him if we wish. Telephone the Thackeray Hotel, Bloomsbury.'

'Well, what do you say?'

'Oh, it's pure waste of time,' said Tarding. 'Such things don't happen, you know. Even if we approved of him, what would the country think and what would the Press say?'

Sir James stuck out his grizzled jaw. 'Damn the country and the Press, too!' said he. 'We are here to follow our own judgment, and I jolly well mean to do so.'

'Exactly,' said Dr Sloper.

Tarding shrugged his broad shoulders.

'We have enough to do without turning down a side-street like that,' said he. 'However, if you both think so, I won't stand in the way. Have him up by all means and let us see what we make of him.'

Half an hour later a very embarrassed young man was standing in front of the famous trio and listening to a series of very searching questions, to which he was giving such replies as he was able. Much of the ground which Scougall had covered in the Forest was explored by them once more.

'It boils down to this, Mr Spedegue. You've once in your life played in good company. That is the only criterion. What exactly did you do?'

Spedegue pulled a slip of paper, which was already frayed from much use, out of his waistcoat pocket.

'This is *The Hampshire Telegraph* account, sir.'

Sir James ran his eye over it and read snatches aloud. '"Much amusement was caused by the bowling of Mr T. E. Spedegue." Hum! That's rather two-edged. Bowling should not be a comic turn. After all, cricket is a serious game. Seven wickets for thirty-four. Well, that's better. Donaldson is a good man. You got him, I see. And Murphy, too! Well, now, would you mind going into the pavilion and waiting? You will find some pictures there that will amuse you if you value the history of the game. We'll send for you presently.'

When the youth had gone the Selection Committee looked at each other in puzzled silence.

'You simply can't do it!' said Tarding at last. 'You can't face it. To play a bumpkin like that because he once got seven wickets for thirty-four in country-house cricket is sheer madness. I won't be a party to it.'

'Wait a bit, though! Wait a bit!' cried Sir James. 'Let us thresh it out a little before we decide.'

So they threshed it out, and in half an hour they sent for Tom Spedegue once more. Sir James sat with his elbows on the table and his finger-tips touching while he held forth in his best judicial manner. His conclusion was a remarkable one.

'So it comes to this, Mr Spedegue, that we all three want to be on surer ground before we take a step which would rightly expose us to the most tremendous public criticism. You will therefore remain in London, and at three-forty-five tomorrow morning, which is just after dawn, you will come down in your flannels to the side entrance of Lord's. We will, under pledge of secrecy, assemble twelve or thirteen groundsmen whom we can trust, including half-a-dozen first-class bats. We will have a wicket prepared on the practice ground, and we will try you out under proper conditions with your ten fielders and all. If you fail, there is an end. If you make good, we may consider your claim.'

'Good gracious, sir, I made no claim.'

'Well, your friend Scougall did for you. But anyhow, that's how we have fixed it. We shall be there, of course, and a few others whose

64

opinion we can trust. If you care to wire Scougall he can come too. But the whole thing is secret, for we quite see the point that it must be a complete surprise or a wash-out. So you will keep your mouth shut and we shall do the same.'

Thus it came about that one of the most curious games in the history of cricket was played on the Lord's ground next morning. There is a high wall round that part, but early wayfarers as they passed were amazed to hear the voices of the players, and the occasional crack of the ball at such an hour. The superstitious might almost have imagined that the spirits of the great departed were once again at work, and that the adventurous explorer might get a peep at the bushy black beard of the old giant or Billie Murdoch leading his Cornstalks once more to victory. At six o'clock the impromptu match was over, and the Selection Committee had taken the bravest and most sensational decision that had ever been hazarded since first a team was chosen. Tom Spedegue should play next week for England.

'Mind you,' said Tarding, 'if the beggar lets us down I simply won't face the music. I warn you of that. I'll have a taxi waiting at the gate and a passport in my pocket. Poste restante, Paris. That's me for the rest of the summer.'

'Cheer up, old chap,' said Sir James. 'Our conscience is clear. We have acted for the best. Dash it all, we have ten good men, anyhow. If the worst came to the worst, it only means one passenger in the team.'

'But it won't come to the worst,' said Dr Sloper, stoutly. 'Hang it, we have seen with our own eyes. What more can we do? All the same, for the first time in my life I'll have a whisky-and-soda before breakfast.'

Next day the list was published and the buzz began. Ten of the men might have been expected. These were Challen and Jones, as fast bowlers, and Widley, the slow left-hander. Then Peters, Moir, Jackson, Wilson, and Grieve were at the head of the batting averages, none of them under fifty, which was pretty good near the close of a wet season. Hanwell and Gordon were two all-rounders who were always sure of their places, dangerous bats, good change bowlers, and as active as cats in the field. So far so good. But who the Evil One was Thomas E. Spedegue? Never was there such a ferment in Fleet Street and such blank ignorance upon the part of 'our well-informed correspondent.' Special Commissioners darted here and there, questioning well-known cricketers, only to find that they were as much in the dark as themselves. Nobody knew – or if anyone did know, he was bound by oath not to tell. The wildest tales flew abroad. 'We are able to assure the public that Spedegue is a "nom de jeu" and conceals the identity of a world-famed cricketer who for family reasons is not permitted to reveal his true self.' 'Thomas E. Spedegue will surprise the crowd at Lord's by appearing as a coal-black gentleman from Jamaica. He came over with

Comedian Tommy Trinder in f
form during a Ball cabaret.

ABOVE: The Twelfth Man draw
lucky raffle ticket while Bruce I
spouts the name of the winner.
RIGHT: Chairman Leslie Frewir
as if he might be discussing Cus
Last Stand with Prince Philip v
Major A. Huskisson (right) – '1
to Taverners – looks on.

The lovely Princess Alexandra arrives for yet another glittering Taverners'
evening at Grosvenor House.

We even pulled in the American 'Globe-Trotters' for one of the Ball cabarets. Here's the Twelfth Man saying 'hello' while John Snagge and Roy Rich look somewhat dwarfed by the big fellas!

LORD'S TAVERNERS' BALLS AND ALL THAT

The first Lord's Taverners' Ball took place in the Great Room of Grosvenor House, London, in the summer of 1951, attended by Prince Philip, the Twelfth Man, and his bride, the then Princess Elizabeth. It was an unprecedented success and quickly became an annual event – the event of the London Season. Packed with celebrities, predominantly from the arts and sport, the Ball continues to be a fine fund-raiser each and every Taverner year. Here are scenes from some past Balls.

the last West Indian team, settled in Derbyshire, and is now eligible to play for England, though why he should be asked to do so is still a mystery.' 'Spedegue, as is now generally known, is a half-caste Malay who exhibited extraordinary cricket proficiency some years ago in Rangoon. It is said that he plays in a loin-cloth and can catch as well with his feet as with his hands. The question of whether he is qualified for England is a most debatable one.' 'Spedegue, Thomas E., is the headmaster of a famous northern school whose wonderful talents in the cricket field have been concealed by his devotion to his academic duties. Those who know him best are assured,' etc. etc. The Committee also began to get it in the neck. 'Why, with the wealth of talent available, these three elderly gentlemen, whose ideas of selection seem to be to pick names out of a bag, should choose one who, whatever his hidden virtues, is certainly unused to first-class cricket, far less to Test Matches, is one of those things which make one realize that the lunacy laws are not sufficiently comprehensive.' These were fair samples of the comments.

And then the inevitable came to pass. When Fleet Street is out for something it invariably gets it. No one quite knows how *The Daily Sportsman* succeeded in getting at Thomas Spedegue, but it was a great scoop and the incredible secret was revealed. There was a leader and there was an interview with the village patriarch which set London roaring with laughter. 'No, we ain't surprised nohow,' said Gaffer Hobbs. 'Maister Spedegue do be turble clever with them slow balls of his'n. He sure was too much for them chaps what came in the char-a-bancs from Mudford. Artful, I call 'im. You'll see.' The leader was scathing. 'The Committee certainly seem to have taken leave of their senses. Perhaps there is time even now to alter their absurd decision. It is almost an insult to our Australian visitors. It is obvious that the true place for Mr Thomas Spedegue, however artful he may be, is the village green and not Lord's, and that his competence to deal with the char-a-bancers of Mudford is a small guarantee that he can play first-class cricket. The whole thing is a deplorable mistake, and it is time that pressure was put upon the Selection Board to make them reconsider their decision.'

'We have examined the score-book of the Bishops Bramley village club,' wrote another critic. 'It is kept in the tap-room of The Spotted Cow, and makes amusing reading. Our Test Match aspirant is hard to trace, as he played usually for the second eleven, and in any case there was no one capable of keeping an analysis. However, we must take such comfort as we can from his batting averages. This year he has actually amassed a hundred runs in nine recorded innings. Best in an innings, fifteen. Average, eleven. Last year he was less fortunate and came out with an average of nine. The youth is second master at the Totton High

School and is in indifferent health, suffering from occasional attacks of asthma. And he is chosen to play for England! Is it a joke or what? We think that the public will hardly see the humour of it, nor will the Selection Committee find it a laughing matter if they persist in their preposterous action.' So spoke the Press, but there were, it is only fair to say, other journals which took a more charitable view. 'After all,' said the sporting correspondent of *The Times*, 'Sir James and his two colleagues are old and experienced players with a unique knowledge of the game. Since we have placed our affairs in their hands we must be content to leave them there. They have their own knowledge and their own private information of which we are ignorant. We can but trust them and await the event.'

As to the three, they refused in any way to compromise or to bend to the storm. They gave no explanations, made no excuses, and simply dug in and lay quiet. So the world waited till the day came round.

We all remember what glorious weather it was. The heat and the perfect Bulli-earth wicket, so far as England could supply that commodity, reminded our visitors of their native conditions. It was England, however, who got the best of that ironed shirt-front wicket, for in their first knock even Cotsmore, the Australian giant, who was said to be faster than Gregory and more wily than Spofforth, could seldom get the ball bail-high. He bowled with splendid vim and courage, but his analysis at the end of the day only showed three wickets for a hundred and forty-two. Storr, the googlie merchant, had a better showing with four for ninety-six. Cade's mediums accounted for two wickets, and Moir, the English captain, was run out. He had made seventy-three first, and Peters, Grieve, and Hanwell raked up sixty-four, fifty-seven, and fifty-one respectively, while nearly everyone was in double figures. The only exception was 'Thomas E. Spedegue, Esq.,' to quote the score card, which recorded a blank after his name. He was caught in the slips off the fast bowler, and, as he admitted afterwards that he had never for an instant seen the ball, and could hardly in his nervousness see the bowler, it is remarkable that his wicket was intact. The English total was four hundred and thirty-two, and the making of it consumed the whole of the first day. It was fast scoring in the time, and the crowd were fully satisfied with the result.

And now came the turn of Australia. An hour before play began forty thousand people had assembled, and by the time that the umpire came out the gates had to be closed, for there was not standing room within those classic precincts. Then came the English team, strolling out to the wickets and tossing the ball from hand to hand in time-honoured fashion. Finally appeared the two batsmen, Morland, the famous Victorian, the man of the quick feet and the supple wrists, whom many looked upon as the premier batsman of the world, and the stonewaller, Donahue, who had broken the hearts of so many bowlers with his obdurate defence. It was he who took the first over, which was delivered by Challen of Yorkshire, the raging, tearing fast bowler of the North. He sent down six beauties, but each of them came back to him down the pitch from that impenetrable half-cock shot which was characteristic of the famous Queenslander. It was a maiden over.

And now Moir tossed the ball to Spedegue and motioned him to begin at the pavilion end. The English captain had been present at the surreptitious trial and he had an idea of the general programme, but it took him some time and some consultation with the nervous, twitching bowler before he could set the field. When it was finally arranged the huge audience gasped with surprise and the batsmen gazed round them as if they could hardly believe their eyes. One poor little figure, alone upon a prairie, broke the solitude of the off-side. He stood as a deep point or as a silly mid-off. The on-side looked like a mass meeting. The fielders were in each other's way, and kept shuffling about to open up separate lines. It took some time to arrange, while Spedegue stood at the crease with a nervous smile, fingering the ball and waiting for orders. The Selection Board were grouped in the open window of the committee-room, and their faces were drawn and haggard.

'My God! This is awful!' muttered Tarding.

'Got that cab?' asked Dr Sloper, with a ghastly smile.

'Got it! It is my one stand-by.'

'Room for three in it?' said Sir James. 'Gracious, he has got five short-legs and no slip. Well, well, get to it! Anything is better than waiting.'

There was a deadly hush as Spedegue delivered his first ball. It was an ordinary slow full pitch straight on the wicket. At any other time Morland would have slammed it to the boundary, but he was puzzled and cautious after all this mysterious setting of the field. Some unknown trap seemed to have been set for him. Therefore he played the ball quietly back to the bowler and set himself for the next one, which was similar and treated in the same way.

Spedegue had lost his nerve. He simply could not, before this vast multitude of critics, send up the grotesque ball which he had invented. Therefore he compromised, which was the most fatal of all courses. He lobbed up balls which were high but not high enough. They were simply ordinary over-pitched, full-toss deliveries such as a batsman sees when he has happy dreams and smiles in his sleep. Such was the third ball, which was a little to the off. Morland sent it like a bullet past the head of the lonely mid-off and it crashed against the distant rails. The three men in the window looked at each other and the sweat was on their brows. The next ball was again a juicy full toss on the level of the batsman's ribs. He banged it through the crowd of fielders on the on with a deft turn of the wrist which insured that it should be upon the ground. Then, gaining confidence, he waited for the next of those wonderful dream balls, and steadying himself for a mighty fast-footed swipe he knocked it clean over the ring and on to the roof of the hotel to square-leg. There were roars of applause, for a British crowd loves a lofty hit, whoever may deliver it. The scoreboard marked fourteen made off five balls. Such an opening to a Test Match had never been seen.

'We thought he might break a record, and by Jove he has!' said Tarding, bitterly. Sir James chewed his ragged moustache and Sloper twisted his fingers together in agony. Moir, who was fielding at mid-on, stepped across to the unhappy bowler.

'Chuck 'em up, as you did on Tuesday morning. Buck up, man! Don't funk it! You'll do them yet.'

Spedegue grasped the ball convulsively and nerved himself to send it high into the air. For a moment he pictured the New Forest glade, the white line of cord, and his young brother waiting behind the stump. But his nerve was gone, and with it his accuracy. There were roars of laughter as the ball went fifty feet into the air, which were redoubled when the wicket-keeper had to sprint back in order to catch it and the umpire stretched his arms out to signal a wide.

For the last ball, as he realised, that he was likely to bowl in the match, Spedegue approached the crease. The field was swimming round him. That yell of laughter which had greeted his effort had been the last straw. His nerve was broken. But there is a point when pure despair and desperation come to a man's aid – when he says to himself, 'Nothing matters now. All is lost. It can't be worse than it is. Therefore I may as well let myself go.' Never in all his practice had he bowled a ball as high as the one which now, to the amused delight of the crowd, went soaring into the air. Up it went and up – the most absurd ball ever delivered in a cricket match. The umpire broke down and shrieked with laughter, while even the amazed fielders joined in the general yell. The ball, after its huge parabola, descended well over the wicket, but as it was still within reach Morland, with a broad grin on his sunburned face, turned round and tapped it past the wicket-keeper's ear to the boundary. Spedegue's face drooped towards the ground. The bitterness of death was on him. It was all over. He had let down the Committee, he had let down the side, he had let down England. He wished the ground would open and swallow him so that his only memorial should be a scar upon the pitch of Lord's.

And then suddenly the derisive laughter of the crowd was stilled, for it was seen that an incredible thing had happened. Morland was walking towards the pavilion. As he passed Spedegue he made a good-humoured flourish of his bat as if he would hit him over the head with it. At the same time the wicket-keeper stooped and picked something off the ground. It was a bail. Forgetful of his position and with all his thoughts upon this extraordinary ball which was soaring over his head, the great batsman had touched the wicket with his toe. Spedegue had a respite. The laughter was changing to applause. Moir came over and clapped him jovially upon the back. The scoring board showed total fifteen, last man fourteen, wickets one.

Challen sent down another over of fizzers to the impenetrable Donahue which resulted in a snick for two and a boundary off his legs. And then off the last ball a miracle occurred. Spedegue was fielding at fine slip, when he saw a red flash come towards him low on the right. He thrust out a clutching hand and there was the beautiful new ball right in the middle of his tingling palm. How it got there he had no idea, but what odds so long as the stonewaller would stonewall no more? Spedegue, from being the butt, was becoming the hero of the crowd. They cheered rapturously when he approached the crease for his second over. The board was twenty-one, six, two.

But now it was a very different Spedegue. His fears had fallen from him. His confidence had returned. If he did nothing more he had at least done his share. But he would do much more. It had all come back to him, his sense of distance, his delicacy of delivery, his appreciation of curves. He had found his length and he meant to keep it.

The splendid Australian batsmen, those active, clear-eyed men who could smile at our fast bowling and make the best of our slow bowlers seem simple, were absolutely at sea. Here was something of which they had never heard, for which they had never prepared, and which was unlike anything in the history of cricket. Spedegue had got his fifty-foot trajectory to a nicety, bowling over the wicket with a marked curve from the leg. Every ball fell on or near the top of the stumps. He was as accurate as a human howitzer pitching shells. Batten, who followed Morland, hit across one of them and was clean bowled. Staker tried to cut one off his wicket, and knocked down his own off-stump, broke his bat, and finally saw the ball descend amid the general *débris*. Here and there one was turned to leg and once a short one was hit out of the ground. The fast bowler sent the fifth batsman's leg-stump flying and the score was five for thirty-seven. Then in successive balls Spedegue got Bollard and Whitelaw, the one caught at the wicket and the other at short square-leg. There was a stand between Moon and Carter, who put on twenty runs between them with a succession of narrow escapes from the droppers. Then each of them became victims, one getting his body in front, and the other being splendidly caught by Hanwell on the ropes. The last man was run out and the innings closed for seventy-four.

The crowd had begun by cheering and laughing, but now they had got beyond it and sat in a sort of awed silence as people might who were contemplating a miracle. Half-way through the innings Tarding had leaned forward and had grasped the hand of each of his colleagues. Sir James leaned back in his deck-chair and lit a large cigar. Dr Sloper mopped his brow with his famous red handkerchief. 'It's all right, but, by George! I wouldn't go through it again,' he murmured. The effect upon the players themselves was curious. The English seemed apologetic, as though not sure themselves that such novel means could be justified. The Australians were dazed and a little resentful. 'What price quoits?' said Batten, the captain, as he passed into the pavilion. Spedegue's figures were seven wickets for thirty-one.

And now the question arose whether the miracle would be repeated. Once more Donahue and Morland were at the wicket. As to the poor stonewaller, it was speedily apparent that he was helpless. How can you stonewall a ball which drops perpendicularly upon your bails? He held his bat flat before it as it fell in order to guard his wicket, and it simply popped up three feet into the air and was held by the wicket-keeper. One for nothing. Batten and Staker both hit lustily to leg and each was caught by the mass meeting who waited for them. Soon, however, it became apparent that the new attack was not invincible, and that a quick, adaptive batsman could find his own methods. Morland again and again brought off what is now called the back drive – a stroke unheard of before – when he turned and tapped the ball over the wicket-keeper's head to the boundary. Now that a crash helmet has been added to the stumper's equipment he is safer than he used to be, but Grieve has admitted that he was glad that he had a weekly paper with an insurance coupon in his cricket bag that day. A fielder was placed on the boundary in line with the stumps, and then the versatile Morland proceeded to elaborate those fine tips to slip and tips to fine leg which are admitted now to be the only proper treatment of the dropper. At the same time Whitelaw took a pace back so as to be level with his wicket and topped the droppers down to the off so that Spedegue had to bring two of his legs across and so disarrange his whole plan of campaign. The pair put on ninety for the fifth wicket, and when Whitelaw at last got out, bowled by Hanwell, the score stood at one hundred and thirty.

But from then onwards the case was hopeless. It is all very well for a quick-eyed, active genius like Morland to adapt himself in a moment to a new game, but it is too much to ask of the average first-class cricketer, who, of all men, is most accustomed to routine methods. The slogging bumpkin from the village green would have made a better job of Spedegue than did these great cricketers, to whom the orthodox method was the only way. Every rule learned, every experience endured, had in a moment become useless. How could you play with a straight bat at a ball that fell from the clouds? They did their best – as well, probably, as the English team would have done in their place – but their best made a poor show upon a scoring card. Morland remained a great master to the end and carried out his bat for a superb seventy-seven. The second innings came to a close at six o'clock on the second day of the match, the score being one hundred and seventy-four. Spedegue eight for sixty-one. England had won by an innings and one hundred and eighty-four runs.

Well, it was a wonderful day and it came to a wonderful close. It is a matter of history how the crowd broke the ropes, how they flooded the field, and how Spedegue, protesting loudly, was carried shoulder-high into the pavilion. Then came the cheering and the speeches. The hero of the day had to appear again and again. When they were weary of cheering him they cheered for Bishops Bramley. Then the English captain had to make a speech. 'Rather stand up to Cotsmore bowling on a ploughed field,' said he. Then it was the turn of Batten the Australian. 'You've beat us at something,' he said ruefully; 'don't quite know yet what it is. It's not what we call cricket down under.' Then the Selection Board were called for and they had the heartiest and best deserved cheer of them all. Tarding told them about the waiting cab. 'It's waiting yet,' he said, 'but I think I can now dismiss it.'

Spedegue played no more cricket. His heart would not stand it. His doctor declared that this one match had been one too many and that he must stand out in the future. But for good or for bad – for bad, as many think – he has left his mark upon the game for ever. The English were more amused than exultant over their surprise victory. The Australian papers were at first inclined to be resentful, but then the absurd-ity that a man from the second eleven of an unknown club should win a Test match began to soak into them, and finally Sydney and Melbourne had joined London in its appreciation of the greatest joke in the history of cricket.

THE FADDIST

There was an old man of Bengal
Who purchased a bat and a ball,
Some gloves and some pads –
It was one of his fads –
For he never played cricket at all!

ALFRED AINGER

74

BARRY TOOK

*'One of the frustrations of living where I do is
that when the leaves fall and the trees are bare
and gaunt, from my study window I can just see
the pitch ...'*

LIVING ON THE DOORSTEP

To live near Lord's, as I do, is a mixed blessing. On the plus side there's the proximity to 'HQ' and the ability, when the sun shines and a game's afoot, to stroll in leisurely fashion to the ground in slightly less than a minute and to be seated in the Pavilion or be leaning nonchalantly, pint in hand, outside the Tavern in under four minutes (three if you run)!

The minus side is that it plays havoc with your work schedule. In spite of any evidence to the contrary I earn much of my living as a freelance script writer/copy writer/journalist. In short, I'm a jobbing scribbler and work at home. Home is an apartment in a block of flats situated immediately behind the bowler's arm as he comes in from the Nursery End. Well, I say immediately behind, but in fact you'd need about four times the distance of Denis Lillee's run-up to reach our front door, and cross a couple of roads and a small public park into the bargain. But behind the bowler's arm we are and I can hear from my study the bell that is rung in the Pavilion to announce that play is about to begin. I can, if I am not strong willed, put down my pen, put on my jacket and be in the ground by the time the first ball is bowled. It's a temptation that is hard, often impossible, to resist.

What is so tantalising about living close to Lord's is not only the cricket but the certainty that in the ground I'll meet friends, chat, drink, put the world to rights, and generally improve what would otherwise be another tedious and humdrum working day.

Cricket, fascinating as it can be, is only part of the joy of Lord's. I love the Long Room and the pictures on the Pavilion stairways, and the welcome 'cuppa' and fruit cake in the tea interval as you sip and munch, staring at the group of photographs of bygone tours or chatting to acquaintances. I enjoy a gossip with the gate-keepers and commissionaires who know me and who are always ready to stop for a chat. I like to watch the youngsters in the nets and the oldsters in the stands dividing their attention between the *Telegraph* crossword and the match in progress.

My local bank looks after many cricketers from Lord's and it's common in the summer to see one or more of the flannelled heroes cashing a cheque or discussing earnestly with one of the pretty cashiers the problems of investment and bank charges. At least that's what I assume they're doing. I mean, what else would cricketers talk to young ladies in Barclays about?

One drawback to living close to Lord's manifests itself at the time of Test Matches and Cup Finals. Local residents park in the street, by courtesy of the Westminster Council, for an annual charge of something in the region of fifty pounds a year. But when the Test Match or Cup Final crowds arrive parking regulations go for nothing and if the unwary resident drives off in the morning he has little hope of parking much nearer than Camden Town until close of play. Still, it's a small price to pay for proximity to the Home of Cricket and it must be admitted that any summer inconvenience is more than compensated for by the months of winter calm.

One of the frustrations of living where I do is that when the leaves fall and the trees are bare and gaunt, from my study window I can just see the pitch. As the cricket season is about to begin I catch glimpses of white clad figures at catching practice or having a workout in the nets. But the inscrutable laws of nature decree that by the time the first ball of the season is bowled the trees are in full leaf, and I can see nothing.

One of the most peculiar experiences I've had was to be in Sydney watching the England/Australia Lord's Test live by satellite. There I was, fourteen thousand miles away, and there, on the screen of our rented television set, were my homely surroundings as clear as if I was still in St John's Wood. The sounds of the match and the applause of the spectators mingled with the occasional engine noise of a jet coming into Heathrow and the odd cry of a seagull (their presence at Lord's has always puzzled me. Is it the cricket or the half-eaten sandwiches that attracts them?). Then suddenly the roar and clang as a fire engine dashed up St John's Wood Road. In our Sydney suburb my wife and I stiffened in our armchairs – was that a plume of smoke rising from back of the trees behind the bowler's arm at the Nursery End? Mercifully it wasn't – and we settled down to the cricket feeling somewhat homesick, for to paraphrase Robert Browning –

> Oh, to be in St John's Wood
> When there's cricket there …

even if it is impossible to park.

WALLY HAMMOND hits a sixer off L. Armanath into the crowd during the England *v* India Test at Old Trafford, 20 July 1940.

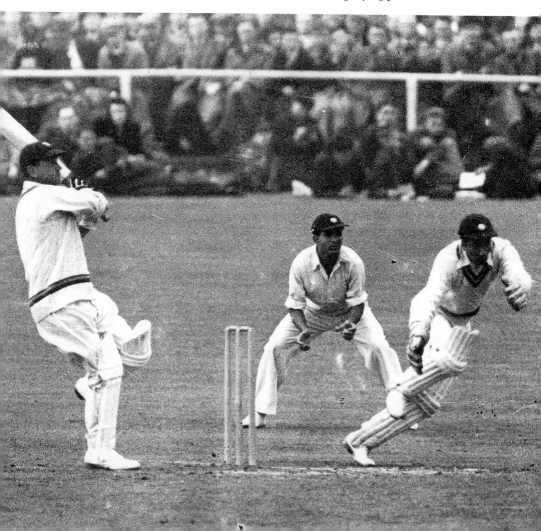

THE THINGS THEY'VE SAID ABOUT CRICKET

Retirement is when no longer can you play; when your box reposes on your dressing-table, a receptacle for spare collar studs; when sex is no more than a Latin numeral ...

– Humphrey Tilling

An umpire *should* be a man – they are, for the most part, old women ...

– R. A. Fitzgerald, Secretary MCC, 1863–76

Send him down a grand piano and see if he can play *that!*

– Yabba, the famous Sydney 'Hill' barracker

I have no memories of cricket except avoiding it at all times ...

– John Mortimer, QC

I hated to see *any* batsman not Lancastrian get runs against Lancashire ...

– Sir Neville Cardus

I felt so much pleasure from the simple idea of your playing a game of cricket ...

– John Keats to his brother, George

During the Middle Ages cricket was popular but frowned on by those engaged in raising military forces: it interfered with the practice of Archery ...

– Ivor Brown, A Book of England

I just don't know how Trevor Bailey came to be born anywhere other than in Yorkshire ...

– Fred Trueman

To bomb a factory is war. To bomb a cricket ground is sacrilege ...

– Sir Robert Menzies, following his inspection of Old Trafford ground after German bombers had damaged it

We have nothing against men cricketers. Some of them are quite nice people, even though they don't win as often as we do ...

– Rachael Heyhoe Flint

The true spirit of cricket requires the bowler to aim at or near the stumps, rather than the batsman's head ...

– Professor Aubrey Jenkins

I know absolutely nothing about cricket ...

– Clive James

There is one great similarity between music and cricket. There are slow movements in both.

– Sir Neville Cardus

A loving wife is better than making 50 at cricket or even 99; beyond that I will not go ...

– Sir James Barrie

Please do not misunderstand me. I am no Wright or Hollies or Benaud, and if I were able to collect half a dozen wickets against, say, East Wittering, I would be completely satisfied ...

– Patrick Moore

English county dressing rooms are such temperate places ...

– John Arlott

Cricket is peculiar in that despite being a big team game, the batsmen leave the field individually, taking their bow for success or hanging their heads after failure, in a way reminiscent of an opera house ...

– Lord Forte

Welcome to Worcester, where you've just missed seeing Barry Richards hit one of Basil d'Oliviera's balls clean out of the ground ...

– Brian Johnston

Oh, God, if there is to be cricket in Heaven, let there also be rain ...

– Lord Home of the Hirsel

I have always fantasised about cricket. Even now, on sleepless nights, I can dismiss the entire Australian eleven for a dozen runs ...

– Donald Pleasance

A substitute has a thankless task on tour; he is reminded before each Test – 'You are only a stomach upset away from playing' ...

– Mike Brearley

E. W. SWANTON

*'When J. G. W. Davies hit Don Bradman's off-
stump first ball at Fenner's in 1934 ...'*

CAMBRIDGE CRICKET BETWEEN THE WARS

University cricket began with a flourish after the First World War, and that of Cambridge especially so. Many men went up more to extend their experience of life in the wider sense than from academic impulse. Games played a larger part in undergraduate life than at any time since, and in the summer the University match at Lord's was one of the events of the season, spelled either with or without a capital 'S'.

The first University match, part of which I saw, was that of 1926; but I came to know later many of those engaged in the matches prior to that, including, of course, several in whose hands rested the destiny of Test matches and the fortunes of many of the counties. Cambridge in 1919 were led by a fruity character called John Morrison, a forceful bat, a better golfer than cricketer, and a better footballer (for the Corinthians and Chelsea) than either. On tour before Lord's that year Cambridge, after bowling out Sussex down at Hove for 172, made 611 – Morrison 168, J. H. Naumann 134 not out, and Arthur Gilligan, going in number eleven against his future county, 101. They won by an innings and 245 runs – and went on to lose narrowly to Oxford.

Morrison became a designer of golf courses and was addicted to drinking sherry from a ($\frac{1}{2}$ pint) tankard. George Wood, who kept wicket for England in 1924, succeeded him as captain, another man of parts who, when the terms for the University match were in course of negotiation with MCC, threatened to take it to the Oval. There followed the era of the three Ashtons, Gilbert, Hubert, and Claude, captains in successive years.

It is generally held that Gilbert's 1921 side was the strongest of the century. They lost to the Australians (against whom Hubert made the first hundred) and with a much depleted side to the Army. Against that their nine victories included five 'straight' against counties. They demolished Oxford, later contributing half the side with which A. C. Maclaren administered to the all-conquering Australians their first and historic defeat at Eastbourne. Hubert Ashton should by all critical opinion have played that year for England, and both he and the fast-medium Clem Gibson must have done so had they not gone forthwith overseas. 'Father' Marriott, Percy Chapman, J. L. Bryan, Claude Ashton, M. D. Lyon – all either reached or touched the fringes of greatness.

G. O. Allen entered the scene as a freshman in 1922, Hubert's year of captaincy, and took nine for 78 against Oxford after the Cambridge batting – Chapman, Graham Doggart (father of Hubert and grandfather of Simon, even more distinguished as a footballer), W. W. Hill-Wood and H. Ashton to the fore – had declared at 403 for four. Not only did three top-class bats not get in but one can count at least ten current or shortly-to-be county cricketers up that year who either had to wait a year or two for their blues or who never got them. Such was the talent – in batting anyway.

Cambridge again beat five counties in 1925 – including Surrey, practically at full strength and despite Jack Hobbs getting 100 in each innings, at the Oval. The great K. S. Duleepsinhji had now arrived and there were such names to conjure with as Enthoven, Jack Meyer, the founder of Millfield, and E. W. Dawson.

When I got to Lord's in 1926 Cambridge were 16 for three, and I had missed seeing all three wickets taken by my contemporary and house-captain at Cranleigh, Maurice McCanlis. Geoffrey Legge had caught them all at second slip. He was, briefly, a high-class out-swinger, and had six for 87 in the match, which Cambridge won by 34 runs. There were two more Light Blue Test cricketers up now, Walter Robins – who would get into my best-ever Cambridge side – and Maurice Turnbull. The next year Tom Killick, a beautiful player destined to play for England while still an undergraduate in 1929, could not make the side.

George Kemp-Welch (killed in the war and in memory of whom those handsomely-inscribed panels of successive Cambridge XIs decorate Fenner's pavilion) was a leading figure in the 1930s, even though with two such future England bowlers as F. R. Brown and K. Farnes under him in 1931, Oxford won at Lord's. That was the famous match wherein Alan Ratcliffe made 201 for Cambridge and the Nawab of Pataudi (father of 'Tiger') elected to demolish this new record and did so with 238 not out. I can see now the hats and umbrellas waving and almost hear the roar when Robert Scott knocked Ratcliffe's stumps awry for 9 in the second innings.

There was a racket then, but when J. G. W. Davies hit Don Bradman's off-stump first ball at Fenner's in 1934 the first reaction was an awed silence, as though something had happened in dubious taste perhaps – or was it only that for the whole crowded ring Jack's innocent-looking straight one with the off-break action had spoiled the day's pleasure. Jove had nodded – Don returned up the pavilion steps summoning a half-smile, no more!

Jack Davies, who since the war has served the CUCC so nobly, wandered about in the covers, sleeves flapping, soft-shoed, almost preoccupied until someone unwisely gave him the chance of a swift pick-up and lethal throw – a splendid all-round cricketer, for Cambridge and for Kent. Those who wish to know more of the history of Cambridge cricket should endeavour to read his article in *Barclays World of Cricket*, if they can lay hands on a copy.

H. T. Bartlett, a devastating bat who might well have played for England but for the war, led a powerful side in 1936, with three future Test cricketers in Norman Yardley, Paul Gibb, and the West Indian, J. H. Cameron, in addition to Jahangir Khan (father of Majid) who had played for India already.

I had the honour of playing at Fenner's for Middlesex in 1937, going in first with George Mann, a future captain of England and past chairman of the TCCB. It was his first first-class match, I being his senior in this respect by one. In the first innings I got an appalling lbw decision from one of the resident Cambridge umpires when feeling quite comfortable. In the second innings we put on 60-odd together, and Ian Peebles led the county to an easy win in a match otherwise memorable for the fact of Rab Bruce-Lockhart, the Scottish rugger international and formerly headmaster of Loretto, getting his only first-class wicket, that of Pat Hendren stumped off a parabolic leg-break.

Mark Tindall, who was to give such invaluable service as master-in-charge of cricket at his old school, Harrow, was captain in 1938 and Peter Studd, a future Lord Mayor of London, in the last summer of peace.

The second Cambridge decade between the wars had been less

glamorous than the first. But they were halcyon days wherein the University sides could mostly give the counties and their other opponents a good run for their money, and sometimes a beating. In cold fact the University won 38 matches against counties between the wars and lost 48, drawing 65. Figures apart, the important thing was – and still is – that Fenner's, beautiful Fenner's, was the nursery *par excellence* for young cricketers of talent, so many of whom went on to refresh their county sides, or to teach the game as schoolmasters, or to do both, and in so many cases to climb the heights to the England XI.

The Cambridge roll-call is a splendid one, and the names, even in the vastly different climate of today, are still coming through. May they never cease to do so.

THE SUPERB JACK HOBBS of imperishable memory, in action.

Snow taking Allan Border's wicket.

Sometime, When I'm Older

Sometime, when I'm older
perchance my mind will range
over days when I was a cricketer
unaware of time's colder ways,
then perhaps in a dusty corner
amongst the jumble of life
I'll recover cobwebbed memories
of past summers and friendly strife.

The vicarage lawn and village green,
church tower shimmering in high summer scene,
honeysuckle days of horses pulling harvest machines,
backyard centuries and boyhood dreams.

Later, in far flung places, meeting idols galore,
F. S., George, Wes and many more,
playing amongst them, as a minnow 'midst whales,
gathering impressions and numerous tales ...

From clamouring Caribbean palm-fringed ovals
with Sobers strong and smooth as Mount Gay rum,
casually batting, rummaging through bowling,
dimming even the tropical sun;
To writhing, wracking Bangladesh birth,
all riots, hardship and blood on dry earth,
matches played on political whim,
Bhutto's anthem, Ayub Khan's funeral hymn;
Then schizophrenic Australians, bottles and cans,
Pommy bastard, 'on yer mate, let's shake hands,
Lillee and Thomson, the Chappells and Co.,
white flannelled undertakers happy you should go.

Laced through these winters, back at home,
Count games, facts and figures for *Wisden*'s tome,
and Lord's on historic Test match days,
the 'Egg and Bacon' and traditional ways.

Finally, after it all, in later years,
games played to assuage some of life's tears
Lord's Taverners friendship, more fun and show,
hoping for others things we were lucky to know.

Sometime, when I'm older ...

JOHN SNOW

JOHN EBDON

*'... We've got enthusiasm on our side, we're
abounding with it – we'll stuff them rotten, won't
we, lads? ...'*

WITH BAT AND BALL
IN DARKEST SURREY

Village cricket is an English institution, and as permanent as poverty. During the period known laughingly as summer, no weekend will pass without the playing of a fixture somewhere. However, closer to Farnham Town in Surrey there used to be a yearly event which was no less noteworthy. It was the annual encounter between the Bat and Ball Inn and the Sandrock Public House, Boundstone; and I treasure the day I first witnessed one.

Wisden has no record of this contest, and few outside the county know of the occasion. They are the poorer for their ignorance. However, an informed minority, the cognoscenti of real rural cricket, spared no effort to attend the spectacle. Nor, as I was to discover, did aficionados of real rural ale. They too supported this unique divertissement and could be seen following the play intently, if glassily, through the bottoms of pint mugs, and evidencing their unwavering and concurrent devotion to both disciplines.

Easily recognisable by the permanence of a glass in each hand from one of which they sipped steadily between deliveries, and only replenishing the empty vessel at the end of each over, their concentration and synchrony was marvellous to behold. But like all zealots they paid a price. Indeed, as still incredulous observers of past events advised me prior to my first-hand enlightenment at the festival, they well remembered seeing many leaving the ground so emotionally disturbed as to be unable to give a coherent account of the day's play, an inability which, my informants added, was also shared by some of the players.

Theirs was a rash assertion, and one which reached the ears of both publicans whose hostelries I visited in search of truth on the day of the match. They were not well pleased. The statement, they said, was a foul calumny, a mendacity. And their knuckles showed white on their beer pumps. In his bar at lunch time, the licensee of the Sandrock was vehement in his rejection of the canard.

'No one from here,' said he from the centre of a group of players, 'is allowed more than three pints each before they take the field. Right lads?' he inquired from his surrounding team mates. 'That's right,' chorused the posse of innumerates around him, 'three only!' 'All except him, that is,' continued their captain, nodding toward a stocky individual who was preventing the bar from falling down. 'He's only allowed two. He's got to be careful, he has.' 'Oh,' I asked, 'who's he?' 'Wicket-keeper,' said the captain tersely. 'His eyes go funny after two. Fourteen extras off the first over last year there were. *And* eleven off the second. Weren't there, Patrick?' he called out to the gentleman under discussion. The maligned one paused in his intake of ale and raised two of his fingers in salute. 'Get knotted,' he said pleasantly, and returned to his tankard.

'All the same,' said the captain returning the gesture without rancour and apparently unconcerned by this show of indiscipline, 'we still won. You see,' said he, 'we've got the bowlers. And', he continued, raising his voice above the hub-bub of the fast filling pub and the rapidly emptying glasses as well-wishers poured in to support their heroes, 'we've got enthusiasm on our side, we're abounding with it – we'll stuff them rotten! Won't we lads?' he shouted. 'Yes,' cried everyone in unison, 'we'll definitely stuff them! If they're lucky it'll rain!' And they gave three cheers and said rude things about the Bat and Ball.

I was much impressed, not only by the show of confidence and support, but by the realism of the Sandrock's captain. Whilst clearly aware of his bowling strength, he was not unmindful of the team's Achilles heel, the wicket-keeper's tendency to double vision. And as I noted the artistry and ease with which that person despatched a pint, I appreciated his anxiety. But the aura within the Sandrock was one of jollity and not concern, the happy Sunday atmosphere of an English country pub, but which that day had a more than usual sense of togetherness. What spirit, I thought as I left them, some flexing their elbows in vertical motions, others with their arms around the waists of lady supporters and, in the case of the wicket-keeper, performing both actions at once – what verve!

I turned into Bat and Ball Lane and walked toward the inn which bears its name. From a nearby church a clock chimed out the quarter. Two-fifteen, and less than an hour to the match. Outside the Bat and Ball a beflannelled young man with a cricket bat drove an imaginary ball toward me. 'Good luck,' I said, entering into the spirit of the mime and returning it to him. 'Do you think you'll win?' He gave a slight twitch and looked uneasy. 'I'm not sure,' he said dubiously, 'not at all sure. I understand the opposition have acquired some very forthright bowling talent.' He licked his lips. 'I'm not very good against pace,' he said; and instinctively massaged his groin. Clearly he was apprehensive – the fact that he executed late cuts all the way to his ear suggested that; and when I went into the Bat and Ball, happy and full as that was too, I sensed just a little edginess at the bar.

Unlike the Sandrock, the Bat and Ball's team was not captained by the publican but by a legal gentleman upon whom greatness suddenly had been thrust. 'Yes,' said that Man of Law, sipping timorously and frequently from his half-pint glass, 'we had a committee to decide who would play, I went away for the weekend, and when I came back I found I was captain! Just like that! Ha! Ha!' He giggled nervously, drained his glass, and showing signs of extreme agitation disappeared into the lavatory to much applause from his fellows, and instructions to have one for them. 'Strewth!' said someone. 'Three bogs in two halves? Bloody hell. Nerves, I suppose.' 'Um,' said another, 'same last year. Remember? Made more runs that way than he did in the middle. And he wasn't even skipper then.' And they laughed uproariously.

Minutes later their leader reappeared, marginally less tense and waving a sheet of toilet paper. 'Batting order,' he cried, 'just worked it out! Have a look at it chaps, and then let's go!' 'Right-oh,' roared the chaps as time was called, 'but do up your flies – it's cold outside!' And to the sounds of 'Land of Hope and Glory' and cries of 'the Bat and Ball for ever!', they departed for the field by divers transport together with their salivating St Bernard mascot.

The chaps were correct in their appreciation of the weather. Outside, the wind was easterly with a bite in it, and as I started off briskly on foot to the Bourne Cricket Club, on whose ground the match was to be contested, I wondered what part the climatic conditions would play in the game. Three pints of beer on a cold day could, I conjectured, cause problems to the fielding side. Particularly to the Bat and Ball captain; and the Sandrock wicket-keeper. And thus occupied, I continued on my way, reflecting that my questions would be answered shortly.

The Bourne Cricket Club has a pleasant oak- and fir-lined little ground a ball's throw from the Churt Hindhead road, and by the time I reached it the teams had arrived; so had their supporters, and so had the beer. A very great deal of it. Promptly inspected by the umpires and other interested parties with the welfare of the game at heart, it was pronounced to have travelled well and to be no worse for its fifteen-minute journey to the ground. That important formality completed, and after only a brief hiatus while the Bat and Ball leader visited the pavilion, the two captains, together with the umpires, inspected the wicket. And so did the St Bernard mascot. The first-mentioned expressed concern about the follow through marks from a previous game, the umpires discussed the specific gravity of the beer, and the St Bernard, showing considerable interest in a leg stump, removed its varnish in five seconds flat before being led off at the gallop to a great ovation, and still smiling.

With the return of decorum, the toss was made, won by the Bat and Ball who elected to field, and the quartet, spearheaded by the Man of Law, jogged from the field exchanging good-natured insults and obscenities as they went, and reported to their dressing rooms. Above them in the roof, scorers sharpened pencils and adjusted their bifocals, the crowd buzzed with expectation, and five minutes later eleven comparatively strong men and true took the field to cheers, counter cheers and boos, and awaited the arrival of the Sandrock's opening batsmen.

'Play!' said the umpire, and the contest was enjoined.

And what applause greeted the first runs, and even greater hurrahs for the first from the bat. Drives to cover, shots to leg, cowshots, mows and sweeps and misses, all were cheered or jeered or groaned at as minute by minute the drama unfolded. An umpire hit in a tender part was transformed into a boy soprano and had to be given a glass of beer, two batsmen collided in mid-wicket and were offered a similar restorative; bails flew and runs came; and at cover point the Man of Law, offering his hands to a descending skier, neglected to close them at the moment of truth. As one man the Sandrock supporters full-throatedly roared their approval of the lapse and asked him to continue the good work. Two balls later he obliged them even more decisively and to even greater approbation.

'Stupid bastard!' screamed the aggrieved and disbelieving bowler in concert with first slip, 'you extremely stupid bastard!' 'Ha! Ha!' said the newly designated love-child self-consciously, and blew into his hands. 'Touch of the old frostbite,' he shouted rubbing them briskly. 'Sorry chaps!' 'Get on with it,' yelled a voice from behind me, 'and pull your finger out!'

Runs came quickly for the Sandrock, but at a price. More wickets fell as the score mounted; and then came the innings for which many had waited with keen anticipation, that of the Sandrock's wicket-keeper – he who had been instructed to restrict his intake to two pints of ale but who, alas, appeared to have lost his ability to count.

With reluctance and difficulty he vacated his seat by one of the barrels and allowed himself to be relieved of his tankard. 'Kew,' he said thickly, 'ver' kind.' Two well-wishers assisted him to the crease, pointed him in the general direction of the bowler, and left him to it. He survived the last ball of the over but then, in a moment of mental abberation, flung himself in the path of a straight drive from his fellow batsman.

'Oh my God,' said his captain in front of me, and buried his face in his hands. 'That's a certain four he's saved for them – I'll do him when he gets back, so help me I will!' 'If he gets back,' said a realist next to him as the wicket-keeper steered an erratic course to cross for a single, blowing kisses to square leg *en route*. 'He can't even see the bowler, never mind the ball – look at him!' We did; and three balls later watched him sit on his stumps.

It was a short, but immensely interesting contribution to the game and one to be unequalled by any other batsman of either side; but there was never really a dull moment in the innings. It was all riveting stuff. Another wicket fell; the Sandrock captain, obviously distressed by his wicket-keeper's cabaret, made only a nodding acquaintance with the black hole, the Bat and Ball's St Bernard, overcome by emotion, committed an enormity in the outfield, another batsman went in and lost a contact lens but stayed, splendid in adversity, and the crowd hummed with excitement and comment. 'Oh, lovely shot!' they cried as he struck two consecutive deliveries for four and hit mid-off's funny-bone with the third; 'take the other one out and you'll do even better! Well done that man, well done!'

It was one of the best one-eyed innings I have ever seen and he returned to a sea of waving tankards and general euphoria, and was immediately given a pint. And so the overs ticked away. The excitement mounted, and so did the score. With one over to go, a flurry of strokes brought the Sandrock's total into the 170s, then to 181; two more runs were added from the first ball of the last over, the next was lofted – and held. The Sandrock's innings closed at 183 for 6 off the allotted thirty overs; and beer was taken at once.

The interval was a hive of activity. Three men, including the family doctor, escorted the Sandrock's wicket-keeper to a bench where, on medical advice, cold water was poured over his head for several minutes; the missing contact lens was discovered at the bottom of a glass and joyously reclaimed by its owner; and the Bat and Ball captain held a conference.

'Well chaps,' he began brightly, and avoiding the eyes of those who had put him out of wedlock, 'one-eight-four to win, eh? Think we contained them pretty well, what? Yes,' he continued, 'jolly good show! One or two chances went down, ha! ha!, but there we are – even Homer may nod! Still,' he went on, and departing from the classics, 'there's no pace in the pitch and their 'keeper's pissed – should be a doddle really. And don't forget, chaps,' said he, placing his index finger to the side of his nose and closing his off-stump eye, 'there's always Plan B if things go wrong!'

'Plan B?' inquired a startled supporting bystander. 'What's that?' 'Ha! Ha!' said the Man of Law, and pointed to the perimeter of the field. 'Bonfires', he explained, 'we'll get the people in those houses to light 'em, smoke'll drift over the ground and we'll appeal against the light. Ha! Ha! Ha! Good wheeze, what? Anyway chaps,' he concluded, 'pads on, toss up for who's going to wear the box, and remember – the honour of the Bat and Ball's at stake! Hip! Hip?' he inquired ·of his team. 'Hurrah!' they responded, stirred by the pre-Harfleur-type exhortation and raising their glasses, 'Hurrah! Hurrah!'

The enthusiasm which greeted the entry of the Bat and Ball's opener was no less than that afforded to the Sandrock's, despite the charisma of their wicket-keeper. Remarkably, and aided by medical science, he appeared to have staged a good recovery, and apart from taking the field accoutred with two left pads and a woman's beret, showed little sign of his earlier extravagances. Nevertheless, the first ball, delivered at some pace by a bespectacled bowler with a suspect action, flew over his head bringing four byes, and cheers from the boundary. So did the second. And the third; and when the fourth was snicked through the hands of first slip to increase the total by three, vulgar singing broke out in the Bat and Ball camp only to be silenced by the sight of a leg stump cartwheeling into the air as their star batsman was dismissed for a duck, and returned to the pavilion accompanied by an unkind chorus of quacking.

Worse was to follow. Pausing only in midfield to avail himself of the outgoing player's box, the new arrival took middle and off and was bowled round his legs for two; his successor hit both his wicket and its guardian with the same stroke, and somewhere a faint heart, acting without the captain's sanction, ordered Plan B to be operated and a pall of smoke attended by an acrid smell of burning rubber began to drift across the ground.

As many a Test match commentator has observed, cricket is a funny game, and this was no exception. Within minutes the situation changed and see-sawed. Rapidly, and following a severe attack of stomach cramp in the pace bowler as the cold and beer took its toll, the score rose to 63 for 3. At 73 for 3 the order went out to extinguish the bonfires, at 88 for 5 instructions were given for them to be re-ignited; and then came another recovery. From the centre came the sweet sound of a ball being hit from the meat of the bat followed by the equally sweet sound, to Bat and Ball ears, of a pavilion window breaking as the first six of the match was registered. Two balls later the music was repeated to scenes of wild rejoicing.

'Boi God!' said a red-nosed collarless rustic above the tumult, 'that's a nasty smell of broken glass! Puts me in moind of ole Bandy Crowe, that does. 'It the charch bell 'e did, old Bandy Crowe. Tharty yur ago that were. Course 'e's dead now, ole Bandy, but that's what 'e done, rung the bloody bell 'e—'

He broke off as more tinkling and cheering signalled the arrival of another massive hit. 'Cor,' he said, 'e ain't 'arf surproisin' they winders. That's three in'it?' 'And the hundred,' said someone. 'They don't know what's hit 'em in the score box!' 'That's roight,' said the ancient, 'that's brought 'em off their arses. Moind,' he continued, ' 'e ain't rung the charch bell yet, not like ole Bandy Crowe done. They sent a chap called 'Airy 'Arry round to get the ball back I remember. Yaas. Vicur said afterwards it were first time 'e'd seen him near the bloody place. Yaas, he were a right old bugger, 'Airy 'Arry was. But ole Bandy Crowe ...'

And so the spate of runs and reminiscences continued. The unex-purgated and somewhat seamy life stories of Bandy Crowe and Hairy Harry were unfolded, revealing them to be men whose strength was not confined to their arms alone, and the esurient batsmen prospered. His was a splendid innings, rich in inventive strokes the like of which will never be illustrated in any cricket manual and one which even drew grudging applause from a visiting Yorkshireman. But, alas for the Bat and Ball, it was not quite good enough. Stumps were drawn, three cheers were given for the winners, and losers, the walking wounded and incapables were led away together with a crestfallen St Bernard; and as the ground emptied, the heavens opened.

'Boi God,' said Bandy Crowe's biographer, 'that'll get in through they winders.' 'Aye,' said the visitor from Leeds as the rain lashed his Gannex, 'dead men are 'aving a right old pee. Just like being at 'ome.'

That evening both teams gathered in the victors' pub and once again the beer flowed as the match was remembered ball by ball, by all except the wicket-keeper. The Sandrock captain, ringing a bell with one hand and holding a tankard in the other, precariously mounted a chair from where he made a speech, and the Man of Law, now untroubled by tension, responded from the floor of the house. Both opined that it had been a great match, and both were cheered to the echo. And when I left the exploits of Bandy Crowe and Hairy Harry both on and off the field were still being related from a smoke-filled corner.

The cartoonist Bill Tidy.

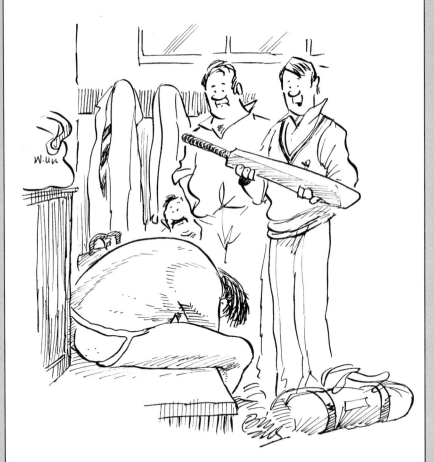

'I thought the purpose of the aluminium bat was to protect the aluminium box.'

SIR LEONARD HUTTON

*'Grandpa, when you made 364 did you hit the ball
on to the roof?'*

MY FAVOURITE
CRICKET GROUNDS

A small frail schoolboy is on his way by bus and train to Park Avenue, Yorkshire's county ground at Bradford, with a good supply of food. The package always contained a cream bun – one of those buns with a lot of cream in the middle – because you could get several cream buns for a penny in those days. He was on his way, sometimes with one or two friends but often alone, to watch Yorkshire play.

I know what that boy was thinking, for I was that schoolboy over fifty years ago, enthralled with first-class cricket and Yorkshire.

Park Avenue became my favourite cricket ground, even though on my first visit in 1926 those stern-looking commissionaires who guarded the gates refused me admission. The ground had been closed a few minutes before I arrived with my elder brother. And ever since, when I've driven to a ground and had my car waved through the gates by commissionaires, I've thought of that schoolboy they once locked out.

It was the only occasion when I have been refused admission to a cricket ground. The next time I went to Park Avenue I got in, to watch Middlesex playing Yorkshire. I sat in the stand that used to adjoin the football ground, before Bradford FC (as opposed to poor Bradford City) went out of existence, and had a very good view from behind the bowler's arm.

Middlesex were skippered by F. T. Mann, the father of George Mann, and their team included Patsy Hendren, Hearne and Durston. Yorkshire had Wilfred Rhodes, Herbert Sutcliffe, Holmes and Leyland, and Abe Waddington, the left-arm opening bowler, who had one of the most attractive bowling actions I ever saw.

All these household names I was to meet or to know in the years ahead, but at the moment I was most impressed, even overawed, by these giants of cricket. They all looked so smart in their immaculate clothes. Their boots and pads were spotless – most impressive to my young keen eyes.

Then Frank Mann had the audacity to hit Wilfred Rhodes for six, the ball striking the seats within a few yards of where I was sitting and ricocheting around the stand as if it had been fired from a gun. Wilfred scowled at such treatment, as he would also do if a catch was dropped from his bowling. Hedley Verity, his great successor in Yorkshire and England sides, was the complete opposite. He would smile, as he did when Jock Cameron hit him for four sixes and two fours in an over at Sheffield in 1935. At the end of that over Arthur Wood, the Yorkshire wicket-keeper, said: 'You got him in two minds that over, Hedley – he did not know whether to hit you for four or six!'

When I see boys today with scorecards and scorebooks, it takes me back to my own schoolboy days in the sun. How delightful they were, so much nicer than facing Lindwall or Miller on the sun-baked pitches of Melbourne and Sydney. Yes, Bradford's ground at Park Avenue was the favourite of my youth, and that sad fire at City's football ground really affected me.

Later in life Lord's became my next favourite. But I disliked it for the first two or three years that I went there, for good reason. In 1937 I made my Test debut there, against New Zealand, and had a bit of trouble with their fast bowler, Jack Cowie. I made nought and one. Then in 1938 I didn't do very well against Australia. It was only in 1939 that I started making some runs at Lord's, and got a century against West Indies. That was the game George Headley made two, one in each innings.

Since then I've come to think that Lord's has the most knowledgeable of all cricket crowds, because most of them have played the game at some time or another. But what struck me when I first went there was the white paint, and the flowers, all those flowers in the Lord Harris garden round the back of the pavilion. Now where I came from we never associated flowers with cricket. We never saw flowers at Park Avenue in Bradford or at Bramall Lane in Sheffield.

At Lord's you never know whom you'll meet: that's one of the attractions of the place. You could bump into a High Court judge, or a famous actor, or a playwright like Harold Pinter. One day a complete stranger – I'd never seen him in my life – came up to me in the pavilion and said: 'Bet on Friar's Fancy in the 2.30 at Sandown.' Simply that, and he walked away. Now at that stage I had never laid a bet in my life, but I thought about this as I went back to the dressing-room (Yorkshire were playing Middlesex that day). Maurice Leyland was there: he had decided he wasn't fit to play, and wanted to go to the races. So I asked him to put a pound on, which was quite a sum in those days, especially for someone who had never backed a horse in his life. And Friar's Fancy came in first at 4 to 1! I was delighted naturally, and the next day when I saw Maurice in the pavilion I went up to him and said: 'I believe you've got a little money for me.' And Maurice turned round and said: 'I forgot all about it!'

Lord's, to my mind, has unrivalled attractions, apart from the people you can meet. There can be nowhere better for a young man to learn his trade than on the ground staff, with those marvellous facilities, and there you can get all kinds of advice.

It was at Lord's again that I made my last Test century in this country, against Australia in 1953. I had to struggle a bit to get there, but I didn't realise then how close we would come to defeat in the second innings. While Willie Watson and Trevor Bailey were making their stand, I tried to keep calm, but I did a lot of pacing up and down, and signed a lot of autographs to help pass the time. I didn't watch much until the day was saved, as I was frightened a wicket would fall.

My last game at Lord's was an afternoon benefit match for the old Middlesex player, Harry Sharp. I remember being hit on the toe and not being able to walk for three or four days afterwards. My last game of all was at the Oval, some time in the sixties, when I played against England Ladies. I remember making 35 against some pretty ferocious-looking bowlers, as ferocious as those commissionaires at Bradford all those years ago. I was so stiff for days afterwards that I decided to give it up for good.

Throughout my long associations with cricket as a player and a watcher, there have been many amusing incidents.

A few weeks ago I was playing in the garden with my two grandsons aged five and eight. Oliver, the five-year-old, was batting; he struck the ball a firm blow into the bushes. Whilst his elder brother Benjamin and myself searched for the ball, Oliver ran between the wickets with great speed calling out 21, 22, 23 and so on, and he had reached 30 when we found the ball.

Whilst I was recovering on the garden seat a little later Oliver came up to me and said, 'Grandpa, when you made 364 did you hit the ball on to the roof?' I was at a loss for a reply!

PRESSURES OF THE GAME

LEFT: A stitch in time seems to be required by Warwickshire's A. M. Ferreir during the Surrey *v* Warwickshire game in the NatWest Trophy Final at Lord's in September 1982. Umpire Dickie Bird obviously had the needle!

BELOW: Lancashire wicketkeeper G. Fowler finds the pressures a bit too much during the Surrey *v* Lancashire match at the Oval in September 1980.

COLIN ATKINSON

*Somerset's ex-captain, now Headmaster, talks
fascinatingly about ...*

CRICKET AT MILLFIELD

As so often happens in schools, the early days of Millfield's cricket owe much to legend, myth and nostalgia, so much so that it is difficult to focus upon a picture based entirely on reality. But colourful, idio-syncratic and possibly unpredictable might be useful adjectives to describe cricket *ab initio* at a school which is now proud of its fifty years' life and that it began in the smallest, humblest fashion. Stories are told in the common room bar of times when the head gardener and the Headmaster's secretary made up the numbers; whilst the then Head-master, himself no mean cricketer at first-class level, captained the side simply because the school wasn't big enough to field a team of boys: though one rather imagines that, since it was his bat and ball, he rather fancied a game himself! And why not?

It was therefore not surprising, if a little disappointing, that the school struggled throughout most of the 40s, 50s and 60s decades to establish itself on an equal footing with the best school elevens in the South West. A glance at the fixture list over this period tells the story. Nevertheless, over the years, Millfield has been helped by visits from such distinguished wandering clubs as MCC, Free Foresters, XL Club and the South Oxfordshire Amateurs.

Throughout this time, amongst other coaches none was more distinguished than Frank Edwards, whose spell at Millfield began only after retirement from Uppingham! He continued to bowl in the nets until he was over 80; and when he died his ashes were scattered over the 1st XI square, which he had created.

When Gerry Wilson joined the coaching and ground staff in 1960, Millfield was fortunate to have one so young and able to follow on from Frank Edwards; and he is still a powerful influence on the game, albeit now aided by a most efficient and positively lethal bowling machine. But so, too, were Barry Hobson, Lloyd Williams and Frank Fenner as successive Masters i/c cricket throughout the period during which Millfield established itself as a school, shedding its tutorial growing pains. Indeed, no fewer than 21 boys have played first-class cricket since Gerry Wilson became coach. Included in this number are, for instance: R. K. Paull, G. I. Burgess, P. W. Denning, P. A. Slocombe, P. M. Roebuck, M. A. Olive, N. A. Felton, P. A. C. Bail, J. C. M. Atkinson (Somerset); D. A. Graveney, J. C. Foat, J. H. Shackleton, P. G. Roebuck (Gloucestershire), V. P. Terry (Hampshire and England), R. D. L. Dudley-Jones (Glamorgan), T. G. Hansell (Surrey), M. J. Bamber (Northants).

Thus it was that the end of the sixties and the early years of the seventies saw the gradual expansion of the fixture list. Clifton, for instance, was first played in 1970. But an indication of the increased strength of the game since then is the number of fixtures at Foals, Junior Colts and Senior Colts levels: and all with A and B teams. Co-incidental with the growth in both interest and strength has been the burgeoning of practice facilities both outdoors and in sports halls. These are also used and enjoyed by the Somerset cricketers throughout their early April training. The excellent grass nets, a dozen or so, have been added to by the provision of four outdoor artificial wickets and six indoor nets, in which the coach is able to nurture young talent during the autumn and spring terms. With delicate handling and diplomatic intervention from the Master i/c cricket and the Director of Studies, even the toughest academic has been known to release boys for the odd period: though bargains often have to be struck and extra work set!

The main cricket field's pavilion overlooks the majestic and famous Glastonbury Tor, whose back-drop is formed by a sweepingly generous arc of the Mendip hills. The wicket itself is biased in favour of the batsman – as is right and proper at school level, or at Test level, for that matter. The out-field is inclined to be fast in fine weather, owing to the clayey nature of the soil, and spectators are often treated to high-scoring games.

In recent years, the policy has been to look for stronger adult sides (e.g. Exeter and Bristol Universities) which could give the 1st XI tougher opposition than some schools. And the introduction of cricket festivals at the end of term has also added 'bite' to the fixture list, for the Welsh Under-16 and Under-18 XIs provide strong opposition for our Senior Colts and 1st XIs as does the ESCA West team, in which several of Millfield's eleven (four in 1985) usually find places when other regions are played.

Finally, during the summer holidays, it is always a pleasant sight to see so many boys of all ages and abilities being coached and using the facilities when the school's holiday courses are in full swing. Most are not from Millfield, and it is a comforting thought that such boys, along with Millfieldians, will swell the numbers of village and club cricketers in years to come. And the odd one or two might represent their county or country. Most will come to appreciate that cricket is a fascinating and, at times, impossibly difficult game.

SLIP-UP FROM SOMERSET

A cricketer Lord's-bound from Yeovil
Turned up by mistake at the Eovil;
   So he said 'Nevery worry,'
   And batted for Surrey,
Though this met with some disappreovil.

DOROTHY SPRING

LESLIE THOMAS

*'The wicket was painted on the hull of the
ship which meant there was no need for a
wicket-keeper ...'*

CAUGHT IN THE DEEP

If you've ever been aboard a vessel jammed in the pack ice around 62°N, 69°W, then you'll know what I mean. If you haven't, then take my advice it's an experience to avoid. Even if you're keen on cricket.

It would probably be all right these days with ski-planes, helicopters, motorised sledges and what-have-you but in 1937 we had nothing like that. Once you were stuck, you were stuck; ice everywhere for miles and seventeen fathoms of freezing water below. Caught in the deep.

There was no one to blame but ourselves. We could have faulted the owners or the skipper but the fact was we all knew the risks. There had been a freak thaw about the second week of March, the ice on the long channel to Port Atuk was reported to be breaking up, and there was a lot of money for everybody concerned with the first ship to get in after the winter. When you've been hanging around in Indian Harbour, Labrador, since November the prospect is too much to resist.

She was called *Fair Sealer*, a gritty, broad, hard-nosed, uncomfortable 8,000-tonner. A lot of the tonnage was in the bow. She was built originally in Finland and she had done all sorts of graft, all of it within the Arctic Circle. The crew were mostly Canadians from Labrador, or Newfies from St John's, a few Eskimoes for the small boat work and for the odd bit of hunting and fishing, four Australians who had worked in the South Polar regions, the rest of us English or Irish and one cook who was Indian. The skipper was a tough old devil called Gerder, Iron Gerder they called him, from Bergen. When the news came through about the early thaw at Great Walrus Creek and the possibility of getting through to Port Atuk there was naturally a good deal of interest because by March everybody in Indian Harbour was short of money. There was also a lot of shaking heads. A thaw before the end of March was something few could remember and even fewer trusted. One drop in the temperature and it would all freeze up again. And that is exactly what happened.

We set sail on 16 March and in 36 hours we had reached the mouth of the Great Walrus Channel. Even the old-timers could never remember seeing the ice so broken up. Bergs and floes sailed past, brilliant with sunlight, as we went north and then north-west. Birds dotted the clear blue skies, always a good sign, and we saw seals basking like sunbathers down in the Florida Keys. Then, in the way it does in those latitudes, it all changed in a few hours. Night came down in the late afternoon with the air still, almost petrified, but as soon as it was set dark – just as if it had been waiting for the cover of night – a grizzly wind came down from the north. There wasn't a man jack of us who was in any doubt about what was coming next. And it did. The blizzard arrived about four bells and when it was light the following morning there we were: jammed, stuck, fixed, iced. Caught in the deep.

Captain Gerder pounded up and down the bridge cursing in Norwegian and the First Officer, who came from Bath and whose name was Forster, kept following him up and down and saying: 'Quite right, sir. Quite right.'

Well, curses nor prayers never did drive pack ice away and we all knew that. There was nothing for it but to sit it out, wait for the natural thaw and forget the bonuses.

Now three weeks in the ice is a long time but Arctic sailors are a patient lot and they know how to live cooped up together like that, going nowhere. There was no danger of us starving because the ship was well-provisioned and the Eskimoes went out hunting and fishing almost every day. There was, goodness knows, plenty of water around and the ship was tough enough to withstand all the pressure of the ice. But time seemed to take a long time to go by.

There was still only about five hours' light each day but the sun was bright, reflecting from the ice and the great snow banks that bordered the sound. Hunting and fishing parties went out with the Eskies, more for something to do than the actual need for food. When the night came down we would be back on the ship, enclosed, away from the cold, and twiddling our thumbs.

It didn't make things easier having half a dozen nationalities in the crew. Politics and religion were banned from the start as subjects for conversation. Now I think of it, they should have stopped the topic of cricket as well. We often talked of sport, football and racing and the Canadians with their ice hockey, but cricket had never come up very much, it not being of much interest to Arctic sailors. At least that's what I thought. But one day it started because somebody had turned up a cricket book in the case of books which had come aboard from the Seaman's Mission at Indian Harbour. I'd never heard anything like it in twenty years at sea. Soon the Aussies and the English were at each other's throats, with the Irish deckhand, of all people, trying to keep the peace. Words like 'Bodyline' and 'Jardine' and 'Larwood' started flying about. Fists were raised. The Canadians couldn't believe it. Nor could I. Not having taken a great interest in the game I still thought it was a gentleman's sport. But here we were on the point of ship warfare.

It went on for a couple of days and in the end one of the Eskimoes complained to the skipper and he came down to sort it out. Being a Norwegian he was as mystified as the other outsiders, so he called Forster, the First Officer from Bath. This started the whole dispute off afresh because Forster said something detrimental to the Aussies and at that point I could see a mutiny breaking out.

Oddly enough it was the Indian cook who came up with the idea of the match. After all there was plenty of space and the ice around the ship was pretty flat. It turned out there was a long piece of thick coconut mat in the for'ard hold. Once it had been used on deck when the owners had a party aboard the ship one summer at St John's, Newfoundland. The carpenter said he could make some bats if someone would show him the shape (he was another Canadian) and the Eskimoes showed how to fashion a ball from blubber and sealskin, the sort they had made in childhood.

Everything was at hand. The first match was to be played the following day and two more would follow. The teams, of course, were England versus Australia, although the Canadians (as fellow Colonials) went on the Aussies' side and the Irish, Eskimoes and the Indian cook played for England. It wasn't perfect but it was the best we could do. The bosun, an Aussie called Ron Grunton, was captain of his side, and Forster the First Officer, who said he had played quite good cricket, whatever that was, was leader of the English. Grunton was a beefy, lurid sort of bloke and Forster was a bit of a lily, so they didn't like each other that much anyway. Me, having my leg where the polar bear got me a few years back, and living most of my life in California anyway, was voted in as umpire. The skipper said he would watch from the bridge and would mark down the runs scored. As he was a Norwegian there were a lot of doubts about this but he said it was an easy game and who was going to argue with the captain.

Not having much experience of the game myself, I am open to contradiction, but I honestly think that the scene on the day of the first Test Match, as they called it, cannot have been repeated many times in the whole history of cricket. There was ice and snow to every horizon, jagged in the distance, smooth as steel around where the ship was trapped. A great arc of sky, blue as sapphire, curved across the scene; not a cloud. The sun shone with a big amber light and the air was cold and sharp. Australia batted first and it was wonderful to see the players all placed about the ice in their furs and hoods, their breaths going up like the smoke from chimneys. The Canadians and the Eskimoes were allowed to wear their skates for fielding.

The wicket was painted on the hull of the ship which meant there was no need for a wicket-keeper. It was a good idea because if he had missed the ball it would probably have gone off over the horizon and never been seen again. The ball, in fact, was a big success. The Eskimoes said it was the sort of ball they had made and used as children – although obviously not to play cricket. But it bounced well on the coconut mat stretched out on the ice, not too high, not too low.

Australia got 143 in their innings, one of the Canadians, a stoker who had been good at ice hockey, hitting 60 of them. The Indian cook turned out to be a good bowler and one of the Irishmen, who had played shinty, where you have to have a fast eye, caught three catches, one of them a beauty, slithering along the ice on his backside afterwards. England got only 98, the same Irishman hitting 40-odd because you have to be able to hit the ball in shinty too.

That night, of course, the Australians were full of it and the Englishmen a bit quiet. The second match was different. England batted first and the First Officer Forster scored 76 with a dazzling array of strokes, as they say in the papers, to all parts of the ice. He hit a six that looked as if it might reach the North Pole and eventually had to be fished from a 'lead', a channel of water that appeared suddenly in the ice. The real thaw was on its way. Ron Grunton, the Australian bosun, was getting more nasty all the time the officer was batting, grumbling at his bowlers and fielders, saying how much luck the batsman was getting, and that sort of thing. Australia only got 81 in reply to England's 187, giving England a victory, so there was a lot of needle in the series.

Everybody on board was full of it. The skipper came down so that the game could be more fully explained. There were arguments and outright disputes and threats on what was going to happen the next day at the deciding match. Some men even went to bed early and one of the Paddies wrote to his parish priest and his mother, something he hadn't done in years, just to tell them about it.

It would not be putting it too strongly to say that excitement was at fever pitch the next day. Everything was forgotten but the cricket. Grunton and Forster practically snarled at each other when they tossed up. Australia won and said they would bat. They made 192, the highest total of the series, Grunton and one of the Canadians scoring a hundred in one partnership. Things did not go well for England and several catches were dropped, it was said because of the low brightness of the reflecting sun.

But they made up for it when they batted. After a couple of early wickets had gone Forster got in again and started to hit the ball all over the ice. He even had the skipper cheering and he was supposed to be neutral. Grunton put himself on to bowl and started to sling the ball down at a tremendous pace. But Forster only hit it further than ever. At the other end there were several useful innings but the First Officer began running out of partners as the total went on and on, closer to the 193 needed to win. With the last man at the other end there were still 20-odd needed. Forster had thrown off his fur hood, sweat ran down his face. His eyes squinted. He waited for the ball.

Grunton, who had been smashed for a final six not by Forster but by one of the Paddies, retired in a nasty sulk and put himself right out on the edge of the ice, on the boundary. One of his Aussie mates, a little chap with matted eyebrows, was bowling and, quite honestly, he was no good at all. Forster got runs easily, almost where he liked. Then, with six needed to win, the Aussie tossed up this childish loop-the-loop thing and the First Officer, his grin widening as he advanced on it, caught it the most tremendous thwack and sent it high, high up into the Arctic sky. The sun caught it as it rose and curved. The English team, leaning over the rail of the ship, started hooting and jogging about and Fraser waved his bat in triumph. But, wait a minute: the ball was coming down. Down and down. And who was right underneath? It was Ron Grunton.

Well, what happened next was the most amazing thing I ever saw in the Arctic, not excluding the time the walrus ate poor Henry McGinty in half-an-hour up at Frobisher Passage. Ron saw the ball falling towards him in the sunlight. He was looking up and his hands were waiting. Suddenly it all went quiet on the ship. Forster stood, half-way down the wicket, staring towards the Australian. Everyone thought he was going to catch it right to his chest, but at the last moment, either through some trick of sunlight, or a touch of a breeze, or just plain misjudgement, it started going over Ron's head. He started to back-pedal on the ice, his feet slipping furiously, like someone riding an invisible bike. A shout rose from the deck of the ship and from the fielders on the ice.

Ron made a desperate, last, truly last, leap, and caught the ball. In the same movement he plunged off the edge of the ice into freezing water.

The cries changed. Everyone started haring towards the place where he had disappeared. Those that got there first reckoned he still had the ball in his hand when he came up.

You only have three minutes. That's to get him out, get him to the ship and start the recovery drill. It took too long. They pulled him from the icy water and scurried with him over the ice. Up the side of the ship in no time and into a hot bath. If the engines had been going they might have saved him with steam but hot water wasn't enough. He was gone ten minutes after taking that catch.

Not before he'd had his last word, though. Opening his frozen eyelids he looked up at the First Officer and a frozen grin cracked across his face.

'Caught you, Forster,' he croaked. 'And we won.'

His last words they were. Only Forster had anything to say after that.

'Not out,' he grunted but with decent respect. 'Six. Fell over the boundary with the ball.'

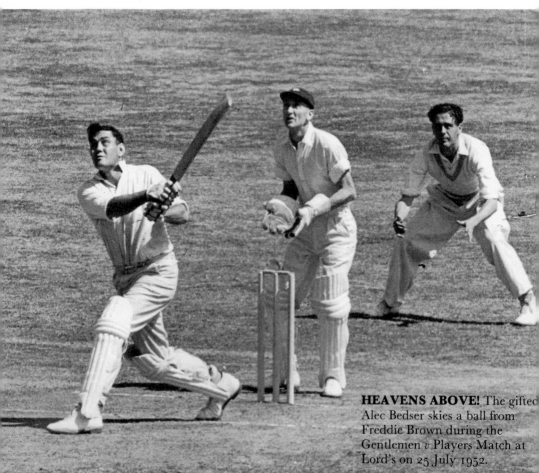

HEAVENS ABOVE! The gifted Alec Bedser skies a ball from Freddie Brown during the Gentlemen *v* Players Match at Lord's on 25 July 1952.

'... I have to say that I'm not one of Nature's
great batsmen ...'

ROOTS

Cricket has been one of the most important themes in my life. I've had plenty of enthusiasms, but the willow and leather have always been a stable factor for me. So it was a memorable day when I first came to Lord's to see Middlesex versus Sussex on Whit Monday, 1956.

I can't remember who won – we only saw the first day – but I remember Don Smith of Sussex scoring 149, I think. Robin Marlar was captain of Sussex. My family was friendly with Bill Edrich – his then wife was a great chum of my mother – and so we got some good seats. By then I must have been eleven but I'd become very keen when I was nine with the fifth Test Match of 1953 against Australia, when England won the Ashes after a long time.

After that I began following cricket avidly. I didn't go to a Test Match in '54, which was the Pakistani year, and '55 I was in Japan with the family – my father was working there with Hawker Siddeley. My brother and I used to play cricket all the time on the lawn of our house in Tokyo. I played quite a bit at my prep school but not much at Lancing. I wasn't very good at cricket. The only sport I was good at was swimming and I was in the school team, so every sports time in the summer was spent swimming.

After I left school I didn't play a proper game of cricket for about ten years – just the odd knock-about – and I'd forgotten what it was like. Then after fame and fortune hit me I was invited to play in a charity match for the Lord's Taverners at Blenheim Palace. So I bought the kit and I really enjoyed it, and I realised what I'd been missing.

On that day I went out to bat with John Gorman of The Scaffold – as usual in those charity matches there were about twenty a side and we were batting about number fourteen and fifteen. I am left-handed and he's right-handed, so we were both able to take our guard at the crease at the same time. It was hardly a very serious game and when the bowler bowled we both missed it.

After that I thought I'd like to play again seriously, but I reckoned if I hung around waiting to be selected it would be a long wait. So I

The Heartaches Cricket Club logo.

decided to form my own team. In 1972 I organised a game against a friend of mine called Bill Heath, who has a team called Heath's Gentlemen. I called my team Heartaches, after my company Heartaches Limited. The game was just a try-out but a big success. The following year we organised five matches and found other teams to play and the year after that we had ten games, and now we've peaked at about seventeen or eighteen matches during the season.

Over the years you inevitably get slightly better – you're bound to after playing regularly for ten years – but I have to say that I'm not one of nature's great batsmen. Once a season I might have a good innings. In 1984 I got 41 against the Abbey Players and my previous best was 39 against Fernhurst in 1980. My highest score remains 41 but I'm determined to get 50 one day.

I bowl quite a lot now, because my bowling has got better though it's terribly slow. (I think it was J. M. Barrie who said, 'I bowl so slowly that if I don't like it I can walk down the pitch and bring it back before it gets to the batsman.') Nobody can accuse me of running the team to boost my own ego – I'm so bad at the game that I get shown up more than distinguished. It's a social event really, a very good way of seeing ten friends every week.

When I first started playing again I'd forgotten what fast bowling was like and I was terrified, but after a while you find that you don't get hit very often. I don't wear protection – except pads obviously, and a box – that's very important. We have a team box. What I try to do, and I don't always succeed as circumstances don't always permit, is to make sure everybody does something. There's nothing worse than asking a friend to come along and give up his Sunday afternoon and then he doesn't bat and he doesn't bowl. Really, I regard myself as a kind of Brearley figure, maybe not automatically worth a place in the side as a player, but indisputably worth a place as a brain. Also I know the names of all the players, which is helpful, and I do know a good few of the rules.

There's a team neck-tie and a team dinner, and I publish an almanack every year which has now gone into its eleventh season – *The Heartaches Cricketers' Almanack*. It's a kind of send-up of *Wisden*. It's the same page size, but it's about 100 pages compared to *Wisden*'s 1200, so it's a bit like writing a short novel every year. My brother Jo does a bit, but I tend to do about eighty per cent of it; Jo's the vice-captain but he's slightly less available these days. When he lived in Tokyo he was always around in the summer; now that he lives in Kent you can never get hold of him.

I watch an awful lot of cricket on television and if there's a Test Match on I don't mind being in a traffic jam because the radio commentary is so wonderful – often as good as TV. I'll always go to the Lord's Test Match – most days usually I'll go to the Gillette final and one or two other days; and I do occasionally go to Test Matches out in the sticks. At the end of meetings and recording sessions I'll always keep an eye on the scores.

Bill Heath – who runs the Golden Hit Line for British Telecom – and I, have an eight-piece pop group. We've suddenly hit the big time rather late, and even played at Lady Rothermere's big party recently. We were called Whang and the Cheviots, I don't know why. Now we've decided to call ourselves The Social Climbers. There's a barrister, a builder's merchant, a racehorse owner and a couple of vaguely professional musicians but we try and keep them to a minimum. The sax player is a Cheltenham restaurant-owner called David Frost – but he's not *the* David Frost.

Then, of course, I've got Pavilion Books, which I own with Michael Parkinson and a marvellous publisher called Colin Webb, and the next lot of Guinness books – we're now up to the fifth volume of hits and the second volume of the quiz book – and radio shows and TV and lots of side things.

I really wasn't interested in musicals as a kid, just pop music and writing, but when I met Andrew [Lloyd Webber] he wanted someone to write for shows – and I found that I really enjoyed it.

I'd like to do something really different next. I've got a feeling that *Chess* could even be the last musical. I think it would have been a fantastic life to be a professional cricketer if I'd been any good, even though real cricketers would say, 'It's bloody hard work, mate'.

SAM

Look out for Sam, O gentle stumper,
For Sam will bowl a fearful bumper,
And follow through with great displeasure
And clock the batsman, for good measure.

'Rhyme' Minister Sir Robert Menzies on Sam Loxton, Australia's most pugnacious cricketer.

SIR JOHN BETJEMAN

CRICKET MASTER

(AN INCIDENT)

My undergraduate eyes beholding,
    As I climbed your slope, Cat Hill:
Emerald chestnut fans unfolding,
    Symbols of my hope, Cat Hill.
What cared I for past disaster,
Applicant for cricket master,
Nothing much of cricket knowing,
Conscious but of money owing?
    Somehow I would cope, Cat Hill.

'The sort of man we want must be prepared
To take our first eleven. Many boys
From last year's team are with us. You will find
Their bowling's pretty good and they are keen.'
'And so am I, Sir, very keen indeed.'
Oh where's mid-on? And what is silly point?
Do six balls make an over? Help me, God!
'Of course you'll get some first-class cricket too;
The MCC send down an A team here.'
My bluff had worked. I sought the common-room,
Of last term's pipe-smoke faintly redolent.
It waited empty with its worn arm-chairs
For senior bums to mine, when in there came
A fierce old eagle in whose piercing eye
I saw that instant-registered dislike
Of all unhealthy aesthetes such as me.
'I'm Winters – you're our other new recruit
And here's another new man – Barnstaple.'
He introduced a thick Devonian.
'Let's go and have some practice in the nets.
You'd better go in first.' With but one pad,
No gloves, and knees that knocked in utter fright,
Vainly I tried to fend the hail of balls
Hurled at my head by brutal Barnstaple
And at my shins by Winters. Nasty quiet

Followed my poor performance. When the sun
Had sunk behind the fringe of Hadley Wood
And Barnstaple and I were left alone
Among the ash-trays of the common-room,
He murmured in his soft West-Country tones:
'D'you know what Winters told me, Betjeman?
He didn't think you'd ever held a bat.'
    The trusting boys returned. 'We're jolly glad
You're on our side, Sir, in the trial match.'
'But I'm no good at all.' 'Oh yes, you are.'
When I was out first ball, they said 'Bad luck!
You hadn't got your eye in.' Still I see
Barnstaple's smile of undisguised contempt,
Still feel the sting of Winters' silent sneer.
Disgraced, demoted to the seventh game,
Even the boys had lost their faith in me.
God guards his aesthetes. If by chance these lines
Are read by one who in some common-room
Has had his bluff called, let him now take heart:
In every school there is a sacred place
More holy than the chapel. Ours was yours:
I mean, of course, the first-eleven pitch.
Here in the welcome break from morning work,
The heavier boys, of milk and biscuits full,
Sat on the roller while we others pushed
Its weighty cargo slowly up and down.
We searched the grass for weeds, caressed the turf,
Lay on our stomachs squinting down its length
To see that all was absolutely smooth.
    The prize-day neared. And, on the eve before,
We masters hung our college blazers out
In readiness for tomorrow. Matron made
A final survey of the boys' best clothes –
Clean shirts. Clean collars. 'Rice, your jacket's torn.
Bring it to me this instant!' Supper done,
Barnstaple drove his round-nosed Morris out
And he and I and Vera Spencer-Clarke,
Our strong gymnasium mistress, squashed ourselves
Into the front and rattled to The Cock.
    Sweet bean-fields then were scenting Middlesex;
Narrow lanes led between the dairy farms
To ponds reflecting weather-boarded inns.
There on the wooden bench outside The Cock
Sat Barnstaple, Miss Spencer-Clarke and I,

At last forgetful of tomorrow's dread
And gazing into sky-blue Hertfordshire.
Three pints for Barnstaple, three halves for me,
Sherry of course for Vera Spencer-Clarke.
    Pre-prize-day nerves? Or too much bitter beer?
What had that evening done to Barnstaple?
I only know that singing we returned;
The more we sang, the faster Barnstaple
Drove his old Morris, swerving down the drive
And in and out the rhododendron clumps,
Over the very playing-field itself,
And then – oh horror! – right across the pitch
Not once, but twice or thrice. The mark of tyres
Next day was noticed at the Parents' Match.

IT WAS EVER THUS

10 February 1841. We got up a tolerably good match behind the Hotel
Royal, on the beach at Dieppe, for the amusement of the Duchess de
Berri, in the year 1829. We mustered, with some difficulty, two elevens;
the bowlers pitched their balls with scientific precision; the batters
defended their wickets with great skill; short and long stops were on
the alert; in fact, all the performers acquitted themselves most admirably. As soon as the first innings were over, one of the party, who had
been most active in the display of his athletic powers, approached the
Duchess's carriage in the expectation of being complimented on his
exertions; instead of which, one of the suite asked the gentleman, to his
utter dismay and confusion, when this game of *creekay* was going to
begin!

The Sportsman in France

ROUGH AND TUMBLE. Cricket at the Oval, one-day international, England *v* India, June 1982. David Gower finds that Indian wicketkeeper Syed Kirmani (with bat) and Kapil Dev (left) will seemingly go to any lengths to stop him making his run!

STEADY, FRED – WATCH YOUR LANGUAGE! Up to his tricks again, the irrepressible Fred Trueman has a go at the photographer watched by a highly amused Sir Gary Sobers, at the Courage Old England *v* Old World Cricket Eleven match, the Oval, 1982.

ECHOES OF A MONTH-LONG HEARING IN THE HIGH COURT

9 November 1977.
The alacrity with which they [the players] joined was frightening.

> *– Kerry Packer*

They want the penny and the bun.

> *– Geoffrey Boycott*

I've heard the only way to get out of a Packer contract is by becoming pregnant.

> *– Raymond Steele* (Australia)

Bob Taylor is one of the best wicket-keepers the world has ever seen.

> *– Alan Knott*

Alan Knott is the best wicketkeeper in the world.

> *– Boycott*

Cricketers [at the Cricketers' Association meeting] thought that if we got rid of a few more [overseas players] it would be nice.

> *– Tony Greig*

We're not a philanthropic organisation.

> *– Packer*

The ban is a disservice to cricket.

> *– Asif Iqbal*

The presence of Greig, Knott and Underwood would have been a great help to bring the crowds along.

> *– Walter Hadlee (New Zealand),*
> *referring to this winter's England tour*

Mr Packer waved a big stick.

> *– Steele*

I don't think John Arlott is very knowledgeable on the game of cricket.

> *– Jack Bailey, ICC secretary*

I'm always open to offers.

> *– Boycott*

We were very anxious, indeed still are anxious, to avoid an horrific situation.

> *– Douglas Insole, TCCB chairman*

The moment that one of my players is banned is the moment you have me for an enemy.

> *– Packer*

There's a little bit of a whore in all of us.

> *– Packer*

It's England first, last and all the time so far as I'm concerned.

> *– Greig, confirming an earlier newspaper*
> *interview*

The press get it right, the press get it wrong.

— *Greig*

It's degrading to have to virtually beg for benefits.

— *Michael Procter*

No one has to have a benefit.

— *Boycott*

We are the poor relations of world sport.

— *Greig*

... makes the language boggle.

— *Robert Alexander, QC*

I'm a press man's dream.

— *Greig*

Gloucestershire want me to go on playing.

— *Procter*

I'm not a legal expert.

— *Derek Underwood*

I'm sure you [Underwood] are far better off being a cricketer.

— *Andrew Morritt, QC*

They thought they could have the best of both worlds.

— *Steele*

Pandora's chest.

— *Bailey*

A more severe ban is justified.

— *Boycott*

Tests are not built in a day.

— *Mutthian Chidambaram (India)*

We were prepared to fly our players home from Pakistan and fly them out to New Zealand six weeks later.

— *Insole, discussing a possible compromise*

I admire umpires.

— *Greig*

I've had nightmares about it.

— *John Snow, on the prospect of becoming an umpire*

I suggest they [the TCCB] are being dishonest.

— *Packer*

Unfortunately the Cricketers' Association is looked on as something of a joke.

— *Snow*

I would say the Cricketers' Association exists full stop.

— *Procter, invited to say what the Cricketers' Association existed for*

It [Test Match revenue] goes to the counties, where it's to a large part wasted.

— *Snow*

I suppose I was a bit young and naive at the time and I let them [*Sunday Mirror* journalists] in.

— *Knott*

Australian players tend to pop out of holes in the ground when the opportunity's there.

— *Ross Edwards, Australian cricketer*

They [Australian cricketers] seem to come out in their thousands when they're knocking hell out of the Poms.

— *Boycott*

Thank heavens I don't have that prospect.

– Edwards, asked what happened if a batsman faced Dennis Lillee and got injured

The next game could be your last. If you're playing against Lillee and he smashes your elbow you'll never play again.

– Knott

I didn't trust the Australian Cricket Board, and I don't trust them.

– Packer

They [the authorities] have undersold the game.

– Greig

I said there'd be a strike or something like this [the Packer series].

– Snow

The tour [England to Pakistan that winter] is very doubtful because of the political situation.

– Asif Iqbal

World Series Cricket is essentially parasitic in its nature.

– Michael Kempster, QC

Test matches are vital to our survival financially.

– Hadlee

They [the TCCB] were trying to white-ant us.

– Packer, using an Australian expression derived from an insect that bores into wood and leaves the shell intact

Someone's white-anted my copy.

– Mr Justice Slade, examining a document in evidence

The establishment could benefit from a jolly good shake-up.

– Greig

The TCCB are not as dishonourable as the Australian Cricket Board.

– Packer

It's very depressing to go into a ground with 400 spectators.

– Greig, referring to county championship cricket

I'm not sure the British public would want four-day matches.

– Boycott

You have to play enough cricket to satisfy 13,000 members at 12 guineas.

– Boycott, arguing that the county championship should not be reduced to 16 matches a county

I would deny that absolutely.

– Insole, asked if the Australian Cricket Board were opposed to any compromise with Mr Packer

Ghulam Ahmed said, 'Soon there'd be 10 Mr Packers on the scene.'

– Chidambaram

Procter is one of the casualties of the battle.

– Peter Short (West Indies)

Being available to go to cocktail parties.

– Greig, explaining the work involved in earning the free use of a car

They [the Australian Cricket Board] were telling me untruths.

– Packer

'You're men of honour.'

– Steele, quoting Mr Packer's reference to the ACB TV negotiating sub-committee

Give them the opportunity to draw back from the brink.

– Insole

I wish I'd never said, 'Draw back from the brink'; there are so many problems.

– Insole

Draw back from the drink, sorry, the brink.

– Kempster

Wars are not won by appeasement.

– W. H. Webster, ICC chairman

Chamberlain's Churchill.

– Mr Justice Slade

We [the West Indies] had grave reservations as to the morality of a retroactive ban.

– Short

There was a deliberate attempt by the ICC to break down the negotiations.

– Packer

After that we had our toes insured.

– Greig, referring to an injury suffered by Fred Titmus in a swimming accident

They can play at Brighton in the water if they want.

– Packer, confirming his players' availability in the English summer

The changes in rules are no more stringent than are required to protect the conventional game

– Kempster

When we went into this we knew exactly what we were doing and it would probably get us banned from county cricket.

– Snow, confirming an earlier interview

When the donkey kicks you know which way it kicks.

– Snow

I did not expect they would blackball us altogether.

– Greig

You didn't have to be an Einstein to foresee the ban.

– Packer

It's everyone for himself now and let the devil take the hindmost.

– Packer

Nineteenth century lockout.

– Alexander

Derek Randall [a big attraction] at Trent Bridge? I thought they were Yorkshiremen who'd come to watch me.

– Boycott

One should go to another county.

– Knott, referring to the competition between him and Paul Downton in the Kent team

Television of Mr Packer's series would have a very serious effect on official Tests. The public could sit at home and watch the circus match.

– Steele

The press, on behalf of the authorities, have always tried to lampoon our games.

– Packer

We were in the gloaming if not in the dark.

– Bailey

We believed they [the players] were going to do irreparable damage.

– Steele

The players should be treated as outcasts.

– Steele

Mr Packer wanted exclusive television rights there and then.

– Bailey

The offer would have had to be quite a big one if I was to be banned from Yorkshire.

– Boycott

The word 'grovel' followed me around.

– Greig

They [his cricketers] must be like Caesar's wife.

– Packer

David Brown [chairman of the Cricketers' Association] and I couldn't have changed anything in a million years.

– Greig

I considered the Cricketers' Association vote [in favour of the ban] unfair and biased.

– Underwood

I would not have got a gun and shot Mr Packer.

– Steele

We're not perfect.

– Bailey

He [Tony Greig] said, 'How the hell did you get involved in this?'

– Boycott

There is no fat at all.

– Insole, questioned about county clubs' finances

Our players had let us down because on their behalf we had negotiated a $350,000 team sponsorship and we'd taken on agreements to which they'd agreed.

– Steele

If there are no good guarantees, tours may have to be cancelled.

– Short

If overseas players are absent from a Sunday League match between Hampshire and Gloucestershire, the cricket ratings will go down and those of 'High Chaparral' will go up.

– Alexander

Any believability in my word would be destroyed.

– Packer, if his series were cancelled

If Tests wane the game as a whole will languish.

– Kempster

The Australian Cricket Board would do anything, even to eating crow or humble pie, to prevent a holocaust.

– Bailey

... Body and soul contract, more on his side than my side.

– Boycott

The series will be considerably better than first-class in the eyes of the public.

– Packer

I kissed them goodbye.

– Steele, referring to players who had already signed contracts

I was riveted.

– Bailey, by Mr Packer's appearance on David Frost's television programme

Kerry Packer picked my brains.

– Boycott

'Fabrication' is your word, not mine.

– Boycott, to Alexander

They found a very good living.

– Insole, referring to engagements in league cricket of Sobers, Lindwall, Ian Chappell and others

They'll fight . . . like Kilkenny cats.

– Packer, of the Australian Cricket Board

Since May 9 [the date of public knowledge of the Packer series] I think that's correct.

– Steele, asked if modern cricketers had become too commercial

They [the ICC] didn't want to compromise in any way, shape or form.

– Packer

We still hoped to prevent a hijacking situation.

– Bailey

We're all getting underpaid, except a few overseas stars who're getting all the money.

– Boycott

The county championship is the lynchpin of English cricket.

– Insole

The effect on the first-class game if the Test match profits diminish would be serious, very serious, or catastrophic.

– Bailey

The world cricket authorities are carrying the can for Australia.

– Packer

I don't know about that [Michael Brearley's double first] but he's certainly very brainy.

– Boycott

When a Yorkshireman shakes your hand that's all you need.

– Boycott

No, you should be expected to play as your form warrants.

– Boycott, asked if he thought Test cricketers should have more security

One can take only so much.

– Greig

A scenario of sorts, written by a celebrated
Private Eye *duo*

BODYLINE REVISITED

(*Brideshead*-style music. Shot of agreeable old car drawing up outside large Victorian gothic house, with kangaroo looking over fence. Caption: 'Winchester College Public School, 1920')

SMALL BOY WITH BRYLCREEMED HAIR (jumps out of car): Jeez, cobbers, it's hard to believe that I am going to be Captain of England's cricket team one day and rule the Empire!

FEMALE VOICE-OVER: When little Duggie Jardine talked about the British Empire he meant the whole world. Britain had just been through the trauma of World War I and desperately needed to beat the Australians at cricket to win back a little pride.

(Cut to shot of Queen Victoria waving to troops leaving for Boer War)

FEMALE VOICE-OVER: At the other end of the world, things looked very different.

(Cut to small Aussie boy without shoes learning how to bat with small stick)

MOTHER: Jeez, Don Bradman, I know we can't afford to buy you a proper cricket bat, but if you go on practising one day you'll smash those snotty-nosed poms right back to England.

FEMALE VOICE-OVER: Mrs Bradman's prophecy was to come all too true. The world was changing. They called it the Jazz Age.

(Irrelevant shot of man drinking champagne and girl taking off her clothes)

FEMALE VOICE-OVER: But then came a new trauma – the so-called Wall Street Crash.

(Shot of modern tower block obviously in Sydney. Caption: 'Wall Street, Washington, 1930'. Cut to old Buffers sitting round table, with koala bear looking in window. Caption: 'The Long Room, Lord's, 1931')

FEMALE VOICE-OVER: Here in the Holy of Holies of British cricket the decision was made that was to shake the Empire to its foundations.

FIRST OLD BUFFER (Lord Harris, for it is he): Look here, chaps, the British Empire is facing the gravest crisis it has ever known. This

*The two captains, D. R. Jardine (left) and W. M. Woodfull, toss up before
the start of the Third Test, 1932, in Adelaide, Australia.*

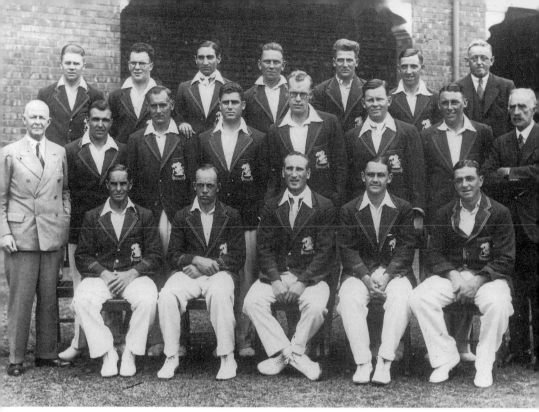

The MCC team visiting Australia for the 1932–3 Australian tour. Back row (left to right): R. G. Duckworth, T. B. Mitchell, the Nawab of Pataudi, M. Leyland, H. Larwood, E. Paynter, W. Ferguson (scorer). Middle row (left to right): P. F. Warner (Manager), L. E. G. Ames, H. Verity, W. Voce, W. E. Bowes, F. R. Brown, M. W. Tate, R. C. N. Palairet (Manager). Front row (left to right): H. Sutcliffe, R. E. S. Wyatt, D. R. Jardine (Captain), G. O. Allen, W. R. Hammond.

young Australian batsman, Donald Bradman, has just made 529 not out in one innings. That makes him the most successful batsman in the entire history of cricket. Do you realise what this means?

SECOND BUFFER IN DINNER JACKET (Lord Pelham Warner, for it is he): Strewth, Lord Harris, I catch your drift. It means that so long as this fellow Bradman is around we shall never win. And that could mean...

THIRD BUFFER: Cripes, Plummy, you mean – the collapse of the British Empire?

(Dramatic music. Shot of Union Jack being lowered over Singapore, 1942)

FEMALE VOICE-OVER: Meanwhile, Down Under, as the Poms call it, Bradman was unstoppable.

(Slow-motion close-up of actor holding bat wrong way round pretending to hit ball. Cut to close-up of ball running along ground and hitting fence)

MAN IN CROWD: Six, Braddy. Good on yer, mate! That means you've reached the fastest double century in the history of the game.

(More slow-motion close-ups of actor pretending to hit ball)

MAN IN CROWD: Six, Braddy. Good on yer.

MAN IN CROWD: Blimey, Donno. Another 25 sixes in consecutive balls. Pretty soon you'll have the best average that any batsman has ever scored.

(Cut to girl taking off clothes in case cricket scenes have become too boring. Man with Brylcreemed hair and dinner jacket dances in background to Beatles record)

JARDINE (for it is he): Cripes, Thelma, there's only one way we Poms are going to stop this chap Bradman.

GIRL: You mean ...

JARDINE: Yes. This is the secret weapon that is going to save the British ruling class.

(Produces machine-gun)

GIRL: Oh, Doug, you're not going to kill him, are you?

JARDINE: No. (Smiles evilly) I'm going to do what the British ruling class has always done. Get some member of the working classes to do their dirty work for them.

GIRL: Oh, Doug, you're a genius!

(*Chariots of Fire*-type music. Close-up of Jardine drinking champagne and smoking oysters. Cut to shot of dirty men in collarless shirts standing in front of a small pile of coal with wallaby jumping around in background. Caption: 'Coal mine in North of England, 1932')

GAFFER (To gormless-looking young man): Ee, Harold Larwood, thou doesn't 'alf bowl fast. 'Appen thou couldst find thysen' playing for t'England one of these days.

LARWOOD: Don't be a t'aft booger, cobber!

(Old agreeable *Brideshead*-style car drives up. Man in top hat, white tie and tails gets out)

LORD JARDINE (for it is he): Larwood, my man, come here. (Gives Larwood a guinea)

LARWOOD (Touching forelock): Thank you, my Lord. What can I do for you?

JARDINE (Producing machine-gun): Can you use one of these, Larwood?

FEMALE VOICE-OVER: And so it was that in September 1933, the British cricket team set sail for Australia on its fateful mission.

(Cut to actors pretending to be cricketers standing around in front of painted back-drop of Sydney Cricket Ground. Close up of Bradman waiting with bat upside down for Larwood to bowl first ball of Test Match)

JARDINE: OK, Harold, you remember our secret plans that we've been working on for months?

LARWOOD: Yes, Skip.

JARDINE: Well, let him have it!

(Larwood produces machine-gun and kills Bradman. Crowd goes wild. Cries of 'It's not cricket!' Shot of British Empire collapsing to strains of 'Rule Britannia' played out of tune on ukelele. Cut to girl taking clothes off in back of agreeable old car)

FEMALE VOICE-OVER: And so it was that, thanks to the game of cricket, the evil empire that had ruled the world for a thousand years was utterly defeated.

(Shot of Hitler reviewing troops)

Pilgertrash Films Pty (as sold to BBC), 1985

A BLAST FROM BUTCHER. Ray Illingworth (Yorkshire) takes evasive action as Roland Butcher (Middlesex) drives a ball from bowler Sidebottom to the boundary at Lord's, 23 August 1982.

MICHAEL PARKINSON

---

*'I was with him the day he perished and it was a
fitting end to such an unorthodox career ...'*

JOHN WILLY JARDINE

I once played for a team captained by a man who thought he was
Douglas Jardine. The fact that his name was John Willy and that the
team he captained swam in the lower reaches of Yorkshire league
cricket did nothing to dissuade the impersonation. He even went to the
lengths of buying himself a multi-coloured cricket cap of the sort that
Jardine favoured, which in the area where we played, constituted an
act of unsurpassed bravery. The cap was finally taken from him in the
most innocent circumstances, when one Christmas John Willy arrived
home from the pit to find it sodden and dejected, sitting atop the
snowman erected by his children in their back yard. He was never the
same without it.

Of all the captains I have played with he was the most impressive,
the hardest, the most imaginative, and I first came across him shortly
after leaving school and joining my first league side. In the coal lorry
going to the match he explained the subtleties of playing in this particular class of cricket.

'Now tha' sees first thing is t'new ball. There's nowt fancy in this
league, we get a new ball every Barnsley Feast so tha' has to be thinking
all t'time abart when it might come and how tha' gets th' hands on it
first,' he said. He explained that he was only telling us this because he

had heard that the team we were to play that afternoon had bought a new ball recently and he reckoned they were saving it for us. That being the case it was important to the outcome of the game that we get our hands on it first.

We arrived at the ground and were changing when the opposing captain came into our dressing room. He was the local headmaster and therefore not very popular with John Willy who thought teachers were layabouts.

'Good afternoon, John Willy, lovely day,' said the headmaster.

John Willy was never a man for pleasantries. 'I hear tha' bought a new ball,' he said. The headmaster smiled blandly. 'You have been misinformed John Willy. This is the match ball.' He produced a battered piece of leather which looked as if it had suffered a lifetime being bounced on concrete wickets. John Willy nodded and said nothing. He went out with the headmaster, won the toss and elected to bat. As he strapped his pads on and prepared to open the innings he said to us:

'Yon teacher's trying summat on. Ah reckon he's got t'new ball in his pocket. If it happens that he brings it out when play starts, then I want you all to stand down by yon hedge at square leg. First chance I get I'll thump t'ball down theer and I don't want it to come back. Understand?' We nodded.

Sure enough, as the opening bowler measured out his run the headmaster, with a superior smirk, handed him a shiny, red, new ball. Halfway through the first over John Willy lay back and pulled the ball hard towards the square leg boundary where it crashed into the hedge. After ten minutes of fruitless searching the umpires, who were worried about the game running into licensing hours, ordered the headmaster to re-start the game using the battered old ball we had seen in the pavilion.

Back in the dressing room someone said, 'Who found it?' Our slow bowler put his hand up. 'Wheer is it then?' someone asked. 'Down a bloody rabbit hole,' said the slow bowler. Overjoyed by his tactical triumph, John Willy played an inspired innings, and when we declared with about 160 on the board he had scored an unbeaten ninety-odd. He came in the dressing room pink with self-satisfaction. 'That's what tha' calls strategy,' he said to the room. 'Now then, wheer's t'new ball?' 'Down a rabbit hole,' said the slow bowler. 'Wheer?' asked John Willy, his face clouding. The slow bowler repeated what he had said. John Willy by this time was trying hard to control himself. Finally he addressed the slow bowler: 'Then go and get t'bloody thing from t'bloody rabbit hole and polish it up nice and shiny.'

Mercifully the slow bowler located the rabbit hole and found the new ball. Polishing it on his backside John Willy went round to the opposition's dressing room and said to the captain, 'By a stroke of good luck we've managed to find t'proper match ball. I tek it tha's no objection to us using it.' The headmaster, aware he had come up against a superior tactitian, shook his head sullenly. Armed with the new ball we got them all out for less than fifty. 'Strategy, that's what tha' needs in this game,' John Willy kept saying, and I came to regard him with the kind of hero worship I had reserved up until that time for The Wolf of Kabbul and Baldy Hogan.

I was with him the day he perished and it was a fitting end to such an unorthodox career. John Willy was batting in a local derby game which contained more than the usual amount of needle when he fell victim to one of cricket's more outrageous whims. He snicked a ball very hard on to his body whereupon it somehow burst through the flies of his trousers and settled inside his pants just above his knee. The wicket keeper and the bowler, sensing an easy wicket and undue humiliation for John Willy, set off towards him with the intention of rescuing the ball while John Willy went through an incredible pantomime trying to extract it and throw it on the ground.

Undeterred by John Willy's dire warnings about what might happen to them if they laid a finger on him, the wicket keeper and the fast bowler both made a purposeful approach toward their victim. What happened next is a matter for dispute. Some say John Willy chinned the fast bowler with a left hook, some say the fast bowler knocked himself out by running on to John Willy's elbow just as the batsman was extracting the ball. Whatever the circumstances, the fast bowler lost two front teeth and spent the next five minutes flat on his back, his thoughts a million miles from the cricket field. Eventually John Willy was given out for 'ungentlemanly conduct' and the fast bowler taken to the local infirmary for a check up. Soon after John Willy was called before the disciplinary committee and severely reprimanded.

The following Christmas he found his cap on the snowman and, being the sort of man who could read the signs better than most, he retired. We gave him a presentation dinner the following season and the chairman of the club, while handing him a chromium plated cake stand, described him as a 'great captain and a gentleman'. We were not sure how John Willy would react to being called a 'gentleman', but he took it very well. Nor did he disagree with being called a 'great captain'. What he said was, 'Me and D. R. Jardine played it t'same way.' So far as I know Douglas Jardine never chinned a fast bowler, but we all knew what John Willy meant.

NORMAN HARRIS

*'Are we doing well or not?' asked a slim figure in
velvet pinstripe, as he sipped a cocktail. 'I haven't
particularly noticed either way ...'*

A WAVE OF A WHITE HANDKERCHIEF, 1975

Poor uneducated fool that I am, I wasn't quite sure if the thing was a charabanc or a coach. However, I was assured it was indeed a coach that was carefully in place by the Nursery sight-screen when play started at Lord's yesterday. The sort of coach that goes with a pair, apparently. But the pair seemed never to have been employed, the coach evidently having been towed there or transported by some other means and set up, like a museum piece, on wooden planks with wheel chocks.

It seemed a bit odd. I thought the idea was that you came in the thing, parked it, then sat on it. Not so. Those who hired it only briefly experienced the novelty of sitting on top before turning to their trestle table and drinks at grass level.

Another perplexity was the sight of a young black man bowling for Eton, Kio Amachree from Nigeria – 'known usually as Chief', said fine leg. 'A great character.'

And in front of the Tavern, while half the young men wore dark suits and silk ties, others were Dylanesque, with hand-rolled cigarettes. Is this the fabric of our society fracturing before our very eyes?

For Harrow, P. D. M. Greig was constantly looking for that purest of strokes, the almost square cover drive, and against Kary he nicked to second slip where he was badly dropped. Otherwise the Harrow openers had everything present and correct. Life at Lord's was good.

Fours were noisily cheered and shouted all the way to the line, the cacophony reminding one of those recent parliamentary broadcasts.

'Are we doing well or not?' asked a slim figure in velvet pinstripe, as he sipped a cocktail. 'I haven't particularly noticed either way.'

There were not really two ways about it. Harrow's openers had brought up the 50 in 20 overs. Compton, who had been playing the quicker bowlers most positively, was being overhauled by Greig, who

Eton v Harrow, Lord's, 10 July 1920.
W. W. Hill-Wood, Eton captain,
is chaired after the game.

came on wonderfully against the slower stuff.

'Mark,' said someone's sister, 'to sit there and talk about your girl-friends is awfully boring.'

'. . . So we went in with them on,' murmured one pater to another, 'and when the girls didn't come in, we took them off . . .'

Greig went at 64, splendidly caught and bowled as he drove. But Compton went on with a much pronounced left elbow – unlike his unrelated namesake, the great D.C.S. – and none the worse for it. On the stroke of lunchtime he drove two fours for his 50.

Eton's young team, however, were already more seriously threatened by Harrow's star batsman, the left-handed M. K. Fosh, who is a prospective Essex player. Strongly built and a croucher, with his hands low on the handle, he proceeded to drive, punch from the back foot, and to swing at anything near leg stump.

At Fosh's hundred an elderly gentleman took out a white handkerchief and waved it. The feat impressed another man's wife sufficiently for her to ask which one was Fosh. Others paused in a discussion about Scimitars and Simcas. 'I hope Michael's boy gets his hundred. I really do . . . Oh, he's got it, has he?'

In 90 minutes after lunch Fosh had scored 122, and in the final over before the declaration he pulled front-foot sixes to the long mid-wicket boundary in a manner that would have done credit to a Kanhai. An announcement said that his 161 was the highest score by a Harrow batsman against Eton since 1913.

Then, with the ball, Harrow emphasised the imbalance of a contest which was seemingly played between young men on the one hand and boys on the other. Pigott tore in like a Lillee and in his first over took two wickets, with the Harrow supporters roaring throughout like – let it be said quietly – crazed West Indians.

FATAL INSTANCE OF OVER-EXERTION

22 October 1805. A match of cricket was played on Friday last, near Totteridge, Herts, between two young men of the names of GREGG and CORDEROY, which was so well maintained, that forty-three and forty-five runs were made in the first innings. GREGG was caught out after making thirty-two runs in the second innings. CORDEROY went in, and made seven runs; he again hit the ball, and ran, but on arriving at the wicket he fell down and expired.

Original Report

LORD'S, 1928

Lord's – Lord's on Wednesday evening!
  Cambridge fieldsmen crowding round,
Oxford's hardly a chance of saving it –
  Hardly a chance, but still you found
    Elderly cricketers gnawing their sticks,
    Blameless Bishops, forgetful of Jix,
    Publicly praying at half-past six,
And prayers and curses arise from the Mound
  On that head of carrots (or possibly gold)
With a watchful eye on each ball that's bowled –
  And a deadly silence around the ground.

Lord's – Lord's on Friday evening!
  Two men out and an hour to play –
Lose another, and that's the end of it,
  Why not call it a harrowing day?
    Harrow's lips are at last on the cup,
    Harrow's tail unmistakably up,
  And Eton? Eton can only pray
For a captain's heart in a captain's breast,
And some decent batting among the rest,
And sit and shiver and hope for the best –
  If those two fellows can only stay!

Stay they did – can we ever forget it? –
  Till those who had bidden us all despair
Lit their pipes with a new assurance,
  Toyed instead with the word 'declare':
    Harrow's glorious hours begin,
    Harrow batsmen hurrying in,
    One and all with the will to win,
  Cheers and counter-cheers rend the air!
    Harrow's down with her colours flying,
    Great in doing and great in dying,
  Eton's home with a head to spare!

C.A.A.
16 July 1928

The initials are those of Dr Cyril Argentine Alington, headmaster of Eton and formerly of Shrewsbury, where he once employed Neville Cardus as his secretary. The Times *paid Dr Alington 3 guineas for this contribution.*

WATCHING BENAUD BOWL

Leg-spinners pose problems much like love,
Requiring commitment, the taking of a chance.
Half-way deludes; the bold advance.

Right back, there's time to watch
Developments, though maybe too late.
It's not spectacular, but can conciliate.

Instinctively romantics move towards
Preventing complexities by their embrace,
Batsman and lover embarked as overlords.

ALAN ROSS

RICHIE BENAUD

*'Old "Slasher" Mackay, even in this, his Test
debut, was never one for long speeches on his way
out to bat . . .'*

1956 AND ALL THAT

Lindwall and Miller! Off the tongue instantly flow McDonald and Gregory, Lillee and Thomson, Tyson and Statham, Adcock and Heine. Great pairs of fast bowlers and they always have hunted best in pairs.

It was good to see Miller and Lindwall together again in London in 1985 and it was a happy coincidence that their visit was at the same time as Australia, brilliantly led by Allan Border, won their only Test of the series at Lord's.

It took me back thirty years to when they were in the 1956 touring team and we played England on the same ground and again won our only Test of the summer, going down eventually 2–1 in the series. It may be of some comfort to Border to know that the 1956 team, despite their victory, was castigated to the same degree as his on returning to Australia.

First, however, in '56 we had actually beaten England at Lord's, almost worth the trip to England just for that, even though the ground happily does seem to be something of a jinx for England when they play Australia.

It is, in fact, an exaggeration to say that both Miller and Lindwall played crucial parts in the 1956 victory, because Ray had damaged a hamstring muscle at Trent Bridge and failed a fitness test. As Pat Crawford then did the same thing on his Test debut in his fifth over, we suddenly found ourselves with a bowling attack of Miller, Ron Archer, Ken Mackay and two spinners, Ian Johnson and me, on a pitch so green it could hardly be distinguished from the rest of the square.

Miller was often at his best when the going was tough and when the opposition would least expect him to lift himself. At 36 years of age he would have been anticipating sharing something like 70 overs with Archer and Crawford during the match. As it was he had to bowl 70 himself.

The first two and a half days of the match were even enough, but when the time came for the drawing of stumps on the Saturday evening Ken Mackay and I were hanging on grimly with defeat easily in sight. England had bowled well and fielded magnificently; Australia were on the run.

Old 'Slasher' Mackay, even in this, his Test debut, was never one for long speeches on his way out to bat. On the Monday morning despite my chatter he settled for 'Don't let's get run out ...' as his admonition before we settled in against Trueman, Statham, Bailey and Laker and Wardle. We made enough between us to provide room for manoeuvre for Johnson the skipper and for Miller the bowler who now never for an instant let up.

It was in that England second innings that I took one of my most prized wickets as a Test bowler: Colin Cowdrey, lbw playing back! It was the time we moved Peter Burge into a close catching position at silly mid-on to stop Colin pushing forward with bat behind pad. No such luxury as the no-stroke section of the lbw law thirty years ago.

Miller had good support in this second innings from Ron Archer whose 31 overs brought 4/71. Even so it was the older all-rounder who kept on producing the unplayable delivery to chip away at the England defences.

First he had Tom Graveney caught at the wicket, then he bowled Willie Watson to make sure there could be no chance of another Watson–Bailey match-saver. Peter May, coming in at number five, held the side together after Cowdrey's dismissal until Miller produced a great leg-cutter for Gil Langley to take his seventh victim of the match – catching Evans and Laker shortly afterwards was to take him to a Test record.

When Miller bowled Wardle, it was the first time he had taken 10 wickets in a Test – what a time to do it, his final Test appearance in the shadow of Father Time! His match figures of 34.1–9–72–5 and 36–12–80–5 bear testimony to the skill and courage he showed on those five days late in June 1956.

Three years earlier we had been defied almost all the last day by Watson and Bailey in that epic stand against a bowling attack of Lindwall, Miller, Ring, Johnston, Benaud and Davidson!

Now in 1956 Johnson led us off, stopping to allow Miller to take the lead through the gate. A great cricketer, bowling his heart out, and successfully too, for Australia to take a 1–0 lead in the series.

Just before leaving the ground he had tossed one of the bails to a youngster in the crowd, a nice gesture from one of the greatest cricketers playing for the last time at Test level at the home of cricket.

The consummate Kapil Dev, in action for India at Lord's.

ANTHONY COUCH

'The Rector's got beri-beri,' he said. 'He's terribly sorry and all that . . .'

THE WEDDING OF NIGEL GRINT

It was never the intention of cricket's founding fathers to challenge the institutions of established religion. Far from it. Personally, I would say that cricket and the supernatural form an obvious partnership. Cricket has learned a lot about self-discipline, playing with a straight bat, etc., from religion, while the church has profitably borrowed the idea of rewards in the life to come – that is to say, drinks after stumps – from cricket. Consider, for example, how many rural deans have graced the middle order across the centuries and, contrariwise, the regiments of crisp openers who have carried the Word into such places as Lake Nyanza, and Swansea. It is only when human weakness and carnal desire are introduced that the easy relationship is disturbed. The point is illustrated by the events surrounding the wedding of Nigel Grint, a chap from Leamington. I never knew Grint personally but I used to arm-wrestle with his brother, Jack, who told me the whole sorry tale.

Nigel Grint played for Spoonfield, a village in Oxfordshire. He was seam-up bowler and a useful man in the deep. He was fairly useless with the bat and seldom went in higher than ten or eleven. But the great thing in his favour was that he cared like mad. Each Friday evening as he alighted from the London train all thought of life insurance, or whatever it was, faded from his mind to be replaced by visions of cartwheeling stumps and celebrations in the Duck and Flag.

However, the smooth surface of Nigel Grint's life was disturbed by the pebble of sexual passion. He fell in love with a girl from St Albans, Miranda Hughes, and so uncontrollable was his delight in her that marriage was proposed. The idea was tabled in the early Spring, and a date for the tying of knots fixed for the second Saturday in July. Fixed, that is to say, by Miranda and her parents. The date had some sort of arcane significance for Mother Hughes, and Miranda didn't want to get into a filthy row about it.

When Grint was told, he turned pale with shock. The second Satur-

136

day in July was the Thrugham match. All matches are important but some have a sort of mystical quality about them. The Thrugham fixture was such a one. Many, many years ago – some say as far back as 1978 – the proprietor of the Duck and Flag, eager to stimulate business, had donated a very small silver cup, to be played for annually by Spoonfield and nearby Thrugham. The visitors had won that match and carried off the trophy. The following year Spoonfield won. When they approached the proprietor of the Bounding Plough, the Thrugham hostelry, they were told that the cup had been lost, or stolen, he wasn't sure which, despite the fact that the object itself was on public display behind the bar. The proprietor claimed that that was a different cup; very similar but different.

Nothing the Spoonfield people could do had any effect on the burglars of Thrugham. Threats of legal action, boycott, arson, grassing to the police about late drinking, all fell on deaf ears. The following year the fixture was cancelled, which wasn't what mine host at the Duck and Flag had had in mind at all. 'Play 'em, and be damned!' he exhorted. 'Show 'em you don't care,' meaning *he* did, profoundly. An extraordinary meeting of the team was called and it was agreed that a succession of crippling defeats might cause the Thrughamites to regret their cupidity.

From that day forward the fixture was special. The result didn't always happen as planned, but every victory had the same sacred significance as did those of the Crusaders recapturing some treasured corner of the Holy Land. For this reason the second Saturday in July was sacrosanct.

Nigel Grint clipped his beloved in his arms and whispered mellifluously in her ear, 'I'll marry you, my darling, any time, anywhere, except on the second Saturday in July.' Miranda conveyed the message back to HQ. Mother Hughes said, 'In my family the girls have always been married on the second Saturday in July, right back as far as 1967. Tradition's important to us. That's the day you get married or not at all!'

Miranda felt uneasy. Mother Hughes, the Wazeer and Chief Executioner of 72 Brickiln Villas, St Albans, had an undinted record when it came to differences of opinion.

'Why is he being so unreasonable?' she demanded. 'Is this what your married life is going to be like, backing down and giving way all the time?'

'He has a prior engagement,' said Miranda.

'More important than his wedding!'

'Yes,' said Miranda.

Nigel didn't like the sound of it either. If Mother Hughes broke off negotiations the soft-skinned Miranda might be permanently eradicated from his life and handed on a plate to his rival, the hated Walter Woodcast, also of St Albans. Nigel wasn't sure whether it was his possible loss, or Walter's possible gain, that troubled him most. Either way, something had to be done. A summit conference was called at Brickiln Villas. Father Hughes absented himself on the grounds that whatever he said he would be treated with contempt, and Miranda kept demurely to her room.

The conference lasted two hours twenty-five minutes, and resulted in a most interesting compromise. Nigel and Miranda *would* be married on the second Saturday in July, but not at St Mildred's, just around the corner from the Villas. The ceremony would take place at St Woden's, Spoonfield, at eleven o'clock. The reception would be in the back room of the Duck and Flag, after which Nigel would join his team mates in the contest with Thrugham. Father Hughes approved the decision (not that anyone cared), but Miranda was less sure. Somehow she was becoming a minor figure at her own wedding. Had she known how it was going to turn out she might well have chucked in her hand then and there and stumped off round to the hated Walter.

One bright spot was the Rev. Plumpstead, the rector of Spoonfield. He was a loud, jovial man who believed that life was to be enjoyed. He adored his work. He thought all his duties were terrific fun, with funerals ranking only a few points behind weddings and christenings. He took an almost embarrassing pleasure in instructing Nigel and Miranda in the responsibilities of married life, and both were agog to see if he would be able to get through the actual ceremony without collapsing with laughter.

The second Saturday in July opened with a flood of sunshine, like a piece of early Delius. Miranda was disappointed. She'd hoped it would rain, thus restoring her and the wedding to centre stage. But the doves and the swallows swooped around the church as if under contract to Walt Disney and the forecast was for unbroken blue skies.

Nigel slipped off early for a clandestine look at the wicket. It was dry, with definite cracks on a length at the church end. Later it would turn. Better to bat first, he thought. But Dick Brainfarm, the skipper, wouldn't hear of it. 'If we bat first you'll have to bowl and field right up to the end,' he said. 'But if we bat second you might be able to get away early ... you know, wedding night, and all that.'

At ten o'clock Nigel changed out of his whites and into his morning greys. The best man, Luscombe, gathered him up, drove him to the church and, together, they had a last gaze across the disordered meadows of bachelorhood before entering the beautiful stone edifice of marriage. But as they turned and walked towards the South Door an odd sight took their attention. An elderly lady on a bicycle was speeding down the village street, waving her hat in the air.

'It's all off!' she screamed at the top of her voice.

Nigel's heart missed a beat.

'What's happened?' he cried, hurrying to the gate where the elderly lady was skidding to a halt. 'What's the matter with them?'

'Beri-beri,' answered the breathless lady.

'What, the whole team?' demanded Nigel.

'The Rector,' gasped the lady. 'He picked it up in Zululand. Gets terrible bouts. Can't leave his bed.'

The Rector!

He and Luscombe looked at each other, then Luscombe hurried off to where the bride's party was gathered in a tight-lipped knot around the Wazeer.

'The Rector's got beri-beri,' he said. 'He's terribly sorry and all that ...'

Mother Hughes looked at him as if he'd suddenly removed all his clothing. But only for a moment. Cool as a knife, she delivered her decision.

'Get another one, immediately.' She snapped her fingers impatiently. 'Arrange it at once. Anyone with the necessary qualifications. I want him here, cassocked and surpliced, in the next twenty minutes.'

Best man Luscombe and the lady on the bicycle hurried to the Duck and Flag where there was a telephone. From memory she was able to produce a long list of possible candidates. Luscombe did the phoning and struck lucky at the third attempt. The Rev. Handiside of Little Yoppley had absolutely nothing to do and would be delighted to rush to St Woden's immediately. A message was sent to Father Hughes and Miranda in their secret hideout to delay their appearance at church until further notice. Everybody then withdrew to the back room of the Duck and Flag, where they steadied their nerves with sherry.

The only absentee was Nigel Grint. He was standing at the edge of the churchyard, hands in pockets, gazing out at the adjoining cricket field. If the ball *did* get up from a length, he mused, he'd need someone at silly point. Also someone at short third man, in case it didn't get up from a length. But who? And taken from where? He'd need three men on the leg side at the very least because of the natural slope of the ground. Damn'd tricky ...

After quite a long time Nigel looked at his watch. It was eleven twenty-five. He wandered back to the pub where he found that the party had divided into two distinct schools. One, headed by Mother Hughes, was becoming tense and slightly hysterical. The other, headed by the best man, was becoming intoxicated. Twice Father Hughes had rung from the hideout to check that he and Miranda hadn't been overlooked in the confusion, and had been reassured with difficulty. At quarter to twelve Luscombe was persuaded to ring Little Yoppley to confirm that Mr Handiside had left. Yes, said the lady who answered the phone, he'd left within minutes of being summoned, but he was a very slow driver. Luscombe examined the map. It was about eight miles from Little Yoppley to Spoonfield. Yes, an average of less than eight miles per hour was very slow ...

Soon after twelve the first of the Thrugham players arrived at the pub. Predictably they found the presence of a wedding party a suitable occasion to display their tastelessness. Two of them gate-crashed the back room and were ejected with incredible speed by Mother Hughes. As she slammed the door behind them she glared. She was not used to her plans going wrong. She had no experience of presiding over fiascos. She was not enjoying herself.

It was suggested that someone should go to Little Yoppley to check that Mr Handiside wasn't lying in a ditch somewhere along the way. The lady on the bicycle offered to go, but this was vetoed on the grounds that if the vicar *was* lying in a ditch the lady might have trouble getting him on to her crossbar. A member of the groom's party agreed to go, and everyone else got back to the serious business of settling their nerves.

At twenty-five past twelve the man returned with the now highly agitated Mrs Handiside. Her husband had left *hours* ago! Why wasn't he here? What had become of him? He was a very careful driver, she assured everybody, but other road users were less considerate. The best man phoned the Nabtonbury police who found it difficult to understand what the problem was, and, when they did understand, found it difficult to work up much interest. The desk sergeant promised to make a note of the information received on the appropriate form.

Dick Brainfarm, the Spoonfield skipper, arrived at about a quarter to one. He quite reasonably assumed from the condition of most of the guests that the wedding was safely over, and was shocked to learn that this was not the case as the vicar, or vicars, was/were indisposed and/or lost.

Mother Hughes, who had been lying down for a while, now re-emerged.

'Where's that woman on a bicycle?' she demanded. 'We must find another vicar immediately. I have no faith in the one that is lost and I refuse to leave this place until my daughter is married. A replacement is required. At once!'

The lady on the bicycle couldn't be found. Someone suggested going through Yellow Pages but this turned out to be a dead end. Mother Hughes cornered Mrs Handiside and insisted that she reveal the names of her husband's co-practitioners. But, as the red-eyed Mrs Handiside pointed out, they'd only been in the district three weeks and didn't know anybody. She knew lots of people in Middlesbrough, where they'd been before, but realized that would hardly be much help.

'What about your bishop?' snapped Mother Hughes.

Bishops have to be booked weeks in advance,' sobbed Mrs Handiside. 'Anyhow, I can't remember his name. Please, all I want is my husband back . . .'

At ten past one her prayer was partially answered. The Rev. Handiside phoned to say that he was at the village of Spinfield. He had almost at once discovered his foolish mistake and was even now on his way to Spoonfield. Spinfield, it seemed, was thirty-five miles on the other side of Little Yoppley. Luscombe did a quick calculation. Thirty-five, plus eight, equalled forty-three. At a steady thirty miles an hour the journey would be accomplished in about one and a half hours, thus the wedding of Nigel and Miranda could take place at two forty-five.

Nigel hurried to find Dick Brainfarm.

'We'll have to bat first,' he said. 'We should be through the wedding and the reception by three-thirty, so I can be changed and padded up by three forty-five. And anyhow, the rough patch should be more useful after tea.'

At twenty-five past two, just as the wedding party was brushing itself down and straightening itself up in preparation for the ceremony, the two skippers wandered out to the middle. Brainfarm tossed. The Thrugham skipper called heads, and heads it was.

'We'll bat,' he said.

'Oh, lor',' said Brainfarm. 'Actually, we've got a small problem,' and explained the small problem to his opposite number. The opposite number was unmoved.

'That's your problem, brother. You should never try and mix business and pleasure. Anyhow, we're batting, and that's that!'

A written message was rushed surreptitiously to Nigel, now enpewed within the church. It read, 'They're batting first. Need you first change from the road end. Be as quick as you can, there's a good chap. R.B.'

Nigel looked at his watch. Two thirty-five. The church, pretty full now, was speechless with expectation. Any moment the organ would bulge into life, the vicar would appear and the whole carnival would be on the road. He would be as quick as he could but, apart from gabbling his bit, there wasn't much he could do to gee it on.

At two forty-two a small boy entered the church and slunk up to the best man. All eyes were on him as he whispered something into the best man's ear, then slunk out. Luscombe, not one hundred per cent sober, rose to his feet, turned and addressed the congregation.

'Mrs Hughes, ladies and gentlemen. I have just received a message from the Nabtonbury police. It seems that the Rev. Handiside has been apprehended by a patrol car and taken, under escort, to the police station. The charge is, driving without due care and attention and exceeding the speed limit. The police regret any inconvenience and hope that Mr Handiside will be with us a little later.'

There was a howl of hysterical laughter from the back of the church and Mrs Handiside was led out. The rest of the congregation broke into subdued muttering and gathered, like beggars, around the Wazeer. Mother Hughes' eyes glinted like frosty glass.

'Nobody leaves!' she announced in a voice that set the ancient stained glass flinching in its leaded lights. 'Nobody sets foot outside this building until my daughter and that person, there, are united in holy matrimony.'

Nigel Grint stepped forward.

'I'm sorry, Mother ...' – he judged that the moment had arrived to use this telling form of address – '... I'm sorry, but we did agree on what was going to happen today. Part One: I, and Miranda of course, were to be married. Part Two: I was going to play cricket. As Part One is unavoidably delayed, I intend moving on to Part Two. If and when his reverence is released from custody and arrives on the premises perhaps you would be kind enough to let me know.'

His exit from the church was dignified yet firm. By the time Mother Hughes had filled her lungs, opened her mouth and delivered the words 'Well, *really*, Nigel...!', Nigel was already halfway across the churchyard. Within minutes he had changed out of his greys and back into his whites, and was directing all his attention towards the rough patch, on a length, at the church end.

The Thrugham batsmen seemed stimulated by the presence of smartly dressed strangers all over the place. They played with fire and style and by tea had amassed 204, all out. Nigel Grint had taken 3 for 33, which was admirable considering all the distraction, but the Spoonfield team knew they had a long, hard furrow to plough.

Luscombe, who had sneaked out via the vestry, informed Grint that the police were just clearing up the business of Luscombe's first telephone call concerning the then lost Mr Handiside. They were just double checking that Handiside wasn't wanted for something, other than the wedding at St Woden's. As soon as that was all cleared up Handiside would be delivered back to Spoonfield.

Brainfarm said to Grint, 'You'd better bat early, then when the vicar turns up you can get married.'

'That's madness,' said Grint. 'We're going to have one hell of a job getting that score, without dickering with the batting order.'

'Only trying to help,' said Brainfarm.

At half-past four the Spoonfield innings opened, and a brave sight it was. Numbers one and two, equally inspired by the unusual goings-on, laid about them like lumberjacks on piece work. Such a display of controlled violence hadn't been seen in the village since Farmer Half-berry's bull, Clive, had destroyed the postman's bicycle, and that was many years ago. At 59 for 0, off twelve overs, it was looking good for the home side. But Thrugham still had a key card to play.

However, before describing the key card another, crucial, event must be related. After being escorted from the church Mrs Handiside had been steadied with sherry in the back room of the Duck and Flag. Now, coincident with the beginning of the Spoonfield innings, she felt the need for air. After wandering about for some time she found herself in the cricket field, near the long-on boundary. For a while she stood and gazed mournfully at the players. How free and gay they were, how careless of their liberty, unlike her own dear Melvyn. She was about to turn away when her attention was caught by the fielder nearest to her. It looked so like . . . Could it be . . .?

'Fabian,' she called nervously. 'Is it you?'

The fielder turned. He gazed at her in amazement, then, with a cry of delight, ran forward and gripped her hands.

'Melissa! But what on earth are you doing here?'

'What on earth are *you* doing here!'

This rather empty dialogue went on for some moments before they came to the interesting bit, which, for the sake of brevity, is best reduced to its essentials. The fielder, Fabian, was none other than the Rev. Fabian Smallwood, only recently inducted into the living of St Crispin's, Thrugham. He was also a very old friend of the Handisides. He was *also* a cracking good cricketer.

Melissa Handiside blurted out the awful predicament in which she and the Rev. Handiside found themselves, to say nothing of the wedding party cowering in the church.

'My dear girl, I must come at once,' declared Smallwood. 'I'll just fix it with the skipper.'

Fixing it with the skipper was not the easiest job he'd had that week. The reason for this was that he, Fabian Smallwood, was the key card that Thrugham were about to play. The vicar was an off-spinner of some ability. The Thrugham committee had only discovered this very recently, but, having done so, had enjoyed a series of unlikely victories. Only the previous Saturday Smallwood had taken 5 for 14, thus helping his side to crucify the Midlands Electricity Board.

The conversation between skipper and key card was brief. Brainfarm was called in and it was agreed between them that the match would be suspended for twenty minutes while the key card joined the happy couple in marriage. Everybody left the field. Smallwood and Grint hurried to the church, the rest to the back room of the pub. Father Hughes and Miranda were instructed to appear instantly and almost before the first illicit pint had been drawn at the Duck and Flag Mendelssohn's merry march was peeling out across the countryside.

It was the first wedding ever at St Woden's where the vicar and the groom wore white and the bride appeared in dark slacks and cardigan. Everybody wept, except Mother Hughes, who was planning a national campaign to make the playing of cricket punishable by death in England as it had been under Edward III. Also it was one of the fastest weddings ever. Everything that could be decently omitted was omitted, an everything else ruthlessly edited or taken *molto allegro*. That is not to say a proper sense of solemnity was absent. Not at all. If anything the pace of the service helped to concentrate the minds of all present on the drama of the occasion. For instance, would the organist and the congregation finish the hymn together? Would the vicar absentmindedly exclude the 'I wills'? Would there be a maddening hold-up in the vestry? Would the photographer know who had married whom?

It says a lot for British common sense and guts that only nineteen minutes and twenty-seven seconds' playing time was lost. The game was played to an exciting conclusion, Thrugham winning by 11 runs. Smallwood took 4 for 29, and Grint, going in last, hit a plucky 14.

Afterwards there was a small party in the back room of the Duck and Flag where all earlier misunderstandings were laughed away and forgotten. Father Hughes danced the tango with the Thrugham wicket-keeper, and the lady on the bicycle did conjuring tricks. There was only one note in a minor key the whole evening. At ten-fifteen they received a phone call from Spanningfield in Shropshire. It was the Rev. Handiside wanting to know if two-thirty, Sunday, would be convenient for the wedding. This provoked a few smiles, but it should be remembered that without people like the Rev. Handiside the rest of us would look ordinary indeed. He may never have scored fifty nor taken three catches in an innings, but I'd bet my life that long after all the other players had left the field because of rain Handiside, M., would still be standing loyally at deep third man, waiting to be needed. And *that's* what cricket is all about.

The Bat and Ball, Hambledon.

SONG OF HAMBLEDON, 1962

I have quaffed ale at The Bat and Ball
At Hambledon,
Told cricket stories of old John Small
Of Hambledon,
Paid my homage in bowling keen
To the great and the late on this players' green
(And ghostly figures I have seen
At Hambledon!)

I've watched John Nyren pen his prose
At Hambledon,
Seen Beldham swipe a four at close
At Hambledon;
Watched Brett and Barker, Mann and May
At glorious cricket the live long day
(And nobody knows that I saw Pilch play
At Hambledon!)

I've touched the grass and the perfumed dew
At Hambledon
While watching these, the peerless few
Of Hambledon;
And loved the mirage of white on green,
The curve of the bat, and the swerve unseen
Of the leather lost (these which have been
At Hambledon!)

O! Never again shall I feel the sun
Of Hambledon,
See phantoms dash at the batsman's run
At Hambledon;
No more the light and the white of May
Nor the lore of the roar of the crowd, O say!
Is death but a dream of yesterday
At Hambledon?

LESLIE FREWIN

*'... Through lorgnettes, field glasses, monocles
and what-nots, Philadelphia society saw today a
real game of cricket played ...'*

SUPER BOSS
THE HANDSOME LORD HAWKE

Lord Hawke was a Christian and a prayerful man. When he was first taking his teams on overseas tours and he found out that matches were sometimes played on a Sunday his moral convictions were shattered. In his agony he sought religious guidance and a clerical buddy gave him what amounted to a heavenly dispensation – provided he attended matins before play began.

So, in India, America, Argentina, South Africa, Australia or wherever his cricketing perambulations took him, he invited his team to accompany him to morning service. And since an 'invitation' from Lord Hawke was tantamount to 'volunteering' in HM Forces, his team would on Sundays enter the cathedral, church, chapel, synagogue or temple nearest the ground – in line of seniority, I suppose, with amateurs, of course, in the lead.

Alas, in later years, after a lifetime of service to cricket, his addiction to speaking to God brought him opprobrium from the Great British Public. For he prayed that no professional should ever captain England, and, thereafter, was consigned to eternal damnation by those enlightened in the modern outlook that all men are, or should be, equal.

As a boy he had more inherent cricket potential than any man ever born. Throughout his life he played billiards left-handed and shot from the left shoulder. When, as a little boy at his prep school he attended his first net, he naturally took up a left-handed stance. Shocked, the hidebound coach explained that while some professional cricketers and village bumpkins might stand that way, young gentlemen did not. Thereupon he turned the child round and insisted that he should bat right-handed.

And so Martin Hawke did throughout his career. He captained Yorkshire, he played for the Gentlemen against the Players, he scored his centuries in first class cricket. And all the time batting the wrong way round. Would even Len Hutton, batting left-handed, or Gary

Lord Hawke ... 'speaking to God' ...

Sobers, batting right-handed, with all their skill and ability, have scored hundreds against Lindwall, Miller, Statham, Trueman and Laker?

Lord Hawke captained Yorkshire for 28 years and was president for 41 years, these offices overlapping from 1898 to 1910. Never had a man such pride in the county. Unlike all other counties, Yorkshire allows none born outside its boundaries to defend the White Rose with bat or ball. Only three men throughout the county cricket club's existence have broken this rule: Cecil Parkin, W. G. Keighley and Lord Hawke himself.

Cecil Parkin was born within spitting distance of the border. In 1906 he played one innings, scoring 0, and took two wickets for 25 runs before it was discovered, in horror, that his birthplace was Durham! Unsung, he was allowed to depart to Lancashire, where he attained international fame. W. G Keighley, born in France of good Yorkshire stock, was allowed to play between 1947 and 1951, it being argued in his favour that a continental birthplace did not make him available for any other county and therefore disbar him from Yorkshire.

And the third off-comer was, of course, Lord Hawke himself, born near Gainsborough in Lincolnshire, where his father was a country rector.

In 1883 he took over from Tom Emmett a team which he later described as consisting of 'Louis Hall and ten ale-cans'. To them he brought discipline and pride and, when he felt the occasion demanded it, the high-handed authority of the martinet.

Ted Peate and Bobby Peel he dismissed from the team at the height of their international fame for minor misdemeanours and, in 1899, at Lord's, sacked Bobby Moorhouse for failing to make an effort to take a catch in the outfield. When asked about it, Moorhouse replied that he didn't think it was coming so far, 'and when Ah seed it up theer Ah said, "Oh, damn it"'. Angrily, Lord Hawke retorted that if he wouldn't try, he'd have to go, and that was the end of Bobby Moorhouse's county cricket.

Nothing pleased his lordship better than to score runs, but his ability did not normally entitle him to a high place in the batting order of a team so powerful as Yorkshire.

In May 1896 Yorkshire scored 887 against Warwickshire without declaring. It is the highest total ever scored in a county match. It left Yorkshire no time to dismiss Warwickshire twice and occupied 274 overs. What was the object of such a useless record? Well, seven wickets had fallen for 448 when Lord Hawke came in at number nine. Santall (65 overs; 2 wickets for 223), Ward (62 overs; 2 wickets for 175), Glover (30 overs; 1 wicket for 154) and Pallett (75 overs; 4 wickets for 184) were already tiring. Here was the opportunity for some fun. Lord Hawke scored another 166 runs and with Bobby Peel (210 not out) carried the score to 740. His lordship hugely enjoyed his slaughter of the weary bowlers and when he was out at last, bowled by the persevering Pallett, decided to give George Hirst an innings. He had been waiting long enough at number ten. So George went in and plundered another 85 runs. And after the innings Lord Hawke had the temerity to ask for the ball as a souvenir!

His plans did not always go so well. In 1898 at Chesterfield against Derbyshire he thought he would like an innings. So, irrespective of merit, he put himself in at number three after Brown and Tunnicliffe and went to put his pads on.

He did not expect to have to wait long. Poor 'Long John' Tunnicliffe had had a series of misfortunes on his way to the ground. He had had nothing to eat since teatime the day before. He had booked in at a dirty inn, found the bed clothes damp and sat up all night in a chair. Obviously, he was in no state to bat long. But Brown and Tunnicliffe scored 554 for the first wicket and it was twelve o'clock on the second day before Lord Hawke got his innings.

It was a natural progression for one of so strong a character to become chairman of England's Test Selection Committee. But here his lordship was torn between two desires. Much as he wanted England to win the Tests, he wanted Yorkshire to win the County Championship even more, and he had built up such a powerful team in Yorkshire that England wanted its players.

For the Test Match at Manchester in 1902 England automatically chose George Hirst, Wilfred Rhodes and Stanley Jackson and then wanted to include, among the thirteen, Schofield Haigh as off-spin bowler. Now Schofie was the best off-spin bowler in England as well as a powerful middle order hitter, but Lord Hawke feared that he would be left drumming his heels as number twelve while Yorkshire were missing his services, so he objected. Fred Tate, of lesser ability, was therefore substituted and Schofie returned to his county duties.

Fred Tate played, missed a vital catch and, going in last when England wanted eight to win, was bowled out with England only four short of victory. After the match malicious tongues were heard to say that Lord Hawke lost more Test Matches for England than anyone else who had never played.

He was adept at winning the toss, particularly on his tours to far flung parts of the British Empire. But it was not all pure luck. He would hand a golden sovereign to his opposing captain, invite him to toss, and, when the coin was in the air, call, 'It's a woman.' And, of course, when it came down with Queen Victoria's head on one side and Britannia on the other, it was! Whichever side was uppermost Lord Hawke would look at it with satisfaction and say, 'We'll bat.'

Another record of which he was proud was that he was the offspring of one of the earliest of all courtships. The first time his father saw his mother was the day he, as a county parson, baptized her when she was a babe in arms.

But he was happiest taking his teams to all parts of the world. Between 1887 and 1912 he toured Australia, India, Canada, the United States, South Africa, the West Indies and Argentina.

In 1889, when thoughts of the Mutiny were still fresh in the minds of the natives, he played at Lucknow. He might have scored a century and demonstrated the superiority of the white raj, but his 'duck' was a stroke of pure genius, probably doing more to cement Anglo-Indian friendship than all the machinations of Foreign Secretaries and Viceroys.

In 1885 in South Africa, he went to gaol to play poker with those condemned to death for the Jameson Raid. His visit was supposed to be an attempt to cheer the prisoners up ... but he won £98 off them. No doubt they could afford it. They paid Kruger £25,000 for their release.

But his greatest moments were in the United States where he and his men arrived almost as beings from another planet, bringing with them some newly concocted ball game.

Rapturously they were met at Philadelphia. 'Quaker City Society bows before the English Gentlemen,' said one headline, and a war correspondent began his account of the first battle.

'Through lorgnettes, field glasses, monocles and whatnots, Philadelphia society saw today a real game of cricket played ... Cricket is English from beginning to end – if it has any end. Consequently society turned out *en masse* today and camped round the big field at Mannheim on coaches, drays, breaks, T-carts and tandems.

'"My, ain't they big fellows," said a Germantown girl, critically overhauling them with a pair of opera glasses. She was right. They looked almost elephantine as they strolled across the field in their white toggery. Then a queer little chap, wearing a white hat and a red nose, set up three little sticks in one place and three little sticks in another. This was all that there was to it.'

With the gentle elegance that was the hallmark of bygone cricket the game continued its amiable course. Whenever an Englishman was out the band struck up 'God Save the Queen'.

But, at last, the moment that all had waited for arrived. The correspondent continued, 'Another tall figure came meandering across the field in a sort of shambling walk – and no wonder. His legs were fitted with a couple of circular washboards and his hands were mailed with lengthy gauntlets. He looked for all the world like Buck Taylor, the King of the Cowboys. For a few minutes his lengthy lordship of Hawke was the bull's-eye for ten thousand pairs of eyes. They did not seem to worry him any. He ranted from wicket to wicket. A wicked ball bounded up and hit Lord Hawke an awful whack on the gauntleted knuckles. Society groaned. His lordship merely put his hand behind his back, tweedled his fingers, looked up at the sky placidly without an audible word. Who can doubt, however, that he talked Parsee to himself?'

The same adulation was not given to the home team. Of one of the Philadelphians a journalist wrote, 'All the morning an imposing individual with a sky-blue coat, a white braided cap, a pair of grey side whiskers and an air of importance had been walking around the ground telling what he knew about cricket. People were appalled at his thorough insight into the game. Out from the club-house he floated, a symphony in blue. What a walk he had! It was a cross between that of Henry Irving and a straddle-bug. It was style though, clear through. He looked at the sky as though to select a favourable cloud to knock the ball over; then he balanced his bat in his hands and pranced along, just as de Wolf Hopper does after a third encore. "That's the boy for Nellie," said somebody. He stepped in front of the wicket, struck an attitude like a petrified Adonis and looked at the unhappy bowler with an eagle eye.

"He is good for a six, anyway. I can tell it by his looks," murmured a dude in the grand stand.

"How handsome he is," whispered a young society woman to her escort, "I'll wager he makes a hundred."

'The bowler was not alarmed. He stepped back a few paces, ran forward, whirled his arm like a cartwheel and let the ball travel. The symphony in blue did not have time to realise that he was alive; he had an awfully pretty bat in his hands too, but the ball whisked by his classic shins. There was a dull explosion at the wickets, and, as far as cricket was concerned, the symphony was dead. He smiled a sort of sickly smile, said "Baw Jawve" below his breath and crawled back.'

They played at Philadelphia, Boston, New York and Massachusetts. There were balls and banquets in their honour. Charming partners devoted themselves to teaching the tourists a new waltz step.

'Lord Hawke,' wrote a correspondent, 'has already made a great impression, and, as he is a comparatively young bachelor, it is a safe prediction that some of the golden girls of the metropolis will find him too nice for anything.'

The tourists did not win back an empire, but perhaps they did more; they captured the hearts of every girl in the Eastern States.

More than one young Yankee had his nose put out by the gay and glamorous Englishmen, and was glad to see the back of them. 'Beefy, solemn-looking men, a more depressingly clad company it would be hard to find,' whined one. But perhaps his girl had given her heart to one of the Englishmen who, at Philadelphia after the match, had drunk sixty-four toasts and was still on his feet at the end of it.

It could only be mental aberration that prevented the Prime Minister from sending Lord Hawke to Washington as ambassador. He had a habit of always getting his own way. There is little doubt he would have made cricket America's national game, caused the Declaration of Independence to be revoked and returned the States to their rightful home in the Empire.

JOSEPH S. F. MURDOCH

*'Earlier Philadelphia teams which had played in
England were generally known as the Gentlemen
of Philadelphia ...'*

THE PHILADELPHIA STORY

Cricket was an importation into the city of Philadelphia introduced by the English hosiery weavers of Germantown, a section of the city, and when first played it appealed to the character of the descendants of English Quakers who had emigrated earlier and probably remembered the appeal of the game as it was played in their former English home villages.

Cricket is, as we recall reading, planned for the participant and the length of time taken to finish a game stems from the idea that it is pleasant and a delight to share some time with friends. Through the sharing of that time, the game becomes a social event which can be enjoyed by young and old.

Thus, these emigrants, far from their native home, sought out fellows who shared the interest and many an enduring friendship in 'the new country' was established by the desire to play the game which provided social contact and a healthy exercise.

The English hosiery weavers of Germantown formed the first club in America in 1842. Here, William Rotch Wister began his cricket. He found a number of his fellow students at the University of Pennsylvania ready to form a club and so organised the Junior Cricket Club there. This was the first club of Americans established in the United States and Mr Wister was its first president. He is regarded as the 'father' of American cricket and played actively and in many matches up to 1861.

After graduating from the University, Wister continued to play with friends recruited from his college and with gentlemen with whom he had formerly played. Through the efforts of this group, cricket began to flourish and it soon became evident that they should organise a formal 'Cricket Club'.

Thus, on 10 February, 1854, a few gentlemen met in Wister's office in Philadelphia and formed the Philadelphia Cricket Club. Wister acted as Chairman of the meeting. It must have been a rather large office for twenty gentlemen were present and, perhaps because of space restrictions, an additional thirty who could not be present were offered membership.

The old Club that Wister had formed in 1842 provided most of the members of the new Club. Because they lacked financial resources, they rented a ground in Camden, New Jersey, across the Delaware River from Philadelphia. A man named Bradshaw was hired as instructor and a shed was put up behind Bradshaw's house as a clubhouse. Mrs Bradshaw 'frequently put up meals' and 'entertained everyone with enthusiasm'. It is presumed that this meant that the good Mrs Bradshaw was a jolly hostess.

On 4 and 5 July, 1858, the first international cricket match was played in America on the Camden (New Jersey) grounds with an English XI, otherwise unidentified, which was 'naturally victorious'. There were 6,000 spectators and it was apparently, from contemporary accounts, 'a notable event'.

Perhaps inspired by the activities of this early Philadelphia Cricket Club many clubs were formed and flourished, so that Philadelphia became the cricket centre of America.

The Philadelphia Cricket Club continued to play in Camden, New Jersey, for some years but because of meagre financial resources they were forced to seek other locations, and in the period from 1854 to 1883, the Club played wherever they could locate a fairly level piece of ground. Finally through the generosity of a benefactor, Henry H. Houston, they secured a parcel of land in the Chestnut Hill section of the city of Philadelphia at the very favourable terms of $1.00 per year. The year was 1883 and Mr Houston not only provided the land but built a modest building which would serve as a clubhouse. This land has remained, to this day, the location of the Club.

When the first railway laid to Chestnut Hill was completed in 1854, the same year in which the 'wandering Philadelphia Cricket Club' was founded, Chestnut Hill was little more than a country village. The stage coaches passing through did little to disturb its tranquillity and the road leading through it was in such a state that it is said that a gentleman mounted his horse to cross from one side of the road to the other. The advent of the railway brought many affluent citizens from the city of Philadelphia to spend the summer and their handsome residences made a considerable impact on the once bucolic scene.

The west side of the village was not developed until after another railway line was laid in 1884, primarily through the vision and enterprise of the same Henry H. Houston who had, a year earlier, arranged for the Philadelphia Cricket Club to have a permanent home on the sun-setting side of the village. A century later, it can only be deduced

Aerial view of Philadelphia Cricket Club grounds at 'St Martins', Chestnut Hill, Philadelphia. Foreground, showing expanse of lawn now devoted to tennis, was until 1924 used for cricket.

that Mr Houston was a visionary who, not without profit, developed the idea that where people will play, they will settle; but if they settle, they will need sustinence. The fact that he owned most of the land in the area may or may not have been a consideration.

This western half of Chestnut Hill became known as 'St Martins', after the Episcopal Church in the area (erected by Mr Houston) which had been built in 1889 and named after the famous church of that name in London. The name persists to this day and the Philadelphia Cricket Club's property which is the location of the main clubhouse, and where tennis, squash, soccer, swimming and field hockey are also played, is known as 'St Martins'. There is also a nine-hole golf course located at this place. Some six miles away, the Club subsequently built, in 1922, an 18-hole golf course which serves as a 'championship course' and, with extra acreage, open fields which serve a selected membership as private shooting grounds.

The Club officially opened their new grounds in Chestnut Hill (St Martins) on 1 October 1884 with a day-long programme that offered the members a cricket match, a presentation of the colours (which were donated by the distaff members of the Club), a choral concert by the 'Orpheus Club', an all-male choral group which to this day continues to serenade the members in an annual concert, and a 'Grand Hop' at a nearby inn. The press report from which much of this account is drawn concludes its article with: 'Dancing was indulged in until near midnight. The residents of Chestnut Hill returned in a special train, which left a quarter before twelve and returned again to the city. In the many carriages drawn up in front of the inn, the guests living in the vicinity were driven home. The affair was a grand success throughout.'

It is noted that a presentation of colours was made at this auspicious opening of the Club on its new grounds and it may be of some interest to a few cricket fans that the colours of the Philadelphia Cricket Club are red, yellow and black. These colours were used to what we must assume to be blinding effect but the adoption of them is lost in history. It is probable that the colours were copied from one of the most famous elevens, the 'I Zingara'. Because the Philadelphia Cricket Club 'wandered' from their beginning in 1854 until 1883, it is believed that the colours of the Zingara, or Gypsies, were appropriate. It may be of interest to note that Bernard Darwin, the eminent correspondent of the London *Times*, thought that the Zingara was the first club to adopt club colours and, quoting from Darwin's book, *British Clubs* (1946), 'There was born one of the most famous and envied of colours when in August, 1845, I Zingara played their first match.'

To continue the quote by Darwin, 'Mr Bolland, one of the founders of the Club, was soon lyrically proclaiming:

> Yes, the Red, White and Blue o'er the ocean,
> Has floated in conquests of old,
> But tonight let us pledge our devotion
> To the folds of the Red, Black and Gold.'

With the establishment of a permanent home through the good graces of Mr Houston, the Club and cricket flourished. A clubhouse was erected and a '500-square-foot platform [sic] for cricket to cost $3,500' was constructed.

The Club records between 1884 and 1893 are lost, probably burned in a disastrous fire which destroyed the clubhouse in 1909, but according to the Centennial History of the Club, published in 1954, and written by the eminent American historian, Horace Mather Lippincott: 'Undoubtedly the Club began at once to enjoy its new home and to play cricket which is steadily recorded each year from now on; mention being made of the First, Second, Junior, Veteran and Summer Elevens, thus showing the widespread interest in the game.'

An examination of the Minutes of the Club from 1893 and after shows that prize bats were awarded to deserving juniors, certain individuals were named 'best cricket player' and, because those annoying 'new' sports tennis and golf were being taken up, the need for a larger clubhouse was expressed.

In the Club Minutes the first international match mentioned is in

1898 resulting in a defeat of the Gentlemen of Philadelphia by P. F. Warner's Eleven 'by eight wickets; the attendance was good and a profit realised but it was very poor cricket.' Many more international matches would take place between the years 1898 and 1924 but the visiting teams from either England or Canada were usually made up of Club players and the Philadelphia teams were usually made up from the best players at the local Clubs, Philadelphia, Germantown, Merion, Belmont and Young America Cricket Clubs.

According to the Club's Centennial History:

> Of all the international matches played at Wissahickon (St Martins), perhaps the most famous and best played was the match between Past and Present Elevens of Oxford and Cambridge and the University of Pennsylvania on September 13th, 14th and 16th, 1895. The Englishmen batted first and scored heavily, tallying 284 runs for the inning. Pennsylvania put a strong side in the field. The English team was in good form and retired their opponents for 138 runs, giving them a lead of 146 and forcing Pennsylvania to follow on. Quite a change ensued through some magnificent cricket. George S. Patterson, W. W. Noble, Crawford Coats and Captain William Brockie gave a fine display of clean, hard hitting so that the total came to 307 runs, 161 to the good.
>
> It was anyone's match but, with the superb bowling of G. S. Patterson and E. W. Clark, the Englishmen were dismissed for 61 and we won the match by 100 runs.

Over the years, either the Club Eleven or teams made up of the better players in the Philadelphia area played visiting teams from Kent (1903), Marylebone Cricket Club Eleven (1905), Hesketh-Pritchard's MCC Eleven in 1907 and, in what was to be the final international match played at the Club, the Incogniti Eleven in 1924.

In only one year did the Club send an Eleven to England, this in 1912, and while the Minutes of the Club reveal that the team's record was 4 won, 3 lost, 3 drawn, only one opponent is mentioned, the Royal Artillery. It is interesting to note that one member's account of the trip explains that 'not wishing to embarrass the Zingari Club in England, whose colours – Red, Black and Yellow – our Club had adopted, this team wore Green and White blazers'.

The Club Minutes do not reveal too much detail of the trip but several of the members who participated recorded their impressions. Allan Hunter mentions the great privilege of playing against the one and only Dr W. G. Grace in two of the matches and 'that event alone made the trip of real value'. Another member stated that 'another unexpected privilege was the witnessing of two days' play of one of the English–Australian Test games at the Oval. To those who saw it, the names of Hobbs, Rhodes, Fry, Barnes and Woolley became the personification of cricket at its best!'

The Club's History mentions that 'the trip produced but one real misfortune. Wherever the team went, they were continually asked to play a few exhibition innings of baseball. During the lunch intermission of one of the early matches, such a game was staged and the reliable Jack Graham had the misfortune to injure his ankle badly enough to preclude his playing any of the remaining cricket schedule.'

In reading ancient reports today, one gathers that World War I dealt a severe blow to cricket in England and in the United States, and following its termination, strong efforts were made to revive interest in the game. Apparently these efforts were successful in England but did not produce equally good results in the USA.

The Club cricketers did not give up easily. Arrangements were made in 1920 for a visit from a team from Toronto and the Incogniti Club of England and this led to an invitation for a Philadelphia team to tour England in 1921.

Earlier Philadelphia teams which had played in England were generally known as the 'Gentlemen of Philadelphia'. They played County teams, including professionals. Whether their deportment maintained the facade of 'gentlemen' there is no record – perhaps mercifully so. However, at this time it was felt that the 1921 team could not be of the strength to play this kind of competition and the team organised was to be known as the 'Philadelphia Pilgrims' and to confine the schedule to amateur competition. Again, as in former years, the team was made up from the better players in each of the Philadelphia-area Clubs. The entire tour covered about seven weeks and was destined to be the last representative team of Philadelphia Cricket Clubs to invade England and, in one of the participants' words, the end of 'this delightful and never-to-be-forgotten association with such fine sportsmen and generous hosts'.

The increased tempo and complexity of life in the 'roaring twenties' brought about a lack of interest on the part of younger players and each year it became increasingly difficult to field an eleven. Finally, in 1925, stumps were drawn for the last time.

If the Philadelphia Cricket Club never fielded an outstanding team, the members were enthusiastic and dearly loved the game. The following members might be mentioned as 'international cricketers' – William Rotch Wister, Lyndford Biddle, Philip N. LeRoy, John H. Mason, Edward Hopkinson, Jr, Cyril G. Woolley, Harry B. Cartwright, Jr, Samuel Goodman, Jr, Herbert Clark, J. Barton King and Joseph S. Clark.

No summary of cricket at the Philadelphia Cricket Club can be complete without mentioning our greatest player, J. Barton King. Lippincott's History of the Club states:

'Bart' King was, of course, the greatest cricketing member of the Club and might well be designated as our most distinguished athlete. At the

J. Barton King, one of America's greatest cricketers, was a member of the Philadelphia Cricket Club.

top of his game he was the greatest bowler in the world and well up as a batsman. He is included in the eleven greatest cricketers of all time by English critics. It is unnecessary to recite Bart's record in detail. Everyone interested in cricket knows it.

He was first noticed in *The American Cricketer* in June 1889 and from then on appeared prominently up to the last game with the Australians in 1912. He was a very fast bowler and kept his pace for twenty years which in itself was remarkable. An English critic says of him, 'Mr. King was a magnificent bowler, very fast, very accurate.'

John Lester, writing in a *A Century of American Cricket*, says: 'It is rather sad to reflect that England remembers so well one whose fame, except to those of us who cherish it, has faded in his native town. He was better known by sight in England fifty years ago [sic] than any other American. There he is still remembered. In a recent article on the deterioration of fast bowling, the famous English athlete, C. B. Fry, writes, "The best swerver I ever saw in my life was J. Barton King of Philadelphia." With us he epitomizes the game and its associations when Philadelphia was the cricket center of North America. He corresponded with the life-span of first-class Philadelphia cricket from blossom to husk, and he symbolizes to us a value that has perished.'

Perhaps a final quote should serve as a toast to the grand game that no longer exists at this fine old Club. Percy H. Clark, one of the Club's early and enthusiastic members and a fine player, was one of those members interviewed on the occasion of the Club's centenary.

He recalled: 'The rivalry between Philadelphia clubs in the Halifax Cup, Philadelphia Cup and Junior competitions was keen, but the relations were friendly and after the matches the home team would see their rivals had refreshments to carry the visitors home with a smile on their faces. We old crocks have happy memories of the battles on the cricket field and I remember with great pleasure the matches played at St Martins. It makes us sad to see the fine turf on which we did our best turned over to tennis, soccer and hockey – something worthwhile has disappeared from our midst.'

If cricket is no longer played at Philadelphia Cricket Club, present members are constantly reminded of any fancied past glories as they sit on a wide verandah and gaze over that which is possibly the grandest expanse of lawn in America and, perhaps sadly to a cricketer, now given over to lawn tennis. In the cool of the evening and with the setting sun sending tall shadows across those courts, few of the contemporary Club members think of the scene that pleased the eye one hundred years ago. This may not be a long time in English history, but it certainly is as American Club-history goes.

The Philadelphia Cricket Club, thoroughly American at this date and in this age, still cherishes the memory of a few Englishmen who so loved the game that they started a Club. Our Club.

CRICKET.

A GRAND MATCH OF
CRICKET
WILL BE PLAYED ON
Dartford Brent,
On MONDAY, AUGUST the 6th, 1832,
AND FOLLOWING DAYS,
BETWEEN THE GENTLEMEN
OF
The Leeds Club,
WITH FULLER PILCH (GIVEN),
AND THE GENTLEMEN OF
The Dartford Club
WITH
E. WENMAN, COBBETT, AND LILLYWHITE (GIVEN),
FOR
TWENTY-TWO SOVEREIGNS.

LEEDS CLUB.		DARTFORD CLUB.	
Mr. A. MYNN,	Mr. T. SHIRLY,	Mr. D. CAVILL	—— MASTERS,
—— B. ROPER,	—— E. BEARD,	—— J. JARDINE,	—— J. HARDS,
—— J. ROPER,	—— W. MAY,	—— C. HUGGETT,	—— A. RICHARDSON,
—— G. BETTS,	—— R. THOMAS,	—— C. HODSOLL,	—— W. BRAND,
—— T. BETTS.	—— T. MAY,	—— J. KEMP,	—— E. WENMAN. (Given)
—— W. CLIFFORD,	—— F. DUDDINGS,	—— T. WENMAN,	—— COBBETT, (Ditto)
—— R. CLIFFORD,	—— F. PILCH, (Given)	—— T. BARTON,	—— LILLYWHITE(Ditto)
—— T. ROBINSON,		—— E. WINTER,	

A Good ORDINARY at the Bull and George, at Two o'Clock.
by Mr. MESSENGER.

PRINTED BY R. J. CUTBUSH, WEEK STREET, MAIDSTONE

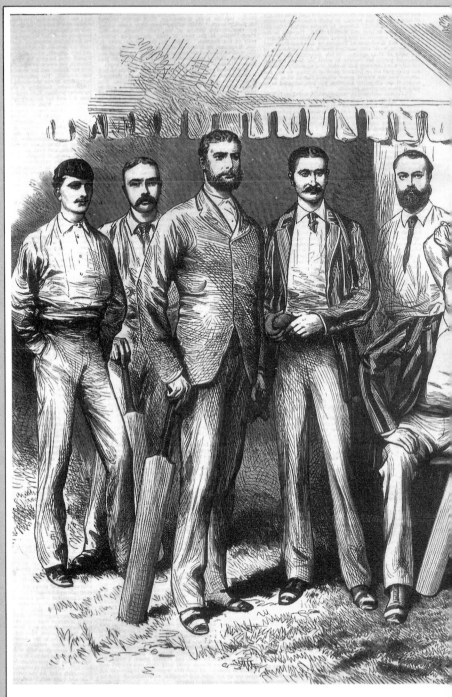

THE AUSTRALIAN T

From left to right, standing: S. P. Jones, A. C. Bannerman, G. J. Bonner, F R.
Spofforth, J. McCarthy Blackman, G. Eugene Palmer, G. Giffen, T. W.

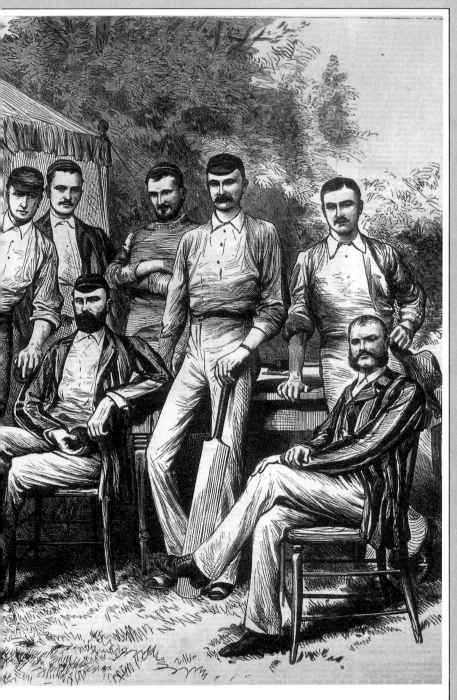

ICKETERS, 1882

Garrett, H. H. Massie and Percy S. McDonnell. Seated in front: W. L. Murdoch, H. F. Boyle and T. Horan.

RICHARD KERSHAW

'... Bats bearing the magic names of Bradman and Miller and Gunn were dragged from brass-bound chests and from beneath beds. And cricket was reborn ...'

BORN-AGAIN CRICKETER

It was James Thurber, that wisest sage among American humorists and the scourge of amateur psychologists, who was the first person to rid me of any residual guilt about cricket. He wrote – in seeing off some magazine psycho who had warned fulminatingly about the dangers of adult day-dreaming – 'Get it straight: ninety per cent of male Americans get to sleep striking out the Yankees.' A reference of course to baseball, not cricket, but still ...

I am a self-confessed day-dreamer. Many is the hundred I have scored at Lord's (let alone the MGC, the Kensington Oval in Barbados, and the Oval in Kennington) and many a good night's sleep I have had as a result. The dangers in other forms of wish-fulfilling escape are palpable, indeed notorious: plot thou not to take over the boss's job, or yet again his daughter, because that way lies envy, a difficult rethink each succeeding morning at the office, and before long, ulcerous disappointment.

But hitting Lillee straight back to the sightscreen three balls in succession; or hooking Thomson twice in an over for six over the head of a stranded Hilditch (ha! ha! ha!) – now, that is clean, positively sanitary fun. What is more, the feedback to Lillee and Thomson is going to be minimal.

So I admit it. But there is another admission: I am in fact a 'Born-Again Cricketer'. I gave up cricket when I got married, and only started to play again when marriage gave me up, and concerned friends thought a day in the country would do me good.

Batting number eleven, with the game all but lost, *I hit four sixes!* No matter that the ground was the smallest in the world – Michael Sissons' watermeadow at Marcham Mill; nor that our team (the Frederick Pickersgill Memorial XI) was playing a group of locals of the most moderate ability. The fact was that a fantasy had taken root, and the vision was rekindled. A vision that would lead to that ultimate mixture of fact and illusion, a mixture which only the game of cricket could possibly achieve – the Lord's Taverners.

The next step on this Road to Tarsus (apart from the purchase of

Best foot forward? Richard Kershaw cops a 'daisy-cutter' during the Lord's Taverners v Charlton FC game at Canterbury in July 1985.

some white clothes and a lightweight bat, and the rediscovery of ancient caps and colours), came in Africa. Visiting the then Marxist-ruled spice island of Zanzibar for a BBC documentary, I was appalled to be told that the game of cricket, once played so widely and interracially in East Africa, had been declared a neo-colonialist relic, and counter-revolutionary in tendency. Therefore not a game had been played in Zanzibar for twelve years.

Standing on the galleried verandah of Zanzibar Television, and looking over a flat green park in the centre of the capital that could only have been made for the enjoyment of cricket, I heard the improbable sound of leather upon willow. Abandoning my producer (whom I think was one of the few ladies James Thurber would have approved of), I went down to find a 'net' in progress. Tentatively, a group of black and brown people were practising for what they told me would be the first permitted revival of the sacred game since the Revolution. The revisionist theology behind all this is unimportant: the fact was that having, as Walter Mitty would himself, seized a bat and given the Zanzibaris a few pointers (any childhood reader of G. H. Henty would have felt it his duty), I was invited to play in the 'First Game For Twelve Years', as the visiting English expert.

The teams the next day were made up largely of policemen and prison officers (we played on the prison ground, and most Zanzibaris had spent the previous ten years locking each other up anyway!) and I suspect one or two prisoners were patrolling the boundary. Bats bearing the magic names of Bradman, Miller and Gunn and autographed were dragged from brass-bound chests and from beneath beds. And Cricket was Reborn.

The game was close and decorously passionate. Tea was served from the back of a prison van, in cups from Staffordshire with roses on the saucers. As Walter Mitty would have admitted even more casually than I do now, I succeeded in making the top score, an innings only halted when a Mozambique terrorist plucked my lofted drive from the air on the boundary with an ease he normally reserved for handgrenades.

What preparation for the Taverners!

I met them in a more orthodox, if no less improbable manner. Shortly after I joined the 'Nationwide' presentation team, Frank Bough passed me the telephone one morning, and I was addressed sharply by none other than Jimmy Sewell of the Yard, a celebrated former head of the 'Sweeney', and a man who brooked no nonsense. He told me that, since Frank could not play, I was therefore to be picked up by a police car the next Sunday, and taken to Bramber Court where I would play for the Metropolitan Police against the Lord's Taverners. ('I've got you and Majid Khan as ringers with my own boys,' he said. 'They've got Snow and Cowdrey and Milburn and Edrich and a few more like that.') I hit many a cover drive in the three nights to come; but on the day I was calm as Walter M. would have wished.

I had to open (naturally; Majid Khan was No. 3). On our way to the wicket I was disturbed by my tall opening partner from the fuzz: 'Do you still live in No. 82, the Mansions?' he said as we passed a couple of retired England captains. It later turned out he was my local Battersea beat crime officer, and one of the nicest of men. But at that moment I could not hear – this was indeed Apotheosis!

I made a few (c&b Milburn, if I recall). I basked and dreamed and glowed. And the Taverners asked if I would join them on some future occasion. That night I was positively drowned by the cup of satisfaction that overfloweth.

And so I came to be a Taverner. That means to discover the secret of indicating to the fiercest opposition that you are just a show-biz amateur who needs help and protection, while bashing a few as quickly as possible before they rethink their charity. It means not listening to Terry Wogan, let alone Henry Kelly, when over the Commentator's microphone they heckle one at the crease for slowness and boredom (would they have done that to Hutton or Washbrook?). It means maintaining a proper gravity when moving Mike Smith wider at cover, or Mike Denness closer at gully, or throwing Colin Cowdrey the ball, realising that captains are made, not born.

In short, it means dreaming. Thurber would, I think, be proud of me. Because I have realised the truth; and then ignored it.

I am not really any good at cricket. I do not even really *think* I am good at cricket. I just *like* and *choose* to think so. And a very good night to us all!

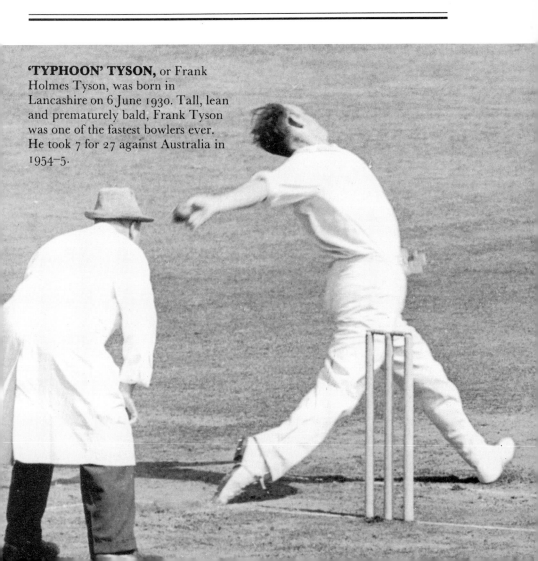

'TYPHOON' TYSON, or Frank Holmes Tyson, was born in Lancashire on 6 June 1930. Tall, lean and prematurely bald, Frank Tyson was one of the fastest bowlers ever. He took 7 for 27 against Australia in 1954–5.

1. E. Barratt
2. A. W. Ridley
3. W. H. Patterson
4. J. M. Read
5. Rev. F. F. J Greenfield
6. E. F. S. Tylecote
7. W. Bates
8. J. Hide
9. G. Ulyett
10. A. G. Steel
11. W. W. Read

12. Rev. V. F. Royle
13. J. Crossland
14. R. Pilling
15. W. Flowers
16. Unidentified
17. Unidentified
18. G. G. Herne
19. Hon. M. B. Hawke
20. W. G. Grace
21. Hon. Ivo Bligh
22. W. Mycroft

CRICKETERS, 1883

23. R. G. Barlow
24. A. J. Webbe
25. I. D. Walker
26. Lord Harris
27. E. Lockwood
28. T. Emmett
29. C. T. Studd
30. A. Shrewsbury
31. A. Shaw
32. A. N. Hornby
33. E. Peate
34. F. Morley
35. J. E. K. Studd
36. G. B. Studd
37. W. Barnes
38. R. A. H. Mitchell
39. L. C. Docker
40. M. C. Kemp
41. A. P. Lucas
42. J. Shuter

HUGH DE SELINCOURT

*'A wily old man came in to bat and, facing
Gauvinier after a one to leg, played the last five
balls like an ancient book ...'*

TILLINGFOLD PLAY
WILMINGHURST

Gauvinier's experience in running the Tillingfold side for some years
had led him to pay small heed to any bad preliminary rumours as to
the composition of the Saturday team. The list was posted in the village
on Thursday evening and unless he had official information that a man
could not turn out, he left it at that.

As in all clubs, of course, on some Saturdays eighteen Tillingfold
men were keen for a game, on others eight; and on the latter occasions
men who groused to the effect that they were never asked to play,
invariably had a prior engagement or grumblingly consented to 'make
one', inferring, as was often painfully true, that they would not have
been asked if anyone else had been available. Getting up a side is no
easier at Tillingfold than it is elsewhere, but the games which Tillingfold
played were better games than he had ever played elsewhere.

The ride to the ground or to the conveyance that was to take the
team from the village square to the opponents' ground was always an
anxious ride for the good Gauvinier, skipper of the Tillingfold eleven.

The ride was more anxious than usual this Saturday, when Tillingfold
were playing Wilminghurst, pet opponents, with whom many close
battles had been fought in past seasons. Two good men were genuinely
unable to play; the team's best bowler was seedy but would turn out if
he could. Report credited Wilminghurst with a specially hot side.

No one was about in the square. The conveyance waited dolefully
empty. Old John Meadows limping by to the 'pub' smiled to Gauvinier:
'Got to scratch the match, I hear.' He had played for Tillingfold forty
years ago and did not approve of the way young fellows went on
nowadays, 'what with motor cycles, pickchers and sech'.

'Oh, I hope not!' Gauvinier answered.

'Can't raise a side, I'm told,' the old fellow continued gleefully.

'Oh, we'll do that if we have to rope in the chaps from the Union.'

'Ah, things ain't what they was: not by a long chalk.'

Gauvinier turned away to meet Tom Rutherford, slow bowler, staunch cricketer, who had spent many years in Tasmania and advocated in gentle undertones drastic measures with slackers and grousers.

'Got a side?' he asked.

'Don't know yet!'

'Not going to scratch?' he inquired.

'Scratch!' snapped Gauvinier.

They both laughed. Then went through the side: eight men and a boy were certainties and among the men were two the mention of whose names caused bitter mirth to the friends.

'We're in for the deuce of a hiding.'

'Damn good job, too.'

Sam Bird, the umpire, trod softly into the square, careful not to jolt himself or to stamp holes in the road with his bulk. He announced like a conspirator, smiling at a secret joke:

'I'm told Mr Marling is playing for Wilminghurst.' He surveyed the sky with beady eyes and addressed it. 'Saw he made ninety-one for 'Orsam against Littlehampton t'other day in twenty-three minutes.'

But Sam Bird could not remain disheartening: his devotion to Tillingfold cricket and the Tillingfold skipper was deep and unshakable.

'However,' he said slowly, tapping the words out with a fat finger on Gauvinier's coat, 'at cricket – you – never – know. Never.'

Eight men and a boy, Gauvinier was grimly thinking; it would be the first time in seven seasons he had come on the field without a full side. Nice thing, Tillingfold turning out short!

It was not a cheery team that left the village square at 1.58 for their Saturday afternoon sport. 'A bloomin' funeral, more like,' as one man put it.

Arrived, they straggled sadly over the field to the pavilion in the far corner of the ground. It was obvious that Wilminghurst had got a hot side, even before their captain Southernhay's bright assertion of the fact to Gauvinier, who was not in the mood to find him disgustingly sympathetic. 'What a pity! It does spoil a game so, doesn't it, when one side is too vastly superior?'

'Oh, we're not beaten yet!' laughed Gauvinier.

'Marling's turned out for us. Hit up ninety-one – '

'Yes, I know. Let's toss.'

'Ninety-one in twenty-three minutes is pretty good going. And this ground's faster. You cry.'

'Heads.'

'It is.'

'You bat first.'

It was the first time Gauvinier had ever put opponents in as the result of sheer cowardice. In their present mood his men were not good for twenty runs. But he felt guilty and ashamed.

'Come on!' he told them in the visitors' room. 'I've put 'em in! We'll get 'em on the run! Then knock off the runs.'

'Some 'opes!' was chorused.

He did not stop to argue, but hurried out to tackle the unpleasant job of asking for a substitute. For two he could not bring himself to ask.

Hardly a catch was flung from one to another as the team (eight men, a boy, and a substitute) proceeded sadly into the field, followed closely by Marling, the cheeriest soul who ever gripped a bat handle, chatting and laughing with Southernhay, obviously awed at opening the innings in such brilliant company. Marling took middle and leg, made his block with two rapid little taps and stood up, twiddling his bat round, surveying the field with a confident beam that meant business.

Gauvinier took the first over; keen as Lucifer to get a quick wicket, knowing well how shaky Marling could be before he felt the ball clean and hard upon his bat. Gauvinier was made to begin the game; once in it, all odious preliminaries were immediately forgotten. There was something to bite into, something good and solid. But he was in for a penitential half-hour, which he vaguely sensed as he eyed his placed field for the last time – three men who were safe to hold a catch, two real good triers, the rest ... oh, well, it was decent of them to turn out at all, especially when one remembered how devilishly hard a cricket ball must seem to them. Gauvinier bowled medium-fast, using his height well. His first ball Marling played out to freely and returned to him at a fair pace along the carpet; his second ball beat Marling and came within a couple of inches of the off bail. The wicket-keeper grinned cheerfully as he lobbed the ball back, wagging his head to one side knowingly. Gauvinier was so braced that he felt no annoyance to hear mid-off, whose fielding was a calamity, draw attention to his presence by remarking, 'That's the stuff to give the troops.'

The third ball struck the edge of Marling's bat and flew straight at short slip, who stumbled back as he saw it coming, stumbled forward as the ball smacked into his large hand, and fell, dropping as easy a catch as short slip will ever have in this wicked world where no catch at short slip is really easy. Gauvinier forced a grin upon his face, forced a shout of 'Bad luck' from his lips to the sorry fieldsman, and turned to deliver his next ball, with black fury boiling through his veins. A yorker: you could see the wicket shake as it shaved the leg stump and went for two byes, which Marling picked himself up to run, after his huge missed effort to wipe a full toss out of the ground.

Gauvinier was not consoled by Marling's kindly remark: 'A squeak, that! Your luck's well out!'

The gay batsman could stand no more of this nonsense: the next ball he drove hard – a lovely shot, bang against the wooden pavilion, terrifying mid-off by his proximity to its flight.

Gauvinier curbed his bitter wish to say how wise it was not to have put a hand out at that one: might possibly have stopped it. He listened without a word to mid-off's remark that he appreciated a good hit when an opponent made it; he was, at any rate, a true sportsman in speech, whatever his more practical deficiencies might be. The last ball of the over was a slower one, which Marling, slightly mistiming, lifted towards Jenkins in the deep. Gauvinier had a vivid imagination, but he never imagined for an instant that the good Jenkins would hold such a catch. He had to walk three steps forward and wait for the ball to fall into his hands: instead of which Jenkins, pleased with himself for noticing that it was a catch at all, ran back, shouting 'That's mine,' then, like a wounded bird, hurried to the right, then to the left, and finally dashing forward as the ball fell, stumbled on to his hands. He got up, walked in a leisurely way after the ball, flipping his stung hand, found it and hurled it in, furious and convinced that the catch was well out of his reach.

During these manoeuvres, the batsmen had run three, and Marling with a laughing apology for bagging the bowling faced the fastish but erratic Longman, who took three little steps to the wicket and delivered the ball with the unexpected suddenness of a catapult. An early success inspired him. On his day he could be deadly, and Gauvinier hoped this might be his day: he hoped it very much, but Longman's first ball was a hot long hop, shoulder high, which Marling hit out of the ground for six.

'I like them,' he remarked to the wicketkeeper, while the wall was climbed and the ball retrieved.

Poor Longman found the wait of an inordinate length. He stood on fire with his blush, silently watching the man climb back over the wall to his place. Longman's second ball was also short, on the off, and beaten past cover to the boundary; his third was driven for two; his fourth went somewhere near the wicket; his fifth, a desperately fast one, was short on the leg, and effortlessly lifted over that accursed wall; his last was outside the batsman's reach on the off.

Runs were coming at a terrible pace; and the pace continued growing faster still when Gauvinier tried a double change. The hundred went up for no wickets. The wicketkeeper supposed grimly that they'd make about three hundred and declare.

'Oh, you never know your luck!' Gauvinier bravely answered.

'We've got ours. This time.'

Never had the Tillingfold team been seen with tails so lowly drooping or apparently with such good reason. Gauvinier put on his first bowlers again, changing their ends. Marling faced Longman, ran out and drove a good-length ball clean out of the ground – a huge hit. The bowler's face was a study. Marling must have decided where the next ball was going before it was delivered, for he was yards out of his ground to what luckily chanced to be a short long hop; he waved his bat at it, fell forward and was ignominiously stumped.

108 – 1 – 89, the score-board read.

A stranger came in, wearing a Sussex Martlet's cap.

'Lord! Look at this!' said Jenkins. 'I'm blowed if we've done with 'em yet.'

But the stranger, deceived no doubt by the queer suddenness of Longman's delivery, played across his first ball and retired, with his off stump leaning well back – a very pleasant sight to the Tillingfold team. No more wickets and no more runs that over. Gauvinier bowled a maiden, which was so refreshing after the orgy of runs that the tails of the Tillingfold team visibly rose; but they drooped during Longman's next, which he started with a juicy full toss and followed by a juicier long hop knee-high on the leg side – a gift of eight runs which was quietly taken; then he settled down and the last four balls were a good length.

Gauvinier is as likely to remember the next over as he is likely to remember that disastrous first. Southernhay, the Wilminghurst skipper, who was set, snicked his first ball and the wicketkeeper took a palpable catch, a good one too, on the leg side. Gauvinier's next ball shaved the new-comer's wicket, and his third, the new-comer being too anxious to emulate the happy Marling, hit the middle peg. Wilminghurst's chief hitter came in next, a familiar figure, obviously resolved to show the visitors what the home side could do in the way of hard hitting, but he, too, began too soon, and drove this first ball back to Gauvinier, who jumped to hold a nice catch. His last ball yorked number seven.

119 – 6 – 0.

Tom Rutherford came up, quivering with excitement.

'One hundred and fifty on this ground means only ninety on ours. Easily. We're not done yet.'

Sam Bird backed him well up. 'That's right!' he slowly declared with immense emphasis. 'And they've not got one hundred and fifty, I may mention.'

'No. Nor will,' declared the wicketkeeper. 'Lord! what a lark to beat 'em with a side like this!'

'We'll make a show, anyhow,' Tom Rutherford remarked quietly, wisely fearful of over-confidence.

'Any of the new crowd bowlers?' he inquired of their umpire.

'Can't say.'

'Man in!'

They sprang to their places – a different side.

Seven runs came from the erratic Longman's first five, then a beauty knocked the off stump clean out of its hole.

A wily old man came in to bat, and, facing Gauvinier after a one to leg, played the last five balls like an ancient book. If only that beggar could keep a length, thought Gauvinier ardently of the solid, unsmiling Longman. But the beggar could not. Came a full toss that went for two byes, a long hop that went for two runs – the two balls would have been a gift of twelve runs to Marling – one that thumped the clumsy batsman on the chest woke him up, perhaps, for he hit the next one for four and the one after for three. One hundred and thirty was up on the scoreboard.

Gauvinier's unuttered curse was modified by hope at having a go at that batsman and not at the wily old man. 'He'll cow-shot a good length ball for four and hit across a half-volley.' He itched to have his chance; bet a hundred to one he'd get him. His chance came. He bowled the ball he wanted to – a half-volley slightly slower – round whirled the bat, well across, down went the wicket. Gauvinier purred to himself like a happy cat, or any bowler who has done precisely what he wanted to do, foreseeing the right ball, and bowling it. An absurd call ran the wily old man out. Longman knocked the last wicket down with a furious full toss. Tillingfold had one hundred and thirty-nine to make to win, after one hundred had been on the board for no wickets.

'That's about seventy-five on our ground,' Tom Rutherford kept quietly assuring every member of the team in turn. Gauvinier in sad silence pondered on the batting order. There was no doubt about number one. Ernest Settatree was a good and careful bat, keen all through, and with any luck might stay there. Lord! how he missed old John McLeod and Trine and Dick Fanshawe and Sid Smith. Still, there were the two Carruthers – the wicketkeeper and his young brother Bill – strong as lions, and, when they got going, dangerous: very dangerous, when, oh! when, they got going! There was half-an-hour's play before tea. If four wickets fell ... hence loathed melancholy.

'Bill,' he cried cheerfully, 'what about first knock?'

Bill blushed and laughed. 'May as well, first as last.'

'Watch the first few, you young fool,' said his brother severely, 'and you'll be right as rain.'

'Not 'alf. You bet. Not if it snows ink!' said Bill, too thrilled at the prospect of going out to bat first to talk perfect sense.

'You've only got to pat 'em to get four here,' said Jenkins, beaming encouragement.

'Oh, I'll pat 'em all right!' quoth Bill.

His elder brother vehemently begged him 'not to act silly' – a way with elder brothers – and Bill replied that he was as Gawd made him –

or words to that effect – while he nervously buckled on his pads, and asked young Settatree to let him take first over that he might 'get his' as soon as possible; and again elder brother adjured him with savage vehemence 'not to act so damned silly'.

'The young blighter!' Ted Carruthers bitterly remarked as the batsmen walked out to the wicket. 'He'd be a decent bat if he wouldn't act silly.'

'Number three, Ted; I'm four, Tom Rutherford five, Jenkins six—'

'Our tail ought to wag, I don't think!' began Ted with grim humour. 'Couldn't raise . . .' But he stopped. The first ball was being bowled. Eyes stared tensely, to see Bill lunge feebly at it, not a hit, not a shot, not even a cow-shot. The ball struck the edge of the bat and soared over slip's head. They ran two.

'Steady, Bill!' roared the enraged Ted, and muttered to his neighbours, 'You'd think he'd never held a bat in his hand before, the young turnip!'

Poor Ted, wounded in his family pride, could only groan as Bill met the next ball with the same futile half-hearted lunge, a shot he never indulged in at the nets, but kept exclusively for matches – hit the ball this time and lifted it high and straight and easy into the hands of deep mid-on.

He came in laughing loudly to hide his miserable discomfiture. 'Haven't kept you waiting long, Ted,' he breezily remarked, and then unable to keep it up, lamented: 'What I needs make that assish scoop for –'

'Yes, you wants a good slap behind yer ears,' growled his brother, choosing a batting-glove. Out he strode, chin forward to maintain the family honour.

Impatience, however, was a family failing, for, much to little brother's glee, Ted viciously lashed at the first ball he received and missed it apparently by feet.

'Look at that now! Look at that! And he tells me not to have a punch!' cried Bill convulsed.

But Gauvinier and Tom Rutherford were thankful to observe that he was steadier after that first absurdity, and he and Settatree settled down to play good, sound cricket, picking the right one to hit, and hitting it hard and clean. Every ball was watched with excitement; every run cheered.

Thirty-two was on the board when the teams came in for tea.

Settatree, not out twelve; Ted Carruthers, not out fourteen.

Tensity relaxed during tea, which was taken on a long trestle-table under trees outside the pavilion: huge plates of bread and butter, piled slices of plum cake, tea from an enormous urn. Laughter and chat and vigorous munching; gulps of hot tea, cup after cup.

Tillingfold ate heartily, talked gaily; after the disastrous beginning they were making a good fight of it.

Gauvinier, lighting a cigarette, urged the reluctant umpires out into the sun. The tensity of the game was resumed. Both men went on batting like books, taking no risks, running well, hitting the loose ones hard and true. There was every sign of a stand. Forty went up on the board.

And then one cocked up at young Settatree, point fell forward, rolled over, held up the ball, shouting: 'How's that?' Young Settatree looked towards the bowler's umpire, who hesitated then half-raised a diffident finger; so he appealed to the other umpire, Sam Bird.

'Ah! I couldn't rightly see,' Sam Bird faltered and called out stoutly to the bowler's umpire: 'How was it?'

'Out!' he snapped, looking at no one, and young Settatree had to retire, a very disgruntled man.

'It hit the ground first, I'll swear,' said young Settatree, almost weeping, to Gauvinier, whom he passed on his way out to bat.

'Rotten luck, anyhow. You were batting better than I've ever seen you bat before.'

'Give it 'em, skipper, for the Lord's sake!'

Gauvinier went out, sincerely hoping that he would, and clearly praying in his own mind that the bowler might not find his blind spot on the leg stump – large and fatal always for his first few balls.

Providence and the bowler were kind, for down came a shortish good-length ball on the off, which went past cover to the boundary, his favourite shot. The next, pitched further up, he used his reach to drive pleasantly back to mid-off, who was glad to stop it, and retreated a few yards at the bowler's suggestion. Thank goodness he was seeing them! Thank goodness, too, it did not occur to the bowler to put a man at extra-cover.

Up to nine he kept count of his runs, though he had no wish to do so; it was unsettling; made him in a hurry. Quietly he stayed there; not feeling that each ball might be his last; not visualising horrid mis-hits, silly mistakes that would be his undoing. The score was mounting; they were putting up seventy. Ted Carruthers was batting soundly, hitting the loose ball hard; two fours: ah! there was eight going up. No disgrace now. It would be fun to put the hundred up. Oh, here was a good one: shortish on the off, again. Full in the centre of the bat. And no extra-cover, he chuckled to himself, watching the ball thump against the wooden pavilion.

The bowler hopefully set mid-off wider and deeper, and forgetting Gauvinier's length and reach, bowled what would have been a good-length ball to a shorter man. The Tillingfold captain stepped out and hit a half-volley straight past where mid-off was standing before his

177

hopeful shifting – a satisfactory drive to watch as it sped over the fast ground to the boundary.

Ninety went up on the score-board, and the fieldsmen looked at the figures with earnest faces. The Tillingfold team, too excited to sit, kept hurrying to the score-box to see the exact score, cheering each run. Every now and then some supporter of the home team would utter a stentorian request to know what Wilminghurst were up to, now.

And the batsmen had that set, unhurried manner that is so depressing to a fielding side.

There came two maidens as the century approached – two maidens which put the field alert on their toes and dug the batsmen in. Why hurry? After the first three balls of the next over, played confidently back, the strain proved too great for the bowler; he sent his first bad ball for five overs, a full toss which Ted Carruthers swept out of the ground for six, and the hundred went up amid roars of delight. Then a long hop pulled fiercely against the wall. He must be nearing his fifty. But out he leapt and lashed viciously at the last ball; he might have been bowled, he might have been stumped, he might have been caught; but none of these sad things happened. He made a complete miss: the ball shaved the off stump; the wicketkeeper fumbled it. Ted scrambled back.

'Steady, Ted; steady!' came the shriek of his young brother, timid to death of the family impatience.

Gauvinier took two nice fours in the next over, and then for the first time the idea entered his mind, anxious till that moment merely to make a decent show and avert disgrace, that they were well on the way towards winning the match! Heavens! They must be near one hundred and twenty now – very near. Curse it! He wished he hadn't realised it, and could just have gone steadily batting on. He finished the over, nervous as when he came out to bat: superstitious really.

Ted hit another four. Shouts of joy acclaimed the fact of his fifty. Then he took another dip, oh! a wild one! There was a nasty snick, slip dived forward, tossed up the ball. 127 – 3 – 52.

'Well played, Ted!' shouted Gauvinier, with a sinking in the stomach at the thought of how long and thin was the tail. Twelve runs – three fours, twelve runs – three fours beat rhythmically through his brain.

Tom Rutherford walked in, his face set, a trier every inch of him. Good man. But the sun was on his glasses; his sight not so good as it had been.

A leg-bye. They ran an easy one.

Marling had been put on. Gauvinier, strung up, had hardly noticed the change of bowling, and had not noticed at all the change of field. Came a medium-fast short one on the off – 'Here's one of them,' he thought; 'a gift,' and hit it full and strong, to look up as he ran forward, to find it travelling straight into the hands of extra cover. He stopped dead in surprise to watch the catch, a good one at the pace the ball was travelling, then walked miserably back to the pavilion, cursing his idiocy. Marling frankly rejoiced. 128 – 4 – 46. Jenkins took his place. Marling sent him down a fast yorker on the leg stump, which the ball shaved. The wicketkeeper side-stepped too late, kicked it: two runs. Jenkins waved his bat at the next ball and was bowled. 130 – 5 – 0. Oh, Lord! To be so near! Well, anyhow it was a damned good game.

'Fancy being such a fool as to beat it straight into his hands!' Gauvinier spoke to Heaven.

Longman was walking in. He had one shot and one only. A little half-step forward, a mighty circular lurch to leg: a good-length ball on the middle or leg stump hit the bat and went for four. At everything else he pushed his bat daintily sideways slowly and cunningly and always ineffectually.

Marling was taking no risks. He bowled a good-length ball on the leg stump – right on to the swinging bat, and, with astonishment, saw it go for four. Gauvinier began to laugh, almost hysterical with amusement and the game's thrill. Wild cheers rent the air. Another good-length ball hit the lurching bat, but not quite full this time, so that it missed the fieldsman, brought up after the last shot. He saved the four, though; and they ran two. Only three more! Only three more! But shortish ones on the off followed, at which Longman dabbed warily, and luckily failed to touch.

The first ball of the next over beat Tom Rutherford all ends up and passed not more than one inch over the bails. At the second, anxious to make sure of the game, he lunged gallantly out, hit, skied, and was caught and bowled.

Followed the boy, and all the fieldsmen crowded cruelly near. But all four balls he gamely managed to stop.

'Will he now, oh, will he bowl on his bat?' Gauvinier ached to think, watching, with horror, Marling place another man on the leg side.

It is difficult for any bowler to realise that a man can have one shot and one only like a mechanical toy. Down came the good-length ball on the middle stump – hit the swinging bat, flew between the fieldsmen – struck the wall.

Too late Marling realised his mistake. He sent a slow, high full toss, an absolutely fatal ball to Longman, who tried to pat it with his bat as with a tennis racket, and was bowled.

But the impossible had happened. Tillingfold with eight men and a boy had beaten Wilminghurst, after a hundred had stood on the scoreboard, for the first time in the annals of Tillingfold cricket, for no wickets.

LEGENDARY LADS

Warwick Armstrong (1879–1947) accompanies Victor Trumper (1877–1915) to open the batting in the Australia *v* England First Test at Birmingham in May 1909. Armstrong was a cricketer on the grand scale who, on the eve of his retirement, weighed 22 stone. He captained Australia ten times without meeting defeat. A spin-bowler and attacking batsman, his unhurried lunge from the front foot made fine use of his powerful physique. He scored 159 against South Africa at Johannesburg during the 1902–3 season and bowled 6 for 35 against England at Lord's in 1909. His companion in the picture, Victor Trumper, first gained fame in Australia with his initial century of 292 not out for NSW *v* Tasmania in 1898–9. In England the following summer he hit 135 not out at Lord's in only his second Test Match. In 1902, during a wet summer, he made 2,570 runs and eleven centuries. A lissom and co-ordinated athlete, he died in 1915 at the early age of thirty-seven, leaving behind a legend of brilliance, skill and personal charm.

J.B. BOOTH

'I cannot write an account of Ranji's batting,
because I am not a really great poet' –
ANDREW LANG

A CHAT WITH RANJI

A GREAT CRICKETER REMEMBERS

26 August 1935. Test matches, whatever may be their virtues or their vices, have, besides a trick of making history, the effect of rousing Laudator Temporis Acti from his slumbers; and in present-day conditions the gentleman is too often more than a little peevish.

When he comes in with his old music, the note is sadly apt to be harsh. Perhaps it was always so, and from now and then having right on his side he has grown to consider himself infallible, and to hug himself joyfully at the thought that he has outlived the best of everything. In such a case, an occasional antidote has its merits. There is nothing new in this; twenty-odd years ago the cricketing Laudator was much the same as he is today, and was all the better for the occasional antidote expertly administered.

Thoughts such as these sent me to an old diary, in which were scrawled notes of a talk with Prince Ranjitsinhji in 1912, when, one evening during the Scarborough festival, he chatted freely of the sportsmen of the past, and of changes in the cricket world. It was a cold, wet summer, and, fresh from India, the Jam Sahib shivered and dug his hands deep in his trouser pockets. Those same hands had not, however, lost their cunning, and more than once brought off the lightning catch that made their owner famous in the field. Age had told a little; the Prince was slower between wickets, but the great batsman was still there, and the panther-like spring at any fielding chance seemed as lithe as of old. Some of the Pavilionites, whose own chests had 'slipped', professed to regret that the Jam was 'putting it on', but most of the girth was amassed in the dressing-room. Feeling the cold intensely, each day he bought something fresh at the hosier's – an extra vest, another cholera belt, a woollen waistcoat – and had the cold lasted he certainly would not have been able to pass out of the dressing-room door.

Shrewd, modest, good-humoured, the Jam had strong views on the game he loved, and in that old diary I find some hastily written notes of his views and opinions as he expressed them one evening that week to a few friends. He didn't believe in 'Test temperament'; in fact, jeered at it. 'There's no such thing,' he said contemptuously, 'except amongst pavilion cricketers.' Then someone asked the obvious question. 'Charles Fry is the best bat in the world at the moment,' he declared roundly, 'because he's the soundest. He can play on any wicket. That's the test. Some fellows are better on slow wickets, some on fast; they're all the same to Fry.'

Then came the obvious question. 'On the whole, I'd call W. G. the greatest cricketer of all time. Not that he was a greater bat than half a dozen, at least, but because he was a pioneer. W. G. was the first of the great all-rounders. Look at the history of the game, from the old top-hat days, the days of Mynn, Carpenter, Pilch, and the rest. One, you read, was a back player; another depended on a forward game; another was a stonewaller; another a hitter. Each had a speciality he relied on. Grace could do anything, and, in spite of his weight, was a magnificent field, to say nothing of his bowling. If it hadn't been for the old man there would have been no Steel, Ulyett, Lohmann, Barnes, Hirst, Jackson and the others.'

'How would you compare W. G. with Trumper?' someone asked.

'You can't compare the incomparable. Each at his best was incomparable. Trumper too, was a pioneer. Twenty years ago at Eton he'd never have got his colours, simply because his strokes were unorthodox. All reformers start as heretics. Look at what they had to say about Jessop.'

As to the greatest bowler, he would not commit himself. In make and action, I remember, he seemed to think Tom Richardson the ideal fast bowling machine. 'In spite of his pace, the naturalness and ease of his action took so little out of him that he could – and did – bowl unchanged for hours, with no diminution in pace, length and sting.' The modern fast bowler – 'modern' being the year 1912 – with a tendency to lose length and become exhausted after a dozen overs, the Jam Sahib seemed to regard a trifle contemptuously, as a sort of hothouse plant.

Taking things as a whole, the Prince roundly asserted that the general average of cricket had vastly improved in his own time. 'When I began,' he said, 'there were only about a hundred really first-class players in the game. Now there are at least four times as many.'

The Jam Sahib had one surprise for most of his little audience. 'Of course, W. G. didn't have modern wickets to bat on,' observed someone. 'Grounds have improved enormously.' And to our vast astonishment Ranji would not have it for a moment. 'Don't you believe it!' he

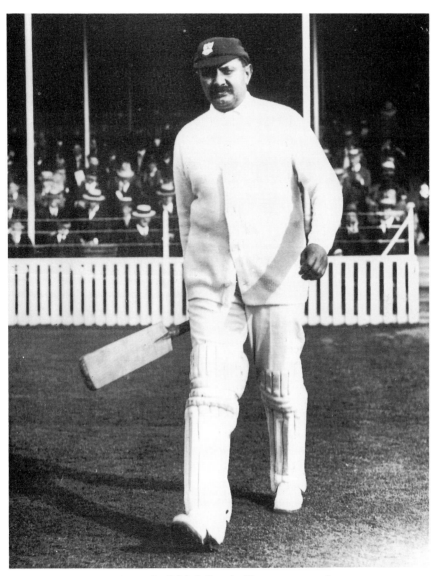

Ranji ... 'he didn't believe in Test temperament'.

retorted. 'Forty years ago there were some wickets every bit as good as the best we have today. W. G. told me that himself. Lord's, the Oval, the St Lawrence ground at Canterbury and about half a dozen others were as good then as now.'

Out of the recent past come these haphazard reflections of one who was, perhaps, the greatest batting reformer in the history of the game, the player of whom Andrew Lang wrote: 'I cannot write an account of Ranji's batting, because I am not a really great poet.'

*'Wilt thou go in at t'fall of twentieth wicket,
Isaiah?'*

FATHER OF THE FLOCK

Probably, and no doubt he would have been vastly disgruntled if any other claimant to the honour had usurped him, Ikey Hodgson was the worst batsman and most slovenly fielder who ever lived.

But nobbut just. His bosom pal, Billy Slinn, ran him a close second. Once, unfortunately, early in his career, when he was raw and unsophisticated, Billy had twice scored double figures in the same match. In the total there would be snicks through the slips which butter-fingered fieldsmen had failed to accept; there would be shots that had bounced in eccentric, non-geometric orbits from a wavering, horizontal bat to points unknown in the glossary of fieldsmanship. Nevertheless, whether through accident or design, and all available evidence points to the former, Billy had suffered the indignity of being unable to prevent the ball and his bat coming into contact often enough, so that ten had twice been registered against his name.

No such misdemeanour ever sullied Ikey's escutcheon. He was not a cricketer. To him, batting and fielding were, as far as personal

participation was concerned, distasteful chores to be avoided or, at worst, evil necessities that the idiosyncracies of the game demanded, and were to be undertaken with the minimum of interest and effort. Had that multitude of iniquitous forms that sift into our private lives been in existence 150 years ago, he would have entered, 'Isaac Hodgson; born 15 November 1828, in the township of Bradford; occupation, professional bowler.'

Or more likely he would have ignored it and been sought by tipstaff and bailiff. They would not have found him, for Ikey was the peripatetic opponent, the shadow of William Clarke's All England XI, the haunter and nightmare of his batsmen.

'The best man for a XXII now living', a critic pronounced him when he was sweeping, like the sword of Gideon, through the ranks of the tourists' champions. Not, mark you, for an eleven. No team of any standing could afford to include Ikey and Billy, to see their last wicket fall at number eight and to field nine players. Once, in a moment of desperation, the United All England XI had invited their co-operation, but in six innings they made a grand total of one run. There is no record extant of the number of catches they dropped or gently bouncing balls they failed to gather, but, it seems, the sad conclusion was reached that their talents were outweighed by their imperfections and the invitations ceased.

But, for a XXII, their very failings were their virtues. With 22 fieldsmen to disseminate, the ground was reminiscent of Piccadilly Circus on Mafeking night, and sixth or seventh longstop were acceptable posts to Ikey and Billy.

A village captain, faced with the unenviable necessity of making out his batting order, risked a vendetta of Corsican bitterness by being compelled to insult one of the rustics by requesting, 'Wilt thou go in at t'fall of twentieth wicket, Isaiah?'

Ikey and Billy lifted that burden from his shoulders. There was no need to tell them. They never looked at the score book or the list of names pinned behind the dressing tent door. Twenty-first and twenty-second were their positions by right, by usage, by custom, and whether precedence was decided by rote, by tossing a coin, by alphabetical order or by seniority was a matter of indifference. In the polite language of the time they rarely 'troubled the scorers' and would probably have lost their way if they had been compelled to cross the wicket.

William Clarke (known as Old Clarke) was a famous cricketer, a native of Nottingham. He once invited the Sheffield Cricket Club to meet Nottingham for £500, with the suggestion that the stumps should be pitched 'half-way between Sheffield and Nottingham, each party bearing its own expenses'; for besides being a man of mighty deeds Old Clarke was a great lover of money.

So he assembled his All England XI playing anywhere, town or village, where he could be guaranteed a 'gate', often taking on 18 or 22 opponents and the two 'home' umpires as well. And, being a man of great cunning, he laid as many side bets as possible with the village yokels, who, when their bellies were full of ale, were apt to think that the sun shone out of their village heroes.

After the match, his top hat brimming with golden sovereigns, Old Clarke assembled his men in the local pub, rewarded them scantily from his fortune, and, if they murmured in dissatisfaction at their miserly stipend, advised them to 'take their hooks back home'. There were plenty more in the South and Midlands anxious to take their places.

The match against All England was a great day for the Yorkshire villagers. The delvers from the quarries, the handloom weavers from their cottages, the wool combers from the water-driven mills, the shepherds, the blacksmith, the saddle maker, the wheel-wright, assembled in the village field. They brought their pints of ale from the pub and stuck them in niches in the dry stone wall. They gobbled their sandwiches in the interval. Mellowed by the sun and the ale, they cheered their heroes vociferously and heckled and tormented their enemies.

Superciliously the Internationals smiled at the cross-batted lunges of the villagers; they laughed uproariously at the incongruous, unorientated swipes of the corn miller and the potter, but, sometimes, they had laughed too soon. For Ikey and Billy would be playing for the village. Not by birth, residence or upbringing would they be entitled to do so. Nevertheless, there they were.

When the villagers went out to field, the grimaces of disdain were wiped away, the mockery and derision stifled. Aided by a splinter or two of outcropping millstone grit, belligerent Billy whistled the ball round the batsmen's skulls, or, hitting the serrated edge of a dandelion root, shot it with supersonic vehemence along the ground. Carpenter and Hayward's billycocks may have wobbled in awe, George Parr and Julius Caesar's shins tingled in dismay, but nevertheless, it was Ikey whom these master batsmen feared the most.

Year in, year out, he and Billy followed the circus round the North of England. Wherever the tourists played, the 'twins' were engaged to bowl them out, and Ikey relied not on groundsman's aid, Pennine undulation or local umpire's bias. The patriarch of Yorkshire's greatest cricketing glory, Ikey bowled slow left arm, relying on his perfect length and subtle flight. Day after day, week after week, year after year, he faced the same batsmen, the stars of their day, the select of England, yet never could they master his sublime skill. In the six seasons 1860–1865 he took 475 wickets against the tourists alone, besides playing in county matches and club matches whenever the tourists had fled to some other corner of the realm.

Poor Ikey. He died in 1867 at the early age of thirty-nine; but he had lit a beacon, a fire that was not to be quenched in a century of cricket. 'I will make thy seed as the dust of the earth,' the Lord had promised Abraham. So it was to be with Ikey. Ted Peate was eleven years old, Bobby Peel ten when Ikey finally left the field. Both might have seen him, as children, when their imaginations were most vivid, at the zenith of his skill. And the line was to continue, forever unbroken, through George Hirst, Wilfred Rhodes, Roy Kilner, Hedley Verity, Arthur Booth, Johnny Wardle and Don Wilson.

Somewhere, in a Bradford graveyard, is an old, moss-encrusted stone. When I retire, like Old Mortality, with rag and cleaning spirit I will etch away the rust and mildew. And there I shall unearth the epitaph to the Father of the Flock:

> Isaac Hodgson, rest his soul,
>   Could never bat but always bowl.
> Through many years the tourists' skill
>   Was subjugate to Ikey's will.
> They took their stance with vain defiance
>   Against his subtle skill and science.
> Progenitor, great Almus Pater,
>   Bowler divine, but batting hater.

THE BAND AT PLAY

In Festivals or Cricket Weeks
Muffled or intermittent squeaks
Denote the presence of a band,
But what I fail to understand
Is why half-hearted use is made
Of local instrumental aid.
If you have music, I submit
That you should make the most of it.
The band might play the batsman in,
That stirring march from 'Lohengrin'
Would fill the bill; now how about
A tune to play the batsman out?
No difficulty here at all,
Handel's C Major 'March in Saul'.
'The Rosary,' 'Lest we forget',
'Funeral March of Marionette',
'Good-bye for Ever' (this to be
A second innings threnody) . . .
Such melodies as these I think,
(Culled and arranged by Herman Finck),
As incidental to the action
Should merit general satisfaction.

RALPH WOTHERSPOON

E. B. OSBORN

*'Let us then consent to the presence of bands at
matches played on the grounds of lunatic asylums,
but refuse to invite them to Lord's . . .'*

MUSICAL CRICKET

30 August 1910. In those pellucid intervals when they are not cal-
culating averages and percentages to several places of decimals or
chronicling So-and-so's 99th wicket or 999th run, certain publicists (let
us choose the name that dignifies rather than the name that degrades
the business of writing round about cricket) wax magniloquent on the
subject of the rights and wrongs of the crowd at a cricket match. Two
years ago it was the question of the tea interval which disturbed the
minds of these friends of the people and dislocated their grammar. Last
year they discussed the subject of suspensions of play while the ground
was recovering from a drenching (last season it was a case of 'the rain
it raineth every day,' and the weather has been even more exasperating
this year) and assured us that such breaks in the entertainment provided
for those who had paid down their money at the turnstiles could no
longer be tolerated.

These agitations, sad to say, were not without effect. Tea intervals
were dropped on several county grounds, where the authorities, for
mercenary reasons, think more of satisfying the sixpenny spectators
than of the comfort of cricketers, who after all are not members of
music-hall troupes, and have a right to indulge in tea-and-talk when
the whole civilised world is doing the same. And this season, as a result
of last year's agitation by the friends of the professional spectator, weird
engines have been provided to protect the pitch from the effects of
rainfall, though nothing has been done – for nothing can be done – to
prevent the drenched outfield from being scarred and cut up by the
men who are scouting out and cannot keep their footing.

It is now proposed to 'enliven' county cricket matches for the benefit
of spectators by means of bands, and the experiment has actually been
tried at Lord's – Lord's of all places in Cricketdom. There can be no
objection, of course, to instrumental music during the luncheon interval
when those who do not care to leave the ground, preferring sandwiches
and cricket gossip to a formal meal, often find that time trickles away

slowly, spasmodically, reluctantly – like the contents of a full bottle. Nor, if the musicians chose to stay and watch the match, would any rational person refuse them the opportunity of performing suitable pieces (such as 'Home, Sweet Home', 'Pack, Clouds, away', etc.) while play is suspended owing to a sudden downpour or the darkening of the heavens by a suspended fog. As long as it is not a case of interfering with the physical and mental comfort of the actual players, everything possible should be done for the greatest possible happiness of the greatest possible number. But it is nothing less than an outrage against the spirit and traditions of cricket to allow a band to perform while play is going on. At athletic sports music is not out of place; but as regards cricket, the good old rule 'Don't mix your arts' comes into full play. Cricket is a complete art in itself – epic, or dramatic, or lyric, as the man and the moment may determine – and the intrusion of the finest and most finely-rendered music is felt by the cricketer who puts brains into his batting, or bowling, or fielding and respects his art, himself, and his fellow-artists as an intolerable impertinence. Moreover, the spectator who really knows the game and is able and willing to concentrate his mind on what is happening on the 'perilous pitch' does not want to be bothered with a band; when deeply moved by the consideration of some crisis, some dramatic turning-point in the history of the *funera nefunera* of a well-contested match, he will describe the most charming music as a noise and a nuisance – adding the appropriate adjectives which, winged words as they are, would be as inappropriate in print as swallows in a cage.

Some cricketers, no doubt, would merely grumble to themselves if a band were allowed to interfere with the business of their game, in which every stroke or stratagem is an 'intellectual thing', like a tear or a laugh. But others will speak out in the emphatic language of the wisdom of intolerance (a kind of wisdom unwisely despised in this complaisant age) if the Lord's experiment is made a precedent. Mr C. I. Thornton, going in to take his innings at Scarborough, once ordered a band to stop playing, and the order was obeyed. He was dismissed without scoring – no doubt there remained something of his *saeva indignatio* at an artistic outrage while he was at the wicket for the first fateful few balls – and his successor, sad to say, went in without rebuking the musicians. There must be other instances of the same timely outspoken common sense in the annals of first-class cricket. To descend from great things to small, the writer himself when going in to try to stop a rot in a village match annexed in passing a concertina which, in the hands of a small boy, had vexed the souls of many that afternoon. The small boy said, among other things, 'Don't excite your silly gizzard' (curious phrase!) and was then taken home by his governess, but the concertina was given into the charge of the home team's umpire. It is perhaps only fair to tell another short story, which shows that in certain circumstances the attendance of a band might make for the betterment of the game. Playing against a lunatic asylum, the writer skied the ball to deep square-leg, and the catch was judged to a nicety and held by the fielder, a gentleman with delusions alleged to be having a lucid interval. Excited by the applause (in which the writer forgot to join) he ran rapidly round the field and was not caught by the attendants, who appeared from nowhere, until ten minutes had been wasted. One of the doctors subsequently said that, though quite harmless, he was very susceptible to the charms of music. Had there been a band in attendance the incident might never have occurred; for example, he might have missed the catch.

Let us then consent to the presence of bands at matches played on the grounds of lunatic asylums, but refuse to invite them to Lord's and other places where cricket is the sport of persons with a whole mind in a wholesome body. All batsmen will agree with this declaration of policy, which has the politic merit of making a concession to the enemy. Bowlers may not be quite so eager to withstand the innovation. They are in the habit of turning all perturbations of the natural order of things (differences of pace in the pitch, cross-winds that help their swerve, etc.) to their own advantage and the confusion of the batsman, their natural enemy; and some of them may regard the music that distracts his attention as an addition to the number of their incidental allies. But they all have to wield the willow, and the majority are anxious to be regarded as batsmen and moved up in the order of going in – a boon for which they will cheerfully resign some portion of their skill in bowling. Let us then appeal to them as batsmen, deceiving them for their own good, to strengthen the forces of opposition.

If their music could be made incidental (in the theatrical sense), the band might be tolerated on county grounds. For each characteristic stroke or bowling stratagem we might have a *leit-motiv*; a late cut or a googly would elicit from the band a characteristic musical phrase. A cricket symphony, composed by an English variant of Richard Strauss, might be permitted. It would begin, of course, by introducing the motive of the mowing machine, the sound of which, heard in the early morning of a mid-summer's day, is so delightful to the ears of cricketers. The time is not yet come for such delicate inventions; until it does bands must not be admitted to the nation's chief playing grounds because a few spectators wish to have their ears tickled. Admit a band for that unreasonable reason, and before we know where we are there will be (as Mr Punch has suggested) side-shows, electric theatres, and small *cafés chantants*, and switchbacks, and flip-flaps, and aunt sallies, and all the rest, doing a brisk business round the field of play. This very thing has happened in the case of American baseball, a fine game till the professional spectator spoilt it and vulgarised its surroundings. Unless the spectator be cockered up, we are told, county cricket will become bankrupt! The sooner, the better – for then county elevens will be chiefly composed of authentic amateurs, which is just what ought to be. Besides, if a band be allowed to settle at Lord's there will be no limit to its depredations. It will get into the *dedans* when a great tennis match is on. Horrible thought!

The Times

'*I forgive you.*'

NAKED RUNNER IS FINED £20

6 August 1975. Michael Angelow, who ran naked across Lord's cricket ground on Monday, was fined £20 when he appeared at Marylebone Magistrates' Court, yesterday.

Mr Angelow, aged 24, a merchant seaman, of St Albans, Hertfordshire, admitted insulting behaviour. When told that the escapade was for a £20 bet, Lieutenant-Colonel William Haswell, chairman of the bench, said: 'The court will have that £20; please moderate your behaviour in future.'

News item

OVER THE TOP! *England batsman Alan Knott is highly amused by the antics of the famous Lord's streaker, seen here in full flight during the Second Test between England and Australia in 1975. A sure case of Knott amused.*

He ran on in his birthday attire,
And set all the ladies afire.
But when he came to the stumps
He misjudged his jumps,
Now he sings in the Luton Girls' Choir!

LES BAILEY,
Wombwell Cricket Lovers' Society

THE YEARS BETWEEN
W. R. Hammond leads out the English team for the England *v* India Test on 22 July 1946.

MISS WICKET

Of your Chloes you poets may sing,
   And you lovers of Delia may sigh,
All the hills with 'Orynthia!' may ring,
   An' you list for your Capulet die,
Carve your Rosalind's name in the thicket,
   With your Thisbe converse through the wall;
But I'll sing the due praise of Miss Wicket,
   Of Miss Wicket, the fairest of all.

E. B. V. CHRISTIAN

WICKET MAIDEN

It is a game for gentle men;
Entirely wrong that man's spare rib
Should learn the mysteries of spin.

Women should not be allowed
To study subtleties of flight;
They should bowl underarm and wide.

Or, better still, not bowl at all,
Sit elegant in summer chairs,
Flatter the quiet with pale applause.

It shouldn't happen, yet it did:
She bowled a wicked heartbreak – one,
That's all. God help the next man in.

VERNON SCANNELL

'NEITHER CRICKETERS NOR LADIES'

It might have been the words of W. G. Grace that discouraged women cricketers from ever turning professional. Back in 1888, a woman could earn 6d (2½p) a day if she was in a team that toured the county fairgrounds. The sporting men found that the Original English Lady Cricketers were a nice change from the usual fare of dogfights and fisticuffs, but Grace diapproved. 'They might be original and English,' he said, 'but they're neither cricketers nor ladies.'

TIM MCGIRCK

RACHAEL HEYHOE FLINT
past captain, England Women's Test team.

WITH ASSISTANCE FROM NETTA RHEINBERG

FASHION IN THE FIELD

The clothing worn by the fair sex for playing cricket – since the first recorded game in 1745 – has often been ridiculed and been a magnet to journalists of both sexes, especially to those who felt women should not be playing cricket anyway!

In 1745, in that first recorded match at Gosden Common near Guildford 'between eleven maids of Bramley and eleven maids of Hambleton', the participants were dressed 'all in white. The Bramley maids had blue ribbons and the Hambledon maids red ribbons on their heads.'

Just over 200 years ago when John Collett painted 'Miss Wicket' the cricketer, to partner 'Miss Trigger' of huntin' and shootin' fame, he dressed her in a long, tight-sleeved, softly-falling gown of the day, worn over what looks like tightly laced corsets which would have made sharp singles rather an effort. 'Miss Wicket' also wore a large trimmed Italian hat embellished with feathers, fruit and flowers.

'Miss Wicket' may have represented an elegant 'lady' cricketer but the women players of the villages in the late 1700s were far more

rumbustious and practical, wearing an everyday full-skirted square-necked gown in any colour with team identification in the form of coloured ribbons or braids on the dress or in the hair.

Thomas Rowlandson, in a water-colour sketch, portrays his women players in hitched-up skirts 'showing a leg'. From the shape of their figures it suggests that these women have literally liberated themselves by peeling off their corsets.

Some reports of village matches in the late 18th century described players as wearing loose 'trousers' with light flannel waistcoats and sashes round the waist, or short fringed petticoats to the knees, and bonnets on the head.

In the early 1800s (exact date unknown), the long, wide, crinolined dress was instrumental in the invention of over-arm bowling by a woman (honestly!). Christina Willes, sister of John Willes, a Kentish squire from Tonford near Canterbury, found that her full skirt hampered her

Rachael Heyhoe Flint ready to go into action – in trousers. She still wears the trousers – in business: she runs a highly successful public relations consultancy.

under-arm lobs while bowling to her brother, so she delivered the ball with a high, round-arm style; her brother fought for many years to seek recognition for the technique. Perhaps the authorities resented the fact that it was a woman who invented it. So the bowling of Willes (not Willis) produced a revolution, thanks to long, full skirts!

The first professional women's team, the Original English Lady Cricketers, formed in 1890, who played exhibition games throughout the country for commercial gain, were attired by Messrs Lillywhite, Frowd & Company in thick flannel, sailor-collared blouses with leg-of-mutton sleeves, heavy calf-length skirts under which white stockings and canvas boots were worn; a man's cricket cap was incongruously perched on Victorian hairstyles.

The first official women's club, the White Heather, was formed in

1887 by ladies of aristocratic birth. The players wore white flannel skirts, white shirts, a girth belt and a white sailor hat and tie and the club colours – pink, white and green – were depicted in the hat ribbon and tie.

One White Heather member, Lady Milner, entreated members not to encase themselves in steel armour – 'the correct corset'. She also warned players that stopping the ball with the petticoat was definitely 'bad form – unworthy of real cricket'.

In fact, the most famous White Heather Club member, who wore the smart tailor-cut blazer with pride, was Lucy Ridsdale who married Stanley Baldwin, the Prime Minister. During the 1926 General Strike, she held a General Meeting of the White Heather Club at No. 10 Downing Street.

The Women's Cricket Association was founded in England in 1926 and gradually, as in all women's sport, fussiness of attire disappeared with the emergence of emancipation. Skirts became shorter, sleeves receded; knees and legs became visible albeit covered by stockings.

Officialdom in England expressed horror at one player who appeared wearing cami-knickers, a flimsy, silky, all-in-one article of lingerie, visible under her skirt. This apparel earned her the nick-name from the spectators of 'Camiknicket at the wicket'.

Five years after the formation of the WCA a demand for uniformity established the wearing of box-pleated gym tunics in heavy linen or serge with a girdle tied round the waist. Underneath long, white cotton stockings, held by suspenders, were worn, and the buckles and straps on pads caused more runs (on the stockings) than on the scoreboard!

The first England Touring Team to Australia and New Zealand in 1934 wore cotton divided skirts of culotte style, but they had to be laundered carefully otherwise they lost shape and the dividing portion hung down like a nappy.

Knee-length socks replaced stockings after the war and since then the basic cricket attire for the players in England, Australia and New Zealand has clung to the same style of short, white, divided skirt, only much shorter in the 1980s than forty years previously.

Women cricketers in the West Indies, India and Holland wear trousers which look very smart; ironically, many male observers are nowadays urging that all women cricketers should wear trousers, particularly when batting, because most international cricketers wear thigh pads and that pad is invariably visible below the hemline which makes it look as though a knicker-leg is emerging!

Now that women's cricket has become seriously accepted as part of the world of cricket I, personally, support the wearing of trousers if we are to be fully recognised as cricketers. No longer then will we gather headlines such as 'Skirts at the Wicket'. Gone will be the well-rehearsed riposte from a woman bowler to a searching male journalist's question, 'How do you like your slips?' Answer – 'One off, one on and two in the wash!'

I approve also the decision taken by the England Women's Cricket Association in 1984 to allow colour trims to be introduced on to cricket sweaters, so now the England team are proudly trimmed with red, white and blue.

Another move firmly to establish women as cricketers was taken at the International Women's Cricket Council in Melbourne in 1985 – 'that all players should be known as batsmen – not batswomen or batspersons.' One newspaper report on England's Test in Brisbane in January 1985 referred to a player as the 'nightwatchbatsperson', which was enough to drive any sub-editor to small type!

MARRIED WOMEN AGAINST MAIDENS

20 June 1793. A match of Cricket was played last week on Bury Common, in the county of Sussex, by *females*, the *married women* against the *maidens*; it was won by the married women, who had 80 notches more than the nymphs. So famous are the Bury women at this game, that they have challenged all England.

News Report

THE LADY CRICKETERS

16 March 1892. At the Lord Mayor's Court yesterday, the case of 'Rowney v. Wood' came before the Assistant Judge (Mr Roxburgh). It was a claim by Miss Agnes Rowney, one of the lady cricketers, to enforce payment of £11 from the defendant, who had taken over the lady cricketers as a financial speculation. At the trial of the action the plaintiff said that the lady cricketers went on tour of the provinces, and when the venture came to a standstill for want of funds the defendant stepped in and became virtually the proprietor, undertaking to pay the salaries of the girls. This the defendant denied, but the jury found against him, and the plaintiff now endeavoured to enforce payment. The defendant said that he was an agent and undertook all sorts of business, but he was doing none just now. He had an office in George-yard, Lombard-street, for which he paid 7s. 6d. per week rent. He lived at Kew in a house rented at £100 a year, but his wife paid that rent. The house was now being given up because

he could not really afford to pay for the journey to and from the City. He had no means to pay the plaintiff: the case was really decided against him on perjured evidence. An order was made for 8s. per month.

The Times

CRICKET-MATCH
EXTRAORDINARY

5 October 1811. On Wednesday last a singular Cricket-match commenced at Ball's-pond, Newington. The players on each side were twenty-two women: eleven Hampshire against eleven Surrey. The match was made between two amateur Noblemen of the respective counties, for five hundred guineas a side. The performers in this singular contest were of all ages and sizes, from 14 years old to upwards of 40; and the different parties were distinguished by coloured ribbons: Royal purple for the Hampshire; orange and blue, Surrey. The weather being favourable on Wednesday, some very excellent play, and much skill was displayed; but the palm of that day was borne off by a Hampshire lass, who made 41 innings before she was thrown out. At the conclusion of the day, the first innings for Hampshire were 81, while those of the Surrey were only seven. Five to one on the Hampshire lasses: any odds offered, but no takers. Thursday the Surrey damsels kept the field with their second innings almost the whole of the day; but it rained so incessantly there was very little play. The game, it is expected, will not be concluded until Monday next; but the general opinion is, that Hampshire will gain the victory. Notwithstanding the unfavourable state of the weather, a great concourse of people attended to witness this singular contention; and although each party seemed to exert their utmost skill and activity against their adversaries, the utmost harmony and good humour prevailed amongst them.

7 October 1811. The cricket-match between the Hampshire and Surrey females, for 500 gs. a side, has terminated; the former won by 15 notches. Another match has been made.

News Report

MARRIED V. SINGLE

14 June 1849. This match, after a contest of three days, was last evening brought to a termination at Lord's in the presence of a numerous assemblage of spectators. The perusal of the score will prove this, – that the batting beat the bowling, or else we scarcely like to say so. On the present occasion the 'fielding' in some respects on both sides was very faulty. At another time, when more space is afforded [*no more space was afforded*], we shall enter into a dissection of the play which has been exhibited as this contest has progressed,

and offer some deductions which it is hoped may lead to an improvement in some points. The final score stood thus:

MARRIED

Dean, b. Wisden	2	c. Nicholson, b. Wisden	19
Clark, run out..	71	b. Wisden	0
Hillyer, l.b.w., b. Wisden	11	s. Nicholson, b. Wisden	32
Box, c. Kynaston, b. Chester	42	b. Martingell ..	37
N. Felix, Esq., c. Kynaston, b. Wisden..	27	b. Martingell ..	0
A. Mynn, Esq., c. Wisden, b. Chester ..	2	c. Armitage b. Wisden	0
Earl Verulam, b. Wisden	2	b. Martingell ..	1
W. Pilch, c. Wisden, b. Armitage ..	4	b. Wisden	18
Daken, not out ..	26	not out..	19
S. Whitehead, Esq., b. Wisden ..	0	b. Wisden	3
Lillywhite, c. Parr, b. Armitage ..	0	b. Wisden	0
Byes ..	16	Byes, 16, wide, Chester, 1, Wisden, 1 ..	18
	203		147

SINGLE

Hon. R. Grimston, b. Lillywhite ..	26	b. Hillyer	76
A. Haygarth, Esq., s. Box, b. Dean ..	24	s. Box, b. Hillyer ..	5
Guy, c. Hillyer, b. Lillywhite ..	0	b. Lillywhite ..	12
Pilch, c. Box, b. Dean .	8	c. Mynn, b. Hillyer ..	5
Martingell, c. Mynn, b. Lillywhite ..	0	c. Whitehead, b. Lillywhite ..	1
Wisden, b. Lillywhite..	0		
Armitage, c. Box, b. Dean ..	23		
Parr, b. Dean ..	61	b. Hillyer	3
Chester, b. Dean ..	3	not out..	22
R. Kynaston, Esq., b. Lillywhite ..	1	not out..	3
W. Nicholson, Esq., not out ..	23	c. Box, b. Dean	32
Byes, 6; no balls (Clark) 5 ..	11	Byes	12
	180		171

The single won by three wickets.

The Times

QUEEN WILLOW

9 September 1936. There is 'sweet English music' in the words men have used to praise the cricket-bat, the pliant, springy, glossy, sweet-sounding blade. With no inkling of its real nature they have honoured it as King Willow. With what now seems masculine cocksureness the poet sang:

> Willow the King is a monarch grand,
> Three in a row his courtiers stand.

For a century there has been no suspicion that King Willow could be a fraud, or that sex might enter into the matter. But presumption must now yield to truth and the world know that the true willow is a 'she', that she is the bat's mother and no other. King Willow has been caught out; his offspring are suspect; they are not chips off the old block. For the experts say that the male willow is too often a hybrid and degenerate, who will wilt and warp in the battle with the ball. Now and then a male will pass the test of true willowhood; then he is a king among bats, a he-bat. But the traditions of cricket, it seems, have descended on the distaff side. Tardy honours must be paid to many scarred and

A ladies' cricket match – Harrow v Pinner – played on the Harrow School grounds and drawn by George du Maurier, circa 1860.

bandaged and anointed 'shes', Amazons of the game, who have stood up to fast balls, lashed at low ones, and stared the googly undaunted in the face. No longer, then, is 'it' or 'he' the bat's pronoun. No ill-advised personification this, as FOWLER might call it. 'She' is the one and only word for a thing that has been found to be feminine.

Habit of course dies hard in a summer game, and the revelation has come late in the season, too late to affect the players and the counties whose exploits our Cricket Correspondent sums up this morning. But in Australia there will be cricket and a whole summer for controversy. Would it be too much to ask of a Test team that they should establish 'Queen Willow' in the language before they reach Australia? Otherwise it must be left to the first match-winner who pats his bat lovingly and calls 'her' a beauty. Or to the first batsman who comes runless from the wicket cursing the fickleness of feminine nature. After all, 'she' will be no intruder; every cricketer with a fancy felt long ago that the manliness of cricket had been exaggerated. The ball, it is true, fierce, red, and glossy, is a masculine thing. But the soft soothing whites and greens of cricket have always shown a feminine touch.

Now that we know the truth about the willow, questions will be asked about the ash, the pine, and the yew. Have the oar and the cue, the racquet and the golf club a similar secret of sex? They too are often blamed for fickleness of form, and, what is more, women have used them as effectively as men. No one can say that of the cricket bat, which is sullen and timid in a woman's hand. The batmakers assert with some scorn that the racquet and the club have felt the cold hand of steel, that even though they might be female in origin they are no longer pure wood. For such hybrids, as for the late King Willow, the only word is 'it'. But the case of the cricket willow is beyond argument. Could there be a clearer claim on the well-known chivalry of cricketers than the cause of one who has served them gracefully, manfully, and anonymously? Let the Gentlemen of England close the season with a toast and the cry: 'King Willow is dead. Long live the Queen!'

News Report

Phyllis at the Wicket

When Phyllis goes a-cricketing,
And revels in the clover,
Then have a care, it's not the thing
To bowl a maiden over.

Yea, when she wields her willow wand
So scornfully to cut you
For three or four or even more,
Don't lose your temper, but you

Should always learn to play the game,
She's bound to give some chances,
And maybe you'll accept the same
Without undue advances.

Observe with what surpassing ease
She follows my suggestion,
Now, for she's left the popping-crease,
It's time to pop the question.

'How's that?' The Umpire Cupid cried:
'Out,' though she barely snicked him,
So exit Grace personified,
A very willing victim.

PERCEVAL GRAVES

SOME OF THEM ARE PRETTY

(Based on a conversation overheard at the Kennington Oval)

Arriving at the Oval
    One bright and sunny day,
I sat near a spectator
    Who'd come to watch the play.
He'd never seen a ladies' match
    And, glasses to his eyes –
'Why! Some of them are pretty,'
    He cried out in surprise.

'Some of them are pretty,'
    He repeated his remark,
'And none of them are wearing slacks,
    In fact they're very smart.
'I thought they'd all be rather large,
    With muscles everywhere
'But these girls look attractive,
    With soft and wavy hair.'

'Some of them are pretty,'
    He uttered, yet again;
It puzzled him, apparently,
    That we could play the game
While looking nice and feminine
    And just the way we should,
And if we're not *all* pretty,
    Then our cricket's pretty good!

MOLLY SHIMEILD

Mrs W. G. Grace

25 March 1930. Mrs Grace, widow of Dr W. G. Grace, the famous cricketer, died at her home at Hawkhurst, Kent, on Sunday, at the age of 76.

Mrs Grace was formerly Miss Agnes Nicholls Day, daughter of Dr Grace's first cousin. They were married at the close of the cricket season of 1873, when Dr Grace was 25. He had then been playing in first-class cricket for eight years, and within a few days of the wedding he took a team out to Australia. The team included his brother, G. F. Grace, his cousin, W. R. Gilbert, Jupp, and Lillywhite. Mrs Grace accompanied the party, and the tour became known as his 'honeymoon tour'. Like Mrs Martha Grace, 'W. G.'s' mother, Mrs Grace always took a keen interest in cricket. On one occasion she attended the Oxford and Cambridge match when her eldest son, the late W. G. Grace, junior, played for Cambridge, and opened the innings for his university. He had the misfortune to register two 'ducks', and as he returned to the pavilion the second time, with all eyes turned towards him, his mother and his sister sat with tears slowly falling down their cheeks.

The funeral will be at Elmers End, Beckenham, at 2.45 to-day.

News Report

The Woman Behind the Hailstones

24 June 1968. Cricket and the occult make strange companions. But last Thursday a woman telephoned Lord's when the ground was covered in hailstones, and said: 'I'm responsible for this storm. And there will be more such storms until the Australians pay their debts.' Mr Donald Carr, assistant secretary of Lord's, told a colleague of the incident at the dinner which the MCC gave on Saturday night to commemorate the 200th Test match between England and Australia.

The Lord's switchgirl, he said, asked the caller for a little more information about herself. 'I have occult powers so far as the weather is concerned,' said the voice. 'Several years ago I used these powers to break the drought in Australia. The Australians have not yet paid me for my services. My spell over their matches will continue.' The Australian fast bowler, Graham McKenzie, received a similar call during the rainy second match at Leicester, evidently from the same person. Again the drought debt was her main theme.

'This woman said she wasn't fooling,' continued Mr Carr, 'and she proceeded to put a spell upon our Jean over the telephone. At the end of a few seconds, Jean felt so dizzy that she cut the caller off.'

In fact, using my own highly developed occult powers, I can tell Mr Carr precisely who the sinister caller was: Mrs Doris

Munday, of Applegarth Road, W.14.

'I've been doing this for a long time,' she confessed, clearly not in the least rattled at being discovered. 'It was three years ago when the Australians asked me to break up their seven year drought, and when I did it, they gave all the credit to the aborigines.

'They also promised to take up a collection for me, and didn't; not that I wanted the money, but I was annoyed. So I started off by smashing the Brisbane Test in 1966. I've been bashing them ever since.'

Mrs Munday, who is 49, broke into the psychic business a long time ago as a hypnotist; then about four years ago she was told by a hypnotist friend that she was a 'weather manipulator'.

Original Report

Test Bowled Two Maidens Over

27 July 1968. In a room with three cricket photographs on the wall, and a view of St Pancras Station, sit some of the most telephoned girls in London.

They are the G.P.O.'s 'Test team', and thousands of people ring them every day – dialling UMP – to hear the latest Test match score. During the present series with Australia more than six million calls have been made.

Four girls provide the voices on a continuous commentary, Miss Margaret Woodin, Mrs Ellen Moelly, Miss Pamela Hawes and Miss Yvonne Biddulph, who comes from Guyana. Miss Biddulph said: 'It got exciting when the West Indians played here. But we didn't exactly come to blows.'

The girls work in teams of three. An editor is in direct link with the ground on which the Test match is being played, and two telephonists take it in turns to record the score or to check the telephone commentary against the information from the ground. The average time between getting a new score from the ground and putting it on record is 25 seconds.

Most of the girls are cricket enthusiasts, and two who were 'not all that interested' are now fascinated by the game. Miss Hawes and Miss Woodin have never seen a Test match, but said: 'We are going to try and get to the Oval for the last match if we can get some tickets.'

The two editors, Miss Pat Weighall and Miss Sheila Keogh, both Post Office telecommunications traffic officers, are self-confessed cricket addicts. 'We've offered to take our equipment to the ground,' Miss Keogh said. 'We have even said we would not mind the overseas tours, but we are still here'.

Although they have no favourite cricketer, all the girls speak affectionately of 'Uncle' Tom Graveney. Mrs Moelly, who supports Sussex, thinks Ted Dexter is 'lovely'.

The Post Office Test team 'reserve' is Mrs Thelma Cumberbatch, a mother of two, who comes from Barbados and is something of a cricket expert because 'I used to play it back home'. She is learning the job, but said: 'I haven't done very much yet. Every time it is my turn rain seems to stop play.'

RITA MARSHALL

A. A. THOMSON

THE LADIES IN PLAY

'*Ron, ron*, or you will *nevaire* egg-sell at the athletics' – thus was I exhorted, some years ago now, with more zeal than precision, by a Swiss governess who tried to initiate herself and me into the complexities of single-wicket cricket, with croquet hoops as stumps and rooks for spectators. It was my first experience of the Cricketing Lady.

There is evidence that the ladies interested themselves, at least verbally, in the game in the earlier years of King George III, when Mrs 'Lumpy' Stevens would scream advice not unmingled with abuse at her famous husband of Hambledon CC. There are many instances, ancient and modern, of wives and daughters, and, in the greatest of all cricketing families, of a grandmother, too, who have at the proper moment ceased to 'mind the distaff' and plunged into disputations on the failure of a relative. Indeed, it is on record that a certain great professional batsman was discovered by a companion wandering in a town at night with a wild mien, because, as he said in low and anguished tone: 'I daren't go home. I daren't. The old woman'll tell me exactly why I missed that ball.'

There hangs in the pavilion of the Kent Cricket Club on the St Lawrence ground, Canterbury, an old print, in the Hogarthian manner, of a ladies' cricket match: Married *v.* Single, I believe. It is not a delicate or æsthetic scene. A burlesque and corpulent figure lies sprawling after a fielding failure. Mid-wicket, too, is an object of fun, having, like the mariner's wife of Mr Jacobs, 'lost her good looks and found others'. The gentlemen spectators, scattered in small marquees, are regaling themselves with culpable abandon.

Far otherwise are ladies' cricket matches conducted in these days. Any who saw the Tests and other matches played a few summers ago between England and the visitors from Australia will recall not only the trimness of these athletes and their skill, especially with the bat, which made tough and crochety old male spectators scratch their heads in surprise, but, more than anything, the exactitude of the organisation (making even the L.G.U. seem haphazard!) and the defiance of the weather. The Oval groundsman and his staff must have regarded the next fixture between men as a rest cure!

I was once present, at all material times, at a ladies' County match,

Ian Botham and Rachael Heyhoe Flint coach Sarah Potter, daughter of film and television writer Dennis Potter.

to which I must give with a sort of military anonymity the title of Wessex *v.* Loamshire, and to the players themselves, in the manner of Edgar Wallace's heroines and villainesses, spurious names that do not, nevertheless, 'have no reference to any living person.' For this is an unofficial and fragmentary account of the proceedings, and of some of the cricketers I can truthfully say that I did but see her passing by.

First, remembering the inhuman ability at catching and stopping shown by 'Twelve Ladies of the District' in schooldays – the much too prehensile fingers and the skirt-protected shins – I remark with fidelity that the fielding of the ladies of Wessex and Loamshire, especially the

Members of the England Women's Cricket Team holding the new St Ivel Trophy, 1976.

latter, was faulty in the extreme. Cricketing ladies have often told me, with an admonishing frown, that it is not their wish to be compared with the men. Quite so; but they must admit comparison with each other, and on this occasion, had I been the Loamshire captain, I would have gathered my team at the close of play and said: 'No, Simpson; certainly not; and you, too, Jackson, and you, Micklethwaite; you may not go off to your sherry party; an hour's fielding practice for all of you; the catching was deplorable, and the throwing-in the limit.'

Perhaps it was the heat; yet this alone does not explain the garrulity of the slips, outdoing any post-prandial discussions among men. Nor am I convinced that the conversation turned solely on the artistry or eccentricities of the opposing batsmen, but rather, I fear, on hats and cookery, or other matters of personal adornment and refection.

Wessex scored some 165 for 8 wickets, and left Loamshire two and three-quarter hours to win, which would appear a little generous were it not that the tea interval bisected the Loamshire innings for three-quarters of an hour! Ah, that's the sort of match I have dreamed of playing in!

A lady to whom I award the prosaic name of Johnson scored 90 odd for Wessex, but let the Loamshire fellows bitterly reflect on the five chances that bumped to earth. In the words of a literary colleague, 'Johnson opened very shakily indeed, and cocked up several that were put on the floor before she became at all menacing.' But she made some lovely strokes, with that full sweeping rhythm which seems to desert man in adolescence, and it took a terrific catch at mid-off to dismiss her, expiation nearly enough for the other fumbling. Sixty-eight of her runs came from boundaries, and the next highest score was a desperate 17 by number nine.

For Loamshire, Sanderson, who must have suffered inward agonies from the inequalities of the fielding, bowled 30 overs in a row, except for negligible respite when changing ends. Three for 53 was inadequate reward.

Loamshire began as if their task, even including the tea, were easy; but they were soon forced to change daring for obstinacy, two players being out for very few runs. The second was bowled by one that seemed to go sharply with the arm, but refinements in definition fall flat before another of my friend's diagnoses. 'She was bowled by a perfect length ball that obviously she knew nothing about.' That's the way that men's Test Matches should be described. A simple brutality. The team was saved, as it turned out, by their number four, who was undismissed, though not entirely unbeaten, for 16, made in a hour and forty minutes. 'There was no moving her.' But there was movement around her in plenty; bowlers came and went and, came again in bewildering permutation. Then one of the opening batsmen suddenly lost control, and, calling for a run for a stroke straight to close square-leg, was amply run out. The lady who had caught that great catch at mid-off, then arrived to make a hurricane 31 in thirty-five minutes. Still number four remained, majestic amid ruin, 4 more wickets falling with a crash. But number eleven not only averted the hat-trick but stayed for the last over and a half, with fielders perched nearly on her bat, and the stumper twice whipping away the bails more in prophecy than in hope.

A great day; but oh! those slip-fielders! If one should chance to cast her eye on these words, may she blush and amend!

BILL FRINDALL

UNVEILING THE LADIES...

The first account of a women's match was published in the *Reading Mercury* on 26 July 1745:

> The greatest cricket-match that ever was played in the South part of England was on Friday, the 26th of last month, on Gosden Common, near Guildford, in Surrey, between eleven maids of Bramley and eleven maids of Hambleton, dressed all in white. The Bramley maids had blue ribbons and the Hambleton maids red ribbons on their heads. The Bramley girls got 119 notches and the Hambleton girls 127. There was of both sexes the greatest number that ever was seen on such an occasion. The girls bowled, batted, ran and catched as well as most men could do in that game.

Village cricket between women's teams had been popular in many parts of Surrey and Sussex before that first report.

The first time that women were invited to play on a major ground was on 13 July 1747 when the 'maids' of Westdean, Chilgrove and Charlton were 'bidden' to play a match on the famous Honourable Artillery Ground in London.

From these inter-village contests, women's cricket spread to the top of the social scale. In 1777 the *Morning Post* reported a match

> played in private between the Countess of Derby and some other Ladies of Quality and Fashion, at the Oaks, in Surrey, the rural and enchanting retreat of her ladyship.

'The Woman of the Match' award seems to have been given to Elizabeth Ann Burrell, daughter of a notable White Conduit Club player, who

> got more notches in the first and second innings than any lady in the game.

and was then aged 20 and extremely attractive. Her prize was the 8th Duke of Hamilton who married her before the next cricket season.

Not all women's cricket was as elegant. The most disgraceful behaviour by female cricketers was reported in the *Nottingham Review* of 4 October 1833:

> Last week, at Sileby feast, the women so far forgot themselves as to enter upon a game of cricket and by their deportment as well as frequent applications to the tankard, they rendered themselves objects such as no husband, brother, parent, or lover could contemplate with any degree of satisfaction.

The first woman to technically assist the development of cricket was Christina Willes, later Mrs Hodges. It is generally accepted that she originated round-arm bowling *c.* 1807 when she practised with her brother John in the barn of their home at Tonford, near Canterbury. Her full skirt of the period made the legitimate bowling style of the time impossible. John, who was to become a squire and sports patron, found round-arm bowling difficult to play, adopted it himself, was the first to be no-balled for employing it in a major match, and had the satisfaction of seeing the style made legal six years later in 1828. It was said that

> Willes, his sister and his dog [a retriever?] could beat any eleven in England.

The first woman to be included in the 'Births and Deaths of Cricketers' section of *Wisden Cricketers' Almanack* was Martha Grace (*née* Pocock):

> Grace, Mrs H. M. (mother of W. G., E. M. and G. F.), b July 18, 1812, d July 25, 1884.

Martha's husband, Dr Henry Mills Grace, was a Somerset man who in 1831 moved to Downend, a village four miles from Bristol, and took over a large general practice. A tremendous cricket enthusiast, he established the Mangotsfield Cricket Club for cricketers in the neighbouring villages, and prepared a cricket pitch for his seven children on the lawn of Downend House. Martha became as keen on the game as her husband and used to coach her sons. She drove her fourth son, William Gilbert – aged nearly six – in her pony-carriage to watch his first game of cricket when William Clarke's All-England Eleven came to Bristol on 22–24 June 1854 to play 22 of West Gloucestershire. The match was arranged by her husband who captained the home side. 'W. G.' wrote in his *Cricketing Reminiscences and Personal Recollections*:

> I was with my mother, who sat in her pony-carriage all day. I don't remember much about the cricket, but I recollect that some of the England team played in top hats. My mother was very enthusiastic, and watched every ball. She preserved cuttings of the newspaper reports of this and most other matches, and took great care of the score books. I have several of her scrap-books, with the cuttings pasted in, and very useful I find them, because in those days *Wisden's Annual* was not in existence, and no proper record was kept.

Two years later Martha Grace mentioned to George Parr that 'W. G.' would do better than his brother, 'E. M.', because his back play was

The touring New Zealand Women's Cricket Team at Lord's for some early practice in June 1964. Picture shows twin sisters Rosemary and Elizabeth Signal making their first appearance for the tourists.

superior. She attended all the matches she could, watched all the play and often criticised vociferously. Once, after 'W. G.' returned at the end of his innings, she rebuked him: 'Willie, Willie, haven't I told you over and over again how to play that ball?'

The first women's cricket club, White Heather, was founded at Nun Appelton, Yorkshire, in the summer of 1887 by eight ladies, the majority of aristocratic birth and independent means. The name was derived from the favourite badge of the founders, who adopted colours of pink, white and green for the same reason.

The club's most celebrated cricketer was Lucy Ridsdale, elder daughter of the Assay Master at the Royal Mint. She married Stanley Baldwin, Prime Minister three times between 1923 and 1937 and a fine batsman who averaged 62 in 1892.

The White Heather Club ceased to function as a playing club after the 1950 season.

In 1890 the English Cricket and Athletic Association Limited organised two teams of women cricketers under the title of 'The Original English Lady Cricketers'. The two teams, the Red XI and the Blue XI, played each other in Exhibition matches on many county grounds around England and were the first to play at Headingley, Leeds. The OELC players were specially selected and coached, bowled overarm, and were forbidden to use their real names. Their uniform consisted of a flannel blouse and skirt, adorned round the hem and collar with striped bands of blue (or red) and white braid. A large blue (or red) bow kept in place the sailor collar, and they wore their colours on sashes around their waists. Caps perched on Victorian hair-styles completed their dress. The OELC was disbanded after two seasons.

The first tour by a women's cricket team took place in 1926 when a scratch team played on college grounds in Cheltenham and Malvern.

Following that successful first tour a number of its members called a meeting on 4 October 1926 when the Women's Cricket Association was formed. Its aims were simply to enable any woman or girl wishing to play cricket to do so, and to play the game with strict order and decorum. The first uniform regulation stipulated that 'WCA teams must play in white or cream. Hats and knickers must be white. Dresses and tunics must not be shorter than touching the ground when kneeling. Sleeveless dresses and transparent stockings are not permitted.'

Other countries followed England's example and official administrations for women's cricket were formed in Australia (1931), New Zealand (1933), Holland (1934), South Africa and Rhodesia (1952), Jamaica (1966), Trinidad and Tobago (1967), India (1973), Barbados (1973) and Grenada (1974).

In 1958 the International Women's Cricket Council (IWCC) was formed to determine tour schedules between member countries.

The first overseas tour by a women's cricket team left Tilbury on the SS *Cathay* on 19 October 1934 bound for Australia and New Zealand. The 15 English players, captained by Betty Archdale, had been selected from those available after trial matches at Old Trafford and Northampton.

The first women's match involving an overseas team took place on 24 and 26 November 1934 at Perth between Western Australia and England and was drawn. Molly Hide scored the first century for a touring women's team.

The first women's Test match was played between Australia and England at Brisbane on 28–31 December 1934, England winning by nine wickets.

The first Test century by a woman was scored in the Second Test at Sydney on 7 January 1935 by Myrtle Maclagan who made 119 for England on the second day.

The first women's cricket tour to England was made by Australia in 1937. They defeated England by 31 runs at the County Ground, Northampton, on 12–15 June in the first women's Test played in England. The tourists were allowed scant opportunity for social licence during the tour as the rules laid down by the Australian WCA ordained that:

> No member shall drink, smoke or gamble while on tour.
> No girl may be accompanied by her husband, a relation or a friend.
> Writing articles on cricket during the tour is strictly forbidden.
> While on board ship, no girl shall visit the top deck of the liner after dinner.
> Members of the team must retire to bed by 10 pm during the voyage.
> Members will do physical drill on deck at 7.15 am daily except Sundays.
> The team will participate in all deck games.

The first women's cricket World Cup competition was held in England in 1973 and won by the host country who were captained by Rachael Heyhoe Flint.

The first women's cricket magazine was first published in England in May 1930, price 6d. *Women's Cricket* was founded by Marjorie Pollard who had been a member of the first women's cricket tour in 1926. A hockey international who, in 1935, had been described as one of that game's greatest exponents of all time, she became an institution in herself. In 1929 the WCA decided to publish its own paper and Marjorie Pollard had volunteered to produce and edit it. She remained its editor until 1949 when she handed over to Netta Rheinberg and Nancy Joy. As a player Marjorie Pollard was 'a mighty hitter, fine fielder and a resourceful captain. No year went by between 1929 and 1936 when she did not excel at one or other facet of the game.' (Netta Rheinberg in *Fair Play, the Story of Women's Cricket*.) Apart from being the first public relations and publicity officer for women's cricket, she was its first reporter, first broadcaster and first commentator. In 1965 she was awarded the OBE for services to sport.

England's past captain of the Women's Team, Rachael Heyhoe Flint, practises in the nets at Lord's.

Netta Rheinberg edited *Women's Cricket* until it failed to win its battle against inflation and appeared for the last time in 1967. She was the correspondent on women's cricket in *The Cricketer* from 1959 to 1970 before handing over to Rachael Heyhoe. Netta Rheinberg captained Middlesex for four post-war seasons, was player/manager of the England team which toured Australasia in 1948–49, playing in the First Test. She also managed the 1957–58 touring team to Australasia, became an umpire and was one of the first women to pass the men's ACU examination, and became the Cricket Society's first female vice-chairman. She has been women's correspondent to *Wisden Cricketers' Almanack* since 1959.

Rachael Heyhoe, who added her husband's name when she married Derrick Flint in 1971, captained England from 1966 until 1977 and never suffered a defeat. A former England hockey international (goal-keeper) and county squash player, she has been an outstanding public relations and publicity officer for women's cricket since succeeding Netta Rheinberg as *The Cricketer*'s correspondent in June 1971. She played a major part in the sponsorship of women's cricket, and in its first World Cup in 1973. She was captain of the England team in the WCA Golden Jubilee Match, on the first appearance of women's teams at Lord's on 4 August 1976 when England beat Australia by eight wickets in a 60-overs match. Commentator, broadcaster, after-dinner speaker (she was honoured with the Guild of Toastmasters' Best After-Dinner Speaker Award in 1973), and organiser of charity cricket matches, she was awarded the MBE in 1973 for services to women's cricket.

ENGLAND v SOUTH AFRICA

Season	Venue	Played	Won by England	Won by South Africa	Drawn
1960–61	South Africa	4	1	—	3

ENGLAND v WEST INDIES

Season	Venue	Played	Won by England	Won by West Indies	Drawn
1979	England	3	2	—	1

AUSTRALIA v NEW ZEALAND

Season	Venue	Played	Won by Australia	Won by New Zealand	Drawn
1947–48	New Zealand	1	1	—	—
1956–57	Australia	1	1	—	—
1960–61	New Zealand	1	—	—	1
1971–72	Australia	1	—	1	—
1974–75	New Zealand	1	—	—	1
1978–79	Australia	3	1	—	2
		8	3	1	4

NEW ZEALAND v SOUTH AFRICA

Season	Venue	Played	Won by New Zealand	Won by South Africa	Drawn
1971–72	South Africa	3	1	—	2

Summary of Official Test Match Results

ENGLAND v AUSTRALIA

Season	Venue	Played	Won by England	Won by Australia	Drawn
1934–35	Australia	3	2	–	1
1937	England	3	1	1	1
1948–49	Australia	3	–	1	2
1951	England	3	1	1	1
1957–58	Australia	3	–	–	3
1963	England	3	1	–	2
1968–69	Australia	3	–	–	3
1976	England	3	–	–	3
		24	5	3	16

ENGLAND v NEW ZEALAND

Season	Venue	Played	Won by England	Won by New Zealand	Drawn
1934–35	New Zealand	1	1	–	–
1948–49	New Zealand	1	1	–	–
1954	England	3	1	–	2
1957–58	New Zealand	2	–	–	2
1966	England	3	–	–	3
1968–69	New Zealand	3	2	–	1
		13	5	–	8

WOMEN'S TEST MATCH RECORDS

Team records

The highest innings total is 503 for 5 declared by England against New Zealand at Christchurch on 16 and 18 February 1935 in the first match between the two countries. The first day's play produced 474 runs with New Zealand being dismissed for 44 and England replying with 430 for 4 wickets.

The highest total in a Test in England is 379 by Australia at The Oval on 26–27 July 1976.

The lowest innings total is 35 by England against Australia on a rain-affected pitch at St Kilda, Melbourne, on 22 February 1958. This was in reply to Australia's total of 38.

The lowest total in a Test in England is 63 by New Zealand at Worcester on 5 July 1954.

England's captain, Jan Southgate, shows what she can do with a nice sweep to pretty leg!

Batting records

The highest individual innings in women's Test cricket is 189 by E. A. ('Betty') Snowball for England against New Zealand at Christchurch on 16 February 1935 in 222 minutes.

The highest individual Test score in England is 179 by Rachael Heyhoe Flint for England against Australia at The Oval on 27–28 July 1976. She batted for 521 minutes, hit 30 fours and enabled England to draw the match.

The highest aggregate of runs in a Test career is 1594, average 63.76, with four centuries, in 25 matches by Rachael Heyhoe Flint for England between December 1960 and July 1979. She also hit the first six in women's Tests – over long-on against Australia at The Oval on 20 July 1963.

Bowling records

The best innings analysis in women's Test cricket is 7 for 6 by Mary Duggan when she captained England against Australia at St Kilda, Melbourne, on 22 February 1958.

The best match analysis is 11 for 16 by Betty Wilson for Australia in the same match. No play was possible on the first day and both teams were dismissed cheaply on a 'sticky' pitch on the second day: Australia

38 (Mary Duggan 7 for 6), England 35 (Betty Wilson 7 for 7 including the first hat-trick in women's Test cricket). They are the two lowest totals and the two best analyses in women's Test matches. In the second innings Betty Wilson scored 100 and Australia declared at 202 for 9. England were 76 for 8 when the game ended. Betty Wilson's analysis of 4 for 9 not only gave her the match bowling record; it also enabled her to become the first cricketer to complete the match double of 100 runs and ten wickets in a Test match. The first instance in men's Test cricket occurred on 14 December 1960.

The best match analysis in a women's Test in England is 11 for 63 by Julia Greenwood against West Indies at Canterbury on 16–18 June 1979 in the first Test match involving a West Indies team.

The most wickets in a Test career is 77, average 13.49, in 16 matches by Mary Duggan for England between 1949 and 1963.

WOMEN'S CRICKET RECORDS IN OTHER MATCHES

The highest innings total in any women's match is 567 by Tarana against Rockley at Rockley in New South Wales, Australia, in October 1896.

The record total in England is 410 for 2 declared by the South against the East at Oakham School, Rutland, on 29 May 1982.

The record individual innings in women's cricket is 224 not out in 135 minutes by Mabel Bryant for the Visitors against the Residents at Eastbourne, Sussex, in August 1901.

The highest score in a Test trial match was recorded by Jan Southgate when she made 201 not out for the South against the East at Oakham School, Rutland, on 29 May 1982. She shared an unbroken third-wicket partnership of 246 with Jackie Court (105 not out).

The highest score in the three World Cup tournaments held in England (1973), India (1978) and New Zealand (1982) is 138 not out in 60 overs by Janette Brittin for England against the International XI at Hamilton on 14 January 1982.

There have been two recorded instances of bowlers taking all ten wickets in women's cricket without conceding a run. The first to do so was Rubina Humphries, aged 15, for Dalton Ladies against Woodfield Sports Club on 26 June 1931; she also scored all her side's runs. Her 10 for 0 feat was equalled in July 1962 by Rosemary White for Wallington Ladies against Beaconsfield Ladies.

The first double in women's cricket was achieved for England by Enid Bakewell (*née* Turton) on the 1968–69 tour of Australia and New Zealand. In 20 matches (eleven in Australia and nine in New Zealand) she scored 1031 runs (average 39.65) and, bowling slow left-arm, took 118 wickets (average 9.77). In the Second Test against New Zealand at Christchurch she scored 114 and 66 not out, making the winning hit five minutes before the close, and took 3 for 68 and 5 for 56. She was just two wickets short of being the first English cricketer to achieve the match double in a Test – Ian Botham was to gain this honour in February 1980. Playing against a New South Wales XI at Manly, she took a hat-trick, all her victims falling to catches by June Moorhouse at silly mid-off.

Island cricket.

LESLIE FREWIN

Behind the scenes – the Honorary Lady Taverners

LORDLY LADIES

The Lord's Taverners have got up to some unusual tricks in their time, one of the most rewarding being their admission of Honorary Lady Taverners. This charming aspect of femininity might accurately be described as 'Ladies of The Cricket Scene' or 'Ladies in the Public Eye' – often both. Leastways, they are assuredly Ladies whose efforts for the Club contribute mightily to the raising of substantial and much-needed cash with which the Taverners fund their work for disabled children and youth cricket.

The Hon. Lady Taverners are an attractive and fiercely-active team who work ceaselessly on distaff-side duties with their appearances at charity cricket matches and the like and with gargantuan effort before and after the annual Lord's Taverners' Ball at Grosvenor House, London. As all who have attended know, the ladies' famous Tombola with its wonderful variety of prizes ranging from motor cars to kitchen sets is an exceptional feature of the gaiety!

Several, if not all, of the fair sex have been doing fine, unselfish work for the Taverners for many years. If any justification were needed for their Membership, it might be added that several of them married cricketers – what better reason is needed? Step forward Anne Subba Row, attractive wife of Raman, the talented Surrey and England Test cricketer, now chairman of the Test and County Cricket Board. Anne first took over the Ball Tombola chairmanship from the delightful Dorothy Carline who worked tirelessly for the cause up until 1973. Anne served four years as chairman and remains active on that same Committee today, fitting in her work with the raising of her family, Christopher, Michele and Alistair. Travelling thousands of miles each year, she also manages to fit in her Taverners duties with valuable work for the Cancer Control Campaign which, incidentally, also benefits from the work of three other Lady Taverners – Judith Chalmers, Barbara Upsdell and Betty Surridge, wife of the great Surrey and England cricketer.

The ever-delightful Marjorie Gover, married to the legendary Surrey and England bowler, Alfred, has been helping to raise fortunes by

LADY MYRA SECOMBE, *tireless worker for The Lord's Taverners, and wife of past-president Sir Harry Secombe, is seen here with her husband who describes her as 'the cornerstone of my life' and who, as Lance Bombardier Harry Secombe, met her at a Mumbles Pier dance in 1946. They were married two years later and today have four children and three young grandchildren.*

ABOVE: *Lady Taverner Joan Morecambe, wife of the much-missed Eric, who became her husband's Girl Friday during Eric Morecambe's three years as president of the Taverners. Joan says, 'It is an immense pleasure and privilege to continue my relationship with the Taverners as an Hon. Lady Member.' It is a pleasure and our privilege to have you with us, Joan!*

RIGHT: *Margaret Thatcher, Hon. Lady Taverner.*
OPPOSITE, MAIN PICTURE: *Ann Barrington.* INSET ABOVE: *Penelope Keith.*
CENTRE: *Liz Frazer.* BELOW: *Marjorie Gover. Hon. Lady Taverners all!*

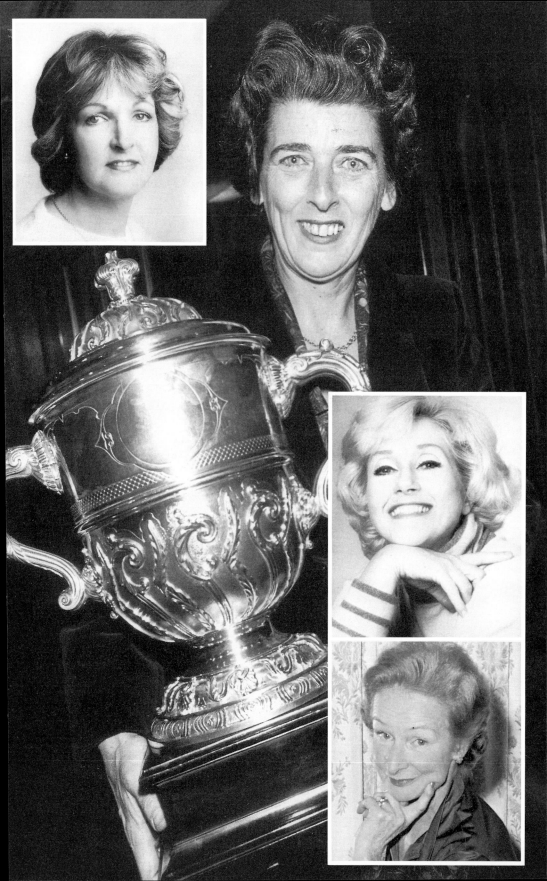

serving on the Tombola Committee for no less than 13 years! Marjorie believes in the Twelfth Man's advice, 'Work hard, raise money and have fun!' which she does with vigour and charm, a charm evident, too, on the boundary watching husband Alf in action at the Lord's Taverners matches.

Television's Jan Leeming confesses that she 'knows nothing about cricket', a fact that doesn't stop her from turning out as a celebrity at matches and other Taverners' functions, appearances which help considerably to pull in the crowds and the cash.

Margaret Thatcher, one among nearly fifty Lady Taverners, is predictably too busy to offer much active help to the Club. What she is unable to contribute is more than compensated for by the presence of husband Denis at many Taverners' 'do's'.

Actress Liz Fraser, for her part, remains a staunch and considerable attraction at cricket matches and functions. Her gay, attractive presence at Taverners matches is perhaps not so surprising when one learns that her gym mistress at St Olave's School for Girls played for the England Womens' XI and never, it seems, stopped encouraging her brood to take up cricket rather than tennis. As a result, St Olave's School team reigned supreme and Liz's wicket-keeping was, I have it on good authority, 'unsurpassed'. As for the lady herself, she avers: 'I must admit that catching balls hasn't done too much for me, but I don't mind being known as "the one who hardly ever dropped 'em".... How-zat?'

And, of course, happily well to the fore among Lady Taverners is the energetic and ever-smiling Ann, wife of the late and much lamented Ken Barrington, that incomparable bastion of Surrey and England for so many years. Ken loved the Taverners and played for them regularly so it is hardly surprising that Ann greatly enjoys carrying on his work for youth cricket. She is seen in the *Daily Express* photograph holding the Ken Barrington Cup presented each year at the Sherbourne Finals of the Under-13 Competition to which the NCA and Lord's Taverners are deeply committed. For the record, Ann, too, is an active organiser of the Ball Tombola and never was a lovely lady more apposite to the scene.

MICHAEL COWARD

*A fine Aussie cricket writer has reason vividly to
recall the Australian team in India during the
1984 golden jubilee of the Ranji Trophy ...*

BAGS OF DRAMA

Looking back, the portents were discouraging, I suppose. The rain fell vertically and with such force it silenced Trivandrum, the capital of the tiny state of Kerala which clings to the elbow of India.

Leaving shrieking children and squawking fowls under sagging canvas awnings, we found an intrepid taxi driver to negotiate the muddy roads to the airport which lies beyond the waving palm trees well away from the hub of the city. Four miles along the track, the battered cab spluttered to a halt. An auto-rickshaw had to be stopped and its owner pressed into service. Petrol, at the expense of the hirer, incidentally, had to be procured urgently. For there was a timetable to be met; a timetable designed, it seemed, by those who have no conception of the vastness of India; by those who have not met the challenges of travelling the sub-continent. Indeed, it was an inauspicious beginning to an extraordinary journey which was to have a quite fantastic conclusion.

In the October of 1984, the Australian cricket team visited India to celebrate the golden jubilee of the Ranji Trophy. For reasons known only to the silent few, the party, on this leg of the goodwill mission, was required to travel from Trivandrum, at the southern tip of India, to Jamshedpur in the far north-east. It is possible to accomplish the journey in six hours. On this occasion, it took 18 hours and yet, in the end, only 31 balls were bowled in anger before a baying mob.

For while the protagonists revealed themselves to be hardy, resourceful souls willing to pacify the game's devotees in Jamshedpur, they had no means to display their wares. To the overwhelming embarrassment of rosetted officials, the clothes and equipment belonging to the elite cricketers of India and Australia had gone missing.

For the only time in the history of the ancient game, an international match approved by the traditional authorities at Lord's could not be played as scheduled because the combatants had nothing to play in or to play with.

This bizarre tale had its genesis earlier in the day at the airport which

229

services the sprawling, iniquitous and desperately poor city of Calcutta which always assaults the senses. It was there, in the wee hours, after a five-hour excursion from Trivandrum which had taken nine hours, that the exhausted players and officials were unsympathetically told that their baggage could not be placed aboard the Fokker Friendship aircraft that was to bump and bounce through scudding grey clouds to Jamshedpur at dawn. There simply was too much of it, said dispassionate airline officials.

The respective team-managers, Mr Bob Merriman and Mr Erapalli Prasanna could not be appeased. Mr Merriman, a member of the Australian Conciliation and Arbitration Commission was, of course, not unused to demarcation disputes. Mr Prasanna, a distinguished Test cricketer, was not unaccustomed to varying degrees of ineptitude and confusion in the country he loved but which aged him so.

Mr Prasanna, inconsolable at such a happening on the day the nation stopped to remember the birth of Mahatma Gandhi, decided, in the absence of assistance from any of the countless deities, to inveigle Sadat into the service of his country in an hour of need.

Sadat, a big happy soul who set off his jet-black moustache by wearing a scarlet tunic and matching turban, was implored to take whatever steps necessary to find a truck to transport the baggage to Jamshedpur, the steel city of India, nestling at the foot at the Dalma Mountains in the State of Bihar.

It is not known what methods Sadat employed, or how many rupees changed hands, but by 3 a.m. the precious cargo was loaded aboard a hijacked truck by apopleptic hotel staff who had set aside rooms for the Australians but had not one bed booked for the pride of Indian cricket.

To ensure an unobstructed passage for the freight, Mr Prasanna enlisted the aid of two eminent broadsheet correspondents, Mr R. Mohan of *The Hindu* and Mr Rajan Bala of *The Express*. They helped load the baggage and Mr Mohan penned a note to the border guards explaining that no commercial value could be attached to the goods in the truck and that interstate duties need not be paid.

At 4.10 a.m., with Sadat back at his post as doorman-cum-driver cum-hijacker for the Airport Hotel, the baggage had started the 140-mile trip to Jamshedpur through some of the poorest areas of India.

Eight hours later, it was officially reported missing, and as cricket officials tried to placate the 25,000 people pressed into the stadium built by Mr J. R. Tata, the steel baron and former owner of Indian Airlines, harassed police launched an extensive posse.

The people flatly rejected the claim of officials that the delay had been caused by a damp wicket and their protests grew steadily louder as rubbish was hurled on to the beautifully-turfed ground and stones were thrown at the windows of the Indian dressing room.

Sensing they were losing control, a sub-committee of countless cricket executives called for an early lunch. No sooner had the boxes of boiled eggs, samosas and apples been presented in the members' enclosure, when word came that the truck had been sighted at Ghatsila, about 30 miles from the stadium. To the dismay of Messrs Prasanna, Mohan, Bala and, no doubt, Sadat, the truck had been impounded for some hours at the border crossing from Bengal to Bihar.

Four hours after the scheduled starting time, a 25-over match was started to jolly the crowd and justify the expense of taking the international game off the beaten track.

Twenty five minutes and 5.1 overs later, rain swept in from the misty valleys of the Dalma Mountains. The rain fell vertically and with such force it silenced Jamshedpur. Again we were with shrieking children and squawking fowls under sagging canvas awnings.

THERE'LL ALWAYS BE AN ENGLAND...

A Labour MP bowled a bouncer to parliamentary authorities yesterday – by confessing he watched cricket on a miniature TV in the Commons chamber.

During 'boring' speeches, Brian Sedgemore, Left-wing MP for Hackney South and Shoreditch, followed play in the first Test on the set borrowed from Welsh colleague Ann Clywd. But reception was poor, and he asked for an urgent debate on the chamber's structure 'before the next Test'.

Commons leader John Biffen played a straight defensive bat and replied: 'I have to confess I cannot understand any of that.' Mr Sedgemore said he would not be watching the rest of the season.

DAILY MAIL

ALAN KNOTT

Alan Knott was voted Young Cricketer of the Year in 1965 and in his Test debut two years later against Pakistan dismissed seven batsmen, all caught. He held the record for most dismissals by a wicket-keeper in Test cricket and his highest Test score was 35 for England against Australia at Trent Bridge in 1977. He scored two unbeaten centuries in a county match against Surrey in 1972. He played World Series Cricket. He runs a sports shop in Herne Bay.

MAN UNDER
A MICROSCOPE

Born Belvedere, Kent, 9 April 1946. 5ft. 8in., 10st. 10lb.
Wicket-keeper, right-hand bat.
First-class career: 1964–
Runs: 14,783 (av. 30.10).
Dismissals: 1,090 (982 caught, 108 stumped).
Tests: 93 (4,211 runs, av. 32.14; 263 dismissals,
244 caught, 19 stumped).
Scored 16 centuries (5 in Tests).

MY CHILDHOOD HEROES: My father was my big hero when I was a boy. He used to play for Belvedere Cricket Club with my uncle, brother, cousin and myself. Dad taught me cricket from the age of four and in the early days of my career he kept wicket to my off-spin bowling. My batting hero was Hampshire's Roy Marshall and Freddie Trueman was the bowler I used to love to watch.

MY MOST MEMORABLE PERFORMANCE: It was the last day of the final Test between West Indies and England at Georgetown in 1968. We were battling to salvage a draw that would give us a 1-0 victory in the series. I shared a four-hour stand with skipper Colin Cowdrey. At the end of play we were nine wickets down and I was lucky enough to be 73 not out. It was the second top score in the innings behind Colin who gave a real captain's performance in scoring 82.

Mushtaq Mohammed (Pakistan) caught by Alan Knott, the England wicket-keeper, off R. Hutton for 57 during the Third Test match, England v Pakistan, at Headingley on 9 July 1971.

BEST BOWLING I'VE SEEN: Michael Holding's 14 wickets for West Indies against England in the Fifth Test at The Oval in 1976 was the most impressive fast bowling I've seen. The best spin-bowling performance came from Derek Underwood for Kent against Sussex at Hastings in 1973. He took eight wickets for nine runs in 10.1 overs.

MY IDEA OF THE PERFECT BATSMAN: Gary Sobers, who was always in command of the situation with marvellous stroke play.

MY IDEA OF THE PERFECT BOWLER: Slow – Derek Underwood, a great bowler on all wickets and just unplayable on any wicket giving him a little help. Fast – Dennis Lillee, who never stops trying and can bowl at pace all day long.

MY IDEA OF THE PERFECT WICKET-KEEPER: I only saw Godfrey Evans play 'live' after he had finished his first-class career but he was still brilliant and I can't imagine there has been anybody better than him at his peak. If I had to pick a wicket-keeper from my era for a world side it would be Rod Marsh. He is a magnificent all-rounder, with gloves and bat.

MY FAVOURITE GROUND: Sydney Cricket Ground. It's large, pretty, has the famous Hill and there are excellent training, practice and changing facilities for the players.

THE SPORTSMAN I MOST ADMIRE OUTSIDE CRICKET: Pat Jennings, the Arsenal and Northern Ireland goalkeeper. If I'd been six inches taller, I would have loved to be a goalkeeper. What an example Pat gives youngsters. He is highly competitive, yet perfectly controlled and he has a wonderful balance that is not easy to acquire.

FREE LUNCH FOR CRICKET WATCHER

30 August 1968. Loudspeakers at the Hampshire and Nottinghamshire county cricket match at Portsmouth yesterday warned a schoolboy on the ground: 'Don't eat the sausage sandwiches – the sausages are off.' It was from his father. The boy, Paul Brown, of Clay Hill Drive, Gosport, was then invited by loudspeaker to lunch in the members' room at Hampshire Cricket Club's expense. Afterwards he confessed: 'I was so hungry that I had three of the sandwiches before I heard the warning. But I feel all right.'

Original Report

SIR JOHN MILLS

'I saw a tiny figure running like mad . . .'

A BOUNDARY, BEGAD!

I have spent many happy days playing and watching cricket but there is one occasion which is etched indelibly on my mind.

Several years ago I was asked to collect together a team of actors to play against a team of politicians.

One of the actors I collected was my great friend Sir Richard Attenborough. He was in the middle of making a film at the time and, as he hadn't played cricket for years, felt he should keep well away from the danger area. I suggested that he field on the boundary, near the drinks pavilion.

Halfway through the innings Denis Compton arrived at the wicket. A short one from our fast bowler arrived and Denis did his usual dance out of the crease and gave it a mighty swipe and the ball soared through five layers of cloud. I saw a tiny figure running like made along the boundary, the ball finally appeared and he put his hands above his head to catch it. The missile returning from Outer Space went straight through them, hit him on the head and he fell to the ground with a thud, out cold and covered with blood.

By sheer good luck, Sir Archibald McIndoe, the famous plastic surgeon, happened to be sitting nearby. He rushed Dickie to hospital and sewed him up with something like twenty-two stitches.

Our Hero was out of action as far as his film was concerned for two weeks. It may have been noticed that he has not turned out for Taverners for the last twenty-five years!

NO!

I must declare a special interest in John Christie, the splendid eccentric who, with his wife, opera singer Audrey Mildmay, created Glyndebourne Opera. John and his family virtually owned the North Devon village in which I live and work. Indeed, he once owned the cottage in which this book was created, a cottage which overlooks the churchyard, hard by the cricket field, in which John and his wife are buried. Christie was at Eton and was later a master there. I am indebted to Wilfred Scawen Blunt's book, John Christie of Glyndebourne, *for the following story*:

L.F.

A number of Old Etonians and colleagues recall John's Christie's athletic activities while a beak. As a bowler he used to lumber up to the wicket, where he delivered the ball in such a manner that it appeared to emerge from behind his head. His bowling was quite innocuous, but he took the wickets of those who anticipated something dangerous. Cyril Butterwick, a colleague of John's, mentions two 'dodges' by means of which John attempted to make additional runs.

He had a theory that if a batsman called 'No' and then ran, he would catch the fieldsman napping. That it certainly did; but it caught his partner napping too, however carefully he explained that 'Yes' meant 'No' and 'No' meant 'Yes'. The second and more complicated theory was that in running between the wickets much time was lost by turning. So his plan was to spin round three yards before reaching the Popping Crease and complete the run backwards so that the next run could be started without delay. This plan was for a time quite successful, because the fieldsmen were so helpless with laughter at the sight of a massive baldish man spinning round like a teetotum that they failed to take advantage of the fact that each run took several seconds longer than the normal procedure.

TEST HERO

OPPOSITE: England bowler Richard Ellison in merciless action during the Fifth Cornhill Test between England and Australia at Edgbaston, Birmingham, on 16 August 1985. Richard took 4 wickets during the morning session of the play – play umpired by North Devon's David Shepherd. David, it has to be said, has one or two superstitious habits which were seen by millions on television. We all have our little foibles and umpire David certainly has his. Whenever either side passes a score of 111, David habitually hops on one leg. Another of his superstitious habits is to poke a matchstick beneath his watch-strap if the day happens to be Friday the 13th. This apparently ensures that he is touching wood all day – and who can blame him!

W. J. FORD

*'Bails often have unaccountable ways of their
own...'*

CURIOUS INCIDENTS
AT CRICKET

There can be no one who has played much cricket who has not a fund
of strange stories about the curious incidents that he has seen or
experienced: indeed, one has only to foregather with some fellow-
cricketers and to listen to their yarns to wonder whether some cricket
stories might not well be ranked with 'fish stories', so hard is it to believe
them. But any reader who perseveres to the end of this article will, I
trust, be less incredulous in the future, and will credit the toughest tales
with at any rate a foundation of truth, for what I have to tell are either
facts that have come under my own observation or are otherwise well
authenticated, many of them being drawn from that great source
of information on matters concerning cricket, 'M.C.C. Scores and
Biographies'. The stories are intentionally given in no set order, as few
things are so dull as a series of anecdotes scientifically grouped under
definite headings; it is better to let them flow forth at random, just as
they would be told in the pavilion or the smoking-room.

Cricket had been played, or at least records kept, for about fifty years
before pads were invented in 1790; queer pads they were, too, consisting
of thin boards set angle-wise to allow the ball to glance off, and the
inventor was one 'Three-fingered Jack', of the famous Hambledon
Club, the original nursery of cricket. He had lost one or two fingers,
and consequently had the handle of his bat grooved, so as to get a
better grip of it. This arrangement was no doubt a necessity, considering
Jack's affliction, but I have seen an arrangement that was almost more
curious in actual use: the batsman, liking a heavy bat for slow bowling
and a light one for faster deliveries, had a hole bored in the back of his
bat about six inches from the bottom, into which he could screw a
loaded disc of wood, thereby increasing the weight of his bat as required.
He has never to my knowledge had any imitators. The bat, indeed, is
often responsible for the fall of the batsman's wicket; but while bad
manipulation is the main cause, yet this trusty friend often proves

'Actually impaled itself on the knife of an old woman.'

untrue, as happened a short time ago when, the batsman having made a good stroke, a splinter was broken off by the force of the hit and knocked the bail off; but Wells, the Sussex player, had a stranger experience in 1860, for the blade parted company with the handle (bats were often made in one piece then) and, leaving the handle in his hand, flew over his shoulder and dismantled the wicket. A third and similar story is equally true: the string that bound a broken bat gave way unnoticed and dislodged a bail, the batsman being in the act of striking: hence, as in the other cases, he was out – hit wicket. But one wonders that the laws do not provide for so untoward an incident, which ought never to be fatal to the striker's innings.

Fast bowlers sometimes break a stump, but I have seen quite a slow bowler do so, hitting it presumably on the exact point of least resistance, while on the other hand I have seen a fast bowler palpably hit the wicket without knocking down a bail, and this happened twice in one innings! One hardly dares to tell the story and be believed, but Shacklock of Nottingham was the bowler.

Here is another almost incredible story, but true. Last year my brother, F. G. J. Ford, hit a ball straight back so hard that it struck the opposite wicket and bounded back within his own popping-crease, while I myself once hit a ball which caught in the edge of the thatched roof of the pavilion and ran about a foot up the thatch, though no one could understand how a ball which was necessarily dropping could take such a course.

But balls are perverse things: one which was hit to the ring is recorded to have struck the pipe of a spectator and to have driven the stem into his throat, while another one actually impaled itself on the knife of an old woman who was dispensing ginger-beer and other commodities to the crowd. Spectators ought not to get hurt, for they are supposed to

239

have their eye on the game; but an unfortunate lady at Eastbourne, who was skating on the covered roller-rink, was hit by a ball which descended through a window in the roof, and so startled her that she fell and broke her arm. Another lady, entering the ground and astonished to find her sunshade suddenly whisked out of her hand, turned round to remonstrate with the aggressor, which proved to be only a little globe of red leather, lately in rapid motion.

'*A cricket ball struck him in the chest.*'

Bails often have unaccountable ways of their own; they have been knocked into the air, but have settled tranquilly in their groove again. One is said – I *don't* vouch for this – to have flown into the air, and turning in the air to have readjusted itself on the stumps, but with the long end where the short should have been; they have been nipped between the middle and the outer stump, and so prevented from falling. We lost one once, and found it at last in the wicket-keeper's pocket, while the ball had struck one something like seventy yards from the wicket. It is not everyone who knows that a former Prince of Wales, the father of George III, died from the effects of a blow from a cricket ball, which struck him in the chest and caused a cancerous growth, the removal of which resulted in death. The man who used to long-stop to a certain very fast bowler named Brown must have heard of this, for he used to arm himself with a pad of hay inside his shirt. He probably needed it, for Brown bowled with such speed that he is said to have sent a ball at practice *through* the coat with which the long-stop tried to stop it, and to have killed a dog on the other side! It must have been a very old coat and a very thin-skulled dog, unless the true version be that, the long-stop holding the coat to one side of him, the ball slipped, as it might do, along and under the coat, and then demolished the dog. Brown's bowling, however, was not always as deadly as this, for we read that in 1819 a player called Beldham – not of course, the famous player who died comparatively recently – hit his bowling so hard that Brown was afraid to bowl to him! Yet Beldham was then fifty-three years old.

The laws of cricket suggest nine ways of getting out, to which Tom Emmett added a tenth, viz, 'Given out wrong by the umpire,' but this method does not often figure on the score-sheet, and usually exists only in the batsman's mind, for there are generally eleven good men and true – on the other side – to support the umpire's verdict; but in a match, played in 1829, between Sheffield Wednesday and Nottingham, Dawson, a Sheffield man, was, according to the Sheffield score-book, 'cheated out', though the Nottingham book only says 'run out'. This match seems to have provoked a good deal of feeling in other years also, as witness the Sheffield Wednesday book again. 'A most disgraceful match! The Nottingham umpire kept calling "No-ball" whenever a straight ball was bowled, and Sheffield were foolish for continuing the game when they perceived that an unfair advantage was being taken.' The Nottingham book still reflects that silence is golden, and ignores the incident. Betting was probably at the bottom of the occurrence, for matches for money, or on which money depended, were so frequent that 'win, tie, or wrangle' has passed into a proverb.

This is certainly the only way in which to account for such entries as: 'Unfinished owing to disputed decision on the question of lbw,' 'Given out unfairly and refused to retire,' 'Side refuses to go out and abide by the decision of the umpire.' But, after all, what is to be done if an umpire gives a decision contrary to the laws of the game, as, for instance, when a man was given out in a first-class match for handling the *bail*? He might just as well have been sent back for blowing his nose. Another curious entry (1843) is 'G. Plank, walked out.' Is this an obscure joke about 'walking the plank'? Or did Plank walk away in dudgeon? Or does it mean that Plank inadvertently walked away from his wicket and was 'run out'? What, again, is 'nipt out'? This sad fate befell Mr Gandy in a match between Eton and Oldfield in 1793; and collateral evidence shows that 'nipt' is not the same as caught, bowled, stumped, hit wicket, or run out. Remembering that to 'nip' a ball meant the same thing as to 'snick' one, I think the expression signifies 'Caught at the wicket', a fate which must have been rare in those days of all-along-the-ground bowling.

'He caught the ball in the course of his jump.'

By the way, there is a charmingly *naive* record about a match between England and Twenty-two of Nottingham in 1818, for the game is said to have been sold on both sides; an umpire changed for 'cheating' (this was illegal, the changing as well as the cheating), and Lord F. Beauclerc's finger was broken by an angry and desperate fielder. Reading between the lines, one gathers that his lordship was bowling too well to please one of the fieldsmen, who, having backed the other side, did not like to see them bowled out, and tried to incapacitate the bowler. The name of 'Lord' is so great a name to cricketers that one does not like to associate it with anything shabby, but it is nevertheless true that though Lord had promised twenty guineas to anyone who could hit out of his ground (the original site of Dorset Square, and now absorbed, I fancy, by the Great Central Railway), yet he refused to pay up to E. H. Budd, who had earned the money by performing the feat. A similar sum was offered, it is said, by a member of the Melbourne C.C. to anyone who succeeded in hitting the clock over the pavilion, and he duly handed over the money to that colossal hitter, G. F. Bonnor, who hit the clock face and broke it. This same Mr Budd once played a single-wicket match, probably for a stake, with a man named Brand. Budd scored 70 and purposely knocked down his wicket; he then got Brand out for 0, and there being no follow-on at single wicket went in again, and again knocked his wicket down after making 31. Brand again scored 0, so he probably had as much of Budd's cricket as he wanted.

Another single-wicket match was played out in twelve balls, off the last of which the solitary and winning run was made. This must be the shortest match on record, but it is only fair to Diver, the Rugby coach, who lost, to say that he was only allowed to play with a broomstick. Here is a nice little bit of bowling, date 1861. The United Master Butchers played twenty of Metropolitan clubs, and got them out for 4 runs; C. Absolon, the well-known veteran, had eighteen out of the nineteen wickets that fell. With my own eyes I have seen the ball run up the bat, cut the striker's eyebrow and bound into a fieldsman's hand, so that he was caught out, and bad luck we thought it; but E. Dowson had worse luck at the Oval in 1862, for one of the opposing bowlers sent down a ball that rose and hit him in the mouth, knocking him on to his wicket, so that he was out for hitting wicket. Worse offenders have escaped unharmed; one for instance – Winter was his name – hit his wicket so hard that 'all three stumps were almost horizontal, but the bails were jammed', and consequently did not fall out, so that Winter continued his innings. In 1860 something similar occurred, but how it happened passes my understanding, for we are told that in a match played at Cambridge, between the University and the Town, the bowler, Reynolds, forced a bail one inch into the stumps, but did not dislodge it! This sounds incredible, but as the occurrence is comparatively recent let us hope that someone who was playing in the match will see these lines and explain matters.

The following score is curious: Chalcot was playing Bow; Bow scored 99, Chalcot 27 and 11; so far all is simple, but one Chalcot batsman, H. Payne, scored 24 and 10, being not out in each innings; wides totalled 3 and 1, so that the other ten batsmen were got out twice each and scored never a run between them – ten 'pairs of spectacles in one match'! 'Pro-digious!' as Dominie Sampson would have said. Another single-wicket match must not escape us: it was played in 1853 between Messrs. Barrett and Swain. Swain scored 5, and Barrett 3 and 1; yet neither made a run, for they were all wides!

I believe 37 is the largest number of runs ever scored for a single hit, the wickets being pitched at the top of a hill, down which the ball was hit, and over which it was thrown when originally retrieved; but F. P. Miller hit a 'thirteener' at single wicket, which must be a record; the ball, of course, was not returned within the boundary stumps, so that the unhappy fieldsman had to chase his own throw what time the batsman was sprinting between the stumps. The mention of hills recalls a famous bowler of old time, Lumpy by name, who always contrived to pitch the wickets, or to get the wickets pitched, in such a way that there should be a little declivity on which to drop the ball; for as the local poet sang – I quote from memory:

> Honest Lumpy did allow
> He ne'er could pitch but o'er a brow.

I wonder what the ground man at Lord's or the Oval would say if Jack Hearne or Lockwood insisted on selecting a pitch to suit them! Where the word 'honest' comes in, few cricketers could see. A tussock of grass once killed a cricketer, who, presumably when fielding, tripped over it, ruptured himself, and died in consequence; luckily cricket is a game of few fatal accidents.

A friend of mine, an old Cambridge man, used to tell a good story illustrative of obstinacy and contempt for rules. A stalwart miner was bowled out first ball, which apparently he regarded as 'trial', and made no move, till the wicket-keeper suggested that he was out and had to go. 'I ain't out,' he replied; 'I ain't out till I'm purred out: happen not then.' 'Purring', the uninitiated should be informed, is good Lancashire for 'kicking'. A match was played last year between one-armed men and one-legged men, and was freely commented on as a curiosity, whereas it was only a revival. Such a match took place as early as 1796, and was played, annually I think, in the fifties and early sixties, the one-armed men generally winning as being the better runners and bowlers.

A violin is a charming instrument, but it has not often saved a man's life; it is credited with such a performance in a good old day, when one Small just interposed it in time to save his head from the ball. Possibly the ball was of his own make, for Small was not only a violinist and a good cricketer, but a manufacturer of cricket balls as well, being originally a cobbler by trade. He lapsed into the poetical when he devised him a signboard, for the legend on it ran:

John Small
Make Bat and Ball
Pitch a Wicket
Play at Cricket
With any Man
In England.

Let us hope his bowling was not so erratic as his final rhyme.

All cricketers can dilate on the extraordinary catches they have seen made, they themselves being generally the victims; but putting those aside which concern them personally, they would, I believe, combine in giving their second votes, as the Athenians gave theirs to Aristides, to a Captain Adams who was playing in Phœnix Park, Dublin, in 1751. The ball was hit to him in the long field, and he not only jumped a fence 3ft. 10in. high, but actually caught the ball in the course of his jump. The story is a hard one to believe, but it is duly recorded in print, with dates and measurements all in apple-pie order.

There are plenty of curious incidents that depend on statistics alone, as for instance in a match of very low scoring, played between South Sussex and North Sussex, when in an aggregate of 89 runs for thirty-two wickets there was only one hit, a three-er, above a single; again in one innings no fewer than seven men were run out; in a single match of three innings there were twenty duck's-eggs; and in an innings of 120 there was no hit for 2, though there were plenty of 3s and 4s. Again, in an innings of 38, no fewer than seven men scored 4 each; while in another match, Gentlemen *v.* Players, Burbidge, the Surrey amateur, caught five men in one innings, 'all of them fine catches'.

The ball occasionally gets played into a man's shirt. This has, indeed, occurred to W. G. Grace himself; but it has played more curious pranks than this, having lodged in a man's pads and once in the wicket-keeper's arm-pit; in this case short slip extracted it and claimed the catch; but the following note does not explain itself very lucidly. Playing for Yorkshire against Surrey, Anderson 'played the ball on to the heel of his shoe, and was there [*sic*] caught by Lockyer', the wicket-keeper. A cricketer's costume was regarded as important even in 1828, for *Bell's Life* has a remark to the effect that 'it would be much better if H. Davis would appear in a cricketing dress, instead of in that of sailor'; but it is hardly probable that it has ever happened before 1899 that only two men turned out to field in a county match properly apparelled; yet so it happened at Dewsbury, where the Derbyshire professionals found that the water had not been turned off at night in their dressing-room, and that all their clothes were soaked through and through. Luckily only about a quarter of an hour was required to finish off the match.

Most of us cricketers recall a match in which H. J. Scott, the Australian, wound up with six, six, six, four; but a certain G. Hall, playing for the Gentlemen of Sussex against the Players of the County, hit the first three balls of the match out of the ground. I myself once received the first and the last ball of a match, each of which went out of the ground, and each of which was bowled by the same bowler.

The dog which Brown killed, as already told, is not the only dumb spectator that has met with an unnatural death at the hands – if I may be allowed the 'bull' – of a cricket ball, for is it not on record that Tom Hearne, the great Middlesex cricketer of early years, was just about to deliver the ball when a pigeon flew across the wicket? Tom stopped, aimed at the bird instead of the stumps, and brought it down dead. F. Cæsar did the same thing in 1847, the victim this time being, however, a swallow; while a good story is told about S. E. Gregory, the Australian cricketer. He was fielding at cover-point, but his attention was astray, when a sudden shout of 'Look out, Sid!' recalled his wandering wits. He made a sudden grab at what he thought was the ball – and fielded a swallow! *Apropos des bottes*, my brother-in-law not long ago decapitated a lark with a golf-ball.

Wenman, a great cricketer early in the century, once experienced a

'*The ball passed between the heads of two ladies.*'

curious piece of good luck, the ball passing clean through the stumps without removing a bail; yet experiment proved afterwards that the ball could not go through without touching them. The explanation must be that the stumps 'spread' just enough to permit the passage of the ball without unseating the bail, and then closed up again, as is quite possible if the ground was hard. But even if possible, it was curious, and scarcely cheering to the other side, as Wenman eventually scored 139, and was not got out. It was not uncommon in early days for a side whose chances were hopeless to give up the game; did not Dingley Dell surrender to All Muggleton? But in so late a year as 1858 the Old Etonians gave up a match to the Old Harrovians, 'because they did not want to come up on the second day'. The Old Harrovians, however, were winning hands down. It is also in the history of the Middlesex Club that the 'secretary courteously gave up the match', rain preventing the opposing side from getting the two or three runs required to win. Of course, this was a 'club' match, and not a county match, the opponents being The Butterflies; still, one would be surprised to find such a thing done in the present day, even in the 'tenthest' of tenth-rate matches.

An interesting match, which certainly has claims to be called 'curious', was played in 1858 between eighteen veterans and England, the veterans scoring 82 and 164, England 96 and 51. The veterans ranged from thirty-nine to fifty-four years of age, though Chester, aged thirty-four, was specially allowed to play for them; yet seventeen years later only three of the older men were dead, two of whom were accidentally killed. In the same year five amateurs played in a game between Kent and England; the scoring was not heavy, only 380 runs for thirty-five wickets, but the ten innings of the amateurs only produced 11 of the runs.

One would think that no stupendous effort, mental or physical, is needed to measure twenty-two yards with perfect accuracy, yet the ground man has failed at least twice in this simple task. In 1861 it was not discovered till four men were out that the pitch was 4ft. short, so the match was continued, not recommenced, on another and a proper pitch, while a similar thing occurred on the Cambridge University ground in a first-class match about 1880, two or three wickets having fallen before the error was discovered: the game, however, was begun afresh, and one of the Studds who had got but few runs in his first try now made 60 or 70. Recommencement was clearly the proper course, but the moral is, 'Trust to a chain and not to a tape, as the latter may easily meet with an accident unobserved or unnoted.'

Here are a few more oddities from my note-book. In an innings of 202 a man made 32 threes and 32 twos; another man struck the ball on to the ground, but managed to hit it a second time as it bounded up, and into point's hands, the umpire actually deciding 'Out.' The same thing exactly has happened to myself, the ball going to short-slip, but the umpire knew his business better, and I went on with my innings.

I have just recalled what 'Narrow escape of two ladies', a memorandum in my book, means. We were playing a scratch game at Eastbourne to fill up an afternoon, and I was fielding in the region of the tea-tent, the spectators standing about rather in my way. Suddenly I saw a hard hit coming that way, and, shouting 'Look out!' went for the ball, which passed between the heads of two ladies busily engaged in chatting, and fell into my hands: their faces must have been within a couple of feet of each other.

I remember, too, nearly robbing our college club of secretary and captain at one fell blow, the ball whizzing between their heads as they were talking: the funny thing was that the net was apparently between them and me, as they stood near where mid-off would be posted in a match, but the ball curled, as a hard-hit ball often does curl on the off-side, and showed them that their security was more ideal than real.

The laws limit the bowler's privilege of changing ends; but as 'nice customs curtsey to great kings,' the M.C.C. once allowed a match to be played at Lord's between the Club and the Gentlemen of England, in which R. Holden, with 'ten picked fields', bowled all through, changing ends at the close of each over. He must have been a good stayer to stand so much work without an 'easy'.

How is this for a case of unfair play? Lord F. Beauclerc, in a single-wicket match between three of Surrey and three of England in 1806, 'unseen took a lump of wet dirt and sawdust and stuck it on the ball, which, pitching favourably, made an extraordinary twist and took the batsman's wicket.' Umpires had to be as 'slim' as the players in the days when matches were played for money.

One could cover pages with such incidents as I have jotted down, but, unfortunately, though the fund of stories is almost inexhaustible, there is a limit to what is generally regarded as illimitable – space; but the reader who, like Oliver Twist, asks for more need only apply to the first cricketing friend he meets, who will, temporarily at least, be able to appease his appetite for curiosities.

Strand Magazine
July, 1900

COLIN COWDREY

*'The helmet is something of a disfigurement on
the cricket field, although hapless batsmen in
certain conditions could make a good case for
wearing it ...'*

SUCH A HARD BALL –
BUT A GENTLE ART

Who was it that decided that cricket should be played with a hard ball?
I have taken so many knocks myself that I feel I shall carry them with
me into old age. It was a tragic mistake not to have a soft ball. Sir
Robert Menzies once told the England team at one of those memorable
dinners he used to give as Prime Minister, and on this occasion as our
host at Canberra, that he had an unstinted admiration for Sir Winston
Churchill: but there was just one reservation. Churchill's wide ranging
attention for everything about the British way of life failed to embrace
the game of cricket. At a very early stage in their relationship, Sir
Robert asked to be excused so as to spend a few hours at Lord's. 'H'm
... h'm ... cricket ... h'm, that damned hard ball game at Harrow' – and
wandered off. Apart from the occasional grunt of approval whenever
England were doing well, he was never known to take much interest.
I sympathise with him over his fear of a cricket ball and a dislike of its
hardness.

I remember opening the innings in a junior school match for nine-year-olds. It was a warm, bright, sunny day and the headmaster produced a new cricket ball. I had never played with a new ball before, and I was struck by the shiny, bright, brilliant red colour of it as I played it away for a single off the first ball of the match. The next ball was a very high full toss, dropping on to the stumps. My partner was completely bamboozled. He adopted what would have been rather a good stance and position for bringing down a high pheasant. It was no surprise when he missed the ball altogether, but something of a calamity when the ball dropped on to the bridge of his nose and broke it. There was a piercing yell and blood everywhere, and the poor boy was carried off to the local hospital. That incident was to give me a healthy respect for the hardness of a cricket ball and the injuries it can cause.

On an early visit to Canterbury, I remember watching Ray Lindwall bowl the first over of the match to Kent opening batsman Leslie Todd, a good player if not the most rugged in the face of fast bowling. Almost at once, he was struck full toss on the toe: a most painful blow. There was a half-hearted shout for lbw, but poor Leslie hopped around in agony for several minutes, and to everyone's astonishment hopped off the field. He had no intention of facing another ball from Lindwall, nor of making an appearance in the second innings. Perhaps he was a good judge.

Bouncers were scarce in my early years, and whilst I was always on the look-out for the odd one, I never had the feeling that the bowler was out to knock me over. It is not quite the same these days – I retired at just about the right time!

The 'bodyline' series started something in 1932–3 which, by general agreement, was buried until the sixties. The seed had been sown by Douglas Jardine and his deployment of Larwood and Voce, and the evil lay dormant. Then, as the wheels of commercial cricket started to gather pace, and there were richer rewards for winners, so inevitably the big strong men came into their own. Brute force began to replace old-fashioned skills.

The administrators have been slow to act, mainly because they have found it so difficult to frame a law which defines a bouncer. Sadly, the spinner has been less of an investment than the fast bowler mixing skill with intimidatory tactics. Protective clothing has become a must. I remember playing in a Test match when Denis Compton put just a pair of socks in his trouser pocket as a thigh pad, and he wore only paper-thin batting gloves. In today's game he would be a prime target and would need to take much more care – yet I cannot see him, or the Don, wearing special headgear.

The first thing one sees on the field at Lord's is a sign of the times. I remember seeing a fielder at a very close short-leg position one over, and stationed at deep mid-off for the next. It happened to be a very

cold day and the helmet may have served to keep his head warm: but there is something rather incongruous about a deep fielder wearing a helmet. This, of course, is one of the problems, for the umpires have made it clear that they will not act as parking spaces for unwanted helmets in the same way as they do for bowlers' jerseys.

On an even colder day a week later, at Chelmsford, Michael Denness produced a new model of helmet, something akin to a balaclava. It kept the head and ears warm and, I am told, is fully protective too. It is less unsightly than the ordinary helmet but still pretty unusual.

I could not help wondering what George Duckworth would have said if I had taken a helmet with me on board ship as we sailed for Australia on my first tour. This great Lancashire and England wicket-keeper was ostensibly scorer and baggage master, but he was much more than that. Having toured Australia on numerous occasions, and won friends in every cricket country around the globe, he was something of a PPS to the captain, a permanent *éminence grise*. To the young players, like myself, he wore a stern, forbidding mask, but beneath, the heart was warm, and I regarded him as father and friend. I'm sure he would have taken one look at the helmet as we sailed out of Southampton Water, and I would have been made to feel so uncomfortable that I could guarantee that the headgear would be floating in the sea long before we reached the Bay of Biscay.

The helmet is something of a disfigurement on the cricket field, although hapless batsmen in certain conditions could make a good case for wearing it. I can think of some desperately sticky wickets in Australia under a fierce sun where Hammond and Hutton played fine innings, but had nothing to show for themselves in the record book – and those innings will never be forgotten by those who watched them. I imagine that they would not have argued if the twelfth man had walked on the field with a helmet. No, my complaint is that the helmet should not really *have* to come into play. That it does do so, and is necessary, concedes that there is too much rough intent.

Violence is, sad to say, very much the order of the day, and shows itself more and more in competitive sport. Soccer has its moments from time to time, and more recently rugby has become outrageously rough. The biting of ears and the hideous scraping of boot studs to tear the skin off a face caught in the scrum are acts which are quite unacceptable; yet they have happened.

In the game of cricket, happily, I cannot remember one player

OPPOSITE ABOVE: *Cowdrey catches Yuile at slip off Titmus for 12 in the Third Test, England v New Zealand, at Headingley, 1965.* BELOW: *West Indians swarm on to the Lord's pitch to congratulate their team following their 1963 Second Test victory. In the centre with a bandaged arm is Cowdrey, who came on for England in a last hope to win.*

striking another. The nearest to that can come when a bowler stands rather firmly on his follow through, directly in the path of the batsman running through and trying to turn quickly for a second. On occasions, when the atmosphere is charged, I have felt the sharp point of a bowler's elbow in the ribs, accompanied by a little word in the ear for good measure. More infrequently, it can happen that a bowler runs across the batsman's path in such a way that it is difficult for the umpire to gauge whether his bulking is accidental. Some years ago there was a rather indelicate incident when John Snow was to be seen in a fair shoulder charge with India's little opening batsman, Gavaskar, knocking him for six.

The only time I have ever really felt like moving into action myself has been when a fielder has come and positioned himself very close to me, square on the offside of the wicket. Such field settings are of nuisance value, and are placed to distract concentration. I would like to see this ruse outlawed, because there is no way that the fielder can keep still throughout, however hard he may try, and in moving he breaks the code which defines fair and unfair play. I have been tempted to let the bat go at the end of my stroke, but when it came to it, courage has failed me, and on reflection, I do not regret that.

Cricket has always been a peaceful game, with the emphasis on skill. In recent years, as commercial sponsorship has improved the reward for winning, it was only to be expected that players would press harder for victory. Bouncers, as a weapon of intimidation, do bring results, for no one likes being hit by a hard cricket ball. In the razzmatazz of World Series Cricket, fast bowlers bowling an unlimited amount of bouncers has made for more spectacular watching, yet to the cricket connoisseur, the development has been hard to bear. The cricketers themselves have not enjoyed it, I am glad to say. As a result, an experimental law has been introduced into English cricket for the summer of 1979 restricting bowlers to one bouncer an over, a bouncer being defined as a ball which rears over shoulder height when the batsman is standing normally. The umpires have been charged to interpret this new rule strictly for the good of the game and, indeed, to put the emphasis back upon skill rather than force.

Violence and strong-arm tactics may amuse those in front of the Tavern from time to time, but it is cricket as a game of skills that we must seek to promote and preserve.

OPPOSITE:
MIDDLESEX MOMENT. Middlesex (later England) captain Mike Gatting hits out off a ball from Northamptonshire's B. J. Griffiths during the Middlesex v Northants match at Lord's on 7 September 1983.

SIMON RAVEN

*'And now it was for James as if all the years
had fallen away and he was back on the Canterbury
green ...'*

THE MCC MATCH

When Harold arrived the evening before the MCC match, he learnt
that the Baron's Lodge team had so far won all its matches but two, both
of these having been honourably drawn. James, who was particularly
anxious that this unbeaten record should be maintained, was in a state
of feverish excitement about the next day. At one point he had even
spoken of not playing himself, in order to 'make room for young blood';
but he had been persuaded that it was proper and even mandatory
that he himself should lead the side on this, the last match of all.

'Quite right,' said Harold. 'And anyhow they tell me you've been in
good form.'

'Not too bad for an old man,' said James with modest pleasure.
'Fifteen not out against the Butterflies and twenty-two yesterday against
some very decent Forester bowling.'

'So of course you must play,' said Harold: and then, leaving James
deep in thought about the batting order, he went to look for Georgy.

'How's Hugo been behaving?' he said at once.

'Rather well. A bit distant, but nothing you could object to.'

'And will he go on coming to see your father?'

'I don't know,' said Georgy. 'He refused at first, then said he would
because of Nigel Palairet. It could mean anything. I no longer understand him, you see. He's become ... alien.'

'Perhaps he always was.'

Then Harold went to find Hugo.

'What do you think of your uncle?' Harold said.

'He seems very well.'

'You know why. All this cricket, and all his friends, and, not least,
seeing you again. After this match, he'll be feeling rather flat. I suppose
you wouldn't think of staying on for a day or two?'

'No.'

'But I thought you'd promised Georgy—'

'I've changed my mind. Because all the reward I've had for coming at all is to have people nagging at me like you're doing now.'

'Your trouble,' said Harold, 'is that you're a second rate man with certain minor capacities which you're too proud to settle for. You're too proud to do the little things you *could* do. You could have been a good schoolmaster, in a modest way, and a great help to James. Even now, you could give him a lot of happiness. But no, not you. You're too grand, too greedy, for such simple things. You must for ever be trying to catch up with some new and more inflated idea of your own importance.'

'I haven't done too badly, Harold. I've become quite rich, you know. I lead a pleasant and civilised life. I read books. I look at things. I think.'

'While you're being so smug about it all, perhaps you'd care to tell me where the money came from.'

'You might say,' said Hugo, 'that I did a lucky piece of business.'

'I might say that you're a bloody little crook.'

'Don't start trouble, Harold. For the moment at least everyone is happy here. You wouldn't want to spoil it?'

Harold grunted and stumped off, but for the rest of the evening he made himself agreeable to everybody, Hugo included. Not that he had to suffer Hugo for long. Although the refreshments were as lavish as ever, James, apologetic but firm, insisted that those who were to play in next day's match should be in bed by ten-thirty sharp. With James and Hugo out of the way, Harold approached Nigel (whom James had pronounced, with regret, to be too light-weight a player for so serious an occasion) and came straight to the point.

'Whatever it is you do in Chester Row,' he said, 'Hugo has evidently reaped considerable benefit. He must be grateful to you.'

'I doubt it,' Nigel said. 'Gratitude is not his *forte*.'

'But you must have *some* influence with him.'

'Perhaps.'

'Then get him to stay here after the cricket's over. Or at least to promise to come again very soon.'

'I see,' Nigel smiled coolly. 'You too want to spare James Escome the truth about his precious nephew.'

'I'm an old friend of Lionel's, of them all.'

'You don't need to explain. I'm on your side.'

'Well then?'

'Hugo,' said Nigel, 'is determined to push off again for good. He is not in the mood to listen to polite requests.'

'So I've found out. It seems he was more docile with Georgiana and Bessie, though. He said he'd do what they asked, because of you. Why was that?'

'At that time he thought I had a hold over him. So I had, but it gets

255

weaker every day. It follows that we must arrange something else. Perhaps you would care to assist me in this? I need someone with a logical and strictly objective turn of mind. I don't know you, of course, but I've read some of your books—'

'—Which?' said Harold, flattered.

'One on the pre-Socratics and another on primitive notions of god-head – a subject that particularly interests me. It seems to me that you may have the qualities needed. Bessie and Georgiana think so too.'

'Qualities needed for what?'

'For what is to be done. Let us go outside,' said Nigel, moving towards the French window, 'and get a little privacy and fresh air. First of all, you'd better hear exactly what our young friend has been up to since he left London. . . .'

The MCC had gathered a side of amateurs, most of whom had played for County Second XIs at one time or another and three of whom had played full seasons in first class cricket, albeit some years ago. This was opposition of a calibre unlike anything yet seen during James's cricket week; there would be no room for error or laxity, as was plainly apparent from the very beginning of the match. The MCC, having won the toss and chosen to bat, sent in two grizzled left-handers, the more grizzled of whom, receiving as his first ball a high and fast full toss, hit it calmly over square leg and out of the ground, thus removing most of its shine and much of the bowler's self-esteem. There followed another full toss and two long hops, each of which was despatched, with an efficiency so spare as to be almost casual, for four runs. After this the play settled down a bit, but no one was left in any doubt how matters stood: the opposition was a tough and old-fashioned bunch of campaigners who would hit bad balls, stop good ones, and drop dead on the ground sooner than give away one run in a hundred.

By lunch time, the MCC had made a hundred and ninety runs for the loss of two wickets. Since this was to be a two day match, there was no prospect of an early declaration, and the Baron's Lodge contingent faced a grim afternoon ahead. The only one who was quite undaunted was James, who remarked that three lucky balls, which could happen at any moment, would be quite enough to restore the balance. After lunch, in the hope of illustrating this principle, he tried a number of quick changes in the bowling; but the MCC batsmen had been in the game too long to be caught out by this kind of trick, and the only wicket to fall before three o'clock went to a grotesque leg break bowled by James himself – a ball which seemed to come back almost square behind the batsman's legs to hit his stumps. This made the score two hundred and seventy for three. There followed another hour and a half of vigorous and unsparing batting, until at tea time, with three hundred and ninety runs on the board, the MCC declared.

The first innings of Baron's Lodge opened with a series of disasters. The first batsman fell inside five minutes to a vicious yorker; number three was out to the very next ball, which went away from him at the last moment, touching the edge of the bat (if he hadn't been a very good player he would have missed it altogether) and proceeding straight into the wicket-keeper's gloves with a dull plop; and two overs later number four called an eccentric run to cover point and was run out by six foot clear. Nor did matters mend when Hugo went in: having driven a couple of balls to the long off boundary and being apparently well set, he received the only shooter of the entire week (all the wickets had been immaculately prepared) and looked round to see the three stumps forming a perfect equilateral triangle on the ground. His scowl was visible from the marquee; and Bessie, who was taking a moment off from clearing up the tea things, laughed so loudly that several MCC men in the field raised their eyebrows, the only facial movement they made during the entire day except to consume food and drink.

After this, however, with a score of only thirty runs for four wickets, Baron's Lodge began to settle down. Number two, a dull but extremely sound player, looked as if he were capable of staying there for life, and number six, who now joined him, was blessed with that quality against which even the dour authority of the MCC must be powerless: he was in luck. He snicked his first ball through the slips for four, chopped the second between his legs for two, and then, having sent short leg the kind of catch one gives a five-year-old child at a picnic, saw it slide like soap through the unfortunate man's hands and drop to the ground with the deliberation of a freshly ejected cow-pat. This mistake cost the fielding side dear; for despite his erratic start, number six was a correct and cool-headed player, just the man for an emergency, and he now proceeded to play the bowling with an unhurried, almost intellectual competence which the MCC players themselves could hardly have improved upon. The score went steadily up, from forty to sixty, from sixty to a hundred; and when stumps were drawn at half past six Baron's Lodge had made a hundred and fifty odd for five wickets (number two having played so far back to a ball that he had hit his own stumps). As James remarked, Baron's Lodge was by no means out of danger but was very definitely still in the match.

Partly because of the dedicated nature of the MCC players, partly because this was the last night but one of the cricket week (the last night on which people could still look forward), dinner was a rather muted affair, more formal than usual and far less gay. Although the match was still a live concern, there was an air of anti-climax, almost of futility, to which most people responded by going early to bed. James, solicitous for the health of his team, was not displeased by this ('When

257

we've won the match we can have a real booze-up'), but when he himself said goodnight he urged all the non-players to stay and drink as late as they wished.

'There are not many nights left,' he said wistfully, and waved his hand from the doorway in what might almost have been a total valediction.

'Now,' said Nigel to Harold when the old man had gone, 'you're absolutely clear about tomorrow?'

'Yes,' said Harold indifferently.

'No doubts?'

'After what you told me last night,' said Harold, 'it is too late for doubts.'

The next morning saw Baron's Lodge battling hard but on the whole successfully to make up ground. Number six continued to cash in on his early good luck with controlled and accurate batting: and by the time the seventh wicket had fallen and he was joined by James, the score had advanced to two hundred and forty. Another hundred runs, and Baron's Lodge would be out of trouble.

James had acquitted himself very decently when playing in earlier matches, but he was now up against a standard of bowling which he had not faced for many years. At first he seemed confused and alarmed: his strokes were played without heart and even without hope, scrappy, aimless strokes, bearing little relation to the balls bowled, like those of a sulky schoolboy who has been forced to play against his will. Then, when the spectators were beginning to feel sad and embarrassed for him, he received a fast, short ball outside the off stump. In the old days this had been his favourite of all things; and even now some reflex stirred from its long sleep and took him into action: over came his left foot, up and across went the bat, all wrist and balance, quick and inevitable as a striking snake, and almost before the shot was completed the ball had flashed past cover and was at the boundary. It was the classical square cut off the front foot, a stroke which had been old-fashioned even when it delighted the Kentish crowds in the 'twenties and which had not been seen in cricket of any consequence since the old Nawab of Pataudi died. It was so unexpected, so beautiful, so absolute in its kind, that for a moment there was complete silence. Then, for the first time since the match started, the MCC players began to clap. Gravely and slowly, without exaggeration but without stint, they applauded what each of them recognised as the work of a master hand.

And now it was for James as if all the years had fallen away and he was back on the Canterbury green in the full pride of his youth and skill. There was no more fumbling and snatching, no more dithering and backing away. Now that he had played his square cut everything was come right. Each stroke was as sure as the one before, neat, essential and precise. Most of them, to be sure, were strokes which scored behind the wicket or not at all (for where should an old man find strength to drive and force?), but they were crisp and firm, models of seemliness and grace. He cut square, he cut late; he glanced the ball to leg off the back foot and off the front: he played back in defence with the calculated suavity of a matador; when he hooked, it was with a feather-light touch, a mere deflection, by which he stole for his own end the bowler's power. It was a captain's innings in time of need: he batted from a quarter past twelve to half past one; and when he came back to the marquee, having declared the Baron's Lodge innings closed for 401 runs of which he himself had made sixty-five, the spectators rose to greet him with a great shout of triumph, many of them turning away to hide the tears which were running down their cheeks.

'Circumstances quite helpful so far,' said Nigel to Harold during the lunch interval.

'I suppose so,' answered Harold, and went on eating his cold salmon with prudence and solemnity.

The MCC batted from after lunch until tea at four forty-five. Swiftly and dispassionately, they made three hundred and thirty-two runs for the loss of seven wickets. By declaring when they did, they left Baron's Lodge with three hundred and twenty-two runs to make in two hours (between five and seven, for either captain could ask for an extra half hour after six thirty). It was, on the whole, a sporting declaration; it left Baron's Lodge with an outside but, given the state of the ground, quite feasible chance. Even so, many captains would have ordered their men to play out time for a draw. Not James. 'All or nothing,' he said as he led his side off the field. 'Never mind the wickets. We want *runs*.'

'Remember,' said Nigel to Harold during the tea interval, 'as soon as the umpires pull the stumps.'

In order to save time, James posted members and supporters of the Baron's Lodge side all round the field so that they might gather the ball the moment it reached the boundary and return it to the bowler. For the first quarter of an hour of the Baron's Lodge innings this precaution was otiose. True, the opening batsman hit a six off his second ball; but he was clean bowled by the ball which followed it, and numbers three and four fared much the same. Number two survived, but he had neither the temperament nor the aptitude for aggressive play; so that when Hugo came in at number five, with the score at twenty for three, it was up to him to take charge without delay.

His behaviour was cool and assured. The first three balls he received he treated with modest deference (time spent in reconnaissance is *never* wasted). The fourth ball, which was only just short of a length, he hooked nippily for four, and the fifth, which was well up to him, and the last of the over, he pushed away towards mid-wicket for a single. Then, facing the bowling at the other end, he once again played three cautious exploratory shots – only to follow them with two rangy drives through the covers and another quick single to mid-wicket off the last ball of the over.

It had been a long day, and tough as the MCC bowlers were, they were beginning to fail in speed and accuracy. For some overs, Hugo cut, hooked and drove with evident ease; then, when the MCC tried the sensible but obvious tactic of putting on slow spin bowlers to tempt him into indiscriminate hitting, he kept his head, refrained from trying to strike the ball half-volley, and scored a quick succession of twos and singles either off the back foot or by leaving his ground and playing the ball carefully yet firmly before it pitched. But although the runs were coming very nicely, the rate of scoring at five-thirty (sixty-seven runs in the first half hour) was still not quite enough to bring the Baron's Lodge total to three hundred and twenty-two by seven o'clock.

At this stage number two, desperate to pay his way, played a pull shot of almost blasphemous ineptness and was succeeded by number six, who was very much more suited to play the kind of innings required. For ten minutes all went well: but at five-forty-five number six, wrought upon by the perennial temptation to hit a leg break at the half volley, mistimed his stroke and was caught by long off. Number seven and number eight both scored a few useful runs, but both got over-excited and before long picked the wrong balls to hit. When James joined Hugo at the wicket the time was ten minutes past six and the score was a hundred and seventy; if Baron's Lodge were to win now, they must score at the rate of three runs a minute.

'You can rely on me to stay here, dear boy,' said James, 'but you'll have to get the runs.'

It was now that Hugo started to put on real pressure. The ground, though of ample size for little boys, was rather on the small side for grown men. It followed that lofted shots, in time of emergency, were often good investments: even if improperly hit, they were liable to sag over the boundary line, immune from being caught, for unmerited sixes. From now on, therefore, and whenever possible, Hugo started to lift the ball. This policy was rewarded by five sixes (two of them at least rather gungy ones) in three overs, quite apart from the runs he scored along the ground. Every time the ball reached the boundary, it was instantly returned by one of the onlookers stationed for the purpose;

and by 6.30 the score had reached two hundred and thirty-eight.

James's part was unspectacular but demanding. Every time he was left with the bowling, he had to contrive to place the ball for a single so that Hugo might renew his efforts. It was a measure of his cunning that only twice in his first half hour at the crease did he receive two consecutive balls and that not once did he receive more than two. Hugo, in a foam of sweat, his face glowing red as a winter's sun, continued game; but he was flagging a little now and badly needed the respite which James could not give him.

'One last effort, dear boy,' James called up the pitch between the overs. 'One last effort. . . .'

For now the shadows were lengthening over the ground and the birds were failing in their song. There were forty runs to be got and twenty minutes in which to get them. The MCC captain, knowing that Hugo must soon make a mistake if only from weariness, was continuing with the slow bowlers who were the more likely to elicit it. One last effort, thought Hugo; now or never. He faced up to a tall, stringy, left-handed bowler, who was giving the ball plenty of air and bringing it in, with pungency, from the leg. One last effort.

The first ball of the over was slightly overpitched and outside the off-stump. Left elbow well up, left foot well across, Hugo drove it into the air over extra cover's head and saw it land just over the boundary line. The next ball was also on the off, but shorter and quicker: this time he put his right foot across and cut it just backward of square; third man, running round the boundary, saved the four, but Hugo and James ran a comfortable two. That's eight of them, Hugo thought. As the bowler's arm came over for the third time, Hugo saw him cock his wrist to turn the ball, for a change, from the off. I'll teach him to bowl Chinamen, Hugo thought; *hit with the spin*. He smashed into the ball with a rancorous cross bat and for the second time that week holed out in the swimming pool. For the fourth ball of the over, the bowler adopted a precisely similar action – wrist cocked for the Chinaman that would come in from the off. But he's faking, Hugo thought; it's going to be a googly, it's going to come in from the leg, and if it's that much higher in the air I'll be certain. It was that much higher. Back over his head then, no time for refinements now, back over his head hard and high. Hugo jumped out of his crease, did not quite get his foot to the ball, and hit it ballooning into the air with a good deal of slice. On the boundary long off waited, shading his eyes with his hands; but Hugo's luck held, and what would have been a catch on seven grounds out of ten cleared the boundary by five yards. The fifth ball was well short on the leg side; his arms felt like lead, but he managed to scrabble it away for two. The sixth ball was straight and quickish; abandoning all thought, Hugo just swished; he caught the ball on the meat, and it sizzled away crutch high between the bowler and mid-on to the boundary. He had scored twenty-six runs in the one over, and he was utterly spent.

'That's it, dear boy,' called James as the fieldsmen crossed over. 'There's time for me to get the rest.'

This he now did, crisply and prettily, and had the honour, some five minutes before the time for close of play. Moving from the wicket half dazed with triumph and fatigue, neither he nor Hugo saw Harold, who, as the umpires pulled up the stumps, walked rapidly away towards the house.

TILL CRICKET US DO PART

26 August 1981. Mrs Mildred Rowley, a nursing sister, of Helming Drive, Wolverhampton, was granted a decree nisi yesterday on the grounds of her husband's unreasonable behaviour. She had complained that he was 'cricket mad'.

After the hearing at Wolverhampton Divorce Court, Mrs Rowley said: 'Cricket was not just a hobby – it was a total obsession. I had just had enough of it.' Her husband, Mr Michael Rowley, was not in court because he is on tour in the West Country with Stourbridge Cricket Club.

He was in Torquay yesterday with his team playing under their touring name of the Worcestershire Marauders, battling it out against Torquay Cricket Club.

When asked to comment on his divorce he said: 'Really there is nothing more that I can say. I cannot stop ... we have got to get on with the game.'

Daily Mail

| *Ready ...* | *Steady ...* | *Go!* |

FRED TRUEMAN

*'It is as a maker of runs that Ken Barrington
will be remembered ...'*

KEN BARRINGTON –
THE RUN MACHINE

The man who came to be known as 'the Run Machine' went to the Oval as a leg-spin bowler in the first place and later in his career, especially in Tests, he took some very useful wickets. He wasn't the worst of slip-fielders, either.

But it is as a maker of runs that Ken Barrington will be remembered.

His philosophy in Test cricket was quite simple: he believed that the longer he occupied the crease, the more the runs would come. He loved playing for England. He worked hard at it – and at making centuries for his country. In fact Wally Grout once said that when Ken walked out to bat one could see a Union Jack waving behind him. It was a tribute I particularly liked because I, too, have always been a very proud Englishman.

For some reason which I have never worked out (because I'm a damn sight better-looking than he could ever have been) we were often mistaken for each other on tour. It became a bit of a laugh because when he was mistaken for me, Kenny would occasionally let it go on by trying to put on a Yorkshire accent. It must have sounded like hell.

In customary laughing mood two greats of cricket, Ken Barrington and Sir Learie Constantine, share a private joke.

Once, when we arrived in Wellington, New Zealand, Ken found a wheelchair and pushed me round the airport in it which caused one of the locals to say, 'How nice to see that chap being looked after by his brother.'

Brother indeed. He'd always be in my Ugly XI!

He'd always be in my England XI, too, because he was a great run-maker and a great bloke to tour with. He loved a joke, a tale, a laugh. As a batsman he no doubt gave the impression of being a dour sort of individual.

Far, far from it. One of his favourite roles in India, for example, was to stand at the crease with the heel of the left foot on the ground, toe pointing upwards, caricaturing one of the pukka sahibs of yesteryear. The Indian crowds recognised at once what he was doing and they were in stitches.

At the time when he was being heavily criticised as a slow-scorer, he began to pace an innings – perhaps 'organise' it is a better way of putting it – so that he reached his century with a straight six back over the bowler's head. Now that takes a bit of doing. Only great players *can* work it out like that, and Ken did it on more than one occasion and in more than one country.

He was probably the last of that long line of England middle-order batsman of the highest class. R.I.P. Ken.

KENNETH FRANK BARRINGTON
(1930–81)

Surrey 1953–68.
England in England 1955, 1959 to 1968; in Australia 1962–63,
1965–66; in West Indies 1959–60, 1967–68; in New Zealand
1962–63; in India 1961–62, 1963–64; in Pakistan 1961–62;
in South Africa 1964–65.

Test Record

	Ins	NO	HS	Runs	Av.	100s
Batting	131	15	256	6,806	58.67	20
Highest score	256 v. Australia (Old Trafford) 1964					
Matches	82					
Bowling	29 wickets at 44.82					

Career Figures

	Ins	NO	HS	Runs	Av.	100s
Batting	831	136	256	31,714	45.63	76
1,000 runs in a season	15 times					
Bowling	273 wickets at 32.61					
Catches	511					

Dedicated conscientious cricketer whose health suffered from his
intensity of application. Strong back-foot batsman, safe fielder,
and occasional leg-spin bowler. An England selector and manager
of MCC in India, Sri Lanka, and Australia in 1976–7.

'Ninety-two for four.'

AT LORD'S

It is little I repair to the matches of the Southron folk,
   Though my own red roses there may blow;
It is little I repair to the matches of the Southron folk,
   Though the red roses crest the caps, I know.
For the field is full of shades as I near the shadowy coast,
And a ghostly batsman plays to the bowling of a ghost,
And I look through my tears on a soundless-clapping host
   As the run-stealers flicker to and fro,
     To and fro:–
   O my Hornby and my Barlow long ago!

It is Glo'ster coming North, the irresistible,
   The Shire of the Graces, long ago!
It is Gloucestershire up North, the irresistible,
   And new-risen Lancashire the foe!
A Shire so young that has scarce impressed its traces,
Ah, how shall it stand before all resistless Graces?
O, little red rose, their bats are as maces
   To beat thee down, this summer long ago!

This day of seventy-eight they are come up North against thee,
   This day of seventy-eight, long ago!
The champion of the centuries, he cometh up against thee,
   With his brethren, every one a famous foe!
The long-whiskered Doctor, that laugheth rules to scorn,
While the bowler, pitched against him, bans the day that he was born:
And G. F. with his science makes the fairest length forlorn;
They are come from the West to work thee woe!

It is little I repair to the matches of the Southron folk,
   Though my own red roses there may blow;
It is little I repair to the matches of the Southron folk,
   Though the red roses crest the caps, I know.
For the field is full of shades as I near the shadowy coast,
And a ghostly batsman plays to the bowling of a ghost,
And I look through my tears on a soundless-clapping host,
   As the run-stealers flicker to and fro,
     To and fro:–
   O my Hornby and my Barlow long ago!

FRANCIS THOMPSON

A. A. THOMSON

'Stay there, Dick!'

'O MY HORNBY AND MY BARLOW ...'

... Barlow was the straight man, the sturdy professional, sober, slow, resourceful and steady; Hornby was the inspired amateur, excitable, dashing, immensely combative and slightly outrageous ...

The best-remembered lines in Francis Thompson's poem, '*As the run-stealers flicker to and fro, to and fro*', draw their inspiration from Hornby's diabolical *penchant* for running short runs, which kept spectators (and his unfortunate partners) in a fever of mingled delight and terror ...

The run-stealing of Hornby and Barlow was not that smooth, well-oiled machine as perfected by Hobbs and Rhodes and afterwards by Hobbs and Sutcliffe. The secret of this technique Wilfred Rhodes explained, as always with a straight face: 'When we're comin', we say Yes, and when we're staying, we say No ... o.' It would be over-simplifying to say that the Hornby and Barlow method was just the opposite. It was much more complicated than that. But sometimes, on a bellow of 'Come on, Dick!', both batsmen would dash madly up the pitch and just as madly back again, with the result that a demented fieldsman would hurl the ball over the wicket-keeper's head for four overthrows. At another time, Hornby would solemnly intone: 'Stay there, Dick', and those two wicked batsmen would slip along the length of the pitch as swiftly and silently as goldfish darting along the side of a tank. But you never knew; you never really could tell ...

Though famous as a run-stealer, Hornby was entitled to the greatest respect as a punishing run-getter. What was remarkable was not so much his tip-and-run tactics as his persistent, relentless driving.

Richard Gorton Barlow, it need hardly be insisted, was different and complementary, particularly in his humour. Whereas Hornby's humour was gay and boisterous, even obstreperous, Barlow's, unlike the climate of his native Bolton, was very dry. He would report with solemn face the observation alleged to have been made by an Old Trafford spectator: 'I'm glad to see t'back of 'Ornby; he's never happy till he's got Barlow run out.'

BASIL BOOTHROYD

*'Going to foreign parts for a game, in my view,
is only asking for trouble …'*

KEEP THE GAME AT HOME

Cricket should not, in my view, be played by foreigners. Where they do play it, they can leave me out. They only got me in once. And out just afterwards. But it's surprising how I feel a twinge in the old wound even now when the summer sun touches it up.

They were Dutchmen, playing at home.

My view that they shouldn't have been playing anywhere was shared by the rest of the eleven. Or ten of them, to be accurate, who, like me, were members of the *Punch* staff barely able to recall the feel of a bat in the hand. The eleventh was Bernard Hollowood, our editor, captain, and owner of a Staffordshire cap. His *Who's Who* entry listed his recreations as county cricket, club cricket and village cricket, his clubs the MCC, the Lord's Taverners'.

County cricket he had played for sixteen years. Minor, it's true, but with a whole family of Staffordshire Hollowoods. One of his brothers, by the grave at their father's funeral, stooped to press his thumb into the churchyard turf and said, 'They'll turn today': an incident Bernard dwelt on with delight.

So he knew what he was doing. So did we, in another sense. Editors are revered figures. When they come up with an idea, however stupid, you don't argue. It's cowardly and shameful, but I told myself that if these aliens really did play the Englishman's national game, or tried to, then (a) I might make the first runs of my life (not counting a great beach innings at Worthing, fathers *v.* under-fives, 54 not out, tide stopped play): and, (b), which I told myself was the reason I went along, at least I should learn the Dutch for lbw.

The match against the over-forties of The Hague would rank, I suppose, as club cricket. We were inclined to take it lightly.

We crossed by ship, on a day of brilliant calm, but took the morrow's engagement seriously enough to practise a little on the deck with folded newspapers and bread-rolls. We should have taken it even more seriously. The receiving party, when we docked, displayed enough Free Foresters and I. Zingari ties to fill Lillywhite's basement, heavily over-shadowing our own status symbols, limited to the captain's Staffordshire cap.

Had our hosts been lighter on the hospitality that evening we might have done better next day, but I don't think so. Apart from Bernard, none of us had ever played a game that started in the morning, on a fully-mown out-field and manicured pitch. Our art editor, Russell Brockbank, looking out from a fresh-painted pavilion the size of Leeds town hall, saw the need to get in some excuses early. 'I'm afraid a few of us are drunk,' he said to the opposing wicket-keeper, who replied, with an impressive command of our language and a sly look, 'Still, or again?'

Their cricket was impressive too. We batted first. Bernard opened, and was there until all but he had fled, including David Langdon, a keen golfer, who took a tee-ing stance and uprooted the off stump with his backlift, Brockbank himself, whose game, from a Canadian upbringing, was ice-hockey, and all the rest of the nine-pins. I experienced no delay in learning the Dutch for lbw, which is lbw. I also learned the Dutch for 'How's that?' (which is 'How's that?'). So they knew the game all right. I didn't even fault their umpiring.

I think we made 52 (B. Hollowood, 43). After that they moved in, or two of them did, and wiped us out without loss. It was quick. All over in time to see the evening paper headline, 'ENGLAND THRASHED'. In Dutch, of course. But we weren't short of interpreters.

Perhaps it was only 'ENGLISH THRASHED'. I prefer the other. It was something to have played for England, after all.

We took the night boat back to Harwich in a force nine gale. I would have stayed over, myself. But captains of ships, like captains of cricket, will take on anything. I think it was Richard Usborne who found a way round the back of the bar and opened it again after it was closed. We retired late to our heaving cabins, until Usborne, who was supposed to be sharing his with Hollowood, spread the alarming word that he was still alone there.

A search party found our captain well for'ard on the thrashing deck, clutching the rail. 'Don't jump, for God's sake,' we yelled, grappling him to safety.

However, it wasn't that. He just didn't want to have anything to do with us. He was obliged, of course, back at the office, to admit us to the Monday editorial conferences. But at least two of them went by, as I recall, without the word cricket so much as falling from his lips.

That was a rare thing, for him.

They play cricket in Corfu, did you know that? I expect you did. I don't want to. I was only once in Corfu Town, where these impertinent rites occur. The hotel barman, somehow spotting me as English, wanted to give me a game, and may still be wondering about the ensuing dialogue.

'What's the Greek for lbw?'

'*Apo podi.*'

'Thank you,' I said, making a note. 'That's all I want to know.'

We are a small island. But big enough to squeeze in the county cricket, the club cricket, the village cricket. And, of course, the beach cricket.

Going to foreign parts for a game, in my view, is only asking for trouble.

OL' MAN RIVER

Botham has become the focal point of much that needs redressing in cricket, but for him to carry the whole can is wrong and unfair. A few players, past and present, lost their suntans overnight when the story broke. So far the Somerset cricketer has not taken anyone down the river with him, mainly because his first scheduled stop, as designated by the disciplinary committee, is not that far downstream. If, however, subsequent events rush him towards the rapids, he may decide that he will no longer paddle the canoe of retribution on his own.

JACK BANNISTER

CHRISTOPHER MARTIN-JENKINS

*'The basis of his game is attack. He wants to be
on top from the first ball he bowls ...'*

BOTHAM – THE MODERN CHAMPION

Even diehard cricket enthusiasts can get a little blasé, in the age of over-indulgence in international cricket, and over-exposure of the star players, when a Richards or a Border, a Lloyd or a Gower comes out to bat. But with Ian Botham it simply is not so. The most hard-bitten critic gets as big a thrill of anticipation as the most starry-eyed schoolboy when this human oak tree surges out of the pavilion bare-headed and belligerent, a brawny right arm swinging his huge chunk of a bat.

Warts and all, Ian Botham is irresistible, the biggest hitter since Arthur Wellard and, before him, Gilbert Jessop but in a quite different class from Wellard and very much more consistent even than Jessop. If he had never taken a wicket, Ian Botham would surely be recognised as a great cricketer. Yet as I write he is not far away from becoming the highest wicket-taker in the history of Test cricket and, to top all this, he has taken some of the most brilliant imaginable catches at second slip where he stands, large hands resting on tired knees, eyes steady, waiting to grasp any victim who happens to have eluded his own attempts to dismiss him with booming away-swingers or deliberately tempting bouncers.

Many a sporting champion has been to some extent the victim of his own success and Ian is no exception. He has performed such super-human feats for his country that people tend to expect them every time, forgetting that he is not in fact superhuman, merely *primus inter pares*. You could argue that he is England's best all-rounder since W.G., though cases could be made for, amongst others, Wally Hammond and Wilfred Rhodes. He is most certainly the best since the war, the superior of both Bailey and Greig, and it is difficult to think of any player in our Test history who has so successfully combined effectiveness with entertainment.

The basis of his game is attack. He wants to be on top from the first ball he bowls and the first one he faces. Very often he is. Cricket is all

Ian Botham at 10. A pupil of Milford Junior School. The demon bowler-to-be is second from right, seated with bat.

about taking the initiative and this is one reason for his amazing achievements. Others are his huge natural ability, his strength, and his boisterous courage.

For a season or two in the late 1970s Ian Botham was as good a fast medium swing bowler as there has been, though perhaps he never had quite the same control as Barnes, Tate or Bedser. Maurice Tate could bat a bit, of course, but not half so well as Botham. In fact only Jessop can be compared as a hitter good enough to turn a match in an hour of fierce assault. None of us who saw them will forget the centuries at Headingley and Old Trafford in 1981. They were 'such stuff as dreams are made on.'

Is he still the best all-rounder in the world? Does it matter much, anyway? For what it is worth I would always put Hadlee, sometimes Kapil Dev and, when fit, Imran Khan ahead of him as bowlers, especially on Ian's form of the last two or three years. But he has more stamina and durability than any of these: and I may yet win my bet with Bill Frindall that he will overtake Dennis Lillie. As for the batting, it is no contest. Botham is much the best player of the famous four.

Let us enjoy his brilliance to the full while we can and hope that, though he has had a very successful benefit, it will not persuade him to leave the game early. If he can afford to lose cricket, cricket certainly cannot afford to lose him!

Botham bowls! The Somerset and England cricketer in fine form at the Oval during the Sixth Cornhill Test, England v Australia, in August 1985.

SCYLD BERRY

*'There's no forgetting either that some of us had
written the match off not an hour before ...'*

SUMMER OF '81

There's a fish-and-chip shop a few minutes' walk from Headingley.
Even by the standards of a county that knows its fish and chips, it's a
good one. Something to do with the excellent batter they use. At any
rate, this fish-and-chip shop was the objective of three journalists at
lunchtime on the Tuesday of the Headingley Test.

Or rather it was just before lunch, about five minutes before the
interval, as we had slipped away to beat the rush. Three wise journalists,
following the whiff of deep-fried batter. But Australia were cruising
anyway; 70-odd to win and eight wickets left. Besides, the last over
before lunch was being bowled by Bob Willis, a museum piece now, on
the last of those much operated-on legs ...

Yes, 1981 was a difficult year for journalists. Now, of course, in
glorious retrospect, professional pride makes us think we saw England's
revival coming all the way. But that is not strictly correct. On the
Monday morning of the Headingley Test several headlines had pro-
claimed the match was lost: 'Farewell to the Ashes'. Even on that
Monday evening I remember Henry Blofeld was incredulous at the
suggestion that Ian Botham – 145 not out overnight – might have
affected the outcome. And I only thought that England might just have
squeezed a draw, given copious rain on the final day.

An ambivalent lot too, we members/gentlemen/bloodhounds of the
press (delete two of three). Being English, we want England to win.
Being journalists, we want to be impartial. And being cricket enthusiasts, for the most part, we can become as worked-up as anyone else
during a close finish, which is my excuse for standing on my feet when
Rod Marsh hooked what was a six until Graham Dilly caught it below
the press box; for having kittens while Ray Bright and Dennis Lillee
hit 35 from four overs; for sighing with relief when Graham Gooch
pointed out to Mike Brearley that the helmet lying behind the wicket-
keeper should be removed from the field, as five penalty runs were not
worth giving away at this stage; and for being fired with animation at
that final moment of victory.

Yet scarcely had the adrenalin drained than we were subjected to the same emotions all over again.

At Headingley the climax came on a cold grey day. At Edgbaston it was a long hot afternoon. As the Australians inched towards victory – or millimetred, so tightly did John Emburey clamp them down for over after over – three wise journalists met again on the steps outside the press box. Australia had passed the 100 with four wickets down: a total of 151 wanted. And we discussed what the day's story – the line, the 'angle' – would be. It had to be 'Captain Fluffs It', we concluded. In the morning Brearley at first slip had missed a very hard low catch; then he had kept Willis going so long, in a do-or-die blood and guts spell, that England's most dangerous bowler wouldn't be able to come back for a final fling. Yes, Willis had shot his bolt and Brearley this time had blown it. Hard on the fellow, but that had to be the story ...

We returned to our seats. Allan Border got out, caught at short-leg off Emburey. The rack of the drama turned another notch, making the tension even less bearable. In fact it was worse than drama, for at least the theatre crowd generally knows the outcome in advance. This one was unscripted. Or if there was a script it said that history couldn't repeat itself, could it? Then with all forces exquisitely poised in equilibrium, another force made itself felt to swing the balance. Firstly Botham was brought on to bowl, that was one factor, and without his inspired performance England's victory could surely not have been achieved. But what inspired him? Some subtly motivating words from his captain, for a start; and then it was the crowd, those 15,000 or so spectators who had been hushed thus far that afternoon. The drama had been working on them, a drip-drip effect heightening their expectation of momentous things as each hour came and went, as each over of Emburey's passed, hitting the defending bat of Border.

Finally Edgbaston found its voice, in an utterly un-British way. Football crowds may chant 'Kill, kill!' but not a Sunday afternoon cricket crowd. This was barracking, as they do it in Australia: not a verbal attack on an opponent, but mass support for the home team. We were to hear it almost two years later when 17,000 turned up at the Melbourne Cricket Ground, not to see if Border and Thomson could score the last few runs to win that Third Test, but to make them do it. It was the same here, and I remember Botham a long while afterwards paying tribute to this Edgbaston enthusiasm – it gave the Aussies a taste of their own un-nerving medicine.

The Royal Wedding had taken place a day before the match, and it must have added to the patriotic, even nationalistic, flag-waving fervour as Botham ran in at ever-quickening speed to sweep aside Kent, Marsh, Bright (what an in-cutter) and Lillee, Bob Taylor clasping the ball to his chest as he rolled in front of the slips. No matter how often the video repeats that sight of Botham, not running in at Terry Alderman but tearing in, the old spine starts a-tingling again. There's no forgetting either that some of us had written the match off not an hour before. For a third time that summer Botham made us scribes look stupid at Old Trafford, or at least those Sunday journalists who had to file for their first editions around four o'clock that Saturday afternoon. At 3.30 the 'story' was that England had batted with pitiful ineptitude, heroically as Lillee and Alderman had bowled. After 69 overs, for heaven's sake, England were 104 for the loss of five wickets, on a pitch which did not make strokeplay absolutely impossible. Even Botham had taken 70 minutes to contribute 28 runs, before the second new ball was taken ...

The next hour was not without its moments. Botham tucked into Lillee and Alderman, and began scoring at some speed, while no less rapidly a nicely drafted manuscript on 'England's Batting Deficiencies' became redundant. It was torn to shreds as fast as the Australian attack. At the start of dictating a paragraph over the telephone to a patient copy-taker in London, Botham was 30 not out; by the end of it he had reached 50. He hit 66 off the last eight overs before tea, whereas England in the whole morning session had scored 29 runs off 28 overs, and for the loss of three wickets at that. If the captain Kim Hughes was at his wits end, in some disarray, so were some Sunday journalists.

Never write anything while I. T. Botham is at the crease; that is the moral of our tale. He can re-write any game in minutes. Since that epic Series, meanwhile, the man himself may have lost a little of his bowling, some of its nip and outswing. But he remains an excellent batter, like that served in those three journalists' favourite fish-and-chip shop in Leeds.

A HAIRY BUSINESS

17 August 1959. About 30 men sitting shirtless in the sun watching the Middlesex-Yorkshire cricket match at Lord's on Saturday were asked by an MCC attendant to replace their shirts. The attendant said this move was a result of complaints from women spectators during the recent hot spell. 'After all, Lord's is Lord's,' he added ...

Original Report

RICHARD FORD

*'W. G. Grace would turn in his grave at the
thought ...'*

I SAY, YOU CHAPS ...

1 September 1980. Has civilisation as we know it ended with the disgraceful scenes in the Members' Enclosure at Lord's before the start of the third day of play in the Cornhill Centenary Test?

Even the august and dignified members of the world famous MCC would appear to have among their number an element who are not averse to using a rather coarser sort of language than one expects on the cricket field.

The abusive language and jostling that took place as the two captains and umpires returned to the Long Room is the kind of behaviour we have come to expect on the football terraces but not from the gentlemen of the Pavilion at Lord's.

It just is not cricket and today the MCC will start an inquiry into this most unsporting behaviour.

Many might prefer a dignified veil of silence to be drawn across the unseemly incidents on Saturday in which Ian Botham, the England captain, was hit on the head and David Constant, an umpire, grabbed by the tie and jostled. But they have received so much publicity that an investigation will begin with Botham and Greg Chappell, the Australian captain, being seen by Mr Jack Bailey, secretary of the MCC.

He had heard a complaint from Chappell that intimidatory and abusive language was being used and that one of the umpires had been jostled as they returned from making a fourth inspection of the pitch, where 22,000 spectators were waiting for play to start. Mr Bailey investigated this and spoke to two members pointed out by Chappell but said he thought, from what they had told him, that they had not been behaving unreasonably.

Mr Bailey said: 'I spoke to the men and felt they were innocent, but of course it could have been a case of mistaken identity. There is no question about it, the members were not pleased at having to wait and made their feelings known, but I thought they were doing it in the reasonable English way and that it would not go beyond this.'

From the hotel where he is staying in London, Botham described the incidents as 'the behaviour one expects from football hooligans'. He added, 'I was walking out to make the final inspection with Chappell and the two umpires when I was hit on the back of the head by a hand.

I did nothing about it but as we were all walking in a man in his twenties grabbed the umpire David Constant by the tie and shoved and jostled him. Greg Chappell and I moved in to break it up.'

He said the man thought he was being clever and added that the abusive language being shouted in the Pavilion had disgusted him. 'It was a disgrace especially as it involved the captain of an opposing team. I feel very sorry and embarrassed about people who to my mind are a disgrace to the game.'

So the language and behaviour of the football hooligan has at last invaded the home of English cricket. W. G. Grace would turn in his grave at the thought.

The Times

GERALD BRODRIBB

*A well known writer and historian of the game
presents some fascinating facts as he takes ...*

A LOOK AT SOME
LAWS

LAW 2, SECTION NINE. A batsman may leave the field or retire at any time owing to illness, injury or other unavoidable cause ...

J. Southerton, in the Surrey *v* MCC match at the oval in 1870, assumed he had been caught and walked out. His dismissal is recorded as: 'J. Southerton ... retired, thinking he was caught ...'

There have been occasions when a batsman has decided that whether he was out or not he wanted to go back to the safety of the pavilion.

H. A. Smith of Leicestershire was facing Larwood at his fastest at Trent Bridge in 1928. He snicked a ball short of the wicket-keeper and promptly left the wicket.

When he was told that the catch was not good, he replied that it was good enough for him.

In a Gentlemen *v* Players match in 1906, one professional was so disturbed by the ferocious pace of N. A. Knox that to his very first ball he retreated to square leg and allowed the ball to crash into his stumps.

'Good afternoon, gentlemen,' he said. 'I've got a wife and family to think of.'

LAW 4, SECTION ONE. All runs scored shall be recorded by scorers appointed for the purpose ...

At Leyton in 1932, Percy Holmes and Herbert Sutcliffe took Yorkshire's score to 555 before Sutcliffe dragged a ball onto his wicket. It beat the world's record opening stand of 554.

While photos were being taken, it was learnt with dismay that the record had only been equalled, since the score was really 554.

The scorers, C. P. McGahey and W. Ringrose, were adamant that 554 was correct but such was the feeling that they were persuaded to 'find' an alleged 'lost' no-ball, and this brought the score back to 555.

The modern score-book lacks some of the flavour of the past. 'Nipt out' ... 'beat his own wicket down' ... 'struck himself out' ... 'shampled out' ... and even 'absent bathing'.

LAW 6, SECTION ONE. The blade of the bat shall be made of wood.

Cyril Poole of Notts. never worried about what bat he used, and was an inveterate borrower. A plan was made to lend him a bat which was a mere shell filled with compressed sawdust.

He scored a brilliant 70 with it and seemed not even to notice the leaking sawdust.

LAW 7, SECTION TWO. Before the toss for innings, the executive of the ground shall be responsible for the selection and preparation of the pitch, thereafter the umpires shall control its use and maintenance ...

After the first day's play between Kent and Sussex at Margate in 1864 four Sussex players were leaving the ground and met a man driving into it with a water-cart.

Upon being questioned the man readily admitted that he was about to water the pitch so Kent should be bowled out for a low score the next day. He added that a bet of a sovereign depended on the result of the match.

LAW 22, SECTION ONE. The ball shall be bowled from each wicket alternately in overs of either six or eight balls according to agreement before the match ...

In the match between British Guyana and Barbados at Georgetown in 1946–47, D. F. Hill bowled an over of 14 balls without any wides or no-balls.

The umpire had simply miscounted after reaching the number of eight – and poor Everton Weekes was given out lbw off the fourteenth ball.

LAW 25, SECTION THREE. If a ball which the umpire considers to have been delivered comes to rest in front of the line of the

striker's wicket, 'wide' shall not be called ...

In the 1890 MCC *v* Lancashire match at Lord's Whitehead (MCC) delivered a ball to A. N. Hornby which slipped and fell very short. Hornby rushed out to hit it but Whitehead raced him for it, seized the ball and threw it to the wicket-keeper who appealed against Hornby for a run out.

Whitehead alleged that Hornby's action had put the ball in play, but Hornby successfully claimed that Whitehead had obstructed him.

LAW 27, SECTION TWO. An appeal 'how's that' shall cover all ways of being out ...

Tom Oates, after keeping wicket for Notts. for many years, later became an umpire and once let out an involuntary appeal when a ball from Reeves, bowling for Essex, was snicked to the keeper.

Reeves, always a bit of a character, promptly raised his finger as in reply and the batsman departed, apparently noticing nothing unusual.

LAW 28, SECTION ONE. The wicket is down if either the ball or the striker's bat or person completely removes either bail ...

In 1924, when he was batting for Cambridge University against Surrey, R. J. O. Meyer received a ball from Percy Fender which caused his leg bail to hop up and balance itself on top of the leg stump.

The umpires adjudged him out, but the MCC later regarded this decision as incorrect.

LAW 30, SECTION ONE. The striker shall be out bowled if his wicket is first bowled down ...

C. H. Titchmarsh was bowled by G. John in the MCC *v* West Indies match at Lord's in 1923, and the off and leg stumps were removed while the middle stump remained standing.

It happened again when Mike Hendrick bowled Madan Lal in the England–India test at Old Trafford in 1974.

LAW 24, SECTION ONE. Failure on the part of the bowler to indicate in advance a change in his mode of delivery is unfair ...

Though the bowler must do this, the batsman may change his position as he wishes.

In 1930 G. Hunt (Somerset), after being hit several times by Bill Voce's vicious in-swingers, batted left-handed to Voce but adopted his usual right-hand stance to other bowlers.

The Indian batsman Sunil Gavaskar was involved in a strange incident in the match between Bombay and Karnatam in 1981–82.

Coming in at No. 7 he batted alternately right- and left-hand as some form of protest, and his action was later condemned by the Board of Control as being a bad example to the young.

There was a very odd incident of no-ball misunderstanding in the Test between New Zealand and Pakistan at Nagpur in 1978–79.

Talat Ali lashed out at a ball from Hadlee and was bowled what he thought was a call of no-ball, but was in fact a loud grunt from Hadlee as he delivered the ball.

In the Europeans v Hindus match at Bombay in 1925–26, N. H. Hughes-Hallett received a note while batting which said: 'Hit out or get out.'

Assuming that it was from his captain, he carried out orders – but when he got back to the pavilion he discovered the note was a hoax.

ONE FOR THE POT!
S. A. R. Silva, the Sri Lanka opener, takes a 6 off the bowling of Ian Botham during the England v Sri Lanka match at Lord's at the end of August 1984.

MISSED!

The sun in the heavens was beaming;
The breeze bore an odour of hay,
My flannels were spotless and gleaming,
My heart was unclouded and gay;
The ladies, all gaily apparelled,
Sat round looking on at the match,
In the tree-tops the dicky-birds carolled,
All was peace till I bungled that catch.

My attention the magic of summer
Had lured from the game – which was wrong;
The bee (that inveterate hummer)
Was droning its favourite song.
I was tenderly dreaming of Clara
(On her not a girl is a patch);
When, ah horror! there soared through the air a
Decidedly possible catch

I heard in a stupor the bowler
Emit a self-satisfied 'Ah!'
The small boys who sat on the roller
Set up an expectant 'Hurrah!'
The batsman with grief from the wicket
Himself had begun to detach –
And I uttered a groan and turned sick – It
Was over. I'd buttered the catch.

Oh ne'er, if I live to a million,
Shall I feel such a terrible pang.
From the seats in the far-off pavilion
A loud yell of ecstasy rang.
By the handful my hair (which is auburn)
I tore with a wrench from my thatch,
And my heart was seared deep with a raw burn
At the thought that I'd foozled that catch.

Ah, the bowler's, low querulous mutter,
Point's loud, unforgettable scoff!
Oh, give me my driver and putter!
Henceforward my game shall be golf.
If I'm asked to play cricket hereafter,
I am wholly determined to scratch.
Life's void of all pleasure and laughter;
I bungled the easiest catch.

P. G. WODEHOUSE

RAYMOND ROBERTSON-GLASGOW

'I wonder if it ever came down anywhere,
Drayson?'

THE CATCH THAT
NEVER CAME DOWN

'What you tell me is very interesting,' said Drayson; 'but did I ever tell you the story of the catch that never came down?'

I stirred uneasily. Distant rumours of this – well – story had reached me some years before. There was a ruminative wildness in Drayson's eye. He helped himself to a cigarette, settled into his chair, and said: 'You don't believe it, of course. No one wants to believe it. It doesn't suit them. It cracks science from top to bottom. It wrecks Newton and Einstein; Jeans and Horstfloobler and that bunch would have to think again. But I know. You see, I was the bowler.'

'What and where was the match?'

'I'll leave you to guess, and just tell you what happened.'

'Ah.'

'We were sworn to secrecy. You see, it would have been awkward for the Club, if it had got around. Either everyone would have wanted to come and play there, to see if it would happen again, or else no one would have consented to play on a ground where a ball might disappear upwards for good. Nervous cricketers could never have stood the suspense. Any moment it might have come. A casual jerk from third-man; gone for good. A promising leg-break; switched away into eternity. Cummings, the treasurer, foresaw the implications; and already he had to answer to the committee for the unaccountable absence of a new ball. But it never happened again; and now the ground is built over.'

There was a short silence.

'It was in the second over that it happened, on the first ball. Curlew, our fast man, had opened in a very erratic manner. His first two balls went full-pitch to Wilkinson, the wicket-keeper, nearly vertical wides. The next two were longhops, which the batsman hooked for four each; then two more full-pitchers. The second of these was immensely, almost inhumanly, fast; and it nearly decapitated Wilkinson. I remember it bounced back an unusual distance from the screen. I asked Curlew at

284

the end of the over what he was up to. He was puzzled, and said the ball was very slippery; dangerously slippery, he thought, and it didn't feel quite like an ordinary ball. It was warm, he said, to the touch. He was right. There was an unearthly warmth about the ball.'

Drayson sat up straight in his chair. He spoke more slowly, and in a lower tone. 'I recall the start of my over,' he went on, 'as if it was yesterday. Two women had begun to settle in front of the screen with a picnic-basket and a small dog. It took some time to move them, also to shift Gandars, a minor poet, who was lost to the world at square-leg when he should have been at mid-on. I was itching to bowl; for the ball was getting warmer. It had reached the temperature of an unsatisfactory hot-bath. You know my style; slow tempters, with a bogus twirl of the hand to indicate leg-break. I tossed it up. The batsman mistook it for a half-volley, as many have done to their cost. The upward sweep of his bat caught the ball on the rise, and it soared skywards.

'A slight breeze seemed to be wafting it towards Wilkinson at the wicket. I called his name, and he began to revolve, in his clumsy manner, underneath it. Gandars, for no apparent reason, shouted "Mine!" and teetered in on his toes from mid-on. Cover-point began to interest himself; and I stood half-way down the pitch, in an alert posture. Then I noticed something. The ball was not coming down. It went on up; slowly, slowly, getting smaller and smaller. Gandars, who is short-sighted, was the first to give up. He shouted "It's gone. Holy mushrooms. That's done it!" and put his hands in his pockets. The batsmen, after running three, stopped, and both stared into the sky. The ball was now only just visible, about the size of a moderate spider, some 150 feet up. There, for a space, it stopped, hovering in miraculous indecision. If it came down, it was going to be the catch of a lifetime.

'One spectator thought we were being funny, shouted something about "horse-play," and left the ground. Cartwright, the groundsman, walked out to the pitch, looked steadily up at the ball, then at me. "Who done that?" he asked, unanswerably; then felt he was a fool; which he is; and began to laugh stupidly. Then the batting side came out, mostly running. Wilkinson wanted to send for a gun. "Extreme range," he explained, "but it's worth trying." Suddenly the ball shot up again, and was lost to view. It just went slap into the void.'

'Did you get another?' I asked.

'Oh, yes,' said Drayson, 'we got another; and we finished the game, though I can remember next to nothing of it. It fell pretty flat, you see. At tea we arranged to keep the affair a secret, and the spectators, just a handful, agreed. But now, of course, it doesn't matter who knows.'

'I wonder if it ever came down anywhere, Drayson?'

'I should doubt it. In fact, I hope not. I prefer to think that for one instant in the world's history the laws of gravity were suspended.'

JACK POLLARD

*A new generation has emerged since the
publication of this article in the original* The
Boundary Book. *For this reason – and the fact
that it has a timeless quality – the editor decided
to give the young bloods of cricket today a chance
to enjoy it, as their fathers did.*

THE HILL
AT SYDNEY

There were those happy summers when I lay on The Hill in the uncut grass, sipped lemonade and watched with other small boys the cricket on the sun-burned field below known as the Sydney Cricket Ground. All around us men would eat meat pies of a brand as notorious as any thrown in Keystone Cops farces, and swig at their bottled beer and occasionally trudge up the tracks they had worn in The Hill to the bar tucked under the big scoreboard which Englishmen think is more informative than a tax-return.

Most of the time the Hillites would chatter noisily and barrack, and one voice, coarse and incisive like the gravel-tones of Louis Armstrong, would periodically holler above the rest. Even the flannelled figures below would smile then. We would all wait for the voice's next shout with a mixture of amused expectation and awe.

Big Bill O'Reilly, adored up there on The Hill, would move splay-footed up to the crease and wheel his heavy arm over in his characteristically defiant style; nimble Clarrie Grimmett would flip leg-breaks up towards the tiny, twinkling, often pained feet of Stan McCabe, each enjoying the other's skill; and Bradman would stride in to bat and soon the crowd on The Hill would start to multiply as men left their offices to attend funerals of grandmothers long since dead.

There were the breath-snatching tensions of Test Matches; Ken Farnes and Gubby Allen unleashing high-kicking deliveries; and the same 'Tiger' Bill O'Reilly smacking Hedley Verity up into the crowded grandstand to the left of The Hill. A wee Tasmanian, Jackie Badcock, one of the first from his island to play for Australia, showed his special type of hook, and a dashing Victorian, Ross Gregory, his lovely driving.

There were the inter-State matches, with a wizard called Don Tallon lashing away the bails and turning his appeals to square-leg, and the comparison of Bert Oldfield, neat and unhurried with flowing hands, swift as a mongoose.

I would watch enraptured all day in the sun, and then sprint out of the ground and up over the slope to the back streets of Paddington, the suburb where Victor Trumper rehearsed in the local district team for Test heroics, to try to imitate strokes seen that day, before the darkness came. The wicket was chalked on a wall, the pitch uneven bitumen, and hits over the fence were 'six and out', and the criticism of S. P. bookmakers' runners substituted for that dominating voice on The Hill.

I had caught the bug. I had joined a privileged group. This kind of initiation, with countless variations, has come to millions all over the world who now enjoy the capacity to watch cricket. When somebody told me that a man once died from excitement at a cricket match and another spectator gnawed the handle off his umbrella in a nervous spasm, it was hardly a shock. It seemed a pleasing way to die.

Now I am saddened because I did not know at the time that rough and friendly voice which sounded above the others during my apprenticeship as a cricket spectator was Stephen Harold Gascoigne, perhaps the most celebrated of all Australians who have watched cricket. On The Hill they called him Yabba.

Yabba was a hawker who sold rabbits from a battered two-wheeled cart around the slums of Sydney. He became more famous than many of the cricketers he chided, a horny-handed rebel who could match his press notices with any film star's. He would hold court on The Hill, standing or sprawled on the grass, with a comical, earthy wit, a great clown's sense of timing, and an uninhibited vocabulary which owed a lot of its striking power to a term he had served as a soldier in the South African War.

He had a vast appetite for life, and he always seemed able to enjoy the antics of cricketers, however dull the play. His confidence was immense, and long before he died in 1942, at the age of sixty-four, he habitually referred to himself as 'The One and Only'. He could skin a rabbit in less time than it takes Ray Lindwall to run up to the bowling crease.

Yabba's kingdom was The Hill and he ruled over it with a touch which enriched the business of spectatorship and left cricket freshly stocked with jokes. Many of them have been drained of their humour now through repetition, or the lack of a voice like Yabba's with which to deliver them. That splendid Australian critic Ray Robinson tells in one of his books of the time Yabba watched a sightscreen being moved. The umpire held his hand aloft to signal the attendant to keep pushing as the batsman wasn't satisfied. The pushing took some time. Yabba gawked at the umpire's upraised hand and called in a schoolboy's querulous tones, 'It's no use, Umpire; you'll have to wait until lunch-time like the rest of us.'

Then, after a batsman had had his stump uprooted first ball by Tibby Cotter, the fast bowler, and was walking disconsolately back to the pavilion, 'Don't worry, son,' Yabba called, 'it would have bowled me.' Yabba, usually in an open-necked shirt and a barman's white coat, rarely enthused about fast-scoring if runs were easy to get. 'Please can I bat with a knitting needle?' he would bellow. When a long partnership was in progress, he suggested in a phrase, since worn to boredom, that the fire-brigade be called to put them out, and once that a nurse of shady reputation be sent for. When J. W. Hearne broke a long runless spell with a single, Yabba shouted: 'Whoa, he's bolted!' He was rich in sarcasm yet free of malice, and he could make a mundane line uproariously funny.

It was men like Yabba, the son of a storekeeper who migrated from Oxford to settle in Australia, who established Patsy Hendren as an idol and clinched Douglas Jardine's unpopularity. They were delighted with Hendren's fielding in the outfield so close to them at the foot of The Hill. He had a habit of jumping the fence to sit among them or swig their beer after the fall of a wicket. They disliked Jardine's Harlequin cap, with its hint of class distinctions, and they laughed at Jardine's stiff-legged running when he was forced to chase a ball to the outfield.

'Mind your stays, old man!' Yabba would call at him, nasal-accented, mocking the English Public School prototype. The apparently hurt, humourless way with which Jardine took these cracks convinced Hillites they were right to chide him so mercilessly. The fervour men like Yabba put into their spectatorship contributed heavily to the Bodyline crisis.

Since that delightful beginning on The Hill I have had many wonderful moments as a sun-bemused spectator on the Sydney Ground: Lindsay Hassett's century in each innings against Tiger Bill at his prime; Colin McCool's slip catch to dismiss Bradman in McCool's first-class début; Len Hutton's incredible 39, superior to most centuries; the impact of Doug Wright's run-up at the first sight of him bowling; Alec Bedser's remarkable determination, still unquenched when Bradman and Barnes had scored double hundreds; Vinoo Mankad driving or bowling out of a curled left hand up towards Miller's floppy hair.

But the joys of watching cricket are happily not confined to one ground. From the beer-swigging on The Hill to the champagne taken in a ribbon-draped carriage at the Eton and Harrow Match at Lord's, from the calm beauty of Canterbury to the calypso-singing galleries of the West Indies, the Festival matches at Scarborough when big hits are as numerous as journalists at a Monaco wedding, and on to the thrills

DAYS OF WINE AND ROSES

Every cricket season teams of Lord's Taverners fan out all over Britain (sometimes overseas) in the pursuit of fund-raising for disabled children and youth cricket. Behind the cricket is a succession of dinners, lunches and other social events which also raise much-needed cash for the cause. Pictured here are just a few such events which have taken place over the years.

ABOVE: *Twenties fun and games at a Taverners' 'do' with (left) Leslie Crowther and Nicholas Parsons.*

TOP: *Holding forth is (second from right) actor Tony Britton with (left to right) MacDonald Hobley, Richie Benaud and Bill Maynard. And isn't that Alec – or is it Eric? – Bedser in the background?*

ABOVE: *The Lord's Taverners' Mansion House dinner on their twenty-first anniversary. Sir Harry Secombe is obviously in characteristic form, standing between City dignitaries. Founder-member Martin Boddey is seen on the right of the top table.*

RIGHT: *Celebrity celebrations. Five past presidents were among the those who celebrated Lord's Taverners' Day in the Circle Bar at the Comedy Theatre, London, late in 1985. Standing in the front of the commemoration plaque are Jimmy Edwards, Michael Denison, Stephen Mitchell, David Frost, Denis Thatcher, Brian Rix, Robert Powell, Alfred Gover, Ted Moult, Bob Bevan, Robin Bailey and Willie Rushton. The wall plaque commemorates the first officially recorded meeting of the Lord's Taverners held in the bar on Tuesday, 3 July 1950. On the day of the celebratory gathering, the Comedy Theatre was presenting* The Little Shop of Horrors!

ABOVE: *Home and Dry! Lord Home of The Hirsel regales a group of Taverners with some cricket reminscences at a Taverners' Charity Luncheon. Flanking him (left) is the late Sir Edward Lewis of Decca and Ronnie Waldman and, in case you want to know, the hairstyle in the foreground is that sported by Stephen Mitchell; the parting on the right belongs to Raymond Baxter.*

ABOVE RIGHT: *Star-gazer Patrick Moore, a Lord's Taverner, talks of higher things with the Twelfth Man.*

RIGHT: *A tie for Sir Gary. The inimitable Sir Gary Sobers is invested with his Taverners' tie at the Cafe Royal, London.*

LEFT: *Taverners' 'terrorists' (left to right) Cardew Robinson, David Frost and Sir Harry Secombe look to be up to a bit of no-good.*

CENTRE: *John Edrich, the Surrey opening batsman, is invested with his Lord's Taverners' tie after the announcement of his award as Lord's Taverners' Cricketer of the Year of 1969. The peerless West Indian captain, Gary Sobers, looks a bit pensive about it all.*

LEFT: *Jimmy Edwards, Martin Boddey and Victor Sylvester appear to be forming a tryst at another Lord's Taverners' function.*

LEFT: *There's obviously something afoot judging by the leg appeal of actress Barbara Windsor seen talking to (left) Richard O'Sullivan and Ronnie Corbett. The Grandee, Michael Parkinson, seems to want to know where the Toastmaster got his insignia!*

of Lock bowling to Neil Harvey in a decisive Test under the shadow of the gasometers at the Oval – the range of absorbing viewing is unlimited.

In Hollywood famous film stars enjoy watching cricket played by expatriate English actors and their pupils; aboard the *Queen Mary* in its berth at Southampton, the crew and passengers watch play, if they are so inclined, on a nearby field from a vantage point even Yabba would have found unique. In Turkey, a spectator in a fez gets just as much fun out of watching as a Gurkha in a turban, in Pakistan.

And who among those who go regularly to cricket matches has not seen the crazy characters who perch precariously on frail tree branches, halfway up telegraph posts, on ladders like firemen at a big blaze, or on sagging roofing? Opposite the Oval there is a rare brand of spectator who views the play from flats outside the ground. They can see only one end of the pitch, and have known half a side to be dismissed without a hint of the causes coming into view.

Of the thrills of watching cricket, among the biggest if visiting famous grounds for the first time, I remember my first trip to Lord's. I was disappointed. Accommodation in the shapeless stands was hard to find at big matches after the vast spaces of The Hill and the towering grandstands of Melbourne Cricket Ground. The scoreboard was so unrevealing it was necessary to undertake a strange ritual common to all English cricket spectators: buy a scorecard. People schooled in Yabba's classes, where money is for beer and meat pies, don't take easily to spending money on bits of paper which further annoys by distinguishing between amateur and professional players.

I remember, too, that the beer from the Tavern, which has since taken on an insidious charm, seemed weak and uninspiring and the Long Room seemed inaccessible. It's a fairly common reaction among Australian cricket followers. It was only later when the traditions and trouble-free atmosphere took hold that the peculiar intimacy of Lord's appealed.

However, if Lord's was slow in winning appreciation, the joys of Hove and Chesterfield and Canterbury and the hundreds of village pitches – Bray tops my popularity poll – were immediate. Old Trafford wove a particular spell because of the thick-accented wit and the surprise of discovering that those around you are as unrelentingly partisan and intractable as the legend says. If Yabba had got among that lot the exchanges would have scorched dry even the dampest Manchester pitch. But who would have won?

It was at Old Trafford that a collector's item for cricket spectators occurred when Dick Pollard hit Sid Barnes off his spot a few yards from the wicket. And the story goes it was at Old Trafford, too, that a spectator, obviously from the south, returned to his seat after lunch to find his hat on the grass under the bench and his place occupied by the large backside of a Lancashireman. 'I say, old chap, that's my seat you're in,' he said, in well-bred tones. Repeated challenges left the Lancashireman's backside undisturbed, but finally moved him to comment: 'Oop here, 'tis rears wat counts, not 'ats,' he said.

Yabba would have enjoyed that ground more than any other cricket field in England, I think, if not its rain, though Trent Bridge, with George Parr's tree and a wholesome brew from nearby breweries and cosy taverns in which to hold post-mortems after stumps, would have earned his respect.

But it would be risky to speculate on what he would have made out of the Eton and Harrow Match, for there is nothing like it in the wide canvas of cricket watching. How would Yabba, who jibed at a man because of his coloured cap, have taken to fellow spectators in top-hats who drink champagne, eat salmon and chicken wings, and stage a parade around the pitch at the intervals, and retire for refreshment to their own exclusive club tents? To less aggressive onlookers it is none the less richly intriguing to watch for the aged dowagers who venture on to the hallowed Lord's turf in wheel-chairs rather than miss the tea adjournment parade.

In a lifetime spent viewing cricket around the world, many common traits among audiences have appeared. They all dote on big hits, the way boxing crowds thrill to knockdowns. They all favour – unless they are from Lancashire – the underdogs, whatever their patriotism. And they all delight to watch a touch of comedy like Ernie Toshack walking down a row of policemen to the field and pinching the last cop's helmet to wear himself. Or Lindsay Hassett's efforts to frighten away uncooperative pigeons from the Oval outfield. Or Keith Miller doing repair work on the pitch with the handle of his bat to a piece of intimate equipment when hit by a fast delivery.

No spectator will forget the West Indian team's victory over a full-strength England side which culminated a remarkably successful English tour. Few can remember the scores, however. What remains in the memory are the acts of the zoot-suited characters who invaded the Oval pitch, plucking guitars, sending coloured balloons aloft, and chanting celebration calypso verses. This, with the bottle-throwing incident on Len Hutton's team's tour of their country, must make the West Indians the liveliest spectators in the cricket-playing nations.

Whatever the nationality, the habit of cricket watching follows a pattern. There is the customary lunch-packing, the familiar turnstiles, the small boys, the arguments over famous feats, the optimistic army of souvenir brochure sellers, the zealots who keep every possible statistic in school exercise books, the squad of cameramen as the players take the field, the men around you who proudly wear old school ties and

England's Tony Greig
and a moment of
truth!

blazers, however worn and faded, the home-made paper hats on a hot day, the rush to buy papers describing the same match at the intervals.

You go out of a ground at the end of the day and then buy these newspapers to read about what happened, to discover if the critics think the ball which bowled Hutton swung late as you thought. You sit among people who reinforce the evidence of eyes intent on the play by listening to broadcast descriptions of it on portable radios. You watch people crush together to get the autographs of famous cricketers in books they discard and forget after they arrive home.

They say the Yabba tradition of spectators taking part in a cricket match is dying, and yet on Frank Tyson's spectacular tour of Australia, when he was running through a side and a tail-ender came to bat, someone raised a voice which would have matched even the maestro's. The tail-ender had trouble with the catch on the gate as he tried to close it. 'Leave it open, you won't be long,' cried the voice. With the right croaky tones it might have been twenty years earlier.

Cricketers agree that the big difference between English and Australian spectators is the lack of gambling in England. Peter May says he was fielding near the boundary during a match in Australia when a spectator asked him if he was an amateur or a professional. He told the man he was an amateur and saw the man pay out five one-pound notes into the hand of a neighbour, his bet lost.

May, incidentally, recalls the time he went in to bat in a New Zealand match and a woman's voice in the crowd commented, 'Look at his sweater, Ethel. I do like that cable stitch, don't you?'

Australian opener Arthur Morris was grimly defending in a match against England in Brisbane when through the heat came a voice on a loudspeaker appealing for the owner of a car jamming the car park to report to the police. Dozens of spectators at once advised stonewalling Morris it was his car.

Then, there is the wisecrack with the Yabba-like ring, for use when a batsman is having difficulty making contact. 'Bowl him a grand piano an' see if he can play that!' someone will shout. No well-stocked barracker's repertoire would be complete without that old chestnut. It's not devastating humour, but it's fun if you're there and cricket would lose something valuable if it stopped resounding across the grounds of the world.

The Yabba tradition has gone, they say, and with him the age of talkative spectatorship, almost as if cricket watchers have tired of scholarly arguments among critics on which country's crowds are the most voluble and witty. The Hill would be poorer if that were true, but one suspects it is but a phase, a pause while the boisterous take a breath – or replenish their stocks of pies and wait for the beer to take effect.

DAVID FRITH
Editor of *Wisden Cricket Monthly*

*'He thumps that cricket ball as if it contained all
the evils of a millennium of mankind . . .'*

VIV RICHARDS:
'IT'S JUST A PIECE OF WOOD'

In the pre-war Depression years, Don Bradman stood for the powers of endurance of the ordinary bloke. His triumphs brought pride and inspiration to masses of struggling Australians in town and bush. Through The Don they saw that life's difficulties were at least not totally universal. Spasmodically they too tasted success on a giant scale, if only vicariously. 'Our Don' took his admirers out of themselves, made their existences less wretched, gave them a kind of hope.

For ten years now Viv Richards has done something similar for the black man.

He has not been alone in this. Clive Lloyd gathered together one of the most powerful cricket teams of all time, with wonderful opening batsmen like Gordon Greenidge and Desmond Haynes, himself and Richards and the solid, phlegmatic Gomes to make runs, and Dujon to keep wicket and add artistry to the middle-order batting, and, most significantly, a brigade of ferocious fast bowlers to keep the opposition in an almost permanent state of submission. They came tumbling out of the pavilion, large and loose and eager: Andy Roberts, Michael Holding, Wayne Daniel, Colin Croft, Joel Garner, Malcolm Marshall, Courtenay Walsh, with keen youngsters queuing up to replace them. For Viv Richards to stand towering above all these as the symbol of West Indian supremacy emphasises the impact he has had on international cricket since the mid-1970s.

Springing from massive local celebrity in Antigua and polishing his game in county cricket with Somerset, Richards quickly made himself comfortable in Test cricket with an innings of 192 not out against India at Delhi in December 1974. There followed seventeen Test innings in which nothing startling took place, and then he recovered his poise with 101 against Australia at Adelaide and 98 in the Melbourne Test which followed. This was the springboard for a most remarkable year in which he established his own utter uniqueness with an unprecedented aggregate of 1,710 runs in Test cricket during 1976.

The core of this batting extravaganza was the 1976 series in England, though the preface, West Indies' home series against India, had more than a touch of intimidation about it: he hit 142 in the Barbados Test, 130 in Trinidad, 177 in the third Test, at the same venue, and finished quietly with 64 in the Jamaica bloodbath when five Indians could not bat in the second innings, most of them injured by the speed assault.

Richards thus came to England for his first Test tour with more than just imposing forenames: Isaac Vivian Alexander. He began that 1976 series with innings of 232 and 63 in the Trent Bridge Test, over twice as many as young Bradman had made on that ground in *his* maiden English Test. Richards struck dread into countless hearts, and caused some analysts, in their desperation, to repeat the mistakes made by several almost half-a-century before, when they concluded that Bradman's technique would be found out on English pitches. He played across the line, they said. So did Richards. His pull shot was too risky, being used to punish balls only slightly short of a length. So was Richards's. Bradman showed them with 974 runs in that 1930 series, skipping to a triple-century, two double-centuries and a century in the five Tests. Richards in the 1976 Tests amassed 829 runs. But he played in only four Tests.

I happen to believe that no batsman has ever approached Bradman for skill, concentration and appetite. And however we judge modern batsmen, we must never lose sight of the crucial fact that they are pampered with covered pitches, protective umpires' light-meters and tasty cash inducements. But to reflect on Viv Richards's performances in that 1976 series is to recall his total dominance over Snow and Hendrick and Old and Underwood and Selvey and Pocock and Willis and Ward and Miller and Greig. Especially Greig. The England captain's clumsy remark about West Indians 'grovelling' when they are in

adversity fired up all of Clive Lloyd's men, but none more passionately than Richards. Never in sport has attempted propaganda backfired as surely as this.

The runs that sparked from Richard's hefty bat that summer came with the rifle-shot crack of the hook, rasping square-cuts as he stepped away to make room, booming drives through the covers, and, in the fashion that became his trademark, meaty persuasions through the leg side, often to respectable balls pitched on or even outside off stump. His attempt at 'art' came in the late-cut, when those heavyweight shoulders lined up square to the crease and the mahogany wrists chopped down on the poor unsuspecting ball: it ran away from him as fast as it could go, bruising the advertising hoarding at third man.

Ironically the one field he did not conquer that summer was Lord's. Injury kept him out of that match. But he would be back several times to entertain the St John's Wood folk in the summers to follow. Not that London missed out completely on the Viv Richards brilliance that season, for he signed off at grimy Kennington Oval with what seemed a certain triple-century, being bowled by Greig, of all people, for 291 after batting a shade short of eight hours. In that first Test series in England, his visiting card had dropped onto the table in the vestibule with a force that rocked the entire house.

Since then he has had his quieter moments, always to boom back with a large innings in which bowlers have been not so much taken for runs as flagellated. There have been memorable duels, such as that with Jeff Thomson, bowling probably as fast as man has ever done. Richards's method is never to withdraw discreetly. Between roaring bouncers which singed his hair he flat-batted the red blur of a cricket ball straight into the stand beyond square leg.

That noble head surmounts a powerful body which has been compared with Joe Frazier's. Richards might have made a fair fighter, from the flash of those eyes as the combatants exchange glares before the first bell to the evident athleticism, coiled in sinister reserve.

He is a conscious leader of the black people, nursing profound emotions, eternally aware of tortured history, injustice, battered pride. He may be as popular in Somerset as in Antigua, and one of his most meaningful friendships may be with Ian Botham, but he is a *black man*, as committed as Frank Worrell and Learie Constantine, if not with quite their natural grace and polish. He shrugs off his deeds with the cricket bat. It is just 'a piece of wood'. With equal modesty, Gary Sobers acknowledged always that he was engaged in nothing more than a sport – to the point where he made a generous declaration against

OPPOSITE: *The indomitable Viv Richards seen in characteristic action.* (*Photo: Bob Thomas*)

England and lost, bringing down heaps of rancour upon his head. Nor did Sir Gary think politics. His ingenuous visit to Rhodesia cost him dearly in Caribbean eyes. Richards, in contrast, has stated that no amount of money could get him to South Africa. (Sobers did not go to Rhodesia for the money.)

So we have here more than a batsman, a quicksilver fieldsman, a teasing bowler, a West Indies captain. Viv Richards is proudly a man of his race, with an unalterable force of opinion which will have been conveyed to team-mates as well as to others in his orbit. Those colourful wristbands, beaming bright red, gold and green, are no mere convenience. When he finishes with cricket he will not finish with life. It could all just be beginning.

At that point what will he have left behind? Almost certainly he will have become the first West Indies player to register 100 centuries. His Test record will be top-shelf. One day in 1985, for Somerset, he slaughtered the Warwickshire bowling and put his name in the distinguished list of triple-centurions. His dominance at Lord's became legend, in Test matches, one-day county finals, and in the World Cup final of 1979. His was the wicket they always needed. When he fell in the 1983 World Cup final, India knew they had it won. And yet more often he seemed to be able to make runs just when he wanted to. His century in his beloved Antigua's maiden Test match in 1981 seemed predestined.

He walks with a swagger; he chews menacingly; he thumps that cricket ball as if it contained all the evils of a millennium of mankind. When he gets settled, the cricket pitch is his domain. Considered literally, there is no such thing as immortality, so Richards will have to leave that domain for good one day. But books and photos and film have a purpose; and if they convey to future generations just how this man's command affected cricket during these past years, they will have served those future generations admirably.

In Certamen Pilae *

(Extract – original in Latin)

The Issue's joined, two chiefs of name
go forth, both heroes of the game.
The word is given, and, urged with might,
speeds the greased ball in level flight,
and o'er the grassy surface sweeps;
with bended knee the batsman keeps
a forward stance, to watch its way
and mark it rise, then *sans* delay,
his arms descend with lightning fall,
to smite again the ringing ball;
and, ringing on, sublime it flies
and disappears into the skies.

WILLIAM GOLDWIN (1682–1747)

** This is the earliest real cricket poem – it first
appeared (1706) in a collection of Latin Poems
called* Musae Juveniles: *translation by Harold Perry.*

C. L. R. JAMES

'No-one I have seen, neither Bradman nor Sobers, saw the ball more quickly, nor made up his mind earlier ...'

THE MOST UNKINDEST CUT

Wilton St Hill. In my gallery he is present with Bradman, Sobers, George Headley and the three Ws., Hutton and Compton, Peter May and a few others. To them he is a stranger. But when he takes his turn at the mythical nets they stop to look at him and then look at one another: they recognise that he belongs. That, however, is what I have to prove. I am playing a single-wicket match on a perfect wicket against a line of mighty batsmen. But great deeds have been done under similar conditions. This is my opportunity to make history. Here goes.

W. St Hill was just about six feet or a little under, slim, wiry, with forearms like whipcord. His face was bony, with small sharp eyes and a thin, tight mouth. He was, I think the expression is, flat-footed and never gave the impression of being quick on his feet. His first, and I believe his greatest, strength was judging the ball early in the flight. When in form he could play back to anything, including George John at his fastest. He never got in front in advance, but almost as soon as the ball was out of the bowler's hand he decided on his stroke and took position. No one I have seen, neither Bradman nor Sobers, saw the ball more quickly, nor made up his mind earlier. Time; he always had plenty of time. From firm feet he watched the ball until it was within easy reach and only then brought his bat to it with his wrists. He never appeared to be flurried, never caught in two minds. With most of his strokes the only sign of tension or effort was the head very slightly bent forward on the shoulders so as to assist the concentration of his eyes riveted on the ball. But you had to be near to see that. I do not remember any more frightening sight at cricket than John running, jumping and letting loose at his terrific pace, and St Hill playing back as if he had known he would have to do so long before the ball was bowled and was somewhat bored by the whole business. You felt that he was giving the ferocious John legitimate reason to hurl the ball at him or take him by the shoulders and shake him. In all his strokes, even the most defensive, the ball always travelled. I have taken people who knew nothing at all about cricket to see him and as soon as they saw this easy, erect, rhythmic back-stroke to the fast bowler they burst into murmurs of admiration. His right toe was always towards point, left elbow high and left wrist as a fulcrum.

Playing so late, he preferred to score behind point and behind square-leg. His famous stroke was the leg-glance. It is a modern fetish that long-leg makes this stroke only decorative and I was glad to see Burke's leg-glance in 1956 repeatedly beat long-leg standing on the boundary. For wizardry Ranjitsinhji's leg-glance, when he crossed the left foot over towards point and flicked the ball to fine-leg, comes first. St Hill's leg-glance was of the same unnatural stamp. To a ball a little over the good length on the middle or middle-and-leg he advanced the left leg a short distance straight at the ball, so that if he missed he was lbw for sure. With the leg almost straight and his body bending slightly over it from the waist, he took the ball as it rose from the matting and hit it where he chose towards the leg-boundary. From accounts and photographs it can be seen that Ranjitsinhji had to make a sharp twist of the body as well as the wrist. St Hill bent forward slightly from the waist and flicked his wrist – that was all. He never followed round with the right foot. He put the ball where he pleased and John, being the finest bowler, was, of course, the chief sufferer. Describing his play in 1928, *Wisden* of 1929 says in one place that he showed fine strokes on the off-side and in another that he was strong on the leg-side. When Wilton was 'on the go' that depended entirely on the bowler. My negative memory may be at fault here, but I do not remember ever seeing a batsman standing straight, waiting for the shortish rising ball and as it passed flicking it between the slips. He didn't cut these down. He merely touched them and then pulled the bat away. That seemed sufficient to send them flying to the boundary.

The short fast ball of ordinary height he could get back to for a slash behind point, but he preferred to cut late. The finest of all his cuts was the late-cut off the slow bowler, to beat first slip and yet give third-man no chance. To save that four on a fast ground third-man would have had to stand on the boundary behind second-slip which would have been both ridiculous and useless. All that it would have meant was his running like crazy back to the usual position. One afternoon at the Queen's Park Oval in 1926 Percy Holmes, fielding at deep third-man and on the boundary behind the bowler, gave a great exhibition. St Hill had him running now thirty yards for the on-drive and then the other way for the off-drive. But it was the late-cuts to third-man that gave Holmes the most trouble. He couldn't anticipate the stroke. We had a wonderful time with Holmes, asking him if he had ever seen in his life strokes like those. The little Yorkshireman never relaxed for an instant and chased each ball like a hare, but he had time and strength to talk to us and admire this superlative batting. Each time St Hill made a stroke we could see Holmes smile as he ducked his head to chase the ball.

I never had enough of talking to St Hill about this late-cut. In so far as it was explicable, his secret was that he never timed the ball from the pitch, as I have seen great batsmen do and get out. He did not lie back and lash across, as George Cox used to do. He didn't hammer the bat into the ground as Frank Worrell does (one of the great strokes of our time). He took up position early, watched the ball well on its way and then launched his wrists into the stroke.

This modern theory that the leg-glance does not pay is a fetish, first because you can place the ball, and secondly if you can hook then the life of long-leg is one long frustration. St Hill did not hook by preference to long-leg. (None of us used the modern theory of getting outside the ball first. We faced the ball square so that if you missed it hit you.) He seemed merely to step inwards and swish the blade across the flight so that when it hit the ball it was pointing at the bowler. The ball went past the square-leg umpire like a bullet. If the square-leg boundary was blocked he might move over and, leaning towards point, flick over his shoulder. But there was no catch to long-leg. The ball dropped twenty or thirty yards from his bat. He was completely master of the on-side. He played the back-glance as well as his own special. To bowlers experimenting around his leg-stump he sometimes upset all calculations by waiting until the ball was almost on him and making a late on-drive, almost all right wrist with practically no follow-through. The ball went between mid-on and the bowler to the boundary, making monkeys of all the fieldsmen on the leg-side.

So far he was all grace, all elegance, always there long in advance. But there was a primitive hidden in him. If a fast bowler blocked his leg-glance – it was no use putting short-legs for he kept the ball down, *always* – or sometimes for no visible reason, all this suavity disappeared. He stretched his left foot down the wicket and, with a sweep that seemed to begin from first-slip and encompassed the whole horizon, smashed the ball hard and low to square-leg. Sweep is not the correct word. It was a swing, begun when the ball was almost within reach, and carried out with a violence that seemed aimed at the ball personally, to hit it out of sight or break it into bits.

One afternoon I bowled the first ball of a match which swung from his leg-stump past the off. He played forward at it and missed. Full of eagerness and anticipation, I let loose the next as fast as I could, aiming outside the leg-stump to swing into him. Out came his left foot, right down the pitch. He seemed to be waiting for hours for the ball to reach, and then he smashed it to the square-leg boundary. Root could get the ball to swing in British Guiana, and in 1926 he was at the height of his form. St Hill made seventy-five for the All West Indies XI and when the players came back they told us that when St Hill was batting, Root's short-legs were an apprehensive crew. They were concerned with him, not he with them. I have seen a bunch of short-legs cower when a batsman shaped at a loose one, but kept my eye on Tony Lock and saw him bend at the waist a little and face it. Time enough to dodge when he had seen the stroke. You couldn't do that with St Hill's stroke because no fieldsman could sight the ball off that ferocious swish.

His off-drive to a fast bowler was of the same ferocity. He used to tell me that on the fast Barbados turf wicket all you had to do was to push forward and the ball went for four. He would outline the stroke, and even though we might be standing in the street under a street-light, his left elbow, and even the left shoulder, would automatically swing over and the right wrist jerk suddenly and check. His body would be curiously straight, but the head would be bent over the imaginary ball and his eyes would shine. On the matting, with its uncertain rise, he put the left foot well over, the toe usually pointing to cover, not to mid-off. He took the bat so far back, at the end of the back-lift it was parallel to the ground with the blade facing the sky. From there he swung with all he had and smashed the fast ball through the covers. A minute later he would be standing almost as if back on his heels (with his head, however, slightly forward) playing the ball back along the ground to the bowler, often as if he were not looking at it. In moments of impishness he would move his feet out of the way, drop the bat sideways on the leg-stump yorker and disdain even to look at the ball racing to the boundary. But this I have seen him do only in friendly games, though I have been told that in earlier days he would do it even in competition matches, and Constantine, who played with him in the Shannon side for years, writes of it as a habit of his. One of his regular phrases in talking about a batsman was 'on the go'. He would say 'When Challenor is on the go ...' or 'When Hammond is on the go ...' For him batting began only when a batsman was 'on the go'. All the rest was preliminary or fringe. I have seen no player whose style could give any idea of St Hill's. The closest I have read of is the Australian, boy, Jackson, and perhaps Kippax.

His play has come to mean much in my estimate of the future of cricket. One afternoon, some time in the 'twenties, Griffith, the Bar-bados fast bowler, was bowling to St Hill from the pavilion end at the Queen's Park Oval in an intercolonial match. Griff was bowling fast, and this afternoon he was almost as fast as John. The ball hit on the matting, and then, s-h-h-h, it plumped into the hands of the wicket-keeper standing well back. All of us noted the unusual speed. Griff was

305

as canny then as he was in England in 1928, and in fact there could never have been a fast bowler who so disliked being hit and took so much pains to avoid it. Griff would not bowl short to St Hill on the matting wicket: he knew he would be mercilessly hooked. He kept the ball well up, swinging in late from outside the off-stump to middle-and-off or thereabouts. The field was well placed, mid-off fairly straight, short extra-cover to pick up the single, deep extra-cover, deep point for accidents, the leg-side was well covered. Griffith had his field set and he bowled to it. That was his way. He was as strong as a horse, he always bowled well within himself, and he would wait on the batsman to give him an opening. He didn't know his St Hill.

St Hill watched him for an over or two while we shivered with excitement tinged with fear. We had never seen Wilton up against bowling like this before and he was surely going to do something. (One thing we knew he would not do, and that was in any way hit across the flight of a pitched-up ball.) Soon he countered. With his left shoulder well up, almost scooping up the ball, his body following through almost towards point, St Hill lifted Griff high over mid-off's head for four. Griff moved away a bit and then came back to be sent hurtling over mid-off's head once more. He dropped mid-off back. St Hill cleared mid-off's head again. *I am pretty sure he had never had to make that stroke before in his life.* But he was 'on the go' and if to remain on the go required the invention of a stroke on the spot, invented it would be. There, for me, is where a future for big cricket lies.

How comes it, then, that all this style and all this fire came to so little? St Hill's record is not negligible. He made his centuries in intercolonial matches, against the MCC team in 1926 and again in 1930. Lord Harris, who knew of George Challenor's form in England in 1923 and saw him at his best in the West Indies in 1926, said of Wilton St Hill that year that he was the finest batsman in the West Indies and certain to be a great success in England in 1928. In England he was a terrible, a disastrous failure, so that even now it hurts to think of it, the solitary painful memory of those crowded cricket years.

W. St Hill was a very curious man of strongly marked character of which the defects belonged more to his time than to himself. He was born in 1893, of the lower middle class. The family was brownish, but Wilton was the lightest of them. By 1912 he was a great batsman and a universal favourite. He got a job selling in a department store, and I believe he worked there for the rest of his life. But St Hill was, as I say, not only an exceptional cricketer. He was an unusual man. I got to know him about 1916 and ever afterwards we used to talk. Even in my youthful days I could not miss his reserve (with sudden bursts of excitement, rapidly repressed as if he had made a mistake), his ironical outlook on life, his tight mouth and, when an issue was over and done with, the slight smile at the corners of his lips that belied the unchanging gravity of his eyes. In all the talk about who should have been selected and who was left out and why, I do not ever remember him saying a word. He may have done so to his more intimate friends – we were never intimate, though if I had been a member of his club I am pretty certain we would have been.

Macartney once scouted the mere idea that he was as good as Victor Trumper. Nobody was ever good as Vic, he laughed, you only had to see him walk. St Hill with a bat in his hand had a similar quality. His smoking of a cigarette while John fixed his field was not mere youthful bravado and baiting of John, who was a man born to be baited. He smoked his cigarette because until he had to play the ball he kept himself removed from all routine details. Even when he was declining and as likely to get out as to score, as soon as he started to stride to the wicket everyone stopped what he was doing and paid attention. As he took guard, all the Maple players or the scratch team used to watch him in a sort of thoughtful silence and none more so than the Maple captain, Hutcheon, a cultivated man with a taste for the sharper contours of life and character. Fires burned in St Hill and you could always see the glow. Whatever his form, whether he was out of practice or not, end of the season or the beginning, he played his own game, letting loose his wrists at the off-side ball and getting caught in the slips, or missing his glance and going lbw.

He was reported to be partial to what the late Aga Khan has defined as 'the good things of life'. On the field he was a martinet. 'Pull your socks up. Pull your socks up,' he would say between overs when things were going badly. Constantine Snr. was captain of the Shannon side, but he no more captained W. St Hill than the Stingo captain did John. That very day that he asked me why I was playing at the lifting ball, Constantine was, as often with him, carrying out one of his experiments. The wicket was slow, he bowled me a short ball and I hooked him for four. This was always the signal for a recurrent blow and counter-blow. Learie bowled short, you hooked him round in dignity bound. But he now aimed to efface the indignity by tempting you to hook again and getting you caught at short-leg. In the same over he bowled short again and I hooked him round again. Then he tried what I presumed was intended to be a fast yorker, but it turned out to be a high full pitch and I would have hit that for four too, but I was almost in position for another hook and only got three. God, how angry St Hill got! He obviously believed that I could hit Constantine for eleven in an over only if Constantine were playing the fool. At such moments he simply took over the side. 'Pull your socks up! Pull your socks up!' he hissed, took the ball at the end of the over, changed the bowler, re-arranged the field and did the same thing at Learie's end the next over. Old

Cons merely stood silent and watched, and Learie strolled off to cover.

John I understood. St Hill I could never quite make out. His eyes used to blaze when he was discussing a point with you; but even within his clipped sentences there were intervals when he seemed to be thinking of other things, far removed. As early as 1921 I had an intimation which I never fully grasped until many years later when I was helping Constantine with his autobiography and he told me some of his own private thoughts. That year there was an intercolonial tournament in Trinidad, the first since 1912. Pascall bowled splendidly and St Hill was in glorious form, making a century. When the tournament was over I wrote some comic verses about the devastating bowling of Pascall. The thing amused everybody. Great cricketers came from everywhere in the West Indies, from England and Australia, to play Trinidad, but Pascall bowled and they were sent away humbled. The last verse went as follows:

> And when to England back they reach
> And tread the sands of Dover's beach,
> And people crowd around to know
> The reason for their wretched show,
> A tear will shine in Hendren's eye,
> Jack Hearne will heave a bitter sigh,
> And Hobbs will shake his head and cry,
> 'Well, friends, we made a decent try,
> Armstrong and Bardsley, Hearne and I,
> But – Pascall bowled.'

One night that week I was paid a visit by a St Hill follower. I knew him as one of those who almost every afternoon religiously watched Shannon practise, and came to the match on Saturdays to see Wilton bat, as nationalist crowds go to hear their political leaders. There were quite a few such.

He didn't beat about the bush. The article on Pascall, he called it the article, was fine. But what about Wilton? Couldn't I do something on Wilton? The man was in dead earnest. I said that of course I would, and he left satisfied. I was in a quandary. He didn't want prose, obviously. Much prose, including my own, had been written on Wilton's batting. A celebrated professor of philosophy had long ago established that what was not prose was verse. Verse it therefore had to be. But my antipathy to writing verse was far deeper than my antipathy to umpiring. The one I had acquired, the other was almost instinctive: you just didn't play with poetry, and I knew that comic verse was out. By ancient tradition sporting prowess should be celebrated by an ode, but a sonnet at least was limited to fourteen lines, and so with much misgiving I sweated out a sonnet to W. St Hill which duly appeared in the next issue of the paper. At the critical ninth line it ran:

> O Wilton St Hill, Trinidadians' pride,
> A century and four came from your bat,
> And helped to win the victory for your side,
> But more than that you did, yea, more than that.

It is just possible that I may have written yes instead of yea. But yea, yea, nay, nay, what did it matter then, much less now? The watchful guardian of St Hill's interests who had commissioned it sought me out and told me it was 'good'. My clique of literary friends who had laughed at the Pascall squib as not beneath a literary man were polite enough to mention that they had read it and passed on. They must have believed that I was serious about it, and in a sense I was. I let them think what they pleased.

It was the earnestness of my visitor which remained with me. Why should it matter so much to him? I think I know now what was being prepared. Wilton St Hill had decided to go to England with the next team (his place was sure) and to stay there and play cricket as a professional. He would leave behind this selling of yards of cloth and ever more yards of cloth over a counter. In those days, at least, it offered little scope. He would finish with it and with the pressures which even on his own field, the cricket field, maintained a reserve which was more than natural. Ollivierre had done it for Derbyshire after the 1900 tour. S. G. Smith had done it for Northants after the 1906 tour. The story was that Small had been approached to qualify for Sussex (or Hampshire) after the war. But Joe refused. Through cricket, steadiness of character and a limited outlook Joe had made a place for himself that was quite satisfactory to him. St Hill was a dissatisfied man. In the most animated conversation about John's off-break or J. W. Hearne's googly (Hearne had visited us in 1911), St Hill, as soon as the discussion flagged, seemed to slip back into some private retreat where he lived alone. A member of my cricket clique once told me that he said to St Hill, 'Maple would be glad to have a man like you.' The reply was instantaneous. 'Yes, but they wouldn't want my brothers.' His brothers were darker than him and had neither his reputation nor his poise.

He never said a word to me about all this, but his friends must have known. The sonnet he did not mention, though there may have been a shade more warmth in his smile when we met after it appeared. I was, of course, quite certain that he had nothing whatever to do with the request. He wasn't one who asked for anything. He continued to bat divinely. One afternoon I was walking in the country with a bat in my hand when I passed a shoemaker's shop with a few men gossiping by the door. I had gone some yards when the shoemaker himself came running after me, awl in hand. 'Excuse me, sir,' he said, 'but are you Mr St Hill?' I looked at the group by the door. All were watching intently. I had to say no, and he was sadly disappointed, as I was. I went back to talk. None of them had ever seen St Hill, but they worshipped him. They knew my name and that I not only played but wrote in the papers. I told them what I thought of St Hill's batting. Their enthusiasm boiled over. One said weightily: 'You know what I waitin' for? When he go to Lord's and the Oval and make his century there! That's what I want to see.' I have to repeat: it took me years to understand. To paraphrase a famous sentence: it was the instinct of an oppressed man that spoke. If further proof of this were needed it is the hostility with which anti-nationalists and lukewarm supporters responded to this now so obvious truism. As for those who believe that all this harms cricket, they should produce ways and means of keeping it out. They are blind to the grandeur of a game which, in lands far from that which gave it birth, could encompass so much of social reality and still remain a game.

SIR DONALD BRADMAN
The first Australian cricketer to be knighted, and perhaps the greatest batsman in the history of the game.

LESLIE FREWIN

*'It is years since someone stirred a tankard of ale
and the Lord's Taverners floated to the surface . . .'*

WE TOLD SOME
CHAPS, WHO TOLD
SOME OTHER CHAPS

The old Tavern at Lord's where it all started was surely a unique place. To those who remember, it was a highly unprepossessing edifice with a slightly beery appearance. It had what looked like a four-ale bar entrance on the road, which let on to a series of fairly gaunt, cast-iron supports of a balcony facing the centre of the field. Unprepossessing it might have been but beneath that portico existed a special kind of magic: it was the place where one could watch the game, pint in hand, and run into all sort of acolytes, chums, friends, acquaintances, adversaries even, there to watch and talk cricket as if one had all the time in the world. As my old friend, the late and delightful 'Crusoe' Robertson-Glasgow once wrote: 'Sydney has nothing like it. Nor Melbourne. Nor Johannesburg. Even the village greens of England have nothing like it for they name their pubs "The Dog and Duck", "The Pig and Whistle", "The Goat and Compasses". But the Lord's Tavern', he claimed, 'has no name. It doesn't need any. The Tavern', he asserted, 'is no respecter of persons. There, a cabinet minister means no more than a junior clerk, and the former will be contradicted by the latter; politely, of course, because the real Taverners don't quarrel – not even after the sixth pint.' Crusoe was right, of course, as he was right about most things to do with cricket.

We who were early or relatively early Lord's Taverners and who are now reaching what Shakespeare called 'the sere, the yellow stage', tend to assume, because of the fame of the Lord's Taverners' charitable organisation, that all cricket aficionados know how the Taverners began, so much of a legend are they today; we tend to ignore the fact that another generation holds sway and is probably unfamiliar with the legend. For the benefit of the new generation, then, it might be apposite to put the young cubs in the picture.

'Mr Cricket', the redoubtable Alf Gover.

The Lord's Taverners, astride its coveted membership, exists today because of a handful of splendid artistic types who in the forties and fifties regularly, come rain or shine, assembled under that rather decrepit cast-iron balcony when they were either, in actor's parlance, 'resting' or, in the services' phrase, 'dodging the column', many of these latter having sneaked off undetected from offices and other such humdrum places to 'be there', where cricket was all.

I think I must plead guilty to coining the sentence: 'It is years since someone stirred a tankard of ale with a cricket bat and the Lord's Taverners floated to the surface.' I wrote it as the opening sentence to my piece, *Tavern In The Town*, in the original *Boundary Book*. And I did so with full knowledge of what I was saying. That lovely old Edwardian edifice was swept away by developers in 1962 when I happened to be chairman of the Taverners. On hearing the news that it was soon to happen, I tried to enlist the aid of several of the early *confreres* in a defence of the place, having received a promise from Madame Tussaud's that they would lend me a dozen pikes with which to ward off the enemy. Alas, my aggressive tendencies came to naught. When we assembled for the fray, Keith Miller was actually in the throes of putting one over the top of the Tavern which landed on a coal lorry trundling up the road outside. That, as they say, was an end to enmity.

And who, one may ask, were those intrepid early Taverners who, celebrating the coming of each Spring, invariably gathered together upstairs in the Tavern, sometimes elsewhere, for a five bob lunch and the passing round of a hat to benefit the National Playing Fields Association? I was lucky enough to count most of them as friends. Taverner Number 1, our Founder Member, was Martin Boddey, a wide-faced Brylcreemed opera-singer-turned-actor, who, in the manner of the great actor-managers, which he was not, elected to call anyone from Laurence Olivier to the parlour-maid 'Dear Boy'. His lovely, resonant voice, like my poor relations, remains with me still. I once spent three months with him and Jimmy Robertson Justice, and a handful of other early Taverners, in a Scottish lowlands hotel where I, then a senior film executive, and they, mummers to the core, contributed our mites of talent to Walt Disney's Royal Command film *Rob Roy*. And what did we incessantly talk about in that lowlands hotel each whisky-washed evening? You've got it in one – cricket and the burgeoning Lord's Taverners! Martin was mightily proud of having nursed the Lord's Taverners into life. I recall that shortly after we all returned from film location to London, Martin received a body-blow: his landlord had given notice that developers were to knock down his home of many years on the Cromwell Road. Martin became very depressed. Happily I was able to persuade a friend of mine who, it seemed at the time, had been left a tenth of Central London by his father, to accommodate Martin and his lovely wife, Bunty (do they still call girls Bunty?), in a block of flats at Hammersmith where I visited them regularly before he died in 1976. There, surrounding him, was always the impedimenta of the very early Taverners' years. He would have loved the Service of Thanksgiving for his life at St John's Wood Church, opposite Lord's, on 7 April 1976, when Ian Carmichael recited Housman's *Loveliest of Trees*, Tony Britton told of Martin's love of cricket and Bach and Elgar filled the Church. And we all repaired to the hostelry opposite joyfully to drink to Martin's life and work.

I don't know who Numbers 2 and 3 of the Lord's Taverners were; nobody does now. I have a hazy memory that Spike Hughes, the renowned opera critic and musicologist, was one of the two 'missing' bods. But if I'm not sure about those two, I know who Number 4 was – the talented Gordon Crier, producer of the pre-war *Band Wagon*, the enormous Arthur Askey radio hit, and other famous radio shows of that period. Gordon, sadly, is no longer with us. Talking recently to Jacqui, his attractive daughter, I produced from her the memory: 'I spent all my childhood racketing around the country with the Taverners, carrying "the rug" (a venerable blanket held by celebrities into which patrons of the matches threw their coins) at charity matches'. Jacqui added: 'The Taverners was something my father cared desperately about.' We all knew that, Jacqui.

The peerless Bruce Seton, who shortly before his death succeeded to his Scottish family baronetcy, was assuredly Number 5 of the Lord's Taverners. Bruce, I'll have you know, was the inseparable companion of our Founder Member. He had earlier starred as the eponymous 'Fabian of The Yard' on television, in a precursor and pale imitation of *Z Cars* and *The Sweeney*. Bruce loved pubs – and he loved the Tavern pub most of all. It was said, and he would have enthusiastically agreed, that if you stood by the Tavern during the cricket season with a tankard of beer in hand, it was inevitable that within minutes you would meet up with somebody you knew. Bruce, of course, knew that full well for he was ever the gregarious actor, full of actor's gossip and chit-chat, the opposite to his wife, Antoinette, herself an actress and daughter of the celebrated actor, Frank Cellier.

When I tackled *The Boundary Book* way back in the early sixties, one of the first questions I asked the hierarchy of the time was, 'Can somebody provide me with an up-to-date list of the Lord's Taverners membership?' A simple enough question combined with a request which was largely lost in an echoing thud of silence followed by a succession of earthy grunts and throat-clearing. Martin Boddey, he with the voice like warm treacle, looked quite pale. 'Now, let me see, dear boy', he said, 'I think Brucey (Bruce Seton) has it. Why don't you give him a bell?' 'Brucey', who had shared the secretaryship with John Varley (Taverner Number 11) and was at the time acting in cohort with another in that joint role, on further enquiry said, 'Now, look here, me old mate, I've an idea that Johnny Glyn-Jones has the list. Why don't you have prayers with him?' John Glyn-Jones, you should know, was a peerless actor of many parts on screen and stage. 'I *did* have it', he admitted, 'but I gave it to Jimmy Gleeson (Number 129) a few months ago; let me see, yes, it was either Jimmy Gleeson, Pinky Green or Bluey Hill. Enquiry of these 'colourful' gentlemen – the first a movie production manager, the second Australia's exported top assistant movie director – produced Bluey's contention that the last he saw of the Taverners' Membership List was when it was poking out of a dirty old sock at a cricket match at the Mote Ground at Sevenoaks, traditionally an early fixture of the Taverners. Just as press day loomed critically close for *The Boundary Book*, it turned out that *somebody* – nobody could remember who – had found the dog-eared pages, had pounced on them and decided, after a hastily-convened conference in the saloon bar of The Clarence Arms, to bring the list 'bang up-to-date'. This was duly done, it seemed, by Martin, Bruce and John Glyn-Jones, sitting in the saloon bar of the hostelry, pints at elbow, trying to remember who had paid their subs after buying their tie from Paul Whiston. Whiston was a Macclesfield silk manufacturer whom Martin had met when another early Taverner had done a BBC programme on Whiston's town and whom Martin had conned into producing a tie.

The list was finally produced for me by Martin, amid noises of approval all round, and foaming pints. I accepted it in good faith. When it appeared in print, howls of horror, rage and dissent split the skies over London. Several bona-fide members, it seemed, had been missed off the list altogether; some had been totally forgotten, others had been entered twice under wrong names, some hadn't paid their

Sitting in the sun – Johnnie Glyn-Jones doing his Moroccan alfresco bit!

subs and had been quietly excommunicated, their names remaining on the list. What a to-do! The cock-up was raised in Council, but it all simmered down. The thing was that Taverners who knew they were Taverners knew they were and it seemed it didn't matter that much. Even then, twelve years after the Taverners had been brought into life with the aid, so to speak, of quantities of hop-filled breath, it was a signal honour, as it is today, to be accepted into membership, thus to be granted the privilege of wearing the tie with its now famous representation of the halo and crown of St Mary-le-Bow, the symbol of the Taverners and, well, bugger the bumph! All of which indicates that the administration of the early days was a bit hit-and-miss, to put it mildly. It was, indeed, administration of sorts which was largely effected beneath the same cast-iron portico as well as in various other saloon bars.

One has, of course, to realise that the early initiates of the Lord's Taverners were predominantly professional actors, some writers, several BBC types, one or two stage producers, a handful of Fleet Street fellows, a couple of theatrical impressarios, the odd artist, one or two naval chaps like Jackie Broome, a covey of cricketers and a Roman Catholic priest named George Long whose upper lip was as stiff as his dog collar. Apart from the naval chaps, the foregoing are not, it must be admitted, individuals or fraternities freely given to exemplary administrative skills. In short, the Lord's Taverners had happened, as Wodehouse's Bertie Wooster would have put it: 'Because we told some chaps, who told some other chaps, who asked them to pass it on to some other chaps'.

Writing the name Jackie Broome revives the memories of a marvellous man and a peerless Taverner. Jackie died in April 1985 and, according to his charming wife, Joan, was 'cheerful and jokey to the

end'. Jackie, a distinguished naval captain, honoured by a DSC, commanded a convoy of ships on the perilous PQ17 Murmansk run during the war ferrying supplies to a near-beleaguered Russia, our wartime ally. He had served in the Navy with Prince Philip. It was he, as I wrote in 1962, who suggested that His Royal Highness might be interested in the formation of the Taverners. Together with Martin Boddey, he was invited – helped by the cunning co-operation of Lieut-Cmmdr Mike Parker, then Prince Philip's Equerry-in-Waiting – to meet the Duke of Edinburgh at Clarence House. His Royal Highness listened attentively. It was cautiously put forward that he might consent to become the Taverners' first president. Prince Philip's reply was typical of him. 'I could not do that,' he said. 'If I became your President I should expect to chair your meetings – indeed I should insist on doing so – and I really haven't the time. But I will be your patron if you like.'

The overjoyed visitors, as I also later recorded, prepared to take their leave. Before doing so, they casually mentioned that the honorary and honourable position of 'Twelfth Man' had been hopefully left vacant. Much amused, Prince Philip enquired the significance of the position. He was told – if he needed to be told! – that the traditional duties of that indispensable and always keenest member of a cricket side were (a) to carry the bag from the station, (b) look after the score-book, (c) bring out the drinks, (d), 'sub' in the field and (e) run for anybody who didn't feel like it after lunch ... 'Exactly what I thought you meant,' said Prince Philip and, thereafter, claimed the right to fill the role.

I have written elsewhere of the genesis of the Taverners and have named the well-used spas and other watering places, among them,

'The Yorker' in Piccadilly, 'The Bear' at Walton, 'The Gloucester' in Victoria Grove, 'The Devonshire Arms' in Earls Court, 'The George' in Great Portland Street – just a few of the hostelries in which the Taverners took form, helped by liberal libations of good English and Scottish brews.

Many of the founder members of the Lord's Taverners aren't on the membership list today; they've left, as Martin would have put it, 'to play games with God'. How good it was to know and work with so many of them – Sir John Barbirolli (Number 7), a dear and long-time friend who was there upstairs in the Tavern at Lord's for the launching of *The Boundary Book* when Prince Philip 'looked in for half-an-hour' and stayed over three hours. There were, too, Nigel 'Paddy' Patrick, the West End producer and actor; Naunton Wayne (did I really work and talk cricket with him and Basil Radford on the sets of Hitchcock's *The Lady Vanishes* in the disused power-house-cum-film studio hard by the canal in Poole Street, Islington?); Garry Marsh (Number 32), a stalwart star of the pre-war movies and a man totally *obsessed* with cricket who called everybody, male and female, 'Old Sport'; Jack Payne, ebullient always and as locquacious as a mynabird; Guy Middleton (Number 39), the thin, urbane, movie and stage public school 'cad' who taught me to play tiddley-winks in 'The Running Horseman' off Berkeley Square. Many of them have since disappeared, into the outfield, and those who remain are still full of reminiscence of those early, dream-filled and quite remarkable days; men like Johnny Glyn-Jones, who now lives out his happy days in sun-filled Essaouira, Morocco, and who claims in letters to me that with an annual heating bill of £34 and 'suffering' one wet month a year, life at his age of 77 is good, very good. That fine actor Denholm Elliott (Number 34), is still at the top of the movie and stage pile in the nineteen-eighties and Clarence Wright (Number 33), he of *Itma* radio fame, an inveterate cricket-lover who did the first Test Match public address commentary at the Oval in 1966 when England played the West Indies, is nowadays holed up on the island of Alderney – a cricket ball's throw away from him is John Arlott (Number 19) on that Channel Isle. And Dickie Attenborough (Number 93) is, would you believe it, still vibrantly around mixing filmic Indian curries with *Chorus Line* legs, if you please.

I rather suspect that Michael Standing was the missing Lord's Taverner Number 2, though there's nothing extant to prove it except that he was a *very* early Taverner. Michael was the son of Sir Guy Standing who played in a number of movies with Sir Aubrey Smith and was a member with him of the original Hollywood Cricket Club. Michael, too, was a fairly flashy medium-fast bowler in his day, playing for the Butterflies and Free Foresters. In 1927 he and Howard Marshall gave the first ball-by-ball commentary on a Test Match. Michael finished

Clarence Wright – the boy from 'Itma'.

up his working life as the BBC's Controller of Sound Broadcasting, as it was called then. Jean, his widow, tells me with great pride that today Michael's grandson is captain of his school Colts.

Of course, there was, and happily still is, John Snagge (Number 9), now in his eighties and still 'batting' energetically. John, lumbering and silver-voiced, made history with his Boat Race commentaries and wartime news reporting for the BBC. His love of cricket is still equalled by his love of rowing. 'Leander's out today, must get to the river!' was a familiar morning cry of John's outside the Tavern in what Neville Cardus called 'those burnt-out Junes'. As John now reminds me, in those heady, early days the Taverners had no offices and everybody worked in their own time from their homes. I took over from John as chairman in 1962 and recall that he it was who 'did a deal' with MCC member Ralph Wade (Number 175), then in charge of offices and office buildings for the BBC. The 'deal' was that in exchange for membership of the Taverners, Ralph was persuaded to make room for our early Council meetings in Broadcasting House. Fair dos!

Jack Hawkins (Number 97), Terence Rattigan (Number 84), Boris Karloff (Number 293), Tony Hancock (Number 289), Richard Burton (Number 101), Robertson Hare (Number 53), Leo Genn (Number 265), Sidney James (Number 110), Roger Livesey (Number 102) and Honorary Taverners 'Plum' Warner, Air Marshal Tedder (who was married to Bruce Seton's sister), Sir Jack Hobbs, Harry Altham, Sir 'Bob' Menzies, Charles Frend, the Ealing movie director, Douglas Bader, Bernard, Duke of Norfolk – all are among the toll of early Taverners who have gone to the Elysian shades. But, as I have said, many, happily, remain: Johnnie Varley (Number 11), now heads up the ebullient 1,000-strong membership of the Australian Lord's Taverners, and Sir John Mills (Number 54) is as active today as ever. Mike Parker

Hand in the till again – for a good cause! John Snagge (left) draws some loot at his local bank and gives his fee to the Lord's Taverners.

(Number 63) enjoys life down-under; Colin Cowdrey, Peter May, Stuart Surridge are all still mightily active and Sir Len Hutton (Hon. Member), Michael Denison (Number 233), Tommy Trinder (Number 170) and Donald Sinden (Number 282) are among the Taverners suns who continue to shine.

I am slightly hesitant to recall the first Lord's Taverners Ball at Grosvenor House in July 1951. It was a Ball, let it be remembered, that was embarked upon by the Taverners who at the time boasted only fourteen pounds, four shillings and eight pence in the kitty. The merry band of Taverners had committed themselves to the hire of the stately Grosvenor House Ballroom at a cost of several hundred pounds. God knows what would have happened had it all gone wrong! There were many additional bills, too, like the cost of mounting a 'cod' cricket match between nets on the ballroom floor, and the expense of two dance orchestras – Victor Sylvester's and Claude Cavalotti's (both early Taverners). It was said at the time that when Prince Philip learned of the fragile state of the Taverners' financial affairs he very speedily offered his resignation as Twelfth Man – an offer which was equally speedily refused! In the event, the Ball turned out to be a great, great success. That evening I had arranged to go on a bit of a club crawl with David Niven whom I collected at Claridge's hiding behind one of the reception area columns to escape the eager, searching gaze of the lanky Duke of Marlborough who was running around the entrance looking for him. But that's quite another and separate story! David and I landed up at that first Taverners' Ball at about ten-thirty and to this day I have little memory of what happened after that which, again, is yet another and quite separate story! But I do have a memory of the elegant presence at the Ball of our Twelfth Man and his gracious lady,

At the sign of the samovar.
(Drawing by Jackie Broome.)

the then Princess Elizabeth. 'What a lovely party,' she said at the end. That is exactly what it was and what the Taverners' Balls have invariably been ever since.

A long time ago I wrote that the Lord's Taverners, tankard of ale in hand, standing beneath the shadow of the old Tavern at Lord's, was really a living symbol of a determination to do everything possible to help prosper the game of cricket, the game all Taverners love. They have come a long way since then. On the way, the Taverners have gathered in members from many unlikely callings, often widely dissimilar to the callings practised by the early members. And, too, the old Tavern has hit the dust, literally, and a new Tavern, hard by the Grace Gates, stands invitingly to remind the young men and women of Lord's today that way, way back a few artistic types started something that has endured and will continue to endure as long as cricket is played on old Thomas Lord's ground. Praise be for such civilised mercies!

LORD OLIVIER, OM

'*I often think what a better life I would have had
... if I had been a cricketer instead of an actor.*'

MY LIFE IN CRICKET

In December 1940 I sailed home from America and arrived back in England during the first week of January 1941. Thanks to splendid staff work by some of my friends, one of them being Ralph Richardson who was already in the Service, I was able to present myself at the Admiralty without any delay – and joined the Royal Navy. For the next two years I flew aeroplanes in the Fleet Air Arm.

I owe a tremendous amount, as an actor, to those two years of flying, for they taught me, more than any other experience of my life, the true value and importance of co-ordination – of the balance of mind and body. It is the essence of good flying and, to my mind, it is without doubt the essence of good acting too.

I have often been asked what I consider to be the most important physical attribute for an actor. There is, I think, no such thing. One *could* be tempted to say that the eyes are *almost* the most important – for me, at any rate, that is near the truth – or that, on the stage, it is the voice. But the answer really is that an actor is, or should be, a finely balanced piece of machinery. And since one part cannot work without the other, it is idle to speculate which is the most important bit of the engine. If one word were essential, that would be 'stamina'.

One of the best co-ordinated of men whom I have ever met is Douglas

Bader. At a time when his life seemed for him, as he would say, somewhat unpromising, it was this nice balance of mind and body which enabled him to face it with a rare blend of courage and audacity, and make of it a triumph of good humour and distinction. I met him only once during the war – but not for the first time, for we had been at school together. In fact he figured in a most memorable day of my life.

He was a natural athlete and very good at all games, whereas, as a boy, I had a very poor physique – very poor indeed. All my life I have been at great pains to improve and develop it, and to this day I still go to a gymnasium at least twice a week, to relax and keep me strong. I may be wrong, but I have always imagined that a strong body means a strong heart.

Despite my lack of natural endowment I had every schoolboy's longing to excel at games, and of them all I craved most earnestly to be a fine cricketer. My father whom, all my life, I had sought to emulate, was a very, very good cricketer. He played for his college at Oxford and was a triple Blue when he came down and went to Durham. He later played for Hampshire and for the MCC; it was natural therefore that both my brother and I were keen on the game and longed to play it well. We rather regarded it as part of our heritage. I have often thought what a pity it is – how much better a life I would have had, what a better man I would have been, how much healthier an existence I would have led, if I had been a cricketer instead of an actor. But it was not to be. I don't know what it was – the finger of God had not touched us with a stump or something. It just wasn't there.

It was not until my final term at school that, to my utter joy, I was picked to play for my house. At this school 'houses' were called 'sets', and there on the set notice-board was my name – Olivier, L., Number 11. It is true that there were some six or seven sets in the school, but here I was, in my last summer term, maybe eightieth in line for my First Eleven cap. The full glory of my selection was not immediately apparent to me, indeed it was still swimming into focus when I found myself putting on my pads and my batting gloves, taking my bat firmly in my hand and stomping out to the middle. Seven runs were needed to win, and as I walked out to the wicket I thought – 'This is the moment I have been dreaming of.' I reached the crease, requested the umpire for 'middle 'n' leg', surveyed the field as I had been taught to do, and faced the bowler. To the first ball I played a somewhat defensive stroke, and as I did so I thought – 'This will not do. Time is running short – I must be bold. This is my great chance – none of that cagey stuff,' I thought, 'I must be bold and resolute.' I made two runs off that over.

The field changed over and it was my partner's turn to take strike.

This gave me time to dream a little. Only five more runs for victory. Now I was beginning to have that glorious creepy feeling, a tingling behind the ears. I knew that triumph was within my grasp. Already I could see myself being marched up through the dining-hall, having been sent for by the senior prefect, to be congratulated on winning the day. Not only that – to be told of their deep regret that they had never before appreciated my talents and that it was time to put me in the First Eleven straight away. We ran a single bye, and I faced the bowling again. Four more for victory. The full glory was now upon me. In my mind I was already beginning to shape the first century that I would make for the First Eleven . . . and I was clean bowled by Douglas Bader. He ended my cricketing career.

PETER MAY

Surrey and England (captain). Peter led England forty-one times (thirty-five of them consecutively) and made over 4,000 runs in Test cricket. He played his first Test at the age of twenty-one, celebrating it by hitting a century against South Africa. In 1957 he hit 285 against the West Indies (Birmingham). A peerless man and player, now Chairman of the Test Selectors, he is pictured here by a Daily Mail caricaturist.

ARTHUR MARSHALL

' There was also a bat signed by Hobbs which
was proudly displayed to the opposing players in a
spirit of unconscious Gamesmanship . . .'

PLAYING THE GAME

I was not gifted at cricket. For nine years I was a youthful sacrificial victim on the altar of our dreaded national game. I was not alone. Hundreds of thousands of young persons suffered with me, and suffer still. I estimate that nearly two thousand hours or about eighty-four days or twelve whole weeks of one's whole life were spent in beflannelled misery in the middle of a green field, longing to be elsewhere. No, luckily enough not always right in the middle. Having proved myself a duffer at anything requiring speedy action near the bat and wickets, I spent a comparatively happy two years in a position well known at prep schools but without any official recognition. I refer to the vital post of Long Stop. It is to be found immediately behind the wicket-keeper on the very boundary of the field of play and it has a great deal to recommend it.

Its chief charm lay in the fact that there was only one chance in five of you ever being drawn into the picture. The ball when bowled might hit the batsman, the batsman might hit it, it might hit the wicket, it might hit the wicket-keeper. When it missed all these hazards and came towards you, you found yourself in the very thick of it. All, however, was not lost. The grass in the outfield tended to be long and lush and if it had not recently been mown there was a good chance of the ball stopping before it ever got to you. No point in meeting trouble halfway. Ignoring unmannerly shouts to run, you waited for the ball to come to rest and then, leaping smartly forward, you picked it up and threw it briskly in, thus skilfully preventing the batsmen from crossing for the fourth time.

At school we faced the tyranny of cricket, and of all games, in the same uncomplaining way that we faced surds, fractions, Canada's exports, Euclid, Africa's imports and the Hundred Years' War. It was all part of the scholastic merry-go-round. Daily we put on those hot and unsuitable clothes, the bags supported by a school belt with snake clasp, and on our heads we placed those enormous, shapeless, white flannel bonnets without which small boys were thought to succumb instantly to sunstroke. Beneath a tree was the visible scoring apparatus, a selection of white numbers on sheets of black tin hung on a discarded blackboard and mysteriously known as the tallywag. The boys who worked this were a sort of walking wounded, boys recovering from boils or headaches or lunch or asthmatic attacks and they had behind them a long tradition of indolence and lack of co-operation. They lay on their stomachs chewing nougat and reading another chapter of *Tarzan of the Apes* or *Bulldog Drummond*. When they tired of that, they would just aimlessly hit each other for five minutes or so. From time to time a despairing cry would reach them from the pitch – 'TALLYWAG' – and they would then reluctantly change the tin plates to a score that was possibly accurate to the nearest ten. At the end of play they were allowed their little joke, which was to leave the blackboard showing that the final score had been 999 for *one*, the last player making 998.

For matches against other schools, the school pavilion was much in evidence. Its interior smelt strongly of disinfectant and linseed-oil and for its construction reliance had been largely placed on corrugated iron. Within could be found cricket nets and spiders and grubby pads and spiders and old team photographs and older spiders. There was also a bat signed by Hobbs which was proudly displayed to the opposing players in a spirit of unconscious Gamesmanship. But despite this trophy, a sad air of failure and decay pervaded the building. From its window, innumerable cricketing disasters had been witnessed; for example, our defeat by Dumbleton Park when our total score had been eight, three of which were byes. There had been, too, the shaming day when our captain, out first ball, had burst into a torrent of hysterical tears.

But cricket did have one supreme advantage over football. It could be stopped by rain. Every morning at prayers, devout non-cricket-lovers put up a plea for a downpour. It being England, our prayers were quite frequently answered!

Mike Brearley
in action

JOHN WOODCOCK

The Times *cricket correspondent's valedictory piece on Mike Brearley's cricket career . . .*

A MASTER OF THE MIND-GAME STEPS DOWN

14 September 1982. Garlanded with honours, the latest of them the county championship of 1982, Mike Brearley retires today from first-class cricket. His next career will be as a psycho-analyst; his first was as a university lecturer. Such is his knowledge of the game and those who play it, as well as the goodwill which attaches to him, that his recent election to the cricket committee of the Test and County Cricket Board is much to be welcomed.

It is 21 years ago that a Cambridge undergraduate, a little under medium height and a scholar to St John's from the City of London School, began to be talked about as a batsman of unusual promise. When the 1961 Australians came to Fenner's, three weeks after Brearley had played his first first-class match there, he made 73 and 89, batting at No. 8 in the first innings and going in first in the second. Jack Fingleton commented that he had seen a great batsman in the making.

In the event that was something Brearley never became. His record during his four years at Cambridge was so outstandingly good, and he has scored so consistently for Middlesex in the years that he has played regularly for them, that it has to be one of the disappointments of his career to have no better a batting average in Test matches than 22.88 and in 66 innings for England never to have made a hundred.

Despite that, he was a winner of Test matches, more so than many a great batsman, and a veritable thorn in Australia's side, because of his qualities as a captain.

Some captains are Olympian, some genial, some bluff, some autocratic, some are confused, some fussy, some anonymous. Brearley was brilliantly analytical. He has worked out the modern game better than anyone else except perhaps for Ray Illingworth. Few have had more to do with the most recent stages of cricket's evolution on the field or more strongly influenced trends off it.

He looked more objectively than most at the Packer intrusion, his aim, right from the start, being that some good should come out of it. He has been ruthless in his pursuit of success for Middlesex, whether that has meant going against the wishes of many of the county's members by importing fast bowlers from South Africa, West Indies and Australia, or preferring, as he did last week, a young Oxford Blue, Richard Ellis, to such a trusty servant as Clive Radley.

Owing, though, to Brearley's reputation for clear thinking, his decisions, although they may not always have brought agreement, have inevitably been respected. Rodney Hogg, the Australian fast bowler, once said of him that whatever other degrees he may have, he certainly has one in 'people'. When it has come to getting the best out of his players he has had few failures.

Having, some years ago, been a sort of cricketing Wedgwood Benn, he retires from active service more as a Joe Gormley, prepared, as it were, to take a seat in the House of Lords so long as that did not mean having to wear a tie. If he were, in fact, the next cricketing knight, it would be no surprise.

His fellow players will miss his counsel, the game his prestige, the reading public his fascinating books on the Ashes. He has scored 44 first-class hundreds and over 25,000 first-class runs. He led England to 11 victories over Australia (as against four defeats), the most gratifying of them coming last year when he returned and pulled together, so dramatically, a dejected and disjointed team.

Under Brearley's captaincy, Middlesex have won four county championships and two Gillette Cups, and if, at some time in the future, they find themselves in desperate straits, and he has no patients for a day or two and has been playing a little, he would help them out. As someone who likes to be fully stretched he probably will.

DONALD TRELFORD

The joys and frustrations of amateur cricket are remembered by the editor of the London Observer.

WHAT A WAY TO GO!

My first cricket bat still stands in a corner of the garden shed at my parents' house – a heavy great thing made even heavier by a metal plate that was screwed on later to stop the handle falling off. How I ever managed to hold it upright at the age of six or seven, when my father brought it home during a war-time leave from the Army, I can't imagine.

I certainly wasn't required to hold it for very long in my debut innings at cricket. That took place on a flat piece of ground next to the railway line in the Durham village to which I had been evacuated. Some older boys had heard about the arrival of the bat, a great luxury in those austere days, and invited me to join them in a game. I was flattered by my new popularity and readily agreed.

As the owner of the bat I was accorded the honour of first knock. At this point my total ignorance of cricket became apparent. After some initial uncertainty as to which way round to hold it and whether I was left-handed or right-handed, I was given my first lesson in how to grip a cricket bat. I recommend it to any young starter today.

I was told: 'Lay the bat on the ground with the handle towards you and pick it up as if you were about to club someone on the head with it like a caveman. Then bring it down into position by your legs without changing the grip.' I've never played any other way. Not that it did me much good on that first occasion, for I found I could barely lift the bat and was quickly bowled out for the first of many ducks.

Property rights having been perfunctorily acknowledged in this way, and the basic courtesies observed, I was thereafter dismissed to sit on the fence overlooking the railway line while my bat was put to more productive use by the other boys. The fence was one of my favourite places. The whole village had rushed there one night as the royal train passed through, and we often came to jeer at the Italian prisoners-of-war labouring on the tracks. They used to grin back, some of them, and invite us to share their hunk of bread.

These nostalgic thoughts have been provoked by the sight of my present bat – undoubtedly my last – standing in the corner of my study. Having ripped a calf muscle in the field at the end of the season and hobbled around on crutches for several months since, I am naturally inclined to wonder if I shall ever hold it again.

If that last match was the end, it was a most inglorious way to go. I had turned out for the *Observer* for the annual match against the *Sunday Times* at Teddington's lovely tree-lined ground in Bushey Park. We had only just started to play and it was already raining. Because it was so wet under foot I had decided to wear my old school cricket boots with extra-long spikes. I dived forward for a catch at mid-on but only got my finger-tips to it. One ball later our wicket-keeper, John Parker – whose son, Paul, the Sussex batsman, has played for England – threw the ball back to me. It fell short and I moved forward to catch it. My spiky boots, however, stayed in the ground for a fraction longer, and the leg must have snapped with the strain. Exit editor, pursued shortly afterwards by everyone else as the rain put paid to the match.

If it has also put paid to my cricket career, then so be it. I have some happy memories to look back on, starting at school, where I was captain of cricket. Two close reflex catches – one high at slip and the other at forward short-leg off a beamer – are as vivid today as the bruises they brought to my palm. In the Air Force, where I spent more time on the cricket field than in the air, I remember a tour of Germany for which words like riotous and rumbustious would be pallid euphemisms.

The high points at Cambridge, apart from the sheer delight of walking out to bat at Fenner's, were three sixes off successive balls at Selwyn and a 65 on Jesus Green. There was also a lively tour of Ireland on which I was stopped in Dublin as an IRA suspect while walking home from a dance in the early hours. To the eye of an Irish policeman, especially one unfamiliar with cricket, my bag looked as if it might well contain a rifle. In later life I shall recall a 74 (out of 109) in my first match for the *Observer* against the *Sunday Times* and 5–12 (and man of the match) at Chelmsford.

330

But my strongest memories of cricket will not be of personal triumphs, of which there were few, but of many curious incidents. One was of batting against the doctors at a mental hospital in Warwickshire while the patients clapped wildly at all the wrong moments, and of fielding on the boundary while they lobbed bricks perilously close to my head!

I shall never forget playing several seasons with the Adastrians. On one occasion my train from the North was very late, with the result that I dashed from King's Cross by taxi and arrived at Westminster Square in time to be told we were batting, that I was opening and the other side were already in the field. I changed in a blur and was out second ball without stopping for breath. I looked up at the clock as I walked back to the pavilion and saw it was 11.32. The game would go on until 6.30, I reflected, but my part was already over!

I was determined to score a fifty at Vine Lane, the Adastrians' HQ. One year I made 44 and then 46. The next time, when I was 49 not out, I felt sure that I would make it. But I hadn't allowed for a stubborn flight lieutenant at the other end, who refused to exert himself for anyone else's runs. Several times I cut the ball to short wide third man and went for the vital run, but he always sent me back. Finally, in exasperation, I played it to the fielder's left hand and charged down the pitch for what I judged to be an easy run. When I got to the other end I found my partner leaning on his bat and flatly refusing to budge. I turned back and was run out by a mile.

Not surprisingly, I was rather put out by this. When I reached the dressing room, I noticed that it seemed to be empty and hurled my bat across it with a string of violent oaths. What I hadn't seen was that a huge air marshal, one of the luminaries of RAF cricket, was emerging from the wash-room at the back.

He watched my antics with scarcely concealed mirth, then muttered from under his dark brows some words of wisdom that I shall never forget and which I recall whenever I feel the need to keep a sense of proportion about life's little frustrations. 'Never mind,' he said. 'You'll get over it. Japs tried to cut my balls off in the war. I got over that'!

SOMETHING FISHY?

Play in the village match between Dowdeswell and Foxecote and Marle Hill was held up when local publican Mike Farley's wife marched onto the pitch and presented him with his lunch on a silver salver – an incident that followed a domestic argument.

DAVID FRITH

331

LESLIE AMES

*'When eventually I went in to bat, Sandy was
270 not out ...'*

THE FORGOTTEN
TEST

Most cricket devotees have memories of the famous unfinished Test match against South Africa that was played at Durban in 1939, but probably few remember another unfinished Test played at Kingston, Jamaica, in April 1930. As far as I know these two matches are the only instances of Tests that were to be played to a finish but were never completed. I have the unique distinction of being the only cricketer to have played in both these remarkable games.

The West Indies then were not quite the force that they were to become in the post-war years, but in George Headley, often referred to as the 'Black Bradman', was one of the greatest batsmen produced by the West Indies, and therefore in the same class as Worrell, Weekes, Walcott, Sobers and Richards. It is very difficult if not impossible to say who was the best batsman. (There is no argument as to who was the greatest cricketer. That honour automatically goes to Gary Sobers.)

In one aspect Headley was not unlike Bradman as he seldom padded up and was looking for runs from almost every ball. Suffice to say George Headley stood head and shoulders above all his contemporaries in the pre-war era of West Indies cricket.

Small in stature, he was equally at ease with fast and spin bowling. Twice in England/West Indian Tests he scored a century in each innings, once at Lord's. In the West Indians there was also Learie Constantine who was a very fine fast bowler, a most dangerous hard hitting batsman and perhaps the finest all round fielder I have ever seen. For some reason which I cannot now remember he did not play in this somewhat forgotten match. Had he done so there is little doubt that we should not have amassed the huge score of 849 in our first innings. Of this mammoth score Andrew Sandham made the record Test score of 325 (since of course exceeded by Bradman 334, Hammond 336, Hutton 364 and Sobers 365). Sandy, as he was always known, who was a lovely character, with a dry sense of humour, batted over

10 hours in a very humid temperature of 85°. When eventually I went in to bat Sandy was 270 not out round about tea time on the second day. I was quickly off the mark with an easy single to 3rd man and a possible 2 if I hurried. As I was running to the danger end I called for the second and would have made it comfortably but the fielder chose to throw Sandy's end. Had the ball hit the wicket he might well have been run out. At the end of the over he beckoned me and said, 'Young man do you see that score under No. 1?' to which I replied, 'Yes, of course, and congratulations.' 'Never mind the congrats,' said he. 'I've been out here over 10 hours in this bloody heat, I am weary and my toes are blistered, and I don't intend having you run me off my feet. If you do,' he added, 'it will be you who will get run out – not me!' I heeded this advice for the rest of his innings. It was perhaps thoughtless on my part as I was 18 years his junior. After our tremendous score the West Indies failed to get the large score we anticipated, the whole side being out for 285. It was then a rather extraordinary decision was made. The England skipper, F. S. G. Calthorpe, decided to bat again, I suppose because there were still 6 clear days before the departure of our ship. After we had scored 272 our second innings was declared closed and the West Indies were set the task of getting 836 to win. This time Headley did not fail, but just before the close of play on the 7th day I was fortunate enough to stump him off Bob Wyatt. He had made 223 and the score was then 408 for 5. Another day would surely have seen the finish; victory was now in sight. However, the weather now had its say. After 8 days of intense heat and humidity the heavens opened and there was never a chance of another ball being bowled before our ship sailed for home. The players on both sides were physically exhausted by the heat and this was not helped by the lack of sleep; in those far off days there was no air conditioning in the hotel bedrooms, and the continual buzz of mosquitoes did nothing to ensure even a reasonable night's rest.

Perhaps it was fortunate that the last two days brought rain. With this experience and ten years later of the Durban unfinished Test, it was decided by the cricket authorities to dispense with such games. A wise decision, I'm sure.

RAMAN SUBBA ROW

*Surrey and England, Lord's Taverner
and Chairman of the Test and County
Cricket Board.*

*'Indians have what can only be described as a
fanatical love for the game of cricket ...'*

INDIAN SUMMERS ...
AND WINTERS

India seems to be a fashionable topic of conversation these days. Perhaps it is films like *Ghandi* and *A Passage to India* or the Mountbatten television series which have focused our attention on the sub-continent.

Whatever the reason, India arouses a curious fascination in the minds of those who have never been there, and inevitably the great majority of visitors to its shores become instant Indophiles.

Of course, I am biased. My father left his village 300 miles north of Madras when he was nineteen to qualify as a barrister in Dublin and practise in London's Privy Council for more than thirty years. I grew up amongst Indian friends although I had passed my 21st birthday before setting foot on Indian soil.

Friends became cricketing friends in 1946. The arrival of the Indian tourists in the first post-war season afforded some of us the opportunity of seeing serious cricket for the first time. Vijay Merchant and Mushtaq Ali who had been successful here ten years previously again delighted the crowds – as did the Nawab of Pataudi, Rusi Modi, Lala Amarnath and Vijay Hazare. Vinoo Mankad was the original left handed oriental magician with the ball and little Gul Mahomed at cover point seemed bent on destroying all wicketkeepers with his lethal left arm.

Yet pride of place in the record books went to none of these heroes. It was left to Messrs Sarwate and Banerjee in their capacities as Nos 10 and 11 respectively to arrive at the crease shortly after one another at the Oval against Surrey and from nought not out they both made centuries in adding 249 for the last wicket. Alfred Gover, the great Surrey and England fast bowler, tells the story of the groundsman coming out so many times to ask the Surrey Captain which roller he wanted that he was told one more enquiry would get him the sack.

Friendships were renewed in 1952 by actually playing at Cambridge against the Indians – including the scourge of Cambridge cricket, 'Buck' Diveche, who had bowled us out in the 1951 University match. But the real thrill was to follow in October 1953 with an invitation from Manager George Duckworth to join a Commonwealth Team captained by Australian Ben Barnett on a five month tour of India.

The thought of going to a country with which I had had so much association – and to be playing cricket as well – was unbelievable. We flew out in one of the early Comet aircraft to Bombay where we linked up with our West Indian and Australian colleagues at the famous Brabourne Stadium which is the home of the Cricket Club of India.

Indians have what can only be described as a fanatical love for the game of cricket. Everywhere we went we were garlanded, fêted and spoilt. We saw some of the most beautiful palaces in the world – Baroda was breathtaking – and we stayed in some of the strangest hotels away from the main cities. The Ritz Hotel in Ahmedabad conjured up all sorts of exciting prospects, including tea and cucumber sandwiches, but it flattered only to deceive us with its name. The hotel sign hung at 45 degrees on one nail and we were plagued by monkeys in the roof, yet somehow we had a laugh and relished the prospect of meeting an Indian off-spinner, Jasu Patel, who had bowled the Australians out. Life was different in the large centres: I seem to remember most vividly the beautiful architecture of New Delhi, the desperate poverty of Calcutta and the marvellous food and hospitality of native Madras.

After that unforgettable trip it was another five years before I renewed Indian contacts. A Test Match at the Oval in 1959 was followed in the sixties by two fleeting visits to Bombay and a Club Cricket Tour for three weeks in 1976 to Bombay, Baroda, Jaipur and Delhi. We were, I believe, the first club to undertake such a tour and again we were overwhelmed with hospitality. Our good friends of the 1953/4 Tour – the Maharaja of Baroda, Raj Singh, Madhav and Arvind Apte – all demonstrated the value of building international friendships by organising a memorable visit.

Raman Subba Row hits Benaud for 2 during his 69 not out innings for England on the fourth day of the Fifth Test at the Oval, August 1961.

Then out of the blue in 1981 came another chance to renew old acquaintances when an invitation arrived to manage the England team on its tour of India that winter. I couldn't but reflect on what George Duckworth would have thought of my assuming his role – 28 years later!

The Tour was subject to problems even before it started. Doubts were expressed in India as to the acceptability of some players in respect of their South African associations, but the timely intervention of the Indian Deputy High Commissioner in London, Pushka Johari, enabled the trip to proceed.

With my seeming wealth of experience of India, I warned the touring party of the potential accommodation problems outside the main cities, but the building of a number of new hotels made my predictions somewhat foolish in the event. With the odd exception, we had superb accommodation and in most places a choice of Western, Chinese or Indian food.

Hospitality abounded once more. We were inundated with invitations to functions and receptions, most of which had to be refused to allow the team to rest after some fairly warm days.

After a good start to the Tour we made the mistake of losing the first Test Match in Bombay and with it the series. With a typical sense of oriental shrewdness, the authorities ensured that all five remaining Tests were played on the slowest and flattest wickets one could imagine. An expert groundsman, Mr Sitaram, kept about three weeks ahead of us monitoring the preparation of each wicket with considerable skill!

For all that it was a fabulous tour. Visits to the Taj Mahal, the President's Palace in Delhi and Mother Theresa's Hospice in Calcutta were undertaken by some or all of the touring party. Our hosts really could not do enough for us – typical, I suppose, of the genuine friendship which exists between our two countries despite several centuries of rule. Perhaps we have Lord Mountbatten mainly to thank for that legacy of goodwill but I know at first hand that cricket has made its own contribution.

NOTICE

A droll old magistrate once put up this notice on a wall adjoining a wood, his property, near Goudhurst in Kent, birthplace of Alfred Mynn.

Take notice all – that from this thicket
You may cut stumps for your cricket.
But never let me catch you at
Cutting down a tree for a bat.
For if you do and want a ball
I tell you plainly fellows all
I'll give you a manufactur'd one,
Made for my trusty well-tried gun.

ANON

HAROLD ('DICKIE') BIRD

The Test and World Cup Final umpire remembers: 'That's when one of the West Indies supporters pinched my white cap off my head ...'

THE GREATEST MATCH OF MY TIME

I think the greatest match that I have ever seen in my time as a player and Test Match umpire must be the 1975 World Cup Final, West Indies *v* Australia, at Lord's.

I stood in the match with Tom Spencer, and I have had the honour of umpiring in all three World Cup Finals, West Indies *v* Australia 1975, West Indies *v* England in 1979, and India *v* West Indies in 1983.

I also umpired the ladies' World Cup Final, Australia *v* England, in New Zealand in 1982.

The 1975 World Cup Final had everything, a match that will remain in the memories of all cricket lovers throughout the world.

West Indies won by 17 runs. In the tea interval the press, radio and T.V. commentators were all saying it was impossible for Australia to get the 296 runs to win off the 60 overs.

Australia came so very close to winning the match, if they had not had three men out in their innings I think they would have done it, and that would have been a tremendous performance – especially as they were running each other out when the batsman was really set.

Ian and Greg Chappell and Turner had all got good scores when they were run out. It was Viv Richards who did the damage in the field. He was a young lad then and he fielded beautifully. It was some of the best fielding I have ever seen. It was he who ran them out.

I can also remember Clive Lloyd's great innings for the West Indies. It was a match winning knock. It was wonderful to watch, full of power and grace and timing. It was probably the best innings I have ever seen in all my time as a player and Test Match umpire. One of the greatest centuries ever. He came in to bat when the West Indies were in trouble.

At the end of the World Cup Final thousands and thousands of West Indies' supporters came on the field when they thought the match was

Have you heard this one? Dickie Bird listens to Ian Botham after Australia won the Second Test at Lord's in July 1965.

all over as Jeff Thomson was caught off a no-ball bowled by Vanburn Holder. That's when one of the West Indies' supporters pinched my white cap off my head. I always have to have a box of white caps sent from a firm in Luton before a West Indies series starts. While travelling on a London bus I saw a West Indian conductor wearing similar headgear and asked him where he got the white cap from. He answered, 'Have you not heard of Mr Dickie Bird, man? This is one of his white caps.'

After the Final it was a tremendous honour when the players and we umpires received our medals from Prince Philip. He had a kind word with me when he presented my medal to me.

He said, 'Dickie, you have had a very long day, well done.' It was then 9.00 in the evening, and I had arrived at Lord's at 8.00 that morning. So it *was* a long day.

I hope I shall be umpiring for many, many more years. Cricket is my life, my love: you could say I am married to cricket. I have given my life to the game.

MILES KINGTON

'This was one of those days . . .'

TROUBLE AT T'CREASE

Dithering Heights – a rip-roaring novel of passion and searing emotion.

'There's trouble up at t'crease!' The dread cry went up and was taken round the little Yorkshire town of Hutton-on-t'-Moor. A beautiful little town it was, although the grimy and dreary moorland was only 10 minutes' walk away, and its one industry was cricket. Generations of Hutton men had gone to work on the county ground, patiently hewing runs out of the resistant pitch. It was man's work in which women took no part, yet when a disaster was reported it was the womenfolk who crowded round the pavilion doors, weeping and waiting for the worst.

This was one of those days. The flag had gone up over the pavilion, meaning that men were trapped inside in a sudden and violent committee meeting. They could be there for days, and nobody knew who would come out alive. The crowd was silent.

'They do say as 'ow big Geoff Boycott has bought it,' said an old man whose crouching stance showed him to be an ex-middle of the order batsman.

'But there have always been Boycotts at the ground!' exclaimed a woman.

'It only seems that way, lass,' said the old man. 'It's always been Geoff, the greatest cricketer Yorkshire ever produced.'

'Any news of Ray Illingworth?' someone asked. Ray Illingworth! The greatest player Yorkshire had ever produced. The man who had gone down south to seek his fortune and had come back again to Hutton-on-t'-Moor as they all did with the possible exception of Mighty Brian Close, the greatest cricketer ever to come from those parts.

Suddenly the crowd pressed forward as the doors opened, then fell back slightly as two stretchers were carried out. The women gasped and the men went pale as the two recumbent forms proved to be those of Boycott and Illingworth.

'Are they dead?' asked the old man. No one answered him. In true gritty, direct Yorkshire style he went up to Boycott and bent over him. 'Art tha dead, lad?'

There was no reply. The women moaned. Then a microphone was thrust in his face and a soft voice said: 'BBC here, Mr Boycott. Have you any comment to make in the light of today's disaster?'

The words had a magical effect. The eyelids fluttered, the lips opened and with a great effort the wounded man said: 'I am fighting fit and raring to play for Yorkshire every day of my life and I demand to see my solicitor.' The roar that went up from the crowd awoke the other man, and Ray Illingworth suddenly sat up from his coma.

'I am the manager!' he cried. 'What I say goes! I think, therefore I am! Consider the spinners of the field! Tha shalt have no other manager!'

Exhausted, both men fell back and were carried off. Before the crowd could look grief-stricken again, the doors opened once more and out strode a spruce figure carrying a suitcase. It was the greatest cricketer Yorkshire had ever produced – John Hampshire.

''Appen you'll not see me round 'Utton again, lads!' he cried. 'I'm off to bonny Derbyshire. If you need a new manager or captain, give me a ring!'

'I always doubted he were a true Yorkshire lad', growled the old man. 'There's got to be summat wrong wi' a man who names hisself after a southern county.'

As Hampshire pushed his way through the crowd, a young man came the other way with all his worldly goods in a small bag. 'I have come to play for Yorkshire, good folk,' he said loudly. 'Tell me to whom I should apply.'

They looked at him. They noticed that he was jet black. They smiled. Even the women laughed. 'Th'art a gradely lad,' said the old man to him, 'but no one not Yorkshire born can ever dig for runs on 'Utton pitch.'

'Know then, old man', said the black youth, 'that I was born and bred in Bradford and proud of it.' There was a short, stunned silence. 'Lord be praised!' shouted the old man. 'We've got our own West Indian at last!'

And that is how Heathcliff, the greatest cricketer Yorkshire ever gave birth to, came to play at Hutton-on-t'-Moor.

THE CRICKET BAT

I'm a cricket bat, a cricket bat
Is what I'm proud to be.
My father was Alf Gover
And my mum a willow tree.

My single life-time mission,
Which of course is known to all,
Is to smite my mortal enemy,
The hard, cruel cricket ball.

Balls – how I love to smash 'em,
Balls – to frustrate and to foil,
As they try to hurry past me
Or try sneaking past – with guile.

And believe me, I can do it,
Be I called on soon or late,
Just provided that my master
Lets me stand up nice and straight.

I'll send that round red rotten thing,
Just where it ought to go,
If I'm only standing upright
With my face toward the foe.

And that, for many happy years
Is just what I have done,
Because my batsman owner
Was an England number one.

But one day, to my horror,
This base, ungrateful star
He signed my chest and gave me
To a charity bazaar.

And if that wasn't bad enough,
Thrown out by number one,

I'm bought by a Lord's Taverner
Who only plays for fun!

Where once I stood up proudly
Waiting each ball to be struck,
I now lean limp and loosely,
Like a badly ruptured duck.

Balls – now they all get past me,
Balls – whenever they do please.
Balls with leers and balls with sneers
All balls; with ball-faced ease.

And when I get within a mile
Of those red, wretched things,
They always find my edges,
Or my oil-hole, where it stings.

So now I'm a sad picture
In a bad state of decay,
A bat with battered edges
With oil-hole worn away.

A far cry from that bat of old,
For now I know full well,
The bat I most resemble
Is a bat straight out of hell.

My appearance at the wicket
Now brings tears to purists' eyes,
I once so firm and rigid,
Like a lucky bride's first prize.

The effect upon my owner,
Every day more clearly shows.
Yes, my sale brought him no century
As only Parsons knows.

CARDEW ROBINSON

Constantine came to the wicket, five of his team
overwhelmed for 79 . . .

LEARIE CONSTANTINE
LIFE, SUNSHINE AND LUSTRE

Learie Constantine was the first West Indies cricketer to reveal to his fellow islanders the 'promised land', the vision of a national cricket typical of his race, the brilliant cricket which has today given the game new life, sunshine and lustre. There were superb West Indian players before Constantine's advent. There was, for instance, George Challenor, whom I herewith call the W. G. Grace of West Indies cricket; for it was Challenor who rationalised instinct for bat-and-ball amongst his Caribbean companions and, by example, taught them first principles of batsmanship. And Learie was fortunate to be born son of a father who also had cricket in his bones. Father Constantine coached the boy, his mother sometimes joining in the instruction as she kept wicket. Constantine, the father, came to England in 1900, a pioneer long before West Indian cricketers were good enough to challenge England in a Test match.

But Learie absorbed theory into his every nerve and muscle. He played like a sort of elemental instinctive force. Principle became impulse in him. He expressed in all of his motions on the field the West Indian temperament. His swift darts and twistings in the slips were directed by intuitions heated by West Indian blood; he bowled terrifically fast as every natural West Indian boy wishes and loves to bowl. He batted with a power, positiveness and agility – again as every West Indian boy wishes and determines to bat. As much as Ranjitsinhji, Constantine was a genius of his own habitation, his place of origin. His cricket was a prophecy which has gloriously come to pass; for it forecast, by its mingled skill, daring, absolutely un-English trust to instinct, and by its dazzling flashes of physical energy, the coming one day of Weekes, of Worrell, of Headley, of Walcott, of Kanhai, of Sobers. All of these cricketers remain, for all their acquired culture and ordered technique, descendants of Learie, cricketers in Learie's lineage. One day at Lord's

343

in 1928, the West Indies were losing easily to Middlesex. Middlesex batted first scoring 352 for six, declared. Then the West Indies lost five wickets for 79. To watch his dusky compatriots, a West Indian had come to Lord's obviously for the first time. He had dressed himself as no doubt he thought necessary at Lord's, on any summer day. He was attired in a light grey frock coat, striped trousers, a brilliantly-spotted neckerchief, a 'stock', glossy shoes and white spats, grey topper and he carried a rolled umbrella. He watched the West Indian collapse in unconcealed dolour from near the 'Green Bank'. (No hideous stand in those days to obscure the view from one of the most gracious parts of Lord's.)

Constantine came to the wicket, five of his team overwhelmed for 79. In an hour he scored 86 out of 107. He drove with a velocity and power quite terrifying. From the high Press Box I looked down on this fury of primitive onslaught, beautiful if savage and violently destructive. And the sight and grandeur of it proved too much for the West Indian visitor by the Green Bank. Far away in the seats at the Nursery End a group of West Indians were rejoicing, as Constantine rode the whirlwind. The West Indian visitor darted on to the field and ran round the boundary towards the Nursery Stand. He waved his rolled umbrella at his exalted West Indians there, and racing along the grass, spats and knees at full gallop, he cried out: 'I'se comin' to join you, boys – I'se comin!' He, like his cheering frantic compatriots in the 'shilling' seats, had seen a great light. Constantine was leading West Indian cricket from the captivity.

In this match at Lord's in June 1928, Constantine was West Indian cricket *in excelsis*. Leading by 122, Middlesex went in again and collapsed for 136 – Constantine took 7 wickets for 57, five clean bowled, with one or two stumps split asunder. At one period of six overs and three balls, he overwhelmed six batsmen for 11 runs. The West Indies, set with 259, were surely a beaten side when five of their wickets were lost for 121. Again Constantine's genius shot out lovely streaked lightning, swift cuts, punctuated by the thunder of his drives. He scored 103 out of 133 in an hour; and the West Indies won by three wickets. He hit a ball back at J. W. Hearne, the bowler, so hard and fast that poor Hearne couldn't play again that season: fingers paralysed out of action! I remember that as I watched this wonderful innings from the Press Box's altitude, I actually (but only temporarily) decided that there were not enough fieldsmen available. Nine were ridiculously inadequate to assist bowler and stumper. The laws should be altered! Moreover, I was really scared at the power and velocity of Constantine's strokes: scared that somebody in the field might not merely be hurt – this was to be expected – but perhaps killed. Yet there was no excess of muscular effort in Constantine's swift plunderings. It was the attack and the savagings of a panther on the kill, sinuous, stealthy, strong but unburdened. The batsmanship of the jungle, beautiful, ravaging, marvellously springy, swift as the blow of the paw. His eye was rapid, comprehensive, and voraciously quick. He would pull the pace of Larwood square. His footwork leaped. He even played back defensively baring teeth. At the same time, inexplicably and fantastically, it was happy genial smiling batting, true to the good nature of Constantine himself. Like a schoolboy with a catapult he killed without intent to kill.

'Ah, but', say our modern scientists, 'but he couldn't really bat. He didn't get behind the line of the ball!' Well, I am today writing of Constantine in this strain, more than thirty years after seeing the glory of him. What shall be said thirty years hence of Bloggs of Blankshire, and the way he got behind the line of the ball under the blazing sky of Kanpur, while he amassed runs at the rate of twenty every mortal hour? Constantine's performances in Test cricket, taken by and large, do not make abnormal reading statistically. You can't really measure cyclones by rain-gauges, thermometers or even seismographs. Grandeur and genius don't add up arithmetically. A talented cricketer – and not more than talented – has been able to establish impressive statistical records in batsmanship – Barrington, for example. But on the comparatively few occasions when Constantine revealed his best in a Test match he contributed unforgettable pages to cricket history by incomparable revelations of himself.

In his own country, in 1934–35, West Indies won a rubber against England for the first time. And in the second game of the series Constantine scored 90 in the first innings, 31 in the second, and in two innings took five wickets for 52, and bowled Leyland, winning the match, with only one more ball to go. At Kennington Oval in 1939 he ran riot against Perks and Nichols; from ninety-two balls scored 79, with nearly every England fieldsman in the deep! It is useless, though, to try to convey any impression of Constantine's skill and fascination by recounting details from the score-book. He was square-shouldered, well-built, but not tall or small. His legs seemed a little longer than you might have proportionately endowed him with – that is, seen in his flannels. He seemed to walk with a straight back as he went to his bowling mark. Then he would turn abruptly and, slightly crouching, right arm a piston, send down a ball which might well be, as Sir Jack Hobbs once said, the fastest seen (and heard) in a lifetime. Am I romantically looking back on a memory-picture of long ago? Well then, let me quote from myself a passage written thirty years ago, when I had seen Constantine a few hours before taking up my pen: 'Constantine's strokes are always made late. He doesn't lift up his bat high behind him as the ball is coming. Constantine waits until the ball is on him; then, swiftly he cracks his bat like a whip. No man living or dead has hit a ball to the boundary with more than the strength and speed of Constantine. He can cut from the middle stump, clean down to third-man. . . . He will lie back on his right foot and crash the ball past mid-on, from a good length. He causes the largest cricket field to look small for a while. . . . His strokes are not blind. There is a calm pivotal spot, a clear brain, around which the whirlwind revolves . . .'

As a bowler, he brought his arm over high, leaning sideways a little, but balanced, so that his action could well have been a trot rendered into 'quick motion'. But while the arm was coming over the whole man of him, nerves and muscles, became hostile – concentrated hostility. The rapid fiery flight of the ball seemed somehow part of his run up to the wicket. The pace of the ball apparently pulled his body after it. His run followed the ball, so that you could never see to an inch at what point Constantine ceased to be a bowler and changed into a fieldsman. He gave the impression that he had power to be in two places at the same time. In the slips his agility, accuracy and rapidity have never been excelled, not even by J. M. Gregory or Hammond. Constantine in the slips sometimes looked to have as many arms as an Indian god.

Constantine made his own and inimitable contribution to cricket and at the same time told the tale of his people. No bowler could enslave him, no opposition could put him in bondage.

The Pavilion at Lord's, designed by Verity. (Drawing by Jack Wood).

LESLIE FREWIN

A tale of Three Johns

THE TAVERNERS 'DOWN UNDER'

The Lord's Taverners in Australia have lifted off like Concorde!

The now highly-successful Aussie club was motivated by the arrival in Sydney in October 1981 of actor-producer John Varley, one of the original dozen who formed the Taverners in Britain in 1950. An avid watcher of cricket from the old Tavern at Lord's, he first met Founder-Member Martin Boddey in 1948. Shortly after that meeting, he set to with Boddey, Bruce Seton, actor Michael Shepley and radio producer Gordon Crier to help lay the foundations of the Lord's Taverners in England, holding the first formal meetings in his family home in South Kensington, London, and in his dressing room at the Whitehall Theatre where he was playing Mark in *Worm's Eye View.*

The Provisional Committee elected John and Bruce Seton as Joint Honorary Secretaries, positions which were confirmed at the Inaugural Meeting in July of that year. John chose to become Lord's Taverner Number 11 as, he claims, that was always his position in the batting order at school!

John lost most of his hair playing in 2,500 performances at the Whitehall Theatre. As a result he decided to concentrate on theatre production and management, staging the theatrical half of the Royal Command Film Performance at the Empire Theatre, London, in 1952. He subsequently managed the Phoenix Theatre, London, and Amalgamated Players, retiring from theatre work in 1976.

Chairman of Crufts Presentation Committee (he is an international Judge of Hounds), he visited Australia, returning to Britain to submit a report to the Taverners' Council urging the formation of the Lord's Taverners down-under. Given the go-ahead, he went back to Australia where, with actor John McCallum, he formed the Lord's Taverners, Australia, roping in John Darling, an influential businessman, as Chairman.

The Inaugural Meeting was held in Sydney on 22 October 1982. At the end of 1985, only three years after its foundation, the Aussie

347

ABOVE: *The winning Taverners' team on the occasion of the 2nd Annual Spring Ball of the Aussie Taverners in 1984. The Taverners' team of four took on the Olympic Gold Medallists and beat them. The two teams were level on points until the last event – the Marathon. On leaving the Regent Hotel, Sydney, the opposition were sent the wrong way and naturally the Taverners came home easy winners! The winners pictured here are (left to right): Barry Knight (ex-England cricketer), Len Evans, OBE (Bon Vivant), Katrina Lee (Australian newscaster) and Gordon Elliott (television presenter).* RIGHT: *John Varley, Lord's Taverner Number 11, and today Chief Executive and Secretary of the Lord's Taverners, Australia.*

Taverners became truly national with state branches in New South Wales, Victoria, Western Australia, Queensland, South Australia, ACT and Tasmania. Membership, much-coveted, today stands in excess of 1,000, the branches having contributed greatly to helping thousands of disadvantaged children to play and enjoy cricket.

The Lord's Taverners in Australia is a fine success story of the eighties, due largely to the unstinting efforts of Founder and Chief Executive John Varley's energetic activities which, not to put too fine a point on it, may one day develop young cricketing talent to knock the stuffing out of the Poms!

GEOFFREY WATKINS

*'Sometimes the batsmen were hit in the tenderest
of places . . .'*

WHERE CRICKET IS 20-A-SIDE AND RICH IN LAUGHTER

Samoan cricket has to be seen to be believed. It is rich in laughter, has elements of farce, echoes of tribal warfare, a touch of the Glee Club, gives a nod or two in the direction of MCC laws and is played in noisy enthusiasm against exotic backgrounds of blue lagoons, waving palms, rubber trees and the beautiful feathery tamalingi with its red flowers.

It is a game that is played with pleasure by men and women equally. In Apia, the capital of Western Samoa, it is played on an area of land recovered from the sea called the Eleelefou. The concrete wicket is slightly longer than ours and four feet wide. It is raised about three inches off the ground so this makes no-balling virtually impossible. The bats are three-sided and 44 inches long, tapering to a rounded handle bound in coconut cord. Individual marks in bright colours are painted on the base part.

Some people are reminded of baseball when they first see the bats, but I see them as tribal clubs, smashing the hard rubber ball – which the players make themselves from strips of raw rubber off the trees – as they used to crack the skulls of their Tongan or Fijian enemies. There are no bails as the strong sea breezes would keep shipping them off.

The teams are 20-a-side and it is a picturesque sight when they take the field in their colourful lavalavas (cotton wrap-around skirts worn by both sexes), wearing T-shirts and bare-footed. Each side brings its own umpire. In the harbour tall-masted yachts gently sway at anchor, and overlooking the town and the pitch is the thickly wooded Mount Vaea where Robert Louis Stevenson lies in his simple tomb on the summit in the paradise he made his own.

The batting side does not repair to the pavilion when the game begins as there is no such place. Instead the other 18 players sit in a semicircle in the position of the slips. Most of the fielders being on the leg-side as the game proceeds – runs are called points – the seated batting side will break into song: sad traditional melodies or war chants accompanied by handclapping. Leading the musical entertainment is 'the teacher', a chorus master-cum-cheer leader of charisma, and whatever he does the rest of the team dutifully follows. He also has a whistle which he blows from time to time and he will go into rhythmical gyrations as if on a dance floor, followed by his team.

Now it might be thought that this is done to encourage the batsmen at the wicket or to put the bowlers out of their stride. Not a bit. It is just done out of Polynesian *joie de vivre*. But the fielding side have their secret weapon also.

The 'teacher' blows his whistle, leaps in the air with whoops, twisting and turning in impromptu dance and grimacing like a gargoyle. He ends by jumping up and clapping his hands above his head with his team emulating him. This, too, is an expression of uninhibited joy and has nothing to do with intimidation.

When a wicket falls, however, the performance is intensified with leaping and shouting and laughter and with the more athletic doing cartwheels and somersaults. It made me think that Derek Randall might have visited this pearl of the Pacific; he would be in his element in this game.

The batsmen have two stances. Some will rest the bat over their shoulder as if waiting to brain some creature emerging from the swamps, while others point it to the ground like a golfer lining up for a prodigious drive; and both men and women, perhaps a little inelegantly, thrust the folds of their lavalavas between their muscular thighs before taking guard.

All the bowlers are fast and they only take three or four paces before hurling the ball down. Women bowl underarm. The ball is always well pitched up, usually middle and leg, and rises sharply. Sometimes the batsmen were hit in the tenderest of places. As they scorn such sissy aids as helmets, boxes, gloves and pads, I winced for them. But they seemed unaffected and just laughed when they were hit.

In fact, whatever the players did they laughed in doing it: dropping a catch, being out first ball, missing a run-out or whatever were causes for loud laughter, and they laughed just as loudly when making a mighty hit into the sun or into the long grass in the outfield where fielders were up to their waist in couch grass.

The ball is bowled from whichever end it lands – there are no overs – and the bowlers are also the wicketkeepers. Although most of the batting reminded me of the village blacksmith having a bash after a skinful of scrumpy, the other aspects of the game were more skilful. Men and women throw straight and hard – learned from their child-hood when they threw stones at tins and other objects – and they all seemed to have a flair for wicketkeeping, going through the motions of whipping off the imaginary bails like a Rodney Marsh.

Batsmen always go for the big hit as it is too tiring to run for singles in the heat. When it was time for a break – the lunch or tea interval – both teams sat on the grass drinking soft drinks and eating biscuits and chatting.

One of the happy sights in Apia between 4 p.m. and 6.15 p.m. is to see a few hundred women of all ages and shapes, and in a variety of costumes, playing cricket on the Eleelefou. The scene is a happy blend of colour, noise and enthusiasm and when it comes to the histrionics of the game the men pale beside the women.

The woman 'teacher' will grimace grotesquely, thrusting her arms to her side and waggling her fingers. Then she will bend her knees, roll her buttocks, kick out in puppet-like movements, straighten up and jump up and down as if demented, all the time blowing her whistle. Then she will kick her left leg as if getting rid of a persistent admirer and leap into the air with both arms extended. She was followed in all her actions by the rest of the team.

On occasions the performance would end with the women facing the men and lifting up their lavalavas for what could have been a full frontal if they had not been wearing a kind of cut-down cotton long johns. It must have frightened the living daylights out of their enemies in the old days.

The men's cricket season has now ended and I saw the last game between the town area and the village of Ifilele Aasa. The town team had 15 Mormon bishops playing for it and one of the umpires was Bishop Afamasaga Laulu, who is also the tribal chief of Fasitootai. He was a splendidly dignified figure in his creamy jacket, ecclesiastical purple lavalava and his clipboard.

As each side had won a game they played a decider – but only 15 players each this time to shorten the proceedings – and the game was won by the visitors.

The start of the women's cricket season began with a game between Vineula ladies, of Apia, and Miliemo. The home team scored 60 points, the visitors 24. So it was a comfortable win of 36 points for the locals, ranging from slim-legged, doe-eyed schoolgirls to muscular, big-busted and broad-beamed ladies.

Although Samoan cricket is fun from beginning to end it once had a tragic sequel. In a match not far from Apia a visiting batsman was given out when the ball was caught by a young spectator. The batsman protested, but the home umpire, proud of his young brother who had made the catch, stuck to his decision. The batsman killed him with one savage swipe of his bat.

But things like that do not happen today. Samoan cricket seems to make many of its rules as it goes along. But who cares? It has a logic of its own, and so long as it is an occasion for so much laughter and pleasure, long may these Polynesian 'flannelled fools' in their cotton lavalavas make a spectacle of themselves and make an entertainment for us.

Peter Ustinov

Park Av
NYC

Dear Leslie

This is the closest to
Cricket you'll ever get me!

Leslie Frewin asked **PETER USTINOV** *to help with his book* Cricket Bag.
Peter's reply is republished here.

E. W. SWANTON

*'What a match Marlar had with those truly spun
and flighted off-breaks – twelve for 143!'*

THE ASHES IN CORONATION YEAR

There cannot be a cricket-lover aged, say, 45 or over who when the Coronation year 1953 is mentioned does not immediately think of England's recovery of the Ashes. I could fill my allotted space three or four times over by reviewing the Test series and the lessons to be drawn therefrom. But this is well-trodden ground surely even to those historically-minded readers then either unborn or too young to have been enthused. So allow me to settle for a rather broader picture.

When the Australian side was announced in the spring the now-defunct *Evening News* was speaking with two voices, their astringent critic E. M. Wellings saying it would prove the weakest since 1912, while John Arlott beneath a youthful photograph prophesied a great series and pointed to Australia's all-round potential. Since at the end of the summer eight Australians shared the wickets ranging in number from Ray Lindwall's 85 to the 45 of Keith Miller, and the only defeat suffered by Lindsay Hassett's team was in the final Test, that particular round went retrospectively to Arlott.

The Chancellor of the Exchequer, Mr R. A. Butler, cheered us all before the season started by absolving cricket clubs from Entertainment Tax, while Lord Justice Birkett gave his usual felicitous welcome to the Australians at the Cricket Writers' Club dinner at which 'Mr F. S. Trueman was presented with the Club's trophy for the best young cricketer of 1952'.

The only regret recorded by the Australians throughout their stay concerned the clash of the last day of their game against Notts with the Coronation, but the county happily waived their rights and Hassett and Co. saw the great procession after all.

A week later at Trent Bridge the *Daily Telegraph* was marvelling at the fall of 12 wickets for 92 runs, six of each side's, mostly at the hands of Bedser and Lindwall, on a 'completely placid and easy' pitch.

Ah, but the conditions were damp and raw for these two masters of

The coveted Ashes.

swing – the shadow surely of things to come.

The weather robbed England of highly probable victory at Trent Bridge. The Lord's Test is remembered rightly for the Watson-Bailey rear-guard which defied all probability on the last day, but other fine deeds led to it, notably with the bat by Len Hutton and Lindsay Hassett. When else, you budding Frindalls, did rival captains make hundreds in the same England-Australia Test? And Keith Miller, always responsive to the St John's Wood air, made a hundred, too, uncharacteristically but of necessity slowly. Lindwall had a splendid all-round match, and let it not be forgotten that Freddie Brown, aged 42 and chairman of Selectors, was persuaded to fill an all-round gap and made his bow to Test cricket with four wickets and 50 very valuable runs.

Let us stay at Lord's and note that Cambridge won by two wickets on the brink of time, the closest margin since 1908, thanks mostly to their captain, the present cricket correspondent of the *Sunday Times*, Robin Marlar, and the Warden of Radley, Dennis Silk. Never shall I forget the captain dawdling in to join Silk when, with 37 minutes and only two wickets left, 52 were needed. Seemingly enjoining continued caution at a mid-pitch conference, Marlar saw Silk exchange the role of a Scotton for a Jessop, add 39 in 30 minutes to the 77 he had needed more than four and three-quarter hours to collect and run in to a hero's welcome.

Perhaps the Editor might persuade the central figures to throw light on a scene that evoked memories of the cricket match in Macdonnell's *England, their England*. But, captaincy apart, what a match Marlar had with those truly spun and flighted off-breaks (twelve for 143)! A few days later he was taking nine of the Players' wickets for 117 and helping to bring about a famous victory for the Gentlemen by 95 runs. Such was the strength of amateur cricket over 30 years ago. One must resist the temptation to linger over several other admirable cricketers short of the highest fame who figured in that G and P: George Emmett, for instance, Reg Simpson, Roy Tattersall, and, not least, Bruce Dooland of Australia and Notts, a charming fellow whose leg-breaks and googlies brought him the season's highest bag of 172 wickets.

A wet and gloomy Old Trafford Test was lightened only by not the least of Harvey's 21 Test hundreds. Only Sir Donald Bradman and Greg Chappell of his countrymen exceed Neil's tally of hundreds, and no others get within distance of them. Yet one thinks not of figures in his case but of the particular charm that belonged only to a handful of the great left-handers: it is the quality that of today's batsmen marks David Gower apart. Come to that, there is something akin in the approach to the game of these two – as well as in their surpassing excellence in the field.

In most ways the Headingley Test of 1953 was, from the English view-point, a slow-drawn drama best forgotten. The *Daily Telegraph* heading after the first day was 'One of the worst days for English cricket' – wherein Lindwall, Miller, Davidson, Archer and Benaud confined their opponents to 142 for seven with 'hardly a buffet made in anger'. Thereafter Australia called the tune. Another marathon defensive effort by Bailey obstructed them in the second innings for 260 minutes, the only apt comparison being with H. L. Collins' 40 in 310 minutes at Old Trafford back in 1921. Even so, England would have lost but for an unexpectedly adventurous 48 by Jim Laker – almost the only positive English batting of the match – and by some less laudable bowling outside the leg-stump by Bailey when Australia were chasing victory on the last evening.

What a relief it was after all this to get down to the hospitable tents and cheerful bunting of Canterbury. Kent were in the middle of the only truly weak period in their history and they took a beating, their thirteenth of the season, from Middlesex. Yet such is the depth of Kentish support that the aggregate gate for the week was 35,000.

Middlesex, at the top of the table, engaged in a spiritless contest with the 1952 champions, Surrey, at Lord's, both sides getting it in the neck from *DT*'s number one man. He recorded that 75,000 had seen the match and suggested that, rather than patronising the return match due shortly at the Oval, the crowds might 'seek cricket of skill, spirit and character elsewhere. As the coloured comedian used to say to his partner, "Boy, even if this was good I wouldn't like it." '

Morally speaking, England had a good deal to make up when the final Test came round. Six days were allotted but only four needed, and at the end, of course, England collected the Ashes with what on paper seems the utmost ease by eight wickets. But for those of us who had been watching the struggle for so long the truth was hard to believe until the crowds surged in a multi-coloured mass in front of the Oval pavilion. The country was taken up by the euphoria of the moment to a degree unknown before since the great boom in the sale of television sets occasioned by the Coronation allowed millions both to see and to listen. To Brian Johnston, Peter West and me fell the joy of telling them the story. For Hutton it was the culminating triumph, made despite losing the toss all five times. Hassett, who had so misread the pitch that he included not a single spinner, took the result like the sportsman England had taken to their hearts. Laker and Lock had undone his side in the second innings as had Bedser and Trueman in the first. Bedser's 39 wickets were the achievement of a series which marked the turn of the tide. This was Peter May's second Test against Australia, Fred Trueman's first – and there were others of their generation due shortly to stiffen the ranks.

Dark days indeed there were to be for cricket – but not yet. Upwards of half a million people at the Tests produced a profit of £130,000. The most popular Australian side in my memory took home all but half of this, and for the counties their share in those days was riches.

Postscript: Chapman and Woodfull, the two captains, each made hundreds in the Lord's Test of 1930, and Hammond and Bradman, also at Lord's, did likewise in 1938.

*'His stoop to retrieve the bails was like a bow to
a parting guest...'*

THE GENTLEMAN IN GLOVES

As the most courtly of all wicket-keepers, William Albert Oldfield, settled into his preparatory stance, he seemed to greet the incoming batsman with a curtsy. He spoke a few words of welcome, as if he were receptionist for the fielding side.

He did not carry politeness to the point of graciously sparing a batsman – like a courtier in a duel allowing his disarmed adversary to regain his rapier. Oldfield darted in for the kill as eagerly as need be; but no matter how quickly he despatched his opponent he never forgot his manners. He did not cuff the stumps or grab rudely for catches. His appeals were not raucous – nor were they apologetic. His stoop to retrieve the bails was like a bow to a parting guest.

Oldfield's actions in pauses of play were similarly genteel. Between balls and at ends of overs he constantly patted his gloves together, almost daintily, first one on top, then the other. I asked the reason for this mannerism; he said he always liked to feel that his fingers were making a perfect fit in his gloves, so he patted the palms with a crosswise action like a slithering clap. A tidy soul, he would go pat-a-patting from end to end with precise stride, the knee-flaps of his pads giving rather a strutting effect which seemed to call for minuet music. The short, dapper man would have made a fine courtier in Louis XV's day. You could picture him in the ballroom at Versailles, with powdered wig, gleaming shoe-buckles and snowy lace at his wrists. On the field his flannels were as spotless as a cravat. Never a thing out of place – except a bail flicked from its groove as a dandy might whisk a speck of snuff from his jacket. As a courtier he would have fitted blandiloquently into the cultivated conversation between minuets and quadrilles. Oldfield was so gentlemanly that he always had the air of being an intent listener, even to bores. I have seen him standing on a burning deck in the tropics, easily caught by an ear-basher when all but he had fled, nodding his head understandingly and cooing agreement in his light voice. Yet I suspected that his thoughts were often far away, engrossed in calculations about dozens of bats, boxes of balls and other stock on his shelves. He has had few superiors as a straight-faced leg-puller, with the lively corners of his mouth kept in order by an enclosing crease in each cheek (like a couple of brackets). He has one of those smirky smiles and a quick habit of turning his expressive face half-sideways, looking at you aslant out of the top corners of sharp-set eyes. He could easily double for George MacReady, the film actor.

When Bert Oldfield, as a fair-haired youth of seventeen, played his first match for Glebe against Waverley in Sydney in March 1915, the opposing keeper was Carter. The Test veteran's swift efficiency was an eye-opener to Oldfield, who assumed that his technique must be the best and ought to be taken as a pattern. Oldfield played only one more match before going to the war. Practising with the AIF team at the Oval in 1919, he saw Strudwick in action and perceived that the Surrey man's methods would repay study better than the brilliant unorthodoxy of Carter. Oldfield and Strudwick were the same height, 5 ft. 5½ in., but the Australian was heavier at 10 st. 7 lb. In the AIF team he was reserve keeper to jolly Ted Long; whenever Oldfield was chosen, selectors C. E. Pellow and C. B. Willis used to notify him with such remarks as: 'You can have a game, Hercy, because Gregory wants to knock someone down.' The 'Hercy' was short for pocket Hercules, a reference to his build; it was superseded by the nickname 'Cracker', a backwash from his habit of addressing all fellow-players with 'Hallo, Crack'.

Looking back from the heights he attained, Oldfield told me he could not have done so well with Carter's method of starting farther back from the stumps. He was sure that Strudwick's policy of taking catches close to the bat was sounder, because the farther the deflected ball travelled the more the gloves had to be pushed sideways to cover it.

Oldfield differed from Carter in mental approach, too. When the pair shared Australia's keeping in 1920 and 1921 the older man occasionally borrowed Oldfield's fingerstalls, but he mostly preferred not to use them for fear of lessening the quickness of his hands. The punctilious Oldfield bound tape around the first joint of each finger and thumb, the most vulnerable spots. He wore two pairs of chamois inner gloves which he always wetted first. On each finger he placed a strong leather stall, like an outsize thimble about an inch wide and coming down almost to the second joint. Inside were rubber tips to absorb whatever shock penetrated from the outer world. By the time he drew on his brown leather gloves with reinforced palms his hands seemed to be as encumbered as a bankrupt's estate. He preferred to sacrifice brilliance, if necessary, to ensure safety and fitness. He never lost sight of the fact that a fielding side which lost its keeper was in a mess, that a substitute stump-jockey could lose the match, the bowlers lose heart and the fieldsmen lose aim.

As far as I could see, that sacrifice of brilliance was largely theoretical. Standing up to the fast-medium bowling of Ryder, who slammed the ball along at Loxton's pace on the fast Melbourne wicket of 1925, Oldfield stumped Hobbs (66) on the leg side – the most brilliant stumping of his career. In the first over of England's next Test innings, at Sydney, Oldfield was standing back to the fast bowling of Gregory with a north-easter when Hobbs leg-glanced the sixth ball down-wind and started to run. Oldfield was already on the move to leg; yards across, he gathered in the catch at top speed, yet with the poise of a tennis champion taking a wide return on the back-hand. It was Hobbs' first o in Australia. In the second innings Oldfield stumped him for 13 off Grimmett. Hobbs must have felt like saying: 'It's that man again.' The stumpings were brought off with a quickness the eye could hardly follow. Nor the camera, because a photograph showed the great English batsman stretched forward with the tip of his toe behind the line. The picture started a warm discussion: 'Was Hobbs out?' – mostly among casual cricket followers who could not have been expected to know that Hobbs' toe could have lifted momentarily or that Oldfield had a name for scrupulous fairness in appealing. (He had absorbed more from Strudwick than how to take the ball.)

Oldfield's keeping began long before the ball passed the stumps or before he stepped on to the field. He was Bradman-like in his alertness to detect every factor that could contribute to success, in cricket or business. He had a mind like a compass needle, as his old cartoonist friend, Jim Bancks, put it. He improved his fitness with deep-breathing exercises and early-morning walks. At the practice nets he studied the bowlers to familiarise himself with their deliveries and finger-spin, so that he could anticipate the ball's behaviour. His grey-blue eyes were ever watchful for clues to the nature of the pitch and the effect of the atmosphere on the ball's flight. As a result, he took up his stance full of unostentatious confidence in his ability to make the most of every opportunity. He was always wide-awake, never lulled by his own air of quiet certainty into mechanical routine. These attibutes – which in private life took him from a tramway depot to proprietorship of W. A. Oldfield Pty. Ltd.'s sport store – gave him forewarning which helped greatly in those dismissals of Hobbs. He was prepared for the Melbourne stumping because he had taken account that the slope of the ground would accentuate the effect of Ryder's inswing. At Sydney, in the five balls which Gregory bowled before Hobbs' fatal leg-glance, Oldfield had noticed that a strong wind over mid-off was blowing the fast bowler's inswinger farther to leg.

Oldfield was so correct in style that photographs of him in action

Ian Botham, on his knees, runs out Hadlee for 5 during the England v New Zealand Third Test (fourth day) at Lord's on 28 August 1978. Phil Edmonds looks on at the 'carnage'.

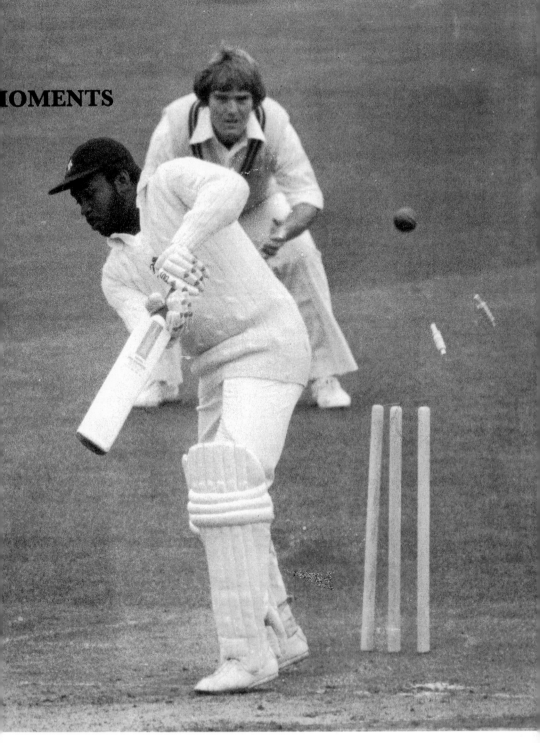

ABOVE: *The wicket goes flying as Chris Old bowls out John Shephard of Kent after 4 runs during the MCC v Kent opening game of the season on 21 April 1979.*

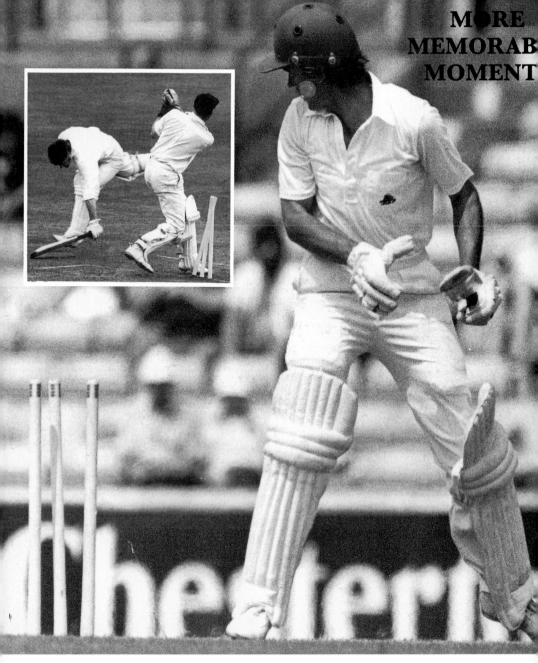

ABOVE: *Chris Tavare (England) bowled by Kapil Dev (India) for 39 runs at the Oval Cornhill Test, England v India, on 8 July 1982.*

INSET: *Gentlemen v Players, Lord's, third day, 20 July 1962. Peter Parfitt (Players) narrowly avoids being run out by A. G. Smith (Gentlemen's wicket-keeper) as he reaches the crease on his 50th run.*

RIGHT ABOVE: *Second Test Match, England v New Zealand, Lord's, first day, 19 June 1958. New Zealand wicket-keeper E. C. Petrie loses his cap as he catches Tom Graveney behind the wicket for 37.*

RIGHT BELOW: *England captain Peter May edges a ball from A. Davidson past wicket-keeper Wally Grout for a single during the Third Test, England v Australia, second day at Headingley, on 7 July 1961.*

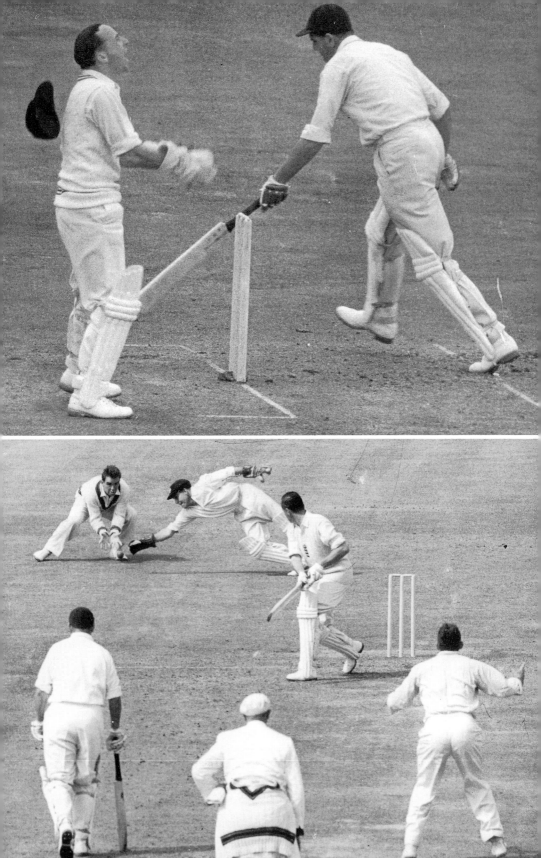

could be used as models for young keepers. With feet slightly wider apart than his shoulders, he went down in two movements: as the bowler came to the crease he lowered himself from a stoop to a squat on his calves, heels down. His right toecap twisted out towards cover, and the left pointed past the leg stump. His arms lay along his thighs, his mouth was at bail level, and his eyes just outside the off-stump. Usually he rose with the ball to whatever height was needed to take it comfortably. That rising with the ball helped keep the fingers down – No. 1 safety-first rule for keepers – but sometimes he had to move earlier, especially if he judged that the ball would come through on the leg side; then, he aimed to step across in time to see the ball pitch and to cover it without reaching to the left. In covering off-balls he did not believe in transferring the body so far that he might unsight first-slip. He preferred to lunge smartly with the right leg to bring his hands to the line of the ball. That made it easier to avoid a ball kicking dangerously from a sticky wicket, he said.

Such wickets are as nasty for the man behind as for the batsman in front of the stumps. After Australia had won the rubber in the first three Tests of 1921, Carter suggested standing aside so that Oldfield could keep in the two remaining Tests. But when rain at Manchester made a treacherous wicket likely in the fourth Test, the captain, Armstrong, kept the veteran battler in the side and did not bring Oldfield in until the final Test. After a ball from O'Reilly jumped from a sticky Melbourne wicket in the New Year Test, 1937, and almost hit Oldfield in the face, Maurice Sievers' fast-medium bowling struck him three times on the back. Such incidents were the only criticism I ever heard thrown into the scales by old-timers in discussions in which Oldfield was weighed against his greatest predecessors – rather in the same way that Bradman is weighed against all-wicket heroes of the past.

Oldfield developed all-round skill, with no preference for catching or stumping. In his Anglo-Australian Test record of five in an innings at Melbourne, 1925, he stumped four of his victims. For polished safety in handling varied bowling in England's heavy atmosphere on grassy wickets, the Oldfield of 1926–34 has not since been equalled. After the 1926 tour, his captain, Collins, could not recall his having made one mistake. After he dismissed 15 batsman in the 1930 Tests (a record for either side on English soil), Somerset's M. D. Lyon, himself a keeper, classed the urbane Australian as the best wicket-keeper he had ever seen. Sir Pelham Warner, who had been a first-class cricketer since 1894, wrote in 1934: 'Oldfield is a wicket-keeper equal to any the world has ever seen.'

No other keeper has approached his feat of getting 22 Test wickets for one bowler (Grimmett). Oldfield thought some of his quickness of eye had been cultivated by his schoolboy habit of always carrying a tennis ball which he bounced against inviting walls and footpaths. His neat efficiency often made difficult chances look easy, as in stumpings after batsmen hit over yorkers. His methods were so quiet and undemonstrative that when he spilled chances on his unlucky days they went down so quietly that you were hardly aware of it and no angry buzz came from the crowd. Once when I congratulated him on a day's fine wicket-keeping at Lord's, he murmured modestly: 'Ah, but I should have had another – I dropped Wyatt.' His blackest days were in the 1928–9 Tests, when some gremlin caused him to miss half-a-dozen chances to stump or catch Hammond off Grimmett, and the times late in his career when Fleetwood-Smith's left-arm googly bowling turned everything topsy-turvy. It must save young keepers from disheartenment to know that even the greatest masters have sometimes been all fingers and thumbs. In such a difficult art the wonder is that misses do not exceed successes, even in Test ranks.

Apart from thickened joints on the first two fingers of his left hand and a leftward tilt of the topmost knuckle, Oldfield's hands bear few traces of his twenty years of wicket-keeping between the wars, including five tours of England. Despite his precautions, he had a few fingers broken but he was never out of action long. Taking a ball from H. L. Hendry wide of a Victorian left-hander's legs, he broke the longest finger of his right hand. Four days later he was keeping in a Test Match. Another time he played with two cracked ribs. He suffered them at Adelaide, in January, 1921, the first time he took the fast bowling of E. A. McDonald. In England's first innings McDonald's smooth run and well-oiled delivery masked the real speed of the ball; though Oldfield was standing back it thudded against his chest. The little keeper clutched it to him. Though the injury was painful he stuck to his post throughout the match, stumped a couple off Mailey and was unaware of the extent of the damage until an X-ray examination after the game. As a batsman he was knocked out in the Adelaide Test, 1933, when his attempted hook against a short ball from Larwood outside the off-stump deflected the ball to his right temple. Oldfield's head was bathed by the wicket before he was helped from the field. His injury – one of the incidents which caused the long-rumbling bodyline volcano to erupt – put him out of cricket for seven weeks. Oldfield played in 16 Tests after that and retired at forty. He is the only man with the Test double of 100 wicket-keeping dismissals and 1,000 runs. In 56 Tests against England, South Africa, West Indies and New Zealand he stacked up the record of 135 dismissals[1] and scored 1,432 runs at an average of 22. He is the only Australian keeper with 500 victims and 5,000 runs, having dismissed 630 men in 244 first-class matches (378 caught, 252 stumped) and made 5,462 runs, including six hundreds.

The example of Oldfield's artistic soundness helped to keep the standard of Australian wicket-keeping high, and his influence extended to other lands. It was visible in the keeping of Willie Clark, of far-off Stirling, where Robert the Bruce's statue looks out across Bannockburn, the place where the English were run out.

Jack Ellis, thirty-four when he toured England as Oldfield's understudy in 1926, had a complexion like an apple in autumn. He clapped his cap on at a rollicking angle and came out to the middle with a don't-care gait which his pads converted into a kind of knock-kneed swagger. Once there was a great to-do when he kept for Victoria in brown pads (a utility model made to save park and outback cricketers cleaning troubles). The consternation broadened Ellis' grin, and he enjoyed his after-innings cigar all the more.

This Prahran contractor had a municipal councillor's talkativeness and was a rival for Lyon, the Somerset orator, and Levett of Kent in candid commentaries on the proceedings, as viewed from near the off bail. When he thought Bradman had scored enough he told the slips so; when the hint wasn't taken he would address remarks to the unheeding batsman's shoulder-blades – especially if someone had missed a catch. Some batsmen feared that Ellis' chatter would disturb their concentration, but many found him amusing. In a match up against NSW, the Victorian slow bowler, Bert Davie, came up against Alan Kippax in top form and ran short of fieldsmen. As Davie bowled the third ball of an over and Kippax simultaneously danced forward with visions of another boundary, Ellis stood upright, planted his gloves on his hips and called down the pitch: 'Take him off!'

In his briefer stays on the other side of the stumps the outspoken Victorian was often at a loss for a stroke but never for a word. Groping with the bat at Kelleway's swingers, he was beaten by an outcurve which narrowly missed the off-stump. Ellis looked scornfully at the bowler and demanded: 'Why don't you put 'em where I can reach 'em?'

Friends who grouped around him by the wall south-west of the Melbourne dressing-rooms were entertained by a succession of cogent and penetrating observations – the best of them out of the side of his mouth.

In hue and humour, an English counterpart of Ellis was sturdy Arthur Dolphin, who kept in the Melbourne Test in February, 1921. As round in the cheek and much deeper in the chin, Dolphin looked like a lobster in the Australian or Indian sun. His nippers were alert to seize their prey, for Dolphin was England's quickest stumper. He was unorthodox in style. Instead of facing the wicket squarely he had his left foot farther forward, so that his broad chest fronted between the bowler and mid-off. He felt that his stance helped him in stumping off balls which spun away, especially when the left-handers Rhodes and

Kilner were turning them unpredictable widths and heights from the soft wickets common in the North of England. In his slewed attitude the happy Yorkshireman had an extra foot in which to take the ball outside the off-stump, yet the nearness of his left foot kept him within close range of the bails. Covering leg balls from that starting-point was more difficult than from the square stance, and Dolphin's left fingers were so twisted from breaks and dislocations that he could hardly hold a golf club with them. His successor, chubby little Arthur Wood, travelled 125 miles from Nottingham to London by taxi-cab when he was called in at short notice for the Oval Test, 1938. The taximeter clicked up £7 15s. Wood was a comical and capable keeper who was behind at Bramall Lane in 1935 when South Africa's great batsman-keeper, H. B. Cameron, hit Verity for 30 in an over: 4, 4, 4, 6, 6, 6. After that slaughter Wood said quietly to Verity: 'Keep 'em there, Hedley; tha hast him in two minds – he doesn't know whether t'smack thi for four or six.'

[1]Totals of Australian wicket-keepers in all Tests, compiled by E. H. M. Baillie of Melbourne.

	Tests	Ct.	St.	Wkts.		Tests	Ct.	St.	Wkts.
W. A. Oldfield	56	82	53	135	B. A. Barnett	4	3	2	5
H. Carter	28	45	20	65	C. R. Gorry	2	4	1	5
J. J. Kelly	36	43	20	63	W. McGregor	2	3	1	4
J. M. Blackham	33	36	24	60	H. S. Love	1	3	0	3
D. Tallon	15	38	8	46	P. M. Newland	2	0	2	2
R. A. Saggers	6	15	8	23	W. L. Murdoch	1	0	1	1
A. H. Jarvis	9	8	8	16	F. J. Burton	1	0	1	1
W. Carkeek	6	6	0	6	A. Ratcliffe	2	1	0	1

Hands Up

The scene: the players' dressing room at Lord's where Freddie Trueman was captain of the Players against the Gentlemen. I entered, having been caught out by the Reverend David Sheppard. 'I'm sorry, Skipper,' I said, 'but it was a good catch.'

'That's all right, Peter,' replied captain Freddie. 'When the Reverend puts his two hands together he stands a better chance than most of us.'

PETER PARFITT

'... I meant to say no-ball, but I dropped my teeth.'

TO THE EDITOR, THE TIMES...

BALL AND BEARD
From Mr Arthur Porritt,
for many years editor of the *Christian Herald*.
10 August 1944

Sir, The Evidence concerning the time-honoured story of Ernest Jones sending a ball through 'W.G.'s' beard is curiously conflicting. I collaborated with W. G. Grace in writing his Cricketing Reminiscences and Personal Recollections, and in 1899 spent hundreds of hours with him as he revived his memories. He never mentioned the 'ball and beard' incident, and no specific reference to Ernest Jones appears in the book. 'W. G.' had an ingrained objection to fast bowlers who, bowling short, bumped the ball high and dangerously (Ernest Jones and Arthur Mold were notoriously addicted to that practice), and my own theory, for what it is worth, is that when Jones bowled the ball that flashed past 'W.G.' face-high 'the long-whiskered Doctor' (as Francis Thompson called him) expostulated testily and drew from Jones the apologetic 'Sorry, Doctor, she slipped.' This may indeed have happened more than once.

ARTHUR PORRITT

UNCAPPED
From Dom Gregory Murray,
of Downside Abbey.
12 July 1974

Sir, It was unfortunate that Mankad lost his wicket in the recent Test match when his cap fell off and dislodged a bail. But, surely, the lesson is obvious. The traditional cricket cap is not suited to the current long hair fashion, being designed to sit firmly on the head, not to balance precariously on a shifting mass of hair. Perhaps our cricketers will now abandon either the trendy flowing locks or the cap – unless, of course, they prefer to wear hat-pins.

A. GREGORY MURRAY

FROM THE CAPTAIN, POETS' AND PEASANTS' CC
2 September 1980

Sir, Not all mid-wicket conferences concern matters of import. Last season, I once came to the wicket when the score was 12 for five. The other batsman, who had been there from the outset, solemnly beckoned me to mid-wicket to give, I assumed, some useful advice as to what I should do. 'I'm sorry to trouble you', he said, 'but I've just lost a fly-button. Would you mind keeping a look-out for it?'

Unfortunately, I did not remain long enough to assist him in the search.

DAVID A. PEARL

A STRANGE INNINGS
From Mr Richard Harman, 18 August 1949

Sir, Opening the innings for Aylesbury on Whit-Monday in 1922, the curate of the parish church was still not out at the lunch interval. Having to officiate at a marriage service at 1.30 p.m. he hurriedly cycled one and a half miles to the church, donned his robes, and cycled back just in time to resume his innings. Surely this is the only time in the history of cricket that the batsman should have performed, between the start and the end of his innings, a marriage service in church.

RICHARD HARMAN

From Canon Lancelot Smith, 22 August 1949

Sir, I had an experience in 1926 very similar to that quoted by your correspondent under the above title, when as a 'not out' at the luncheon interval I left the ground to take a funeral and returned from the cemetery to the batting crease to resume the innings with my pre-lunch partner at the wicket. The match was at Spalding against a team of Indian students which included the Nawab of Pataudi and Nazir Ali.

LANCELOT SMITH

VILLAGE UMPIRES

From Mr Charles Ponsonby, 12 August 1935

Sir, I am glad that Mr Aidan Crawley has called attention to the horrible suggestion made by Mr F.G.J. Ford that alterations in the leg-before-wicket rule should apply to village cricket.

Umpires in village cricket are all honourable men and try to temper their judgments with discretion, but they often suffer from defects both in training and physique. The majority of them have no training in the art of umpiring; some have never played cricket themselves, and many would frankly admit that they are unfit for cricket, too old, too fat, or too slow. Some even have defective dental arrangements which interfere with a quick decision.

I was playing in a match last year and as the bowler delivered the ball the umpire ejaculated 'brr', and after a pause, 'I beg your pardon, I meant to say no-ball, but I dropped my teeth.'

Of course not every village umpire suffers from defects. Some are very good and all do their best in this very difficult position.

CHARLES PONSONBY

MY BIRD, I THINK...

From Major H. C. Dent, 12 September 1919

Sir, The undersigned was on tour through Essex in 1888, playing for Charlton Park CC. In the match against Felsted Long Vacation CC a fast ball was put down to me in the course of the game, which I seemed to lose sight of, but was fortunate enough to put through the slips for two. A dead swallow with broken beak was then found midway down the pitch; the bird had evidently flown head on into the ball. The incident was not noticed by the umpire, and I remember there was a lively discussion in the pavilion after the match as to whether I should have been given out had I been caught or bowled, as, although 'No ball' had not been called, the flight of the ball had obviously been obstructed.

The bird was sent to a taxidermist, and was exhibited in the Field office for some little time, and subsequently was on view in the Charlton Park clubhouse for many years. I have known of rabbits and birds killed by golf balls in their flight, but imagine the incident I have recorded quite singular as a 'cricket curiosity'.

HERBERT C. DENT

DOWN THE HATCH
From the Headmaster of Wallasey Grammar School, 24 June 1955

*Sir, Cricket balls in flight do strange things. Their impact has ignited
boxes of matches in umpires' coats. And there was the sparrow killed
by a ball bowled at Lord's, the heroic bird thereby attaining the
immortality of a glass case in the Long Room of the pavilion. But
is there precedent for what happened here yesterday? A boy playing in
a junior match mightily smote a towering hit high above this two-
storey building. The ball, descending with the steep trajectory of a
howitzer shell, fell clean into the mouth of a chimney pot whence by
devious ways it issued soot-stained in a downstairs classroom.*

*The pity of it is that this happened just after school was over. Had
it been half an hour earlier when the room was occupied the boys would
have had the enjoyment of this uniquely dramatic interruption of a
lesson. And in future years what a splendidly improbable tale they
could have told of a sudden rattle in the chimney and the startling
emergence of a high-velocity missile which, however suspicious it may
have looked to the master, was in fact a cricket ball legitimately going
about its lawful business.*

F. L. ALLAN

THE OTHER CRICKET MATCH
From Lieutenant-Colonel H. B. T. Wakelam, 9 August 1956.
Sporting journalist, author and BBC commentator. Gave first
running commentary – England *v.* Wales at Twickenham, 1927 –
and first television Test match commentary – England *v.* Australia
at Lord's, 1938.

*Sir, Mr Isaac Foot's report, in his letter of 2 August, of 'Werrington
versus St Dominick' recalls to mind the reply given by a village
cricketer, when asked, on his return from an 'away' match, how his
team had fared. 'First we went in, then they went in and we went
in, and they went in, and they won. Then they went in and we went
in, and they went in, and we went in, and we won. And then it were
tea-time.'*

H. B. T. WAKELAM

FORCEFUL BATTING

From Mr H. C. Broadrick, 9 August 1949

Sir, The writer of your amusing article on 'Forceful Batting'
maintains that no side can hope to better the performance of the
Stratford Police eleven. (A 'posse' of eight constables and one cadet,
led by an inspector and a sergeant, failed to trouble the scorers.) I
can claim, however, that the opponents of a school with which I was
connected for many years at Harrow succeeded in making what might
be described as a 'minus quantity'. Our opponents, a large South
Kensington preparatory school, were dismissed for four runs, and
when we went in to bat their opening bowler proceeded to bowl three
wides and two no-balls. Thus we won the match without touching
the ball with the bat. This, I think, should remain a positive record
for many years to come.

H. C. BROADRICK

OBSTRUCTING THE FIELD

From Mr A. A. Milne, 23 August 1928.
A member of the Westminster School XI in 1899 and 1900 with
a modest record: 294 runs (average 10.50), highest score 44, and
28 wickets (23.11).

Sir, I must make my contribution to cricket history; the only one I am
likely to make. In 1899 I was playing for Westminster v.
Charterhouse, the match of the year. Somehow or other the batsman
at the other end managed to get out before I did, and the next man
came in, all a-tremble with nervousness. He hit his first ball straight
up in the air, and called wildly for a run. We all ran – he, I, and the
bowler. My partner got underneath the ball first, and in a spasm of
excitement jumped up and hit it again as hard as he could. There was
no appeal. He burst into tears, so to speak, and hurried back to the
pavilion. Whether he would have run away to sea the next day, or
gone to Africa and shot big game, we shall never know, for luckily
he restored his self-respect a few hours later by bowling Charterhouse
out and winning the match for us. But here, for your Cricket
Correspondent, is a genuine case of 'Out, obstructing the field.'

A. A. MILNE

The errant batsman was one H. Plaskitt, who won a lawn tennis Blue
at Oxford. He must have been practising his smash.

CRICKET ON THE ICE
From Mr C. E. Boucher, 8 March 1929

Sir, May I add a reminiscence concerning the winter of 1878–79?
At the close of the Term, when many had already gone down, in
December, 1878, an attempt was successfully made to arrange a three
days' cricket match, Town v. Gown, on the ice of the flooded
Grantchester meadows. The veterans Hayward and Carpenter played
for the Town, and Charles Pigg, the subject of a memorial notice in
The Times *today, headed 'A Beloved Figure in Cambridge',*
captained the Gown team. We had a large field of perfect ice kept
for us. Scoring was heavy and the game was drawn, though we led
easily on the first innings. Fielding was delightful, and the chase of
the ball into 'space' when it eluded you most exhilarating. Bowling
was our weak point; we could only try lobs, and the umpires were
severe on 'no-balls'. The Town took first innings, and Pigg put us
all on in succession for two overs apiece to see what we could do. I
still recall my delight when I sent up a full toss to Hayward, who,
seeing visions of the ball travelling half a mile, over-balanced himself
with the effort, with fatal result to his wicket. The Sportsman *at*
the time gave some account of the match.

C. E. BOUCHER

The winter of 1878–79 lasted from October until May, although a brief
thaw in February put an end to cricket on the ice. *Wisden* records a dozen
such matches, including one by moonlight in Windsor Home Park and
this one in Cambridge. In 1983 *The Times* recorded cricket on ice in
China – and an England XI playing in the desert.

CRICKET REMINISCENCE
From Mr H. C. Troughton, 18 August 1919

Sir, May I say that I saw George Anderson's famous drive for eight.
It was made on Monday, 4 August, 1862, and was, of course, a
stupendous hit, but it ought not to have realised eight runs, and would
not have done so had not the fieldsman thrown the ball into the middle
of my back.

HERBERT C. TROUGHTON

Anderson was playing for North of England against Surrey.

'LE ROI EST MORT...'

From the Revd Hugh Hunter,
Vicar of Riddlesden, Yorkshire.
26 August 1938

*Sir, I called out to a very small boy in the village here this evening
(24 August) as he was slogging a ball up the street, 'Hello,
Bradman!' He replied, 'I'm not Bradman, I'm 'Utton!' I apologised
instantly.*

HUGH HUNTER

On 23 August Hutton's 364 against Australia at the Oval had broken
the previous Test match record of 334 by Bradman.

A PROBLEM OF CRICKET

From a Puzzled Foreign Sportsman, 14 July 1932

*Sir, On a recent visit to your beautiful England I went to see your
national game of cricket. Kind friends told me how the game was
played, but I could not find out why the umpire could not give a
decision without being appealed to. In other games one considers it
unfair to ask the umpire for a decision. Will you kindly explain to
me why it is so in cricket.*

A PUZZLED FOREIGN SPORTSMAN

Now is September Passing Through

Now is September passing through,
The golden days are over, swift they came
With soft expectancy and magic new
Tempting our senses with ephemeral fame.

O, there has been much laughter, much that's fine
Where flannelled fools have roved, and umpires called
Not Out! and now the darkness sets in other time
To hush the scene which once the wickets ruled.

The night has come, let's close the echoing bar
Where evenings, after match, good fellowship was all,
But thoughts again will wander to a summer far
Ahead of winter, and to bat and ball.

Now is September passing through
The rusted gates of wind and storm and rain,
The cold is cold, and fires leap anew
Until the cricket season comes again

As come it will, when winter's chafing hand
Conjures the dreamed-of scores that might-have-been,
When pads will re-emerge, and wickets proudly stand
Once more upon the village and the county green.

And who shall play again? Whose names be on the card,
In some new season, by pavilion door?
Who, too, shall toast with sadness and regard
The bowled September men who'll play no more?

LESLIE FREWIN

375

BRIAN JOHNSTON

Come into the commentators' box with the
irrepressible 'Johnners' and the gang – it's cramped but great fun ...

SEPTEMBER SONG, 1985

It may have been one of the wettest summers ever but somehow in the TMS Commentary Box we seem to have had plenty of sunshine, fun, and laughter. It's been my fortieth season of cricket commentary and once again I am amazed that in all that time I have never had a quarrel with anyone in the box. It's extraordinary, really, because we are all extroverts, different in character, and crowded together in boxes far too small to contain us all comfortably.

Nothing much changes. We still receive a vast mail together with the much publicised chocolate cake, sweets, wine and other delicacies. There is a constant stream of visitors in the box, including our Saturday lunch-time guests in 'View from the Boundary'. One of these was Roy Hattersley, a really keen cricket follower. When I introduced him I gave him his full title of 'The Right Honourable, etc.' but after that I told him that I would be calling him 'Hatters'. He seemed mildly surprised but took it in good part. Later in the season he told me that when he returned home, his wife had opened the door and said: 'Hello, Hatters' – something she had never called him before!

Blowers still has his attacks of Busitis ('... as that ball goes for 4 through the covers, I can see a No. 2 bus going up the Wellington Road...'). At the Oval he once even had 'a good-looking' bus. On certain grounds he cannot see any buses from the box. But he's never stumped. He substitutes helicopters, 'rare' pigeons, butterflies flying alongside the bowler or, triumphantly at Lord's this year, an airship.

The Boil still speaks like Mr Jingle ... 'Young, well built, strong, nice action, good line, good length, good bowler.' I usually catch him out once a season, and was once again successful at the NatWest Final. I asked him why the Essex wicket-keeper could never be interviewed by Peter West on TV. He had to give up, but I expect you have already guessed it: 'West is West, and East is East, and never the twain shall meet.'

Sir Frederick still smoked his big curly pipe in the mornings and his cigars after lunch. (We call them his Adam and Eve – when he's Adam, we Eve.) He had a minor operation after the 5th Test but was back at the Oval for the final Test a week later. He obviously returned too soon, because he had a relapse and had to go back into hospital. But a few weeks in his Spanish villa soon put him right.

The Bearded Wonder still brings his briefcases full of reference and record books, most of which he seems to have written himself. He continues to smart at the mildest of jokes and is attended by a bevy of beautiful hand maidens who attend to his *every* want.

A.R.L. brings good looks and a breath of Welsh air into the box. He adds lustre to our call as the only commentator on TMS – as opposed to summarisers – to have captained England.

Jenkers continues to arrive with 5 or 10 seconds to spare and throughout the day regales us with the voices and accents of famous people. I have always said that there is a danger of him making us all superfluous – he can do all our voices to perfection.

The Alderman has spent much of the summer signing his two bestsellers – his autobiography *The Best Job in the World*, and his fair but candid *Boycott*. I am sorry to report that I once again beat him easily in the word game which we play during rain or dull periods. Just why I win I am not sure. He is a keen student of the English language and far better read than I am. Maybe he tries for too many exotic words, whereas I stick to the basics, like sewer and truss.

Bachers, our producer, has once again kept order in the box with his usual tact and judgement. He conducts us on a light rein, but is quick to stop us going over the brink with some of our absurdities.

We have had three welcome guest summarisers *Illy*, *Jackers* and *Barners*, who have all adopted themselves well to our unusual style of broadcasting.

That leaves *Mcfillers* who, on his last ever tour, has been ferried around the Test Grounds. The BBC gave him a dinner and a decanter with the figure of Don Bradman engraved on it. We – his colleagues – gave him an enlarged framed cartoon of the occasion when, after giving him a slice of chocolate cake, I immediately asked him to comment on the last delivery. The cartoonist has captured well the explosion of crumbs all over the box as he attempted to speak.

He will be sadly missed in this country. He has received shoals of letters and all ours too have contained messages of farewell to him. It was sad that the final ball on which he will ever commentate in a Test should have been the last Australian wicket to fall, so giving England victory and the Ashes.

We shall all miss him both as friend and broadcaster – certainly the fairest and least biased commentator with whom I have ever worked. We all wish him a long and happy retirement.

Editor's note

For the benefit of the uninitiated and those who live outside the United Kingdom, 'Blowers' is Henry Blofeld, 'The Boil' is Trevor Bailey, 'Sir Frederick' is Freddie Trueman, 'The Bearded Wonder' is Bill Frindall, 'A.R.L.' is Tony Lewis, 'Jenkers' is Christopher Martin-Jenkins, 'The Alderman' is Don Mosey, 'Bachers' is Peter Baxter (the BBC producer), 'Illy' is Ray Illingworth', 'Banners' is Jack Bannister, 'Jackers' is Robin Jackman and 'McFillers' is Alan McGillvray, now back on his native heath, Australia.

THE DUCK'S EGG

Written on the shell of a duck's egg and found on the cricket field of Amersham Hall, on 17 July 1886, after a match

Two balls I survived,
   But the third one came straight,
For the Bowler contrived
(Seeing what I survived)
To bowl at a rate
   I did not contemplate.
Two balls I survived,
   But the third one came straight.

ANON

J. A. R. SWAINSON

---

*The Director of the Lord's Taverners weighs in
with some pertinent facts*

WHERE THE MONEY GOES

In the first 21 years, the Lord's Taverners raised £210,000. Since 1972, the Charity is now raising in excess of £700,000: well on its way to its first million. It has 18 regional cells all over the country and operates from London with a full-time staff of four plus a part-time accountant. 82p in the pound goes directly to beneficiaries. Charitable objectives include:

1. Youth cricket: The provision of equipment, artificial pitches and the running of competitive games for young schoolboys, particularly the disadvantaged.

2. Cash contributions towards the provision of hard-surface playing areas in urban districts such as Brixton and Toxteth.

3. The provision of 'New Horizon' mini-buses for the mentally and physically handicapped young. At the time of writing, the Taverners put one mini-bus on the road every 10 working days. The overall cost for each vehicle is about £16,000. Every bus is specially equipped for the handicapped.

4. Special projects: the provision of sports facilities for the mentally and physically handicapped.

The Lord's Taverners is unique in that it is both club and charity. The Club now embraces well-known personalities from the world of sport and entertainment as well as businessmen prominent in their profession who are invited into convenanted membership. Anyone can become a Friend of the Lord's Taverners upon payment of £10.00. – a form of Associated Membership. Covenanted Membership of £25.00 per annum over a minimum period of four years enables a company or an individual to become a Full Member of the Lord's Taverners. All monies so convenanted go towards the 'Terry Wogan Covenant Appeal' and enables the Taverners to buy 'New Horizon' buses.

THE LAST BALL OF SUMMER

'Tis the last ball of Summer
    Left rolling alone;
All his artful companions
    Are smitten and gone;
No trace of his kindred,
    No shooter is seen
To relate all the glories
    Of Briggs and Nepean.

I'll not leave thee, thou lone one,
    To curl on the stumps;
Since thy brothers were slogged so,
    Partake of their thumps!
Thus kindly I smack thee
    Afar in the heavens,
Where the mates of thy tribe went
    For sixes and sevens!

And soon may there follow,
    Ere sinews decay,
A capital season
    To get thee away!
For muscles must wither,
    Our cricket be flown;
And we shall inhabit
    Pavilions, and groan!

NORMAN GALE

Good night, sweet pints ...

ACKNOWLEDGEMENTS

Acknowledgement and grateful thanks are extended to the following:

His Royal Highness The Prince Philip, KG, KT, for graciously consenting to write the Preface, and for his interest, suggestions and help. Brigadier Clive Robertson of Prince Philip's staff. Mr Michael Shea and Mr John Haslam, respectively Press Secretary and Assistant Press Secretary to the Queen. Mr M. V. Mavor, Headmaster, Gordonstoun School, Elgin, Moray.

The Executors of Mr C. E.Hughes for *The Infant Cricket*. The Executors of the late Mr Edmund Blunden and Ms Helen Hayward of A. D. Peters Ltd, for *The Season Opens*. Mr Harold Pinter, Methuen (London), Ms Judy Daish and Mr Ivan Kyncl (photographer) for *Hutton and The Past*. Mr Ian Wooldridge, Sir David English, Editor, London *Daily Mail*, and Associated Newspapers Group, plc, for *The Day Cricket Stood Still* and for the facilities afforded by the Group's librarians, Mr Johnston and Mr Dignum. Mr John Arlott and Cassell & Co. Ltd, for *Cricket for Breakfast* from *The Twelfth Man*. Mr Christopher Martin-Jenkins for *From The (Near) Nursery End* and *Botham – The Modern Champion*. The Executors of the late Mr A. A. Milne for *The First Game*. Mr and Mrs Michael Pearce for *The Oldest Double-Act in the Business*. Mr Norman Harris and Mr Andrew Neill, Editor, London *Sunday Times*, for *David Gower – Right Handed!* and *A Wave of a White Handkerchief, 1975*. The Executors of the late Mr G. K. Chesterton for *Lines on a Cricket Match*. Times Newspapers Ltd, and Mr Ralph Nodder, Syndication Manager, for *Cricket: From Bible to Bunyan* (Mr Simon Barnes); *Echoes of a Month-Long Hearing in The High Court*; *Musical Cricket* (Mr E. B. Osborn); *Test Bowled Two Maidens Over* (Ms Rita Marshall); *Such a Hard Ball – But a Gentle Art* (Mr Colin Cowdrey); *A Master of the Mind-Game Steps Down* (Mr John Woodcock); *Trouble at T'Crease* (Mr Miles Kington); *Where Cricket is a 20-A-Side and Rich In Laughter* (Mr Geoffrey Watkins); *To The Editor, The Times*; *A Chat With Ranji* (Mr J. S. Booth); and *I Say, You Chaps . . .* (Mr Richard Ford). Mr Peter West for 'On Compo'. Mr Dick Brittenden for *Bert Sutcliffe – Third Ball Unlucky!* and Roy Palenski for his Sutcliffe photograph. Mr Michael Melford for '*Johnners' At The Helm!* The Executors of the late Sir Arthur Conan Doyle for *Spedegue's Dropper*. Mr Barry Took for *Living on the Doorstep*. Mr E. W. Swanton for *Cambridge Cricket Between The Wars* and *The Ashes in Coronation Year*. Mr John Snow for *Sometime, When I'm Older*. Mr John Ebdon and Mr Nigel Hollis of David & Charles Ltd, for Mr Ebdon's abridged version of *Ebdon's England* entitled *With Bat and Ball in Darkest Surrey*. Sir Leonard Hutton, Messrs Benson & Hedges and Ms Karen Earl for *My Favourite Cricket Grounds*. Mr Colin Atkinson for *Cricket at Millfield*. Mr Leslie Thomas for *Caught in the Deep*. Mr Tim Rice, Mr Ron Hall, Editor, *Sunday Express Magazine*, and Mr Tim Satchell for *Roots*. The late Sir John and Lady Betjeman and John Murray Ltd, for *Cricket Master*. Mr Christopher Booker, Mr Ian Hislop and Mr Richard Ingrams of *Private Eye* for *Bodyline Revisited*. Mr Michael Parkinson and Ms Julie Ivelaw-Chapman of International Management Group for *John Willy Jardine*. Mr Richie Benaud and John Farquharson Ltd, for *1956 and All That*. Mr Harry East and Opax Publishing Ltd, for *Super Boss* and *Father of the Flock* from *Laughter At The Wicket*. Mr Anthony Couch and John Richard Parker of MBA Literary Agents Ltd for *The Wedding of Nigel Grint*. Mr Joseph S. F. Murdoch, historian of the Philadelphia Cricket Club, for *The Philadelphia Story*. Mr Richard Kershaw for *Born-Again Cricketer*. The Executors of the late Mr Hugh de Selincourt for *Tillingford Play Wilminghurst*. Mr Alan Ross for *Watching Benaud Bowl*. Mr Ralph Wotherspoon for *The Band At Play*. Mr Les Bailey of the Wombwell Cricket Lovers' Society for his untitled limerick. Mr Vernon Scannell for *Wicket Maiden*. Mrs Rachael Heyhoe Flint for *Fashion In The Field*. Mr Cardew Robinson for *The Cricket Bat*. Ms Molly Shimeild for *Some of Them Are Pretty*. The Executors of the late Mr A. A. Thomson, Ms Vivienne Schuster of John Farquharson Ltd and Pavilion Books Ltd for *The Ladies In Play* and *O My Hornby and My Barlow* from *Odd Man In*. Ms Laura E. Bamford and Guinness Superlatives Ltd for *Unveiling The Ladies* from *The Guinness Book of Facts and Feats* (Bill Frindall). Mr Michael Coward for *Bags of Drama*. Mr Alan Knott, Norman Giller Publications and The Lord's Taverners for *Man Under A Microscope* from *Cricket Heroes*. Sir John Mills for *A Boundary, Begad!* The Executors of the late Wilfrid Scawen Blunt for the quotation from *John Christie of Glyndebourne*. The Executors of the late Mr Perceval Graves for *Phyllis At The Wicket*. Mr Simon Raven and Blond & Briggs Ltd for *The MCC Match*. Mr Fred Trueman and BBC Publications for *Ken Barrington – The Run Machine* from *Arlott and Trueman on Cricket*. Mr Basil Boothroyd for *Keep the Game at Home*. Mr Scyld Berry, Mr Donald Trelford, Editor, the London *Observer*, and Mr Raman Subba Row, chairman of the Test & County Cricket Board, for *Summer of '81*. Mr Gerald Brodribb and Pelham Books Ltd for *A Look At Some Laws* from *Next Man In*. The Executors of the late Mr P. G. Wodehouse for *Missed!* The Executors of the late Mr Raymond Robertson-Glasgow and Dennis Dobson Ltd for *The Catch That Never Came Down*. Mr Jack Pollard for *The Hill at Sydney* from *The Boundary Book*. Mr David Frith, editor of *Wisden Cricket Monthly*, for *Viv Richards: It's Just a Piece of Wood* and *Something Fishy?* Mr C. L. R. James for *The Most Unkindest Cut* from *Beyond A Boundary*. Lord Olivier, OM, Ms Shirley Luke and Cassell & Co. for *My Life In Cricket* from *The Twelfth Man*. Mr Arthur Marshall, the BBC and Mr Brian Johnston for *Playing the Game*. Mr Donald Trelford for *What A Way To Go!* Mr Leslie Ames for *The Forgotten Test*. Mr Raman Subba Row for *Indian Summers ... and Winters*. Mr Harold ('Dickie') Bird for *The Greatest Match of My Time*. The Executors of the late Mr Ray Robinson and William Collins Sons & Co. Ltd for *The Gentleman in Gloves* from *From The Boundary*. Mr Brian Johnston for *September Song, 1985*. Mr J. A. R. Swainson, Director, The Lord's Taverners, for *Where The Money Goes*. The Executors of the late Mr Norman Gale and Methuen (London), for *The Last Ball of Summer*.

Thanks are due also to the many individuals and organisations who either helped in aspects of the creation of this book or who extended courtesies to the compiler and editor, notably:
Mr Marcus Williams, editor of *Double Century* and *The Way To Lords* (William Collins Sons & Co. Ltd) for his unstinting help and encouragement and for his footnotes to *The Times* letter feature; Mr Michael Pirie Frewin for his valuable suggestions; Mr Roger Kemp; Dom Gregory Murray of Downside Abbey; Mr Jack Rayfield, Editor of *The Lord's Taverner*, for the provision of archive photographs; Mr Murray Haines of the C. Christopher Morris Cricket Library Association of Haverford College, Pa, USA; Ms Anne-Marie Schaaf of The Historical Society of Pennsylvania, Mr Peter May; Mr Colin Cowdrey; Sir G. O. Allen; Mrs Veronica Trueman; Mrs Michael Melford; Mr Timothy Booth of Aycliffe Press, Barnstaple; Mr and Mrs Alfred Gover; Miss Jenny Secombe; Mrs Joan Morecambe; Mrs Ann Barrington; Ms Liz Fraser; Mrs Joan Broome; Mrs Jean Standing; Ms Jan Leeming; Mrs Anne Subba Row; Ms Jacqui Crier; the late Mr Gordon Ross; Mr Don Cameron of the New Zealand High Commission, London; Mr Spike Milligan, Mr Clive James, Mr David Puttnam, Mr John Varley, Chief Executive and Secretary, the Lord's Taverners, Australia; Mr George McWilliam, Mr Dennis Silk, Mr John Snagge, Mr Dennis James, chief photographer of the *Berks and Bucks Observer*, Mr John Glynn-Jones, Mr Tom Newton, Mr Ronnie Corbett, Mr Robin Marlar, Mr Jasper Carrott, Mr John Moody of Lord's Cricket Ground Shop and Sporting Handbooks Ltd.

Thanks, too, to the directors of the Sport & General Picture Agency and to Nikè, their archivist, who helped so much to provide illustrations. Here grateful thanks must be extended also to Mr Tim Morris, chairman of the Press Association Ltd, and his General Manager and Chief Executive, Mr Ian Yates, for waiving library research and reproduction fees for several photographs used in this book, and for facilities so expertly given by their photo archivists.
Additionally, the compiler and editor is most grateful to the Governors of the BBC for help given to him by the BBC Hulton Picture Library, London; thanks, too, to Ms Marjorie Wallis and her colleagues at that Library for their patient and productive help. Warm thanks are also due to Mr Patrick Eagar for his fine jacket illustration and to the contributing artists and cartoonists, in particular Mr Bill Tidy, Mr David Langdon, Mr Reg Smythe, the late Mr Jackie Broome, Mr Peter Ustinov, Mr Reg Varney, Mr Tom Newton and Mr Jack Wood.
The compiler and editor's best thanks go to Pelham Books Ltd's publisher, Mr Dick Douglas-Boyd, and his associates, Ms Ruth Baldwin, Ms Clare Ford, Ms Patricia Walters, Ms Sally Partington and Ms Zena Kvicky, for their encouragement and expertise.

Finally, sincere gratitude is extended to Lord Deeds, lately Editor of the London *Daily Telegraph*, and to Mr John Anstey, Editor of the *Sunday Telegraph Magazine*, for their immediate and enthusiastic help to the compiler and editor of this book.